ACE IN A DAY

ACE IN A DAY

The Memoir of an Eighth Air Force Fighter Pilot in World War II

LIEUTENANT COLONEL WAYNE K. BLICKENSTAFF

Edited by

GRAHAM CROSS

CASEMATE
Philadelphia & Oxford

Published in the United States of America in 2022 by
CASEMATE PUBLISHERS
1950 Lawrence Road, Havertown, PA 19083, USA

Copyright 2022 © Gayle F. Wellborn and Jayne P. Blickenstaff
Introduction, supplementary information, and photographs contributed by the editor, copyright 2022 © Graham Cross
Artwork by Vincent Dhorne

Hardcover Edition: ISBN 978-1-63624-209-5
Digital Edition: ISBN 978-1-63624-210-1

All rights reserved. No part of this book may be reproduced or transmitted in any form or by any means, electronic or mechanical including photocopying, recording or by any information storage and retrieval system, without permission from the publisher in writing.

Printed and bound in the United Kingdom by TJ Books

Typeset in India by Lapiz Digital Services, Chennai.

For a complete list of Casemate titles, please contact:

CASEMATE PUBLISHERS (US)
Telephone (610) 853-9131
Fax (610) 853-9146
Email: casemate@casematepublishers.com
www.casematepublishers.com

"War will exist until that distant day when the conscientious objector enjoys the same reputation and prestige that the warrior does today."
—*John Fitzgerald Kennedy*

"Older men declare war. But it is the youth that must fight and die."
—*Herbert Clark Hoover*

Contents

Editor's Introduction   ix
Foreword   xii

One	1
Two	4
Three	14
Four	24
Five	37
Six	43
Seven	55
Eight	61
Nine	65
Ten	77
Eleven	83
Twelve	87
Thirteen	93
Fourteen	105
Fifteen	109
Sixteen	114
Seventeen	122
Eighteen	127
Nineteen	132
Twenty	136
Twenty-one	141
Twenty-two	145
Twenty-three	152
Twenty-four	162
Twenty-five	167
Twenty-six	171
Twenty-seven	175
Twenty-eight	183

Twenty-nine	194
Thirty	206
Thirty-one	211
Thirty-two	217
Thirty-three	229
Thirty-four	241
2011	245
Epilogue	247
Appendix 1: Blick's War Diary	248
Appendix 2: "Captain Blickenstaff Gives Good Dope on Bombing"	317
Appendix 3: Blick's Aircraft	319
Appendix 4: Blick's Aerial Claims	323
Appendix 5: Blick's Promotions	324
Appendix 6: Blick's Awards	325
Appendix 7: Blick's Missions	326
Appendix 8: 350th Fighter Squadron Losses	333
Index	335

Editor's Introduction

The name Wayne K. Blickenstaff, or simply "Blick," is not as well known among historians and enthusiasts of the Eighth Fighter Command's operations in the skies over Europe in World War II as it should be. Blick was a stalwart of the 350th Fighter Squadron of the 353rd Fighter Group based at Goxhill, Metfield and Raydon, England, as part of the Eighth Air Force prosecuting the strategic air campaign against Germany. As an original cadre member, he rose steadily through the ranks from a second lieutenant element leader to flight leader, squadron operations officer, squadron leader and finally to a lieutenant colonel and group operations officer. His combat record was equally impressive. Flying the P-47 Thunderbolt and P-51 Mustang he flew two tours of operations encompassing 133 missions, 456:55 combat hours and claims of ten enemy aircraft destroyed in the air. His double "ace" status included a ME262 jet fighter and the destruction of five aircraft in one mission giving him "ace in a day" status (one of nineteen pilots of the Eighth Fighter Command to achieve this accolade). He was awarded the Air Medal (with seven oak leaf clusters), the Distinguished Flying Cross (with three oak leaf clusters), the Silver Star and French Croix de Guerre. These bare combat statistics, however, do not do justice to the totality of his war record. He took over the reins of the 350th Fighter Squadron amid the disastrous losses of the June 12, 1944, mission and rebuilt it into an effective fighting force. His methods were controversial, but ultimately effective. With such an impressive war record, it is truly astonishing that his story is not more widely known. This is undoubtedly down to Blick's unwillingness to place his role in the European air war ahead of others, who he believed were more worthy of historical attention. Blick's original title for his book, *The Quiet Warrior*, reflected this personal modesty and we hope *Ace in a Day* is more emblematic of his military achievements.

I grew up in the sleepy, rural village of Raydon, Suffolk, in the United Kingdom, the wartime home of the 353rd Fighter Group. In my early research into the group, one name that always stood out was "Blickenstaff." It was certainly an unusual name. The 350th Flight Surgeon, "Doc" Canipelli, told a great story about how he and Blick once landed at an RAF airfield while on a cross-country errand in one of the group's liaison aircraft. Their signing of German and Italian surnames into the tower visitor book prompted one of the RAF duty personnel to exclaim, "We've been invaded!" Fascination with that unusual name led me to make contact with Blick in 1990. In the days before the internet and email I wrote him a letter, and a few weeks later the eagerly awaited reply appeared. Blick, as he signed himself, was open, friendly and very curious about why I had written to him. He said he looked forward to hearing from me again and, from that first letter, we struck up a firm friendship that endured until he passed. In later years when the internet made contacting him very easy (Blick was very much a pioneer technologically), I was always impressed by the time he was prepared to give complete strangers who could well be asking him questions about his wartime experiences that many of his generation chose not to discuss. We first met in person at the 353rd Fighter Group Reunion in Williamsburg, Virginia, in 1991 and again in Orlando, Florida, in 1996. It was at these reunions that I witnessed how deeply he cared for, and was concerned for, the welfare of the men he had served with and commanded.

One of the reasons we connected as friends was that neither Blick nor myself were obsessed with aircraft serial numbers, versions or code letters (although I have incorporated much of that data into the editing process for those readers who desire it). We were, instead, both intensely interested in human character. Blick was a keen and reflective observer of those around him and an intellectual who thought a great deal about why things were done a certain way. The result is, I believe, one of the sharpest observations of life in an Eighth Fighter Command fighter squadron available. The numerous astute pen portraits of key individuals are historical gold dust in themselves. Yet, what shines through is Blick's honesty and openness in discussing his inner thoughts, feelings and the many command dilemmas he faced.

Blick was a talented artist and illustrator and in his later years became an equally talented writer. From some point in the late 1980s after he retired, he was working on a factual account of his wartime experiences and he graciously shared excerpts while I was working on my group history, *Jonah's Feet Are Dry*, in 1998. Fiction attracted him as a medium for the ideas it allowed him to explore and he developed the manuscript into a novel loosely based around his experiences. At some point around 2006, he began converting this earlier fictional account back to a more factual representation of his wartime experiences. Then, in late 2011, he asked if he could send me his memoirs. I did not need him to ask me twice. He was apologetic that some of the "third person" writing from the novel might still be in there but was very insistent I confirm I had received all the chapters safely. A couple of weeks later, just before Christmas 2011, came the shocking news that he had passed away suddenly. Looking back, I think he knew his time was short and wanted to get the book to me so that it might reach a wider audience at a future date.

In 2018, two of Blick's daughters, Perry and Gayle, got in touch wondering whether the book was publishable. Keen to honor my friend, I quickly agreed and the result, some four years later, is this book. In editing the book, I have looked to maintain Blick's authentic voice, and my changes have therefore been minimal.

Where I have added or changed text, I have clearly identified what I have amended. I have a good deal of material from official records, Blick's correspondence and his earlier factual account sent to me by him in 1998. Where it is useful, for further information or clarification, I have included this material and identify it from Blick's text with square brackets. I have also included footnotes to further clarify Blick's account or give the reader relevant information that he did not provide when writing his book. There has also been some minor reorganization of the chronology in the later chapters to ensure it is accurate, but this did not involve actual changes to the text. In places, I have altered the "third-person" or fictionalized names used in the original novel. In a few instances I have chosen to maintain the fictionalized names so as not to risk any upset to families—something Blick would certainly not have wanted. Blick also makes wide use of dialogue in the text. The reader must appreciate that this is his memory of the events and not an exact reporting of the words spoken. For this reason and to reinforce the historical credibility of the account presented here, I have included Blick's personal "War Diary" (written during his two tours) and further appendices on 350th losses, aircraft, missions and all of Blick's combat reports. A copy of Blick's original manuscript will be included in the 353rd Fighter Group Archive for the reference of future researchers.

I should like to thank the kind assistance of Perry Blickenstaff and Gayle Wellborn, who have ensured Blick's manuscript has become available to the wider public. My longtime friend and fellow researcher, Joe Canipelli, has been of invaluable help. I should also like to thank Dan Cather and Valerie Stabenow for their kind assistance with additional photographs. I extend my further thanks to all the 353rd Fighter Group veterans and families who have helped my research over the years.

We are now at a time when Blick's generation have mostly passed from the scene. There are unlikely to be many major new autobiographies of American fighter pilots from that era published. To have a new one from a pre-eminent example of the breed is a welcome treat and a valuable addition to the historical record. Blick was a very talented man and his family and friends miss him a great deal. He was modest, but also an idealist, believing that humanity had the capacity to achieve great and good things given the chance and opportunity. He was painfully aware that many of his comrades did not live to see that opportunity and was, I believe, surprised, to the end, that he himself had survived the war.

Graham Cross
Ely—July 4, 2021

Foreword

Yesterday, I was looking at my old wartime photo album and saw my picture, taken when I was a cadet in the Army Air Corps (now called the Air Force). I was shocked. It was hard for me to believe I was ever that young—I am now over four times that age. There I was, dressed in my uniform, just as so many young people are today, and I can't help but wonder what it's all about. After all of these years, I realize how immature, how naïve, I was about the world and its affairs. At the time, however, I didn't think so, but I was still a child, no different than the children who are sent to Iraq to fight in a war they know nothing about. Yes, they are still children, and they are told, in effect, that they are protecting our freedom. We were sure that's what *we* were doing, also. There was a difference, though—a mighty big difference. We had been attacked and we were fighting back. Along with all other parents, my heart cries out now, saddened when I see those scared and lonely boys and girls who have been trained too early to be men and women and sent off to a land they have probably never heard of to fight and kill other boys and girls they don't know and have no reason to hate.

I have wondered many times why we use our young people to do our dirty work. They are physically superior of course, but we also know now that their brains are not yet fully developed, and that they sometimes do stupid, illogical things because of it. And we capitalize on that. It's enormously exciting to be dressed in a uniform and handed a gun and sent off to a faraway land to do duty for our country. I know. I went through it.

This is my story. I have changed the names of some individuals for their protection and for the protection of their families, but the story is real and true.

WKB
December 2006

One

Until I was twelve, almost thirteen, years old, I lived in Chino, California, a small town six miles southeast of Pomona, and about forty-some miles east of Los Angeles. Pomona was larger, but not quite a city. Its promotional image was a heavily laden cornucopia with all kinds of fruits and vegetables spilling out and with the lettering, "Pomona Valley, Where Everything Grows." My grandparents, on my mother's side, lived in Pomona and we did almost all of our shopping there. It was also host to the huge annual Los Angeles County Fair, the largest fair held in California.

Chino was a typical small town, and we kids were free to roam without fear of harm. There was no need to lock the doors and windows. We weren't what you would consider poor, but we didn't have much money. We learned early on to save our pennies. When the fair was on, our school would close down for a day and furnish transportation for those of us wanting to go. I remember one time I was given a dollar and sent on my way with a smile and an encouraging, "Have a good time!" And I did. I had a wonderful time just watching and listening to all of the sights and sounds. I had been trained to be thrifty, so I spent only two cents of my money. I have no idea now what I managed to get for two cents, but it must have satisfied my spending urge. When my grandfather heard I had been given a dollar and had come home with ninety-eight cents he laughed so hard I thought for sure he was dying. I didn't know if I should feel stupid for not spending the money or proud that I was able to save it.

Those early years were not an easy time for me because I had inherited my mother's shyness. She told me one time that when she was asked a question in school she would say she didn't know the answer even if she did. She was too shy to answer. I wasn't quite that bad, but almost. My brother was four years older, and he did not help at all. He was the social one—outgoing, easy to talk to—and he tried his best to encourage me to be more like him. I didn't like to be pushed. All that did was to make me even more withdrawn. One time he was trying to get me to go with him to some kind of a social event and I kept refusing until he gave up. My father said something to the effect that it was good I had a mind of my own. That upped my ego, of course, but it didn't help my social skills. In fact, I began to think shyness might be a good thing. I was wrong, of course.

Shy people tend to spend a good deal of time by themselves, and I was no exception. Now I say I was a loner, which somehow seems to be a more positive expression than "shy." It's true that there are a lot of pluses for being social, but there are some mighty good ones about spending time alone, too. A big one is that you learn to know yourself—you have time to think about things. People who are always surrounded by sounds and activities sometimes seem to be frightened when forced to delve into their own minds. I found another plus, too, and it was one that my brother, in all of his social life, never really discovered—the wonderful, fantastic and highly imaginative worlds that writers write about. Those vivid images still linger in my imagination—*Tom Sawyer* and *Huck Finn*, *Treasure Island*, *Tarzan*, *Moby Dick*, *Robinson Crusoe*—and it was a time when the adventure strips in the Sunday papers were popular—*Prince Valiant*, *Tarzan*, *Flash Gordon*, *Buck Rogers*, *Mandrake the Magician*, *Superman*, *Batman*. Because of them, I started drawing and making up stories to illustrate. At the time, I didn't know how they were to influence my future.

While in high school, I was busy with friends, as all kids are, involved in my own activities and never giving the news we heard much thought. We knew the world situation was a little volatile, and we sometimes talked about the possibility of war, but only in a kind of light-hearted, breezy manner—untroubled and vague. We had no real interest in it. Why should we? War was something that occurred somewhere over there on the other side of the world. Regardless, sometimes in a pessimistic mood, I had a hazy, nagging feeling there would be a war and that I would be just the right age to fight in it. There was nothing about childhood to suggest I would become a fighter pilot.

In 1937, we were living in Pomona with my mother's parents because my dad was dying from cancer and needed constant care. I graduated from Pomona High School in 1938 and my mother, who had always relied on my dad for major decisions, had to take on the responsibility of my future. I had no idea what I should do. She, however, was determined that I should pursue an art career, and somehow managed to scrape together the tuition money for Woodbury College in Los Angeles. I understood that I would have to work for my room and board and any needed extras. Woodbury was a business school, but they had an advertizing art course, and I signed up for that, along with a few required business classes. It was a two-year course, but because we attended classes through the summers, it was the equivalent of a four-year college course. While there, the world news worsened and we could no longer wish it away. My gloom about having to take part in a war was beginning to seem real.

I graduated in 1940 and went to work as a naïve apprentice for one of my art teachers, a busy commercial artist. Soon after that, France fell to the Germans and in

September, President Roosevelt signed the first pre-war conscription act.¹ It wasn't long before a few of my friends were drafted into the armed services. Two of my old school friends in Chino enlisted, rather than wait for the draft, because they wanted to be able to choose what branch of the service they entered. Both chose to fly. Richard Wright opted for the Navy and Howard Galbreath joined the Army Air Corps. To escape the draft, I rented a small apartment and asked my mother to come to Los Angeles and live with me so I could classify her as a dependent. At the time, only single men with no dependents were eligible for the draft. It was a good idea but it didn't last long.

It was a Sunday afternoon and the December sun was hanging low in our eyes as we drove southwest on Glendale Avenue toward my girlfriend Jeannie's home. I was driving a little two-seater Fiat with the sunroof open. I had picked Jeannie up early in the morning and we had driven into the foothills of the San Gabriel Mountains, hoping to find a good place for a picnic. In those days people in California hadn't yet built a house on every available eighth acre of land and we found an ideal spot—a little grassy area, isolated from the rest of the world under an old and weathered live oak. It was peaceful and quiet; the only noises were those of insects buzzing in the sun, and the water of the stream bubbling over rocks. On the drive home, we were relaxed and content with our own thoughts and feeling no need for conversation.

I drove in a kind of automated haze, but gradually realized that people were passing us—too many people. I glanced at the speedometer, thinking I must have unconsciously let up on the throttle. No, my speed was as it should be, just a hair over the speed limit. Something was different, and I felt a kind of electricity in the air, a nervousness of sorts, an uneasiness. An overactive imagination? Maybe, but why was everyone speeding?

"What's going on?" Jeannie asked, looking out at the road. I had thought she was asleep. She obviously felt something too.

"I don't know," I said. "Look at the cars. Everyone is speeding."

It was weird. The sounds of the cars were muted, pressing into my ears as if I were underwater. I heard my heart beat, and it was racing. What was it? What could it be? What was going on? Jeannie's voice sounded okay. It was happening outside. Something in the air. A shiver of fear ran up my spine. Fear? Of what?

"Are you all right?" I asked.

"Yes. But I feel a little nervous ... kind of jumpy. Something's going on."

"Yeah." I smiled. "Maybe the people from outer space have finally arrived."

"Could be."

"Maybe—" I reached down and turned the radio on and never finished the thought.

The first words we heard were: "... THIS MORNING THE JAPANESE BOMBED PEARL HARBOR AND ... !"

---

1   The Selective Training and Service Act enacted September 16, 1940, as the first peacetime conscription measure in United States history.

Two

As a kid, I was fascinated by airplanes and the pilots who flew them. Charles Lindbergh, Roscoe Turner, Wiley Post, Amelia Earhart and Wrong Way Corrigan were all heroes of mine. I remember a large color print hanging on the wall over my bed—a painting of Lindbergh flying low across the ocean in his *Spirit of St Louis* called "*WE*." I had dreamed that someday I would fly, but never imagined dropping bombs or shooting at other planes. Most of what I knew about war was fiction from books and movie scripts. However, in spite of my naïveté, I knew that if I were going to have to fight, I would rather be in the air than on the ground.

I gave up my apartment in Los Angeles and took my mother back to Pomona. Then, hoping to follow my Chino friends' examples, I set out to enlist in either the Navy Air Corps, or the Army Air Corps. My first choice was the Navy, but unfortunately they had a four-year college requirement. The Army's requirement was two years of college, but they didn't recognize my degree in commercial art. I was discouraged and had no idea what I should do next. I could enlist in the regular Army, which I knew nothing about, with the hope that I would be assigned a job I liked. Or, I could wait for the draft.

Luckily, the Army Air Corps needed pilots desperately. And because of that they soon developed a competitive, day-long written examination that would eliminate the need for the college requirements.[1] I thought it was my pass to flight school until I was about three-quarters through the exam. It was tough, and I had never been good at taking tests. As an art major, it had been a while since I had studied and been tested on the usual school subjects. With sweat and a lot of luck, I squeaked through. Barely. By one point!

Breaking the news of my enlistment to my mother was difficult, to say the least. Even though she was highly sensitive, she hid her emotions from me, determined that I not see her break. When she was young, the horrors of World War I had indelibly

---

1 The Aviation Cadet Qualification Examination, effective January 15, 1942, in lieu of the two-year college requirement. Wesley Frank Craven and James Lea Cate eds, *The Army Air Force in World War II Vol. VI Men and Planes*, Chicago, University of Chicago Press, 1955, p. 491.

impressed upon her and she considered flying risky. Even so, she understood that I had to go to war and gave me the support I needed. Now I realize how much she worried about me before I went away and throughout my years of service. At the time, however, I was still young and naïve and had no idea what a God-awful feeling it was to send your child off to war.

After signing my life away and going through a cursory physical exam, I left Los Angeles on a train, along with approximately fifty other potential warriors. Our train was made up of standard civilian sleeper cars with upholstered seats. It was not unexpected that we have a comfortable, pleasant trip. Why shouldn't we be treated right? We were volunteering our lives to save our country.

An Army sergeant, who was in charge and had all of our paperwork, disappeared as soon as we were loaded on to the train, leaving us with no apparent authority. It wasn't long before we were acting like a group of Boy Scouts without a scoutmaster. Understandable, of course. We were all very nervous, and we expressed it in various ways. Some were outgoing, non-stop talkers, showing their bravura, or describing their fears and apprehensions to anyone who would listen. Many would overreact with too-loud laughter and non-relevant comments. Then there were people like me, struggling with everything we could muster to keep our feelings inside and put up a brave front. Even though I knew it was probably better to loosen up, I just sat there listening to my stomach churn.

The light outside gradually faded into a warm glow as the sun settled behind us. And the window, caked with grime, gave the landscape a softness like an out-of-focus photograph. We passed San Bernardino, which was my last tie to home. The tension of the previous hours finally caught up with me and I drifted into daydreams that I had played out many times before. The details were blurred, but I was always the hero. I flew high above the clouds, but the ugly carnage of the war was forever remote. With victory, I was welcomed home with cheers, and love and tears from my mother. The dream would always stop there. I was a hero, but I had no idea why!

There was a porter, named Joseph, who came around to make up the bunks. He didn't know how to cope with the noisy, rowdy young men, but he knew that they were off to fight for their country and that many would not return, so he put on his best smile and accepted their revelry.

The train was hardly an express, never reaching any worthwhile speed, and stopping completely once in a while, off on a spur for some unknown reason. It would sometimes linger for as long as a half-hour without movement. There might be an occasional whoosh of steam or the squeal of brakes as the wheels jerked slightly. I still remember that metallic, ozone-like smell of the steam on the wheels and rails. For whatever the reason, the stop was an opportunity to get out of the smoke-filled air and stretch our legs. At one of the stops, a couple of guys got off and came back with bread, various cold cuts, bourbon and ice, with heavy emphasis on the bourbon. I was too jittery for partying. I knew I'd feel better if I had a few drinks, but I was afraid I would feel worse in the morning. Instead, my rational thinking led to my decision to climb into my top bunk and get some rest. With a huge sigh of relief, I stretched out and closed my eyes.

Just as my nervousness was finally beginning to ease, and my mind was closing in on more pleasant thoughts, the partygoers decided to make sure everyone was still awake and joining in on the fun. I had no choice but to get up and pretend to enjoy the celebration—of what, I wasn't quite sure. After a while, most eyes were glazed over and words became unintelligible, and I was able to escape back to my berth. Each berth on the train had a curtain for privacy. As I drew my curtain closed, a picture of Marvin Bledsoe was forever imbedded in my mind. He was sitting on the floor, his features in shadow under a weak overhead night light. With a unique grin on his face, he was using an ice pick to whack away at a huge chunk of ice between his legs, while at the same time, performing a running commentary on the advantages of making life in the Army as pleasant as possible. Watching him with the ice pick, I shuddered a little, hoping that drunks have their own special angels watching over them. Thankful to be back in bed again, I was soon lulled to sleep by the clicking of the train's wheels on the rails.

I woke up the next morning tired and feeling the lack of sleep, but I was ready to face the day, and very thankful I had quit the partying when I did. Returning from the restroom, I was surprised to see Bledsoe climbing out of the berth below mine, while Joseph stood by, too, waiting to put the seats back together. Joseph looked at his watch and told us that the dining car would be open in five minutes.

I looked at Bledsoe and smiled. "You don't look much in the mood for breakfast," I said, "but how about some tomato juice or coffee or something?"

He shook his head slightly to clear his vision. "Yeah, well ..." he hesitated. "I don't think so, Blick. You'd better go on ahead ... but thanks."

"Okay." I headed down the aisle toward the front of the train. I was almost to the door when Bledsoe called out.

"Wait, Blick. On second thought the coffee might be good. Give me a couple of minutes." And he headed for the restroom.

Marvin Bledsoe had been my first contact. We quickly learned that everything in the Army was done alphabetically, and he was one of the seven "Bs" that boarded the train with me. He was just ahead of me in line, and not in the least bit shy. He had turned around at one point and started a conversation, forcing me to respond, and I was thankful for the company. He was immediately likeable ... a little taller than I was, maybe five-nine, with thinning, light brown hair and a smattering of freckles. He was outgoing, with complete candor and openness, and had an appealing, slightly crooked smile that was impossible to resist.

We were ahead of the crowd so there were empty tables on both sides of the aisle. As this was my first trip on a train, I was excited to see the tables covered with white tablecloths and set with bright silverware. We would be able to eat our breakfast while watching the scenery. It was a scene right out of the movies. We sat down at one of the tables.

"This is really nice." I said.

"Yeah, it really is. Enjoy it while you can, but don't get used to it. From what I hear, this is not the Army's usual form of transportation."

I couldn't resist. "You're in better shape this morning than I thought you would be. The last I saw of you I didn't even think you would make it to bed."

"My problem now is mostly lack of sleep. Oh, I can feel it—I know I was drinking—but I really didn't have all that much. A little goes a long way with me. A couple of good shots and the rest is mostly water. I learned a long time ago about the payoff in the morning."

"You sound so old. ..."

"Yeah, I suppose I do. It's all relative, you know. Compared to the rest of you guys I am. What are you, Blick? Twenty, twenty-one?"

He was right, and I nodded. "Yeah, twenty-one."

"I've got three years on you." And there was that big grin again. "And, as you'll find out, I imagine, a lot can happen in three years."

That brought up my question, "How come you're here with us?"

"That's easy. I knew they'd need someone who could take care of all you kids. And besides, I thought it would be a good way to get some free flying lessons in real airplanes—something besides those kites I've been flying—"

I broke in. "You're a pilot?"

"Yeah. I have a civilian license. I've been flying off and on for four years, but it's not the same. Like I said, those Piper cubs are so light they're like flying in a kite. I can hardly wait to get into something faster and sturdier."

"But I interrupted ..."

"That's okay;" he thought for a second. "I was just about to say I couldn't just sit around either, with everyone looking at me thinking, 'You 4F bastard, don't you know there's a war on?"[2] He paused for a moment, and his smile turned grim. "But actually, I'm so pissed off with the Germans and the Japs, I can't think about much of anything but getting over there and shooting a few balls off! I *had* to enlist."

"Yeah," I said. "When you boil it down, I guess that's how we all feel."

I found out later that Marvin had thought early on about going into the Air Corps, but until Pearl Harbor, he wasn't completely sure that's what he wanted to do. Even then, he almost didn't make it. He grew up with an overbite and the doctors gave him a hard time on his first physical. They claimed that, because of his mouth formation, he could conceivably have a hard time with oxygen masks—something he had never considered. After a great deal of experimenting and deliberation, however, they relented.

---

2   Bledsoe is referring to the "4F" category of rejection for service on physical, mental or moral reasons under the Selective Service Act that attracted social stigma in the 1940s.

The waiter came and I ordered hotcakes and eggs, which just about made Bledsoe heave. He said he just wanted a cup of coffee, but I told the waiter to bring him a big glass of tomato juice as well.

When the waiter left, I asked, "Tell me a fact, Marvin, where did you get that ice last night?"

Bledsoe, for sure, couldn't be called a handsome, sexy, Hollywood type, but that smile of his would melt the heart of the coolest. "It wasn't that hard," he said. "It's just that the train happened to stop in the right place." He looked at the window, then rubbed it with a finger. "They really ought to clean these windows once in a while. ... It was sort of a spur-of-the-moment thing. I saw that liquor store not far from where we were stopped, and it seemed like a good idea to have a little celebration—you know, sort of loosen everyone up. The guy seemed happy to give me the ice as long as I bought a bottle of hooch. And for another bottle he threw in the ice pick!"

The train arrived in Phoenix about eleven o'clock and we were unloaded and then reloaded into the backs of covered, olive-drab trucks. Then after a dusty, half-hour ride that seemed like two hours, we were again unloaded. We were on the parade ground at Williams Field and ordered to line up as our names were called.

Again, I was standing next to Bledsoe, on my left, and to his left was Bob Bell. We were still together alphabetically. On my right were Joseph Bridges and Brian Buchannan. I didn't know it at the time, but I eventually learned that being a B was a good spot. There were always enough As, so we didn't get all the shitty jobs and the embarrassment of having to go first for things that no one knew how to do. But the best thing was that we were far enough ahead to get whatever it was out of the way quickly, especially the physicals, of which there were many, and it was never very pleasant standing around in lines practically naked. For the doctors, a person at the beginning of the line was a real, live human being, ready and willing to give his life to the cause, but at the end he was just another asshole and penis.

Williams Field [in Arizona] was a newly designated staging area, thrown together practically overnight for the purpose of indoctrinating new recruits into the world of the military. It was set up to outfit us with our uniforms and give us a fast course in military training, which actually turned out to be mostly marching and following orders. Because those people charged with the training didn't know much more than the recruits about what had to be done, there was a great deal of confusion. Bledsoe, who always seemed to know everything about what was going on, just smiled and said we wouldn't be there long because of the Army's need for pilots.

We were marched to our barracks—a long, one-story, wooden building with a pitched roof and doors at each end. As we entered we walked past open toilets on the right and sinks and showers on the left. Then on the right was a small room with a sign that read "Sergeant Ostersen." The rest of the building was one open room, with cots lined up on both sides at right angles to the walls. Between them was a gap of about three feet. The aisle in the center of the building was probably eight feet wide.

Sergeant Ostersen was a regular Army sergeant who was in charge of our barracks. I had the impression he was more concerned with his own importance than he was with our training. He spent a great deal of effort reminding us that we were nothing, neither buckass privates nor cadets.

Our first experience with him was shortly after we found our cots, already designated to us. He was small, but built like a steamroller, and he knew it. His eyes were light blue, and almost disappeared in the shadows of his heavy ape-like brow. He just stood there watching until we were at our cots. Then, with his long arms dangling down like a gorilla's, and without so much as a groan, he strode slowly and deliberately up the length of the aisle and back again, hesitating in front of each person and glaring as if one look was mightier than a thousand words!

We hadn't the slightest idea what we were supposed to do, so we just stood there watching, our suitcases dropped at our feet. I took a quick, sidelong glance at Bledsoe and caught the hint of a smile. We waited, and the more we waited, the more apprehensive we became. The sergeant knew what he was doing.

Finally, when he thought he had created the proper amount of fear, he stood in the center of the building, put his thumbs in his belt and started to speak. I didn't think the anger in his words showed in the eyes. I even thought I saw a glint of humor. His voice was another contradiction. Following the pattern that so often happens—the little man with the huge voice—it was deep and resonant like that of an officious news commentator. The sound was beautiful, but the words were from the street.

In essence, he told us he was a peace-loving guy and he didn't want any trouble, and that he didn't care about us—that we were not going to be there long and he didn't "give a good goddamn if he never saw any of us again." But while we were there we would do as he said. It was the first time we heard him say that we were nothing—that we wanted to be flyboys and that not even half of us would make it. We loved that statement, of course.

He also said there was a bulletin board right outside the PX and that we were to report to the theater at two o'clock for an indoctrination meeting. Then he strutted to his room and slammed the door.

Bledsoe was smiling and said. "I think he was expecting us to applaud."

The indoctrination meeting was a little friendlier and more sympathetic than the sergeant's harangue. The officer at the podium introduced himself as Lieutenant Colonel Phister, Base Adjutant. He was a tall man, close to six feet, and looked to be about forty or a little more—his slightly wavy, gray hair was deceptive. He stood straight, showing two rows of ribbons on his blouse; a perfect picture of a military officer. He smiled and seemed genuinely sincere when he told us, "how good it is to see so many fine young men, eager and ready to offer your services to your country in this time of so great a need."

He explained that we were there to get outfitted and provided with a few basics of military life while waiting for our assignments. He would see to it that we would be as prepared as possible to face our new lifestyle. It would not be easy, because the present emergency required that our training be jammed into shorter hours.

The colonel continued: "That's all I have for now. The next thing on the schedule is to report to the quartermaster for your uniforms. If you don't know your sizes don't worry about it. The men there are good. And, of course, if something doesn't quite fit, go back and change it. You'll be doing a lot of living in those uniforms. … Good luck."

He turned to leave and someone yelled, "TEN-HUT!"

I was at a loss with that, as most of us were, but we finally understood it meant the meeting was over and we got up and started to leave. Suddenly another officer was barking into the microphone. "GET BACK TO YOUR SEATS. YOU ARE NOT DISMISSED!"

He waited until everyone was sitting again, and then sneered, "That was the sloppiest, most irresponsible and disrespectful performance I've ever seen." He was obviously furious, but caught himself and hesitated for a second in an attempt to calm himself. "I realize that you are new and I'll make this one exception, but if it ever happens again you'll be doing a hundred laps around the parade ground. Clear …?

"Now let's do a little practicing. When an officer enters the room, the highest-ranking person yells 'ATTEN-SHUN!' and everyone immediately jumps to attention. That's *up and standing*. Clear? Then he will say, 'As you were,' when he wants you to sit down again. Clear? When he is ready to leave, that same person will yell 'ATTEN-SHUN!' again and, once again, everyone pops to attention. Clear …? And nobody—I repeat NOBODY—leaves without being DIS-MISSED. Now then … have you got it? IS THAT CLEAR …?" He paused, and stood there glaring, letting it all sink in. "Now let's try it out."

We did … about twenty times!

After the trip to the quartermaster and another physical (*what in the world were they looking for?*), we were allowed to go back to the barracks and pack our suitcases to send home with all things civilian. The die was cast.

I was tired. Even with the sleep I had managed to eke out on the train, the strain on my nervous system was beginning to catch up with me. I wasn't the only one, either. Even Bledsoe was slowing down. His smile was still there but it had diminished somewhat, and so had his exuberance. Some kids were strung tight but most were ready to hit the sack. A few were already asleep, still in their uniforms. Down the way a little, Dick Carrington was just sitting there on the cot, spaced out—a long way from his home in Salt Lake. With his light, amber hair and unblemished skin, he epitomized the young, clean-cut, innocent college kid who shouldn't even be out of school yet. I wondered what he was thinking.

My eyes were closed and my mind was beginning to wander into that delightful never-never land of imagination, when suddenly and without warning, a loud, rasping, grating noise came over a loudspeaker somewhere. And then a crackly, somewhat off-key bugle sounded a version of "Taps." There was instant mass reaction, everyone with his own choice obscenity. Someone said, "I thought we were supposed to go to sleep now!"

There was a reply. "We are, asshole; that's Taps—the signal for nighty-night."

"Jesus ... that's great. Wake us up to go to sleep!"

As the last note crackled off, and the sputtering of the recording stopped, we heard the sergeant's door open and the lights went out. Then his door slammed shut.

I was still tired, but the new disturbance had rejuvenated my mind and my eyelids would no longer stay closed. I stared into the blackness, rehashing the past two days. None of my usual go-to-sleep tricks worked. Trying to sleep like this, on a cot, with a roomful of people, was a strange new experience. I heard everything and, as I drifted, all the noises turned up their volume. There were muffled whisperings and groans as people tried to find comfortable positions on uncomfortable beds ... and once in a while a bit of nervous laughter. And Carrington was still rummaging around trying to get undressed and settled. Gradually all those sounds changed to the heavy breathing and light snoring sounds of sleep. For me, however, sleep did not come.

It had been a strange, weird day, and I have never forgotten it. Nothing even remotely resembled what I had expected. But, of course, I didn't know what to expect—in fact, those expectations were more like vague feelings rather than real thoughts. I had just sort of accepted things as they had come along without too much speculation. Early on, I had learned that if I didn't expect too much, I probably wouldn't be disappointed. And it helped to remember what Mr Hazington, one of my art teachers, told me once. He said that in order to be a good illustrator you have to experience all things—that you have to be able to *feel* every situation if you wanted to get that feeling across to the viewer. If you are painting a horse, that horse should *smell* like a horse. ...

We were at Williams only a few days, and thinking back on the experience I have to admit that they did a pretty good job of breaking us in. Some of it wasn't particularly pleasant, but I don't think any of us thought life in the Army would be pleasant anyway. We were there because we felt the necessity to be there and we tried to prepare ourselves for whatever they might throw at us.

First thing in the morning we had a formation outside, while hardly awake—calisthenics to prepare us for our daily activities. I was happy I was in good physical shape. Some weren't, and it was a tough time for them. And we had a lot of drilling. It seemed to me that when they didn't know what else to do with us, we drilled. At one point, they even gave us rifles, which we had to learn to clean and strip. It was hard to imagine what we would be doing with a rifle while flying, but it was good training for something.

One major happening was the trip to the barber. About an hour before lunch on the second day, all training stopped and our sergeant informed us, "This is gonna come as a shock to you, but part of bein' a soldier is to *look* like a soldier. Those beautiful curls and golden locks gotta go! Who knows what's livin' in there." And he guffawed.

There were three chairs and, as always, the line was long, but moving. We were experiencing one of the great Army maxims—*hurry up and wait!* When it was my turn, I had to walk to the third chair, and in trying to be confident, soldierly and business-like, my right foot slipped on the two-inch rug of hair, and I came close to doing a split right there on the floor. It brought a smile to the barber's face. "I guess we'd better sweep up that hair," he said, but made no move toward the broom. I sat down in the chair and watched in the mirror. With all the flair of a matador, he floated the cape over my shoulders and had it tied before it settled. Then, with no wasted motion, he picked up the electric shears and made five passes over my head. The first went down the middle, the next on the right side, taking all of the sideburns, and the third cleared up whatever was left on that side. He followed that with a repeat on the left. The stubble that remained looked to be about a half-inch long. Then with a showy flair, he lit a match and singed the ends of what remained. He removed the cape, shook it, and said, "Next."

The entire procedure took all of three and a half minutes.

On the third day, our regular drill routine was broken and we were herded, once again, into the theater for what we were led to believe would be our final enlightening indoctrination experience. It was a movie, and we found out quickly that we were about to be educated in the pain and miseries of venereal disease.

A soldier went out with a girl who was, unfortunately, all clapped up, but he didn't know it, of course. He just thought she was a virgin. Later on, he was shooting some pool with another soldier friend, and when it was his turn, he put his cigarette down on the edge of the table. His buddy picked it up and took a drag. Oh-oh ... there it was—big tragedy! The poor slob got the clap from that drag on the cigarette!

That was it: *"You never know where the disease lurks,"* and *"Never, never, go unchecked after being with a woman!"*

After the movie, a chaplain took the stage to talk about the dangers of getting involved with girls, and how necessary it was to be wary of them. "It's important to practice abstinence," he said. "I can say proudly that for thirty-one years I have been celibate. Oh, I won't say it has been easy to resist all those lustful temptations, but I know from experience how good it can make you feel."

"Oh my God!" Bledsoe mumbled. "Pardon me while I go puke!"

Someone in the back of us said. "I always thought being celibate meant that you were crazy."

"Well ... !"

Bledsoe was right. Williams got rid of us quickly. The next morning we were told to pack up our stuff—we were leaving. We marched to the parade ground where we were loaded into those same, drab GI trucks. There were more this time, and with their rounded canvas coverings they looked like covered wagons being readied for the trek across the plains.

Rumor had it (mostly from Bledsoe) that we were headed for Thunderbird Field, a country club-like primary training field for pilots, over on the other side of Phoenix. Bledsoe thought we'd be there before noon.

After a long, bumpy and hot ride with nothing but dry, sparsely decorated landscape appearing and disappearing out of the opening in the back of the truck, and clouds of dust from the road rolling in over us, the sound changed. We had pulled on to a graveled parking lot and stopped. We were unloaded before noon.

We looked around and, as implausible as it seemed, we saw an oasis—a real live, honest-to-God oasis, right out there in the middle of nothing. There were a few trees, neat gravel walkways, shrubbery, green grass—it was unreal. Maybe it really was a country club.

I stood there motionless, all of a sudden a strange silence in my head blocking out everything but the eerie whine of an airplane engine somewhere in the distance, an uneasy thrill lurking deep in the hollow of my stomach.

Three

At Thunderbird, our real training began. We had no idea what it would involve, but it didn't take long to find out. We knew nothing about hazing, but we learned quickly. Since then, though, much of it has been discontinued because it is considered too brutal and dangerous and unnecessary.

We were greeted by a cadet officer who, without preliminaries, ordered us to pick up our gear and follow him. "And look a little alert," he said, "you're supposed to be cadets now." With a smirk, he added, "After tomorrow, Misters, you'll wish you were 4F-ers!"

He turned and walked off at a normal pace on a gravel walk lined with olive trees, while we struggled to follow with our B-4 bags. B-4 bags were large Government Issue clothing bags that folded and zipped with pockets on the outside, which were always stuffed and bulging. They were heavy and almost impossible to hold out to the side far enough to keep from interfering with our leg movement.

At the head of the walkway, I noticed a large, weathered, wooden sign, planted in a rocky bed along with an arrangement of small cacti. On it, hand hewn, was a crude but striking, bas-relief of a bird resembling a hawk or an eagle, with wings outspread. "THUNDERBIRD" was carved underneath. I learned later that, in Native American folklore, the Thunderbird caused thunder by beating its wings, and it flashed lightning from its mouth and eyes, causing rain to fall. Most of the tribes also believed the Thunderbird could grant success in wars … that it could conquer evil.

It was interesting, too, to learn later on that Millard Sheets, who was a well-known California artist, had designed this whole field to resemble a Thunderbird. Looking down from the air, the observation tower was the head, the headquarters building the body, the barracks the wings, and the gardens were the tail feathers. We were walking along the Thunderbird's back.

[Thunderbird Field near Glendale, Arizona, was one of the Army Contract Pilot Schools run by civilians to provide prospective pilots with their primary training and expand the Air Corps quickly. A collaboration between the well-known literary agent, Leland Hayward, and president of Southwest Airways, John H. Connelly, it reputedly had a number of famous Hollywood stars as investors. Construction began on January 2, 1941, and the first training flights took place on March 22 of the same year.[1]]

The walk led us to the headquarters building. It was a square, rough stucco, one-story building with a pyramided tile roof. The colors were earth colors—the gray-greens of sage and cactus, mustard yellows of yucca, and grayed-down browns and reds of desert sands. Definitely a tribute to Frank Lloyd Wright's ideals that buildings should fit comfortably into their surroundings. It in no way resembled any picture I had conjured up in my mind of an Army base.

Instead of going into the building, our leader took us around it, into another park-like area shaped like a huge diamond. It was rimmed by long, low structures with eaves hanging over a cement walk and supported by rough-hewn logs. There looked to be about sixteen rooms to a unit.

In the center of the diamond, there was a large well-kept rectangular area surrounding a flagpole. As we straggled to the far side of the flag, our group joined a cadet captain and three cadet lieutenants who were there waiting. We were told to put our gear down and relax a bit. "You Misters will be wise," the Captain said, "to take advantage of every minute you can." We heard, and then looked up to see, a yellow and blue, two-seater, open cockpit biplane, sputtering low overhead as the pilot pulled the throttle back preparing to land.

An officer marched out of the headquarters building and stood, stiff and straight, waiting quietly under the flag. He looked to be about forty-five and stood as if he were wearing a girdle. When all of our lagging recruits finally arrived, he nodded, and our cadet captain asked for our attention. "Gather around, Misters. Colonel Kanner has a few words. ..."

The colonel stepped forward, then waited until all movement and sound ceased. He started to speak, but stopped to let another plane go by.

"Welcome," he said a second time. "I am Colonel Kanner, and this is Cadet Major Odell. I'm sure that most of you are a little nervous and apprehensive ... and that's understandable. This is a school and we run it like a school. But unlike most schools we are military, and we operate under military rules and regulations. We train you to be pilots, but we also realize that a pilot must know more than the technique of flying. We support the flight training with excellent ground-school courses in all applicable subjects—and we make very little distinction between the two. You cannot graduate without passing both. And also, with equal emphasis we train you to be soldiers."

He paused for a moment and flashed a quick smile. "That sounds like a tall order ... and believe me, it is. It's not easy. You will work harder than you ever have in your life. And it will be even harder for your class than the previous ones, because

---

1 See Willard Wiener, *Two Hundred Thousand Flyers—The Story of the Civilian-AAF Pilot Training Progam*, Washington, Infantry Journal, 1945, pp. 144–145.

we've had to accelerate the program. What was a year's effort before, from start to finish, has now been cut, because of the emergency, to eight months.[2] Here at Thunderbird you will have to accomplish in about two and a half months what used to take four. We've tried to condense the courses and we've managed to do it with a few, but we haven't had the time, yet, to adjust everything. I assure you, however, that if you make it through, you will always look back on this time as one of the most memorable experiences of your life."

He paused and looked up to watch another plane. "You will soon discover that this academy is, for all intents and purposes, governed by you and your peers. Cadet officers will be chosen from your class, and they will take over when the present class is graduated.[3]

"Cadet Major Odell is your commanding officer and he will prepare you for your duties as upperclassmen, which in turn will help you with the awesome responsibilities you will face in the future.

"I am always here and available for questions of any kind that can't be answered by any of the upperclassmen or Major Odell. We believe in running a strict military organization, but if you study hard, follow the rules and obey orders, you will have a good time here. I must say, however, that if you don't heed them, we will not hesitate, even for an instant, to eliminate you from the program. We do not tolerate insubordination, unruly conduct of any kind, or any breach of honor." With that, he exchanged salutes with Odell, did a wooden about-face and marched back to the building.

We were divided up into four groups, with each of the cadet officers taking a group. I was assigned to Cadet Captain Sangar. We followed him to our quarters and he patiently showed each of us our room. The rooms were duplexes—dormitory style—with two people in each room and a bathroom between. There were two windows in each room overlooking the courtyard, with a desk and two chairs between. The entrance was from a recess between the two rooms. On the wall opposite the door there was a large closet, and the two beds were butted head-up against the wall opposite the windows. My roommate was Clyde Bressler, and Bledsoe and Hilary Blevins were in our adjoining room.

Sangar left us to "take some time and get settled in," and said he'd be back in an hour or so to give us all the poop. I was familiar with most of the "B" names at Williams, but I didn't really know much about them. Clyde had caught my attention

---

2   Blick is rounding here. Pilot training reduced from one year to nine months on July 1, 1939, and then seven and one-half months on May 24, 1940. It reverted to nine months as of March 15, 1942, for new classes. Rebecca Hancock Cameron, *Training to Fly—Military Flight Training 1907–1945*, Washington, 1999, p. 566.

3   Cadets policed themselves under the "Honor System" modelled on West Point. See Charles Watry, *Washout! The Aviation Cadet Story*, Carlsbad, California Aero Press, 1983, p. 75.

early because he was so much taller than the rest of us—probably about six-one. It was not so much his height, though, as it was his stance. His shoulders were always humped over in a slouch so common with tall people.

Being short, and always yearning for height, it was hard for me to believe this guy's desire was to be short! He was probably just shy and didn't want to be noticed, but by slouching he drew more attention to himself than he would have by standing tall and straight. I couldn't suppress the thought that he would make a good subject for a cartoonist, and I had to smile. His nose was a little sharp and his chin really did recede a bit, and so, with his long neck and slouch, I could see the drawing looking like a vulture, or more likely, Ichabod Crane.

Cadet Sangar came back and rounded up everyone in his group and crowded them all into our room, which was in about the middle of his unit. It made sense, rather than having to repeat himself several times.

"Today you are free," he said, "but tomorrow you are ours!" That sounded ominous, and as he went on, it got even worse. "It's rough," he said, "but you can make it a lot rougher than it really is if you try to resist. If you ever get that kind of a reputation—that you're a sorehead or something—look out. Every upperclassman here will pounce on you faster than a flea on a dog … and your life will be one miserable hell. You just might even be washed out because the Air Corps frowns on that kind of personality. When things get really hard to take, just remember that we all had to go through it and soon it, too, will be over. Then you will have your day as upperclassmen." He went on to explain that no one was allowed to touch us without permission, but they could shout, scream, give us orders, demand that we say or do anything they tell us—"within reason," he said, and smiled.

He went on. "Most of the upperclassmen will respect your study time at night, but there will be times—especially while you're new—when you will have visitors. The first mister to see an officer or an upperclassman will shout 'ATTEN-SHUN' and everyone will immediately drop what they're doing and jump to attention. There is only one exception—the john. You are safe there.

"In the presence of your superiors you are to stand at attention at all times with your eyes straight ahead. Your rooms are to be inspection ready at all times—and I mean *white-glove-inspection-ready.* You will be gigged for any discrepancy ['Gigs' were punishment demerits]—five gigs means one tour, and a tour is an hour pacing off laps on the parade ground. You will double-time (trot) everywhere—no lower-class cadet is to be seen walking, other than on the flight line. If you approach an officer, slow down to a walk and salute."

He stopped for a bit, then worked his way over to Clyde's bed and pulled up one corner. "Now watch," he said. "I'm going to show you how to make a square corner. All corners must be made this way—study and practice so you can do them quickly and easily." Then he tightened the blanket all along the side and pulled a quarter out of his pocket. "I shouldn't show you this, but maybe it'll save you a few gigs." He tossed the quarter on the blanket and it bounced. "If it doesn't bounce, I guarantee you'll get gigged."

He was thoughtful for a bit. "I guess that's about it. If you're lucky and keep your head out of your ass, you'll have some free time on a couple of Saturdays and Sundays. Now let's go get something to eat."

We spent the rest of that first day following Cadet Sangar around. He showed us the mess hall, where the classrooms were, got us outfitted with cadet uniforms and flight suits, showed us where the daily schedules were, and took us to the PX. The upperclassmen stood around laughing and jeering and giving us greedy looks, letting us know they could hardly wait to get their hands on us. I did my best to walk tall and ignore them, but inside, my stomach was mass of jitters, and I was sure the fear was showing on my face.

It started that night. Clyde was sitting at the desk writing a letter and I was hanging up my new clothes when Bledsoe and Blevins wandered in.

"We're off to the PX for a coke," Bledsoe said. "You interested?"

Seeing Clyde writing reminded me that I should write my mother. I had dropped her a short note at Williams, but that was it, and I was sure she was hungry for more information. She didn't even know we had moved.

"Thanks, Marv," I said, "but no thanks. It has been a strange day, and I haven't had much time to digest it all ... and I don't think a coke would help much."

"Clyde?"

"No, I'll bow out, too. I'd like to get this letter finished, and from the sound of things, we're not going to have much free time from here on. If I'm going to get it done, I'd better do it now."

They started to leave, but never made it. As Blevins opened the door, two upperclassmen were coming in. He turned and yelled, "Attention!"

We jumped to attention—heads and eyes straight ahead.

The two upperclassmen stood looking around for a moment, then one asked, "Who said attention?"

"I did," Blevins said.

"You did ... what ... Mister?"

"I called attention."

"You called attention ... *WHAT* ... Mister?

Blevins was at a loss and said, "Yes."

The upperclassman eased forward until his face was inches away. "Now you listen, Mister. Tell me how you address an officer!"

"Sir."

"Now then, I'll ask again who called attention?"

"I did, Sir."

"What was that? I didn't hear you!"

"I did … SIR!"

"That's better."

Satisfied for the moment, the upperclassman joined his friend, who was staring at Clyde.

"What do you make of it, Dan?" His friend asked.

Dan took a turn around Clyde. "Hard to tell. Never seen anything quite like it before. Whatever it is, it sure does need some help."

He pushed his face close to Clyde's, turned up the volume and said, "Hit the wall, Mister!"

Clyde didn't move. "Sir?"

"I said HIT THE WALL! You know what that means, Mister?"

"No, Sir?"

Dan stepped back a little and stood looking at Clyde with a deliberately pained and incredulous expression. "Well now, there seems to be a little education needed here, don't you think, Chuck?"

"I do believe you're right."

Dan took a step backward and said gently. "Now then, Mister, if you'll just be so kind as to walk over there and stand with your back to the wall."

Clyde moved to the wall as ordered. The temptation to smile was strong, but the thought of the consequences was stronger.

Dan followed, giving him just enough time to relax a little. Then he shouted, "BRACE, MISTER!"

Clyde's reaction was immediate. He stood tall against the wall.

"You call that a brace, Mister?"

"He obviously doesn't know what it is, Dan," Chuck said. "We're just going to have to teach him."

"Right,"

They did … and with the decibels on high.

"STRAIGHTEN UP, MISTER!"

"GET THOSE FEET TOGETHER!"

"MAKE THOSE SHOULDERS FEEL THE WALL."

"GET YOUR CHEST OUT."

"SUCK IN THAT GUT!"

"TUCK IN YOUR BUTT, MISTER. I STILL SEE LIGHT BETWEEN YOUR BACK AND THE WALL, Y'HEAR?"

"GET YOUR NECK ON THE WALL—AND TUCK THAT CHIN IN. I WANT TO SEE WRINKLES, MISTER!"

"ARMS AT YOUR SIDE—AGAINST THE WALL!"

"WHAT ARE YOU LOOKING AT, MISTER? GET THOSE EYES STRAIGHT AHEAD!"

They finally stepped back to admire their work.

"Well, Chuck, what do you think? Any hope for it?"

"Geeze, I just don't know—maybe a glimmer. Might help if he stays there for a while, just so he'll sort of get the feel of it, Y'know."

"Yeah, he can use it. Lot of work there, though. I think I'll take him under my wing, so to speak. Make sure he learns, you know. Help him to get through."

"Good idea. ..."

Dan sat down in one of the chairs and looked around for a moment. "What you see there Misters, is a brace," he said. "Learn from it."

He got up and they started out the door, but Chuck turned quickly to Clyde. "Did you move, Mister?"

"No, Sir."

"I didn't hear that!"

"NO ... SIR!"

"See that you don't. We're not out of here yet. You move when you get permission ... understand?"

"YES ... SIR!"

Chuck started out the door once more, but stopped again to take a last look at Clyde. Then he said, "At ease," and walked out.

Clyde waited until he was sure they were gone, and then unwound from the brace and collapsed on the bed.

"I think I'd like that coke now," he said.

The next week was a nightmare—pure torture. Our flight schedules didn't start until the following week and our time was filled with indoctrination formations, and some extra classes, which required frequent traveling around the area. The upperclassmen were relentless in their torment. Trouble was everywhere.

To try to avoid unwanted confrontations, we'd peek stealthily around corners. Then, when the coast seemed clear, we'd blast off at quadruple-time. It was usually a futile try, of course, because the upperclassmen were street smart and knew all the tricks. They were there, somewhere, waiting to pounce. The one haven was the bathroom, and it was a popular place, even without nature's urge. It wasn't a particularly comfortable place to study, but it was the place for any heavy concentration.

There was no rest. Activities started with a morning formation at five o'clock, and didn't quit until Taps at night. And every night was Halloween—only with no treats, just tricks. The ground-school classes started immediately and they were tough—even tougher because there was never any time to study. Also, I had the weird feeling our instructors were making everything as incoherent as possible. We had to study in whatever free time we could scrape together between classes and formations. Because of the harassment, it was nearly impossible to get anywhere on time, thus opening up the opportunity for more gigs. I was not a fast-moving person, having always been classified as easy-going, but it didn't take me long to learn that if I didn't go full speed at all times I'd be walking off tours constantly. I have bragged since that I could return from running a mile, take a shower, get dressed and be present for the next formation in four minutes! I never said, though, that I was such a lousy runner that I was always the last one home.

Dick Carrington, with his light hair and clear skin, looked much younger than his twenty years. He was either intimidated by his new older friends, or very naïve. I suspected a little of each. He had sisters, no brothers, and they had been brought up in Salt Lake as strict Mormons. To go from being surrounded and mothered by females to this rigid and harsh circumstance had to be a shock to his psyche, for sure. He was bright, but that was overshadowed by his naïveté. He tried so hard to be one of the "fellas"; his questions and answers often bordered on just plain dumb. Old man Bledsoe took him under his wing, but there were times when he just had to stand back and watch.

Carrington never seemed to get mad or irritated at the constant interruptions. In fact, he seemed to enjoy it … and that was part of the problem. Whenever he was put in a brace or ordered to do something, he would do it, but always with the hint of a smile—it was like a game. And that's what really pissed off the upperclassmen—they couldn't stand the fact that they weren't getting to him … deep down. It didn't take long before the word was out—that he was a smart-ass kid who thought he was one of God's chosen. And of course that meant that he needed a little extra help with his training.

They were ruthless. When one group would leave, another would take over. Wherever he went he would be approached, and his unit was the noisiest in the whole compound. Shouts of "TEN-HUT" and screamed orders were heard at night until Taps. Carrington's roommates couldn't all fit in the john at the same time, so they had to spend their evening hours trying to find a place to study. They were persecuted just because they happened to live with him, and because "they were negligent in their duties." They were supposed to show Carrington the way!

We suffered also because of Carrington's relationship with Bledsoe. He was in our rooms much of the time. The routine would be similar to that first night. Someone would come in and put us all in braces, then find something to harangue Carrington about.

"When I say brace I mean BRACE! Do you know what that is, Mister?"

"Yes, Sir."

"What was that?"

"YES, SIR!"

"You sure don't act like it, Mister. Get that chin tucked in—I wanta see those wrinkles!"

"Are you smiling, Mister?"

"NO, SIR!" Try as he might, though, Carrington could not control that smile.

"What's so funny, Mister?"

"Nothing, SIR."

"Get those eyes straight ahead! ... May I touch you, Mister?"

"Yes, SIR."

"Do you know there's a loose button on your shirt?"

"No, SIR."

He yanked one of the buttons off and held it up into Carrington's line of sight. "That's one gig for not being properly dressed."

"Yes, SIR."

There was no escape. After classes, he'd find the bed corner messed up, or something else out of order. Three days into that first week and he was already walking more tours than anyone on the base. He tried to study as he walked, but that negated a third of the tours he had walked by adding more gigs. Fortunately, the classes came easy for Carrington, and he could get by without much studying. Nevertheless he was still looking forward, longingly, to the haven of the flight line, and relative peace for part of the day, at least.

For me, the ground school classes were almost punitive. I had never been a good student in subjects that didn't interest me, and I was one of the first to say, "What in the hell do I need this for?" I'd try to retain the information, but it would just fade right out of my mind when I left the classroom, especially if accosted by upperclassmen. It wasn't long before I became worried about passing.

There were courses in Weather, Communications, Engines, Theory of Flight and Navigation, plus detailed military administration instruction, which made no sense at all. I could relate to Weather, and Navigation seemed important, too, but I had trouble with the math. The concept of triangulation and wind drift came easy because it was visual, but working it out accurately in numbers was tough on me.

I thought the class on engines was excellent for a mechanic, but for a pilot? What was I supposed to do if the engine was balking, stop and fix it? The Communications class was a disaster. We had to learn the Morse Code, not only in dahs and dits, but also in light flashes. I couldn't even tell the difference between a long flash and a short one. Part of the course, though, was learning how to ride a beam into an airport, and I picked that up easily.

I did, however, enjoy the course in flight. Up to then my knowledge of flight consisted of feeling my hand go up and down as I held it out the window of a moving car, and blowing on a toy propeller. I had no idea that a wing gave a plane lift because of the lack of pressure above it. I thought the wind pushed it up. We studied instruments, controls, and all the maneuvers we were likely to encounter, as well as those we weren't. We learned about the G forces on the body—how we could black out—and the "red out" of negative G forces, which left a horrible image of broken blood vessels in my mind.

The first formal inspection was announced ahead of time for two o'clock that first Thursday. It was pathetic. We were dressed in our khakis and overseas caps, and stood at attention at the foot of our beds while Odell and a cadet lieutenant with a clipboard found something wrong with almost everything, including getting the white glove soiled on top of the door jam.

In the bathroom, where the gigs were shared, there was a dark curly hair found in the shower drain, a smudge on the upper right-hand corner of the mirror, dirt on the trap under the sink, a slight, almost invisible yellow ring in the toilet bowl, a pale yellow spot back of the seat, and the toilet paper was not rolled up tightly.

The lieutenant did the coin trick on the beds and I survived, but Clyde's blanket didn't perform well, giving them a good excuse to tear up the bed. He was gigged also for wrinkles in the sheets and uneven corners. The chairs were not positioned at right angles to the desk; there was a little dust on the inside of the lampshade, and the drawers were not neat. The windows were, of course, spotty—if nothing else, they could always pick on the windows.

My shoes were not polished properly, nor was my belt buckle. My cap was two and a half inches above my right eye instead of the required two inches, and my left collar wing was not completely at rest. I was told that my tie could be tucked into my shirt a little neater, but otherwise I was in fine shape! Clyde was okay except for his belt buckle. They probably felt they had done enough damage to him already with his bed.

Bledsoe said later on that they'd probably get more lenient later on—that they had to do that so we'd know what would be required the next time. He was right, as usual. Every week there was a repeat performance and they were mostly okay. We didn't anticipate, however, the "informal" inspections, or what should be called "harassment" inspections. There were numerous occasions when I would come back to my room to find gigs placed around in strategic places, as on the bed or in the closet or the desk drawer. Many times the bed would be torn up, and the bathroom was a favorite. We learned quickly that we had to hit the john accurately, keep everything spotless at all times, and leave no hairs. The last one out of the bathroom in the morning took a last swipe at the mirror and dried every drop of water in the sink, and then stuffed the taps with toilet paper to stave off any loose drips. Later on, after living through it, I had to admit it was good training!

Four

When the long-awaited morning arrived, a notice was posted on the bulletin board listing the lower-class flight assignments, and their instructors. There were six cadets to a flight. My flight was scheduled to meet our instructor by the tower at six-thirty. We were to be in flight suits, ready to fly. Our instructor's name: William Handel.[1]

Finally!

Other than John Balason, who was one of the Bs on the train, I didn't know the others. Their faces were familiar, though. While waiting for Handel we used the time to get acquainted. Raymond Betner was small, with white, bleachy-looking hair and an unmistakable New York accent. I couldn't help thinking that this wide-open Arizona desert must be a tough transition to make from tall buildings and busy streets.

John H. Baer III was about my height, maybe five-eight.[2] He wasn't fat, just a little ample here and there, especially in his face, which seemed a little too fleshy, and made his eyes appear smaller and closer together than they really were. There was a slight puffiness around his eyes, disguising his cheekbones and indicating, perhaps, a little overindulgence in the good life. Because of his very "proper" usage of the language, he seemed a little pompous, but not at all unpleasant. He was also from Los Angeles. I knew immediately that we had walked to different beats. I mentioned that I didn't remember his being on the train, and he smiled. He said he missed the train and had to go by automobile. He was put in with the Zs at Williams.

Henderson Cagle was big-boned, with large, heavy overdone features, a neck the size of a normal thigh, huge shoulders and a chest that would put a wine vat to shame. He wasn't really tall, maybe five-eleven, just thickset and burly—definitely a football player, and someone I wouldn't want to tangle with. He was from Arkansas.

No one could dislike Balason. With his upbeat attitude he was a pleasure to have around. He was young, even younger than Carrington, and in the Air Corps only

---

1 William Handel appears to be a fictionalized name—W.A. Hammett signed off Blick's early flights in his logbook. Given the uncertainty, I have left "Handel" in the text.
2 Baer is a fictionalized name.

because he'd been able to fudge on his age and get away with it.³ A dedicated eager beaver, he was quick to learn, and shrewd enough to keep his mouth closed and listen. Like Bledsoe, he already had a few hours in light planes and could hardly wait to get into the air.

I was mesmerized by the sight of so many planes and had never before seen such a number at one time. My only previous experience was seeing a small run-down, weedy, country airfield with a tin-roof hangar, two fragile airplanes and a windsock. Here there were several rows of planes, lined up at right angles to the tower and the runway—all the same, blue and gold, two wings and two open cockpits.

Handel was thin, lanky and deeply tanned, with dark, neat, straight hair and stood about five-nine. The combination of high cheekbones and leather-like skin gave him a Native American look. I guessed his age as middle thirties. He was dressed in a uniform of sorts—matching gray shirt and pants, called pinks, but with no recognizable insignia. When he approached, we didn't know if we were supposed to salute or not. Balason started to, but then reneged when no one else did, but his action was just enough to make the rest of us think we should. The result was an embarrassing confusion.

Handel's face opened up with a big toothy smile and he touched his right temple in acknowledgement. "I guess we'd better get something straight right off," he said, and went on to explain that he wasn't an officer—wasn't even in the Army; that he was just plain Mister. He said, "Most of us here are civilian instructors. There are a few Air Corps officers, but their instruction is mostly limited to check rides."

He continued. "Here on the flight line, you are at ease. The hardline discipline is relaxed because we want you to be able to concentrate on the flying. Flying is hard enough without a lot of excess disarray strewn around in your mind. That doesn't mean, of course, that I shouldn't get the same respect any instructor does, however. I'm sure you understand that."

He led us over to the hangar, to one of the benches under an overhanging eave, and motioned for us to sit. "I have a few things to say before we get started," he said, and then disappeared into the hangar to get our logbooks, which he handed out. "While you're with me, I'll keep your books up to date, but first turn to the second page and fill in the part [on who] to notify in case of an emergency.

"This is where we'll meet every morning. You'll be spending a lot of time here until you solo, and it's a good place to study, so come prepared. For those of you who don't know, the planes out there that you will be flying are designated PT-17s. They're Primary trainers, made by Stearman, and they are good planes, rugged and

---

3   John Macke Balason of San Diego, CA, born October 18, 1923, would have been eighteen in early 1942. While young, the Army Air Force had changed its age requirement from twenty to eighteen, effective January 5, 1942. See Craven and Cate, *Army Air Force in WWII*, Vol. VI, p. 494.

dependable, with plenty of power—220 horsepower radial engines. You won't have any trouble. Landings are the toughest because the wheels are close together and the plane tips easily. You have to stay right on the rudders—no relaxing.

"Before we actually start in, I'd like to give you a little run-down on what we'll be doing. Flying is a matter of control, and all of the exercises we do are designed to help you learn that control. There are the basic maneuvers like S turns across a road while holding your altitude, figure eights, spins and stalls. Then the more complicated chandelles and rolls. Here, you will learn good, smooth, basics. You'll have plenty of time later to get involved with the more dramatic and complicated maneuvers. It's important to get to the point where you no longer have to think about the technical part of handling the airplane … to where it's automatic.

"Along with control, and even more important, is the matter of judgment. A simple detail like a landing approach is all judgment, and weighs heavily in your final testing. One other thing—probably the most important life-saving exercise you will have—the forced landing. You will have this throughout your training. Your instructor will cut the throttle at the most unexpected time, and at that point you are to handle the airplane as if the engine died. You have to look around, try to determine the wind direction and find a good place to land, then glide in and hit that spot. The instructor will wait until he sees how close you come to making it, and then he'll shove the throttle forward again. You can't fly with the expectation that the engine will quit at any moment, but it *is* just a machine, and sometimes it happens. If you are properly prepared, you'll be able to handle it."

Handel looked down at his list and said, "Okay, it's time to start. I'll take Balason first. The rest of you just wait here." Balason got up and they walked out to the planes. I watched them go, wishing I'd been the first, yet glad I wasn't.

My butterflies were on a rampage. I asked Baer how he was feeling; if he was ready to go.

He said, "Yes, I believe so. I'm a little apprehensive, but I presume that's a normal reaction."

"Have you ever been up before?"

"No … never."

"Neither have I."

Handel stopped at the first plane in the row directly in front of us. He motioned for Balason to get in the front cockpit, hopped up on the wing to check him out, then climbed in back. When he was strapped in and ready, he leaned over and yelled to the crew chief, "Switch off, gas on." The crew chief repeated the statement, reached up and pulled the propeller through a couple of times to pump fuel into the cylinders, then stepped back. Handel called, "Contact." The crew chief repeated "Contact," then put his hands on the prop and gave a big yank downward. The engine popped and sputtered, puffing smoke out of the exhaust, catching sporadically until finally smoothing out into a steady purr. They moved out of the line and started toward the runway. I was reminded of starting the old Model T my friend, Kenny Mongrain, had in high school—it's prop was a crank.

The routine was simple, and the same every morning. We waited and studied while student and instructor flew. The flight time varied, but averaged a little over half an hour. When our time was up, we taxied back to our spot, and Handel would stay in the plane with the engine running while the next student climbed in. We were thus occupied five mornings a week on the flight line—and a welcome relief it was, away from the agony and distress of harassment.

While in the air, communication was less than adequate. We had stethoscope-like tubes attached to a cable, which ran into the other cockpit. There was a metal mouthpiece on the ends we had to shout into. They reminded me of those old tin-cans-on-a-string "telephones" we made when we were kids. They never worked either. We soon found out it was easier to shout back and forth over the sounds of the wind and the engine, and use sign language. It was a little hard on the throat, but gradually, as we became more familiar with Handel's actions and directions, the need for shouting decreased.

Because he wanted us to have confidence in the airplane, and to find out if we had any tendency toward air sickness, he took us cautiously through all the aerobatics, including snap-rolls and Immelmanns. An Immelmann was the start of a loop but with a roll-out at the top. However, he made it clear that we were not to indulge in such maneuvers—that we were to spend our time practicing the basics.

And we did. Over and over, and over again, we did our S's and figure eights over the roads. It was hard to hold altitude because of the lag in the altimeter. And without an airspeed indicator, the difference in the sound had to be picked up quickly to stop the gain or loss of altitude. All instruments, except the altimeter and the needle and ball, had been taped over. "You have to learn to fly by the seat of your pants," we were told, "and listen to the sound of the guy wires as they vibrate in the wind."

Balason, with his avid, youthful enthusiasm, was the most talkative about his adventures, explaining in great detail how he was beginning to master the differences between the Stearman and the Cub he had flown; how this plane was so much heavier, and how hard it was to keep from over controlling. "It's so powerful," he remarked. "If there is so much difference between this and a Cub, what a fantastic thing it must be to fly a fighter! I can hardly wait."

"In due time … in due time," Baer said. "Perhaps it would be better to center your focus on the assignment at hand—one step at a time. Don't you suppose?"

One morning, a little over two weeks after their introduction to the flight line, Handel and Balason were late returning and we were getting a little antsy, for fear something had happened. We began to watch each plane that landed until it taxied to a stop. Finally, one pulled up to our spot and Balason climbed out. We could tell he was excited from the way he hopped down off the wing. His hands went up in a sign of triumph as he ran and danced toward us.

Balason had soloed, at seven hours and six minutes—the first in our flight. He was ecstatic and couldn't stop talking. He had flown twelve minutes all alone and did three landings all by himself at a little landing strip north of the field, which the instructors used for just that purpose.

In answer to a question earlier, Handel had told us that it usually took about eight hours to solo. He didn't say, but we heard from other people that it could go as high as ten. But that was it. If we didn't make it by then we were out—on our way to Navigation or Bombardier School, or some other godforsaken punishment.

I thought about that a lot, and it didn't help my nervousness a bit! I was tense, and much too tight on the controls. The eighth hour came and went, and my concern deepened. It seemed that the more I flew the worse I got. I knew what was going on, and tried my best to calm down, but the minute I wrapped my hand around that stick I could feel it happening … the rush of blood and the muscles tightening.

"Washing Out" was a common fear—something we talked about only rarely and in a hushed voice. We could logically say to ourselves that not all people had the coordination, or skill, or whatever it was, to fly an airplane, and it didn't mean they were useless, but emotionally it was shameful. Those people who couldn't make it were told one day and were out the next—eliminated, just written off like they never existed, and no one ever heard from them again. Of course it wasn't quite that bad, it just seemed that way. Most of the washouts went on to become navigators or bombardiers.

In our flight, we all thought that if anyone didn't make it, it would be Baer. He just didn't seem the pilot type. We thought of him more as a "ground pounder"—an office worker, a teacher, a controller maybe, but as a pilot, never. And he was the second one to solo!

I continued over-controlling everything. On my turns I couldn't come close to holding my altitude, and on landing, I either dropped it in from too high or rammed it into the ground. It was a rugged airplane, for sure, and I was thankful.

Handel seemed to understand, and was sympathetic. He did what he could to help me relax, but nothing worked. Something deeply distressing happened when I got into that cockpit—I just broke apart, and I couldn't understand it. I was a good driver, a gymnast with excellent coordination, and I knew I could fly—that I could be a good pilot. But that cockpit! Why couldn't I just sit back and enjoy the ride like I did in a car? What was so damn different? But then I remembered how frightened and nervous I was on my first driving test.

I was just shy of nine hours when, finally, I was told to go to the auxiliary runway and land. Handel gave me a pat on the shoulder and got out, "Take it up," he said, and I was alone … *all alone!*[4]

---

4   Blick's logbook indicates that he took his first flight at Thunderbird on February 25 and soloed on March 18, 1942, with 8 hours, 57 minutes of flight time.

My take-off was atrocious, but I was determined, and with a bumpy, roller-coaster ride, I leaped into the air on the third try. I let out a huge, audible gasp of elation, and then tenderly lowered the nose to pick up enough speed to circle the field.

Something strange and bewildering happened next. There was a sudden lull, a calmness, as if I had entered another dimension—a time warp of some kind. Even the engine was smoother and quieter. My stomach was calm, there was no throbbing at the temples, and my hands were dry and relaxed on the stick. I felt the tension dissipate—just drain right out—and for the first time I felt at ease. No panic. I maneuvered slightly to the right, my hand gentle on the stick, and leveled off. Finally … and with an overpowering sense of relief, I sat back and looked around. I was alone without the fear of those critical eyes watching my every move. I was free.

Free …! I was an eagle, my wings outstretched, soaring with the wind. I no longer had to fly the plane—I *was* the plane. It responded to my every thought. Never had I known such freedom, such euphoria. The wind talked in new musical sounds, singing and whistling in a different tone for every change in speed. I felt every variation of movement in, as they said, the seat of my pants!

It was truly a miracle—the ultimate escape—and I didn't want to go back to that reality below. But of course I had to. I returned to the landing strip and shot three landings, all so smooth I hardly felt the runway. When I taxied to our spot, I reached up and shoved my goggles up on my forehead to signify that I had soloed. Until we soloed we had to wear our goggles around our neck and suffer the onus of being called a Dodo![5] Handel had a smile on his face, and said, "Nice landings. We can go home now."

A few mornings after most of the lowerclassmen had soloed, Odell announced, "There was an accident yesterday. Cadet Gerald Joseph Bridges was killed while landing. No one knows yet what happened, but either he got foot-heavy on the brakes, or they locked. He flipped completely over on his back shortly after touching down. It may sound callous at this point, but things like this do happen and usually it's because the pilot was careless. We can't dismiss anything like this casually, but our job is to carry on regardless. It's important that we learn from these mistakes and see that they don't happen again."[6]

We had heard about the accident, but it didn't make much of an impression on me until my line shortened. Joe Bridges' spot was just one away, on the other side of Clyde, and when Brian Buchannan moved left to that spot, I felt an emptiness,

---

5 Common to all primary schools and referencing a "flightless" bird.
6 According to his logbook, Blick was flying at Thunderbird from February 25 to April 21, 1942. Of the three accidents at Thunderbird in February, eleven in March and one in April, only one accident appears to have been fatal. Eugene J. Black died in a ground collision in his PT-17 nine miles south of Thunderbird on March 27, 1942. Given the proximity to Blick's solo flight, it seems likely Black is "Bridges" in the text. See https://www.aviationarchaeology.com/, accessed May 6, 2020.

a void that I didn't understand. Death was no stranger to me. I had watched my father, my grandfather and my grandmother die slow agonizing deaths, but this was not the same.

I hardly knew Joe Bridges, yet that simple movement of Brian's to fill Joe's space, literally disintegrated a whole person. He was blacked out, erased, crossed off the list, never again to be seen. Gerald Joe Bridges had never been there. For all we would know, he had never been born.

I couldn't help but think of my own mother—what it would be like for her if I had been Joe, and I thought of all the other mothers who had sent their boys off to do battle with the power-hungry, evil people who caused it all, and never even got the chance.

As the time approached for the upper class to be graduated, much of the talk centered on the customary tug-of-war between the two classes. The contest was held on the last day before graduation, and symbolized the end of the hazing. It was a battle for supremacy. In the history of Thunderbird, the lower class had never won, and the word was out that that was intentional—that no matter how good they were, the lower class always deferred to their superiors.

I was with Bledsoe, Balason and Baer at the PX and we were talking about it, when someone suggested, "It's about time for all that ol' malarkey to stop."

"Right!" We all agreed. Even Baer said, surprisingly, "I feel it would be a major triumph for us to pull those scoundrels through that mass of muck and mire. Yes, it would be a very satisfying experience indeed."

Bledsoe was all smiles. "I'm not sure exactly what the hell John is talking about, but I think I'm all for it. We have to make sure, though, that we don't let it out to them. We think it's tough now, but life would be unbearable if they even had a hint of what we're thinking."

"Y'know," I said. "I'll just bet we could do it. We don't have a lot of big guys, but we have a whole bunch of short, stocky muscle. And we do have Cagle. We could put on a good show anyway."

We had barely a week to prepare. I was voted emissary, and I rounded up the twelve most likely cadets, in my judgment anyway, who would pull with the most muscle and determination. With the exception of Cagle and Clyde, who desperately wanted a taste of revenge, we were all short, under five-nine, compacted, agile and sturdy. Three were weightlifters, and all had played football or some major sport.

Argie (Theodore Argiropulos) was another Californian who was an old hand at tug o' wars and told us the secret was to pull together in rhythm, at the same time, just like the crewmembers rowing in a scull. "On count," he said. "We pull in unison, hard, then ease up and pull again, and keep the rhythm going. They won't know what hit them until it's too late."

We practiced a little, in twos and threes and fours on the flight line when we had a chance, but the upperclassmen sensed that something was brewing, and they wouldn't leave us alone. It was the worst week ever. Their favorite question was "Who will win the tug of war?"

The date was set for Friday at four o'clock, after classes, on the ball field out behind the barracks. I rushed back to my room, changed to my shorts, then hurried out toward the field. I was waylaid before I had taken my sixth double-time step. There was no way I could ignore the bellowed, "HALT, MISTER!"

I stopped abruptly and stood at attention, eyes straight ahead, and the upperclassman circled around like a sniffing dog on the make. I had a terrible thought that maybe they were all over the area keeping the participants away.

"Where are you going, Mister?" He said.

"To the ball field, SIR!"

"Why are you going to the ball field, Mister?"

"The tug of war is today, SIR."

"Are you in it, Mister?"

"Yes, SIR."

"*And who will win today, Mister?*"

There it was—the dreaded question I knew was coming. I knew what I should have said, but I was hyper and a little out of control. I blurted out "We will, SIR."

There was a long, crushing silence, and I knew the wheels were turning, slowly and deliberately.

"WHAT DID YOU SAY, MISTER?"

"WE WILL, SIR!"

Another silence, and then, "Well now, Mister, that's what I thought you said, but I just figured my hearing was goin' bad. I don't know how you managed to get things so twisted around. Why don't you and I take a little walk out to the field and get you straightened out?"

"Yes, SIR."

He started to walk on, then turned as if he had a sudden afterthought. "You know what a duck walk is, Mister?"

"Yes, SIR."

"Glad to hear it. You know how a duck flaps its wings and quacks when it walks?"

"Yes, SIR."

"Good. I want you to show me and all those other people out there how you do that. And I want to see those elbows flapping and hear that mouth quacking. NOW LET'S GO, MISTER!"

With all of my gymnastics, I had developed a strong upper body, but my legs were slight. I was never very good at ground tumbling because I lacked that necessary bounce. It was some crazy, weird, cruel insight that allowed that particular upperclassman to lock on to my Achilles heel. I had to travel all the way around our barracks unit, and then on out to the playing field which was at least another thirty yards.

I didn't see how I could make it, but I had to. It was a matter of honor. I got down on my haunches and started to waddle. I flapped and quacked, and I was a duck—no doubt about it. But no duck had ever been so miserable. I was at the point of collapse at the end of the unit, and there was still a long way to go.

We had picked up several more obnoxious upperclassmen. With all the quacking and laughter it had developed into quite a show. It crossed my mind that I was a little like the Pied Piper.

My legs were the first to go of course, but the flapping and shouting were draining the stamina I needed for those weary leg muscles. I tried to ease up on the arm movement, but it only served to draw added attention. My flaps were already down to about a third of what they were, in movement as well as speed. But the legs—my poor gimpy legs. I was no longer conscious of what they were doing. Automated, they were moving with slow, trembling, unsteady steps like a broken down rusty robot, struggling in the sands of the Sahara. I could no longer raise my feet, and they dragged in the dust leaving tracks like two snakes in formation.

As if in some kind of marathon race, the crowd had joined in. People were cheering and yelling me on, making me even more determined to go until that point of collapse. I was too unconscious to hear them, but I was told later that many upper-class voices were in with the cheers.

My original tormentor finally stopped me near the contest site.

"We all enjoyed the walk, Mister," he said. "Did you?"

It wasn't easy, but I managed to muster up a wobbly, "Yes, SIR."

"Now we can all watch and see who wins."

"Yes, SIR."

I couldn't get up. There was no more push left in my legs. I rolled over on my side and tried to extend my legs, but they were so cramped they wouldn't move. I didn't have the muscle to straighten them. I worried about who could take my place—I hadn't thought about a spare.

As soon as the upperclassman left, Argie hurried over and started massaging my muscles. He was good at it and soon had them straightened out. "I think you'll be okay if they'll just hold the tug of war off for a little while longer," he said.

Argie worked on me until it was time, and we took our pre-planned positions on the rope, Argie on the end as coxswain. I wasn't sure how much good I could do, but I was there anyway. Between the two teams there was a mud moat, about fifteen feet wide. Four people, two from each class, controlled a fire hose to spray water across the center. The object, of course, was to pull the opposing team through the water and the mud all the way across and out the other side.

The upperclassmen were confident—there was no reason not to be. It was a tradition that they win. It had always been thus and thus it would always be. They were dead wrong. They didn't reckon with our determination, our conviction, and certainly our boldness. And the low blow pulled on me fueled our anger. Where before we would have treated it like a highly competitive game, now we were outraged, almost violent in pitch and bent on humiliation.

Tradition also dictated that all members of the losing class walk through the moat and the fire hoses, and they were completely unprepared, much to our delight.

It was a magnificent victory for us, but the graduates were smart and played it down, taking a little of the sting away. On the day of their departure, they made the rounds, congratulated us, as new upperclassmen, and told us what a pleasure it had been knowing us and hoped that we would meet again. And then it was time for our retribution. ...

Gleefully, and barely able to contain ourselves, we watched the new class struggle in. Our pent-up frustrations needed release, and the time had come. It was something akin to returning home after a bad day at the office and kicking the dog. However, we soon realized that it was a frivolous and unsatisfactory sport. We continued with the braces, the "Sirs" and the inspections, because of their potential value—all were part of military training. But we no longer had the heart for deliberate embarrassment and humiliating harassment.

I was relieved to be rid of such time consuming activities—we all were—and I needed to concentrate on my school classes. School had never been easy for me and we had been told over and over that a passing grade was mandatory if we were to graduate. It was necessary, even though a person might be the most exceptional pilot to ever go through the program. It was worrisome, and hard for me to understand the logic. It didn't make a lot of sense that if a pilot couldn't read his dahs and dits, he wouldn't be able to shoot down a Hun.[7]

And there was something else that bothered me, and I just didn't know how to cope with it. I knew I was a good pilot. When I was alone I could fly like I was born with wings, but let someone climb into that other cockpit and watch, my old test-taking nerves would climb right in there with me. My hands would get sweaty and my thought processes would automatically shift into low gear. I'd handle the plane like the stick had a mind of its own. I'd over-control, misjudge forced landings, and louse up simple things like the landing pattern—in general, look about as inept as a newly hatched bird hopping out of its nest.

I talked to Handel about it. He said he understood—that he was a little like that himself. "But," he said, "it's not me that you have to convince. It's your check-rider. It won't matter a damn what I tell him. If you go up there and do a lousy job for him, he'll wash you so fast you won't know what hit you. No quarter—his word is final!" That didn't help—not at all!

"What you have to do is get up there and practice, then practice some more, until you can do all those maneuvers right on the nose, automatically, without even

---

7   Dits and dahs or dots and dashes refers to Morse Code that uses a series of short dits and longer dahs to represent the letters of the alphabet for communication.

thinking about them. Make believe he's back there all the time, checking you out, watching your every move."

"You're right," I said. "I know you're right. I'll try."

"You've got to do better than that. Do it. Don't just try."

It helped. I felt I was getting a little more relaxed. But Bledsoe—the kid that never cracked a book—was no help at all. He was forever optimistic, and with good reason it seemed. He was a natural at whatever he tried. I wondered if he ever went through the exercises. He would come in from a flight with various exciting stories—none, of course, resembling anything like the standard maneuvers we were supposed to practice. He loved to buzz—see how close he could get to the cactus—but the favorite was how he'd go up to 10,000 feet or so, then toss out a roll of toilet paper and see how many times he could cut it before it reached the ground. Never a worry about washing out.

If I questioned him about the exercises, he'd come up with something like, "What I'm doing is going to help me in a dogfight a lot more than perfect S turns over a road."

"Yeah, I'm sure you're right, but we're dealing with a system here that we have to get through. I'd like to see you convince Lieutenant Jacksen that those S turns are not important."

"Oh hell, Blick. They're so easy I can do them in my sleep. You know that … and you can too. What you need to do is relax a little. Go up there and have some fun for a change. It would help, you know." He grinned. "You'll find that you can go back down there and knock those turns off easier than seducing a whore."

I was ready to try anything. The next day I went up to altitude and just flew—once again capturing that remarkable birdlike feeling I had the day of my solo. I needed it. Such a refreshing pleasure! I had been so swept up in the technical aspects of handling the plane, I had all but forgotten the thrill of being up there all alone with just the singing of the wind and roar of the engine for company, high above the problems of the classrooms and technical perfection.

When it was time for my final check-ride, I was as ready as I ever would be. I met Lieutenant Jacksen on the flight line and we walked out to the plane together. The lieutenant wasted no time on cordialities—he got right to the point. He used the walking time to inform me what I was supposed to do, with the explanation that he didn't want to have to shout while in the air. It was a simple routine, one that I had done at least a hundred times, starting out with the higher-altitude maneuvers like the spin and the rolls, then down to 200 feet for the figure eights and S's.

As I taxied out to the runway, I felt the lieutenant's feet riding the pedals, and the nervousness was back, in full. It was not quite the same as having an imaginary person in that seat. I knew my every movement was being watched and graded. My confidence disintegrated to the extent that I even began to doubt my ability to taxi. My turns were jerky and I was heavy on the brakes. I couldn't even keep the speed constant. I'd slow almost to a stop, then shove the throttle forward too fast and have to hit the brakes again.

At the runway, I stopped, revved it up to check the mags, then pulled out to take off. It was a disaster. Jacksen was on the controls continuously, anticipating my every move. Each movement was a battle of wills. The engine's torque pulled the plane to the left, as was normal, and when I countered with the right rudder, Jacksen did also. The combination was too much pressure, of course, and the plane veered to the right. The reaction was to use the left rudder, but the same thing happened. The result was a kind of snake-like slither down the runway, all the way to lift-off. And at that point, I was so swept up in the confrontation with Jacksen and the battle for supremacy, that I forgot there was the matter of getting into the air. When it hit me that it was time to haul the stick back, we both pulled at the same time, much too hard, and the plane literally jumped into the air at an angle that could not possibly sustain flight. My reaction was immediate, and I pushed forward too hard, ramming the wheels back on to the runway. That happened twice before we were finally into the air to stay. I had clear visions of navigation or bombardier school.

As we climbed to altitude, the ride got smoother. I was furious at both myself and Jacksen. I felt foolish for letting the lieutenant influence my control. The madder I got the more confident and determined I became. *I knew I could fly and damned if I would let some crazy lieutenant get in my way because he was so scared to just sit back and enjoy the ride.* I forgot Jacksen as best I could, but it wasn't easy. There was the constant struggle for the controls. Gradually, however, as we went through the various maneuvers and it was obvious I could handle the plane, the pressure from behind eased.

I pulled up into a stall, kicked the rudder, shuddered over, and spun down to where I could do my controlled S's and eights. I did them with no more than fifty feet variance in altitude. Bledsoe had been right. They were easy, once I got over that fear of failure.

After finishing the last series of S's, I turned to go back to the field. Halfway through the turn, in a steep bank, Jacksen yanked the throttle. I had forgotten the forced landing was due and I was totally unprepared. I had planned to make sure I knew what the wind direction was at all times, but the frustration with Jacksen at the onset had erased it from my mind. I felt the old panic coming ... here I was—200 feet, in the middle of a turn, and the engine conks. First things first. I leveled out, then started to look for some sign of wind direction. I looked for smoke but didn't see any. I saw a car kicking up some dust, and then had to find a place to land. There was no time and I picked a spot that looked flat and fairly smooth, set up a glide speed and headed in that direction. I knew I wasn't going to make it—there was just no way to stretch that glide.

As we lined up with the field, Jacksen shoved the throttle forward for a second, and then pulled it back, something all instructors did to "clear the engine." I never knew if Jacksen saved me intentionally or if he was routinely clearing the engine, but that extra boost of power was just enough to put us into the field … if we had landed, which we didn't, of course. As the wheels were about to touch, Jacksen shoved the throttle forward and we climbed back up and headed home. On landing, I was prepared to battle Jacksen for control of the rudders and stick again, but there was none, and I landed on my own.

I never found out how I was graded on that ride, but there was no problem in passing. I had two more flights in order to make the required sixty hours. At the end of the last one, Handel made it official by stamping my logbook and signing it. And we shook hands.[8]

I was worried about the ground school, too, and with good reason. With a lot of cramming I thought I could make it, in everything but the communication. I just couldn't seem to cope with those dits and dahs and the flashing lights.

It was Balason who saved me. For some reason Morse was easy for him, and he kept testing me and testing me until the last minute. Because of him I made it … but just barely. I was sure hoping I'd never have to use it, though, because as I left the classroom, it stayed there, and never popped back into my head again. The only thing I've ever been able to remember is SOS!

Our orders gave us four days to report to Minter Field, near Bakersfield, California, for our Basic Training. Baer asked Bledsoe, Balason and me if we wanted a ride back to LA.[9] His father had sent his car to him when he became an upperclassman. "If we use our own transportation we will be able to enjoy a night or two in town before reporting in," he said. And that sounded good to us. Bledsoe and I could be dropped off on the way into LA but Balason would have to hop a bus to San Diego. Bledsoe lived in Riverside, which was only a few miles northeast of Chino.

---

8   Blick's logbook confirms a half-hour check-ride with Lt H.T. Van Cau on April 16 and a further three flights to make 60 hours (37.01 solo) as of April 21, 1942.

9   In use from June 1941, Minter Field took its name from First Lieutenant Hugh C. Minter, a member of the prominent local Minter family, killed in a mid-air collision over March Field in July 1932. See https://minterfieldairmuseum.com/, accessed May 7, 2020.

Five

Bledsoe decided to drive to Bakersfield, and I went with him. There was nothing in our orders to indicate that we were allowed to have our own personal vehicles on base, but there was nothing against it either, and that was good enough for Bledsoe. He left a 1940 Chevy convertible with his wife and took his 1936 Buick sedan. I learned on that ride that he wasn't much of a mechanic, but he was a born salesman, and he could recognize a good trade. He'd pick up a bargain, use it for a while, then turn it around for a profit. With his ready smile and honest look, he was a natural. He'd sometimes make as much as 150 dollars. He had the thought that he might pursue it after the war—"All of those returning GIs will need wheels."

He picked me up early. It was only 145 miles, give or take a few, so we thought we could be there for lunch and then have the afternoon to get settled. I was a typical car-oriented Californian, not used to buses and trains, and I welcomed the ride.

As we drove north on Highway 99, we could feel the rise in temperature. It was expected. Inland, away from the cool Pacific breezes, Bakersfield was always hot ... even in the latter part of April. I had been through Bakersfield several times, but had forgotten the dry, dusty bleakness of the landscape, with tall banks of eucalyptus trees here and there dividing up the acreage. Phoenix was more interesting because it was supposed to look like desert!

We knew we were getting closer to Bakersfield when the road stretched out, ruler straight, ahead of us, and disappeared into the simmering heat waves.

"You want me to drive, Marv?" I asked. "You look a little sleepy."

"Naw ... I'm all right. My foot gets tired, though. Somebody ought to invent something for long drives ... something that would keep the car at a constant speed."

"Yeah ... set it for the speed you want and just sit here and steer."

"And it would help, too, to put a curve in the road once in a while."

Minter Field was just out of Bakersfield, a mile or so off the highway to the west. We turned left at the sign. The hard-packed, dusty, gravel road dead-ended with a right turn through the main gate, where we were stopped by a sergeant who asked for our orders.

"Just keep going straight," he said. "Headquarters is about three-quarters of a mile up the road. It's on the right, past the barracks. You'll see the mess hall on the left. You can park in front of the building until you find out where you'll be quartered."

The base was bleak, more like what I thought a military base would be like. There were a few isolated trees, some grass and shrubs around some of the buildings, but it was mostly dirt, hard-packed by GI shoes and swept clean by the wind. Thunderbird had spoiled us. Bledsoe drove slowly, and we absorbed it all. The barracks were wood, built like those at Williams, but were two stories. There were outside stairs for the second floor. All of the other buildings we could see looked to be one level and covered with black tar paper. In the distance we heard the sounds of engines.

When we walked into our assigned barracks, we were greeted by the few people we recognized from Thunderbird, including Carrington, Argiropulos, Brian (BB) Buchannan, Clyde, Betner and Boggs.

"Well, well," Bledsoe said, glancing at the door. "Look who just showed—finally." Baer and Balason entered. It had only been a few days since we left Phoenix, but we greeted each other like we were long lost brothers. I wondered later about that reaction, but realized that we were all still nervous and we needed to share those emotions. Baer, I noticed, was especially earnest. He seemed sincere when he shook our hands.

The building was arranged much the same as at Williams, with the latrine at the west end. Instead of the sergeant, however, we had Cadet Lieutenant Schwartz in the little room by the door. He waited until four o'clock, when everyone was supposed to be there, to assign all the bunks.

When the confusion ended, Schwartz called for our attention. "My name is Schwartz, and I'm your barracks officer. I don't have a lot to say. You mostly know your way around by now. I'll try to answer any questions you may have, but you'll just have to catch me when you can. I've got my own flying and classes to attend to. If it's something urgent that can't wait, any upperclassman can probably help you out.

"There's one thing I'm sure you're all wondering about—the hazing. In theory, it exists, and you might run across it once in a while with some of the upperclassmen—I'm sure you will see some of your old upperclassmen around—but by and large, we are busy enough ourselves to not bother you. But just keep in mind a couple of things. Things like 'Sir-ing' the upperclassmen, double-timing to where you're going, inspections; those sorts of things still apply. There will still be tour-walking for those who don't want to cooperate. Just remember that we've been through it all, too, and we don't have any desire to make it rough on you, so we're asking that you respect that and go along with us. Don't make it hard on yourself. There's a bulletin board right outside my room, and I'll keep all the pertinent information on it. You'll find your way around shortly. Anyone have a question?"

Baer's hand went up. "Sir, he said, "are we allowed our own automobiles on base?"

"Yes, for you people who want your own transportation, you can park in the lot by the main gate, which you passed on the way in. For those of you who don't have cars, there are buses from here into Bakersfield, where you can catch a bus to LA or wherever. The schedules are on the bulletin board. I have to warn you, though, you'll be pretty busy, so you won't have a lot of time off. Any other questions?"

The routine was much the same as it was at Thunderbird and, as Schwartz had said, we barely noticed the upper- and lower-class differences. I found the ground school classes a little easier. Either I was getting brighter or the subjects were more related to flying and made more sense—and there weren't any dits and dahs and blinking lights. It helped, too, that there was more time to study without the constant harassment. The Thunderbird "country club" was a thing of the past. But the return of some quiet time more than made up for it.

It was a big mystery how the flights were picked. I drew only two Bs, and I didn't know either. They were Bolken and Boldman. I had heard of neither. Bolken was a quiet, pleasant person, well built and about five-nine, who looked like he had inherited Scandinavian blood somewhere along the way. In contrast, Boldman was a little taller, with dark hair that looked a little like a wet sponge. He wasn't at all fat, but was rounded here and there without much muscle definition. And he talked, sometimes to the point of blab. The other three were all about the same height. Martin and Lemmon were both good-looking kids with smiles, and looked typically collegiate. And McCool was thin, with sharp features that seemed to fit well with his clipped Pennsylvania accent. Our instructor was First Lieutenant Walter Hunt.[1] It was disappointing, of course, not knowing anyone, but we were all in the same boat and it didn't take long to get used to each other.

Two days after our arrival we were scheduled to meet on the flight line at seven o'clock. I had my usual queasy stomach but I was happy we weren't wasting a lot of time prolonging the agony. Not that it really was agony. It was just the anxiety—the fear that I'd somehow foul up with the new airplane. And I wondered if an Army lieutenant would be a tougher instructor than a civilian. But, what the hell, I thought. *I was there to learn to fly, so let's get on with it.*

Hunt was small, shorter than I was, but thin and wiry. His hair was brown and there was too much of it. Standing high on his head in disorganized waves, it looked like he had just combed it back off his forehead with his fingers. His eyes were dark blue and deep-set—hard to see in the bright sunlight. His flight suit was rumpled, with a clipboard, papers, maps and a few pens and pencils sticking out of the leg pockets. His Ray-Bans were hanging by one arm at the top of his zipper and his sleeves were rolled up over his elbows with one cuff holding a Zippo and a crinkled

---

1   Blick's logbook indicates he began basic flight instruction at Minter Field on April 29, 1942. Lieutenant W.M. Hill was his instructor.

package of Camels. It was difficult to tell whether the bars on his shoulders were silver or brass. Obviously, his mind was on something besides passing a neatness inspection.

He stood with a cocky stance that would have made Jimmy Cagney proud—legs apart, slight tilt to his head, arms hanging away from his body, as if a little muscle-bound. To me it seemed a little too [much] … and maybe just carefully thought-out showtime for our benefit.

"First," he said, "with me, here on the flight line, we don't have to go through any of that saluting shit. My job is to teach you to fly. All that other crap you can learn somewhere else. You aren't gonna shoot any of those damn Heinies or Japs down with these Vultee Vibrators, but by God you can learn something about how to do it."[2] He waved his arm toward the field. "These planes are good, strong, solid airplanes, and about twice as powerful as what you just came out of—450 horses. They're nothing to be afraid of, though. They sound like they're gonna fall apart on take-off, but don't worry about it, it's normal. You have a two-position prop, and take-off is made in low pitch. Just keep in mind—all the time—that you're now into serious flying. You're past playtime."

It didn't take long to find out that Hunt was a frustrated fighter pilot, not happy at all with the fact that he was safe in the States instructing, while many of his classmates were in aircraft, learning how to fight a war—*really* flying. He hadn't yet come to grips with the idea that he, too, was contributing to the war effort. Hardly a day went by when he didn't mention something about how he should be elsewhere, flying fighters. It was tiresome, but we found him to be an excellent instructor, even if he did tend to stray from the routine at times to show off his own prowess. He was gentle and considerate in the air, never taking his own frustrations out on his students.

My first ride was a good one. And that's all it was—a ride.

"Just follow me through on the controls for now," Hunt said. I was happy about the canopy—I could finally hear!

We headed northwest and climbed to 10,000 feet and Hunt went through all the aerobatics, including a loop, which was a first for me. Out of the loop, he pulled up into a stall and fell over into a spin.

"Remember to always have plenty of altitude when you start this," he told me, taking advantage of the quiet. "This baby doesn't pull out of a spin easily and you need a lot of room."

After saying that, he spun all the way down to about 200 feet before pulling out. I knew that he was watching me, so I put on a big show of being unconcerned. I

---

2   The Vultee BT-13 Valiant (called a BT-15 with a Wright Cyclone engine instead of the Pratt and Whitney 450-horsepower Wasp engine) was the main American basic training aircraft during World War II. Pilots referred to it affectionately as the "Vultee Vibrator" because the canopy shook in a spin. Watry, *Washout!*, pp. 105–7.

didn't wet my pants, but I was thinking it was a shame to die before I finished my training. Back on the ground, he explained that he just wanted us to know what the plane was capable of so we wouldn't be afraid of it. I knew, though, that he just wanted to fly himself, and show off a little.

Hunt was a little crazy of course, but I liked him. Even though it was cadet to officer, I felt at ease when we were together. I mentioned once, soon after we started flying, that I had a problem when I was being observed and judged—that I knew I could fly, but when the instructor was watching I'd get so nervous I'd go all to pieces.

On my second flight, I flew the whole time, even took off and landed. I could feel Hunt on the controls and it made me nervous. The take-off seemed like a battle to see who would be the first to pull the plane off the ground—that's the impression I had. After a couple of tries, we made it into the air and the pressure eased. I did well for the rest of the time, with Hunt talking me through turns and stalls. The landing was awful, though. I was too fast and the plane wouldn't stay on the ground.

The third flight was better, but I couldn't completely eliminate the nervousness. It wasn't Hunt's fault—he was just there, and I was trying so hard to make every move perfect I over-controlled everything. Back on the ground Hunt said I did fine, that it was a good job. "Thanks," I said. "I wish I could feel it myself, but I know I didn't do well. I get so nervous."

The fourth flight was much the same until Hunt directed me to one of the auxiliary fields. It was normal to shoot landings at small fields away from the traffic. When we were down, he told me to pull up and stop. He slipped out of his parachute, got down and with a grin said, "Go ahead. You wanted to fly. Do it!"

I was shocked. I'd only been up three times and one of them was just a joyride. I had told Hunt I was nervous with an instructor watching, but my God ...! What a mistake! About the only thing I had learned was how to close the canopy!

I looked at Hunt. He was grinning up a storm, and kept motioning me to go. I couldn't hear him but I read his lips clearly and they mouthed, "Go ahead ... go."

I just continued to sit there, staring, but finally I thought *okay, dammit, nothing to do but do it!* Hunt's theory was obviously sink or swim, but he wasn't the one sinking. ...

I goosed it a little—cautiously—and holding the left brake, turned to taxi out to the end of the runway. At least I could taxi. At the runway I tried to settle down—and to remember. *Rev it up, check the mags, roll down the flaps, prop in low pitch* ... okay, all that's left is to shove the throttle forward and steer it down the runway.

I had already forgotten the power of the engine and it veered to the left before I was ready. I reacted too quickly with too much pressure on the right rudder. Then, while still trying to get it rolling straight, the plane decided, all on its own, that it was time to lift off. It leaped into the air too soon, before either I or it could cope with it. I shoved the stick forward and of course bounced the wheels back on the runway. When finally I had enough speed to stay in the air, I was still having trouble keeping the plane straight. As a consequence, I was at a near stall with the nose high and the right wing down. I must have looked like a duck hit by a gust of wind.

It didn't last, however. It couldn't—I'm still alive. Somehow I did what had to be done automatically, and the plane was soon righted and climbing smoothly. I kept it straight and settled back into the seat, relaxing as best I could until I could breathe easily again. I started a climbing turn and then remembered I hadn't rolled up the flaps, or changed the prop pitch. I hoped I was far enough away from the field so Hunt wouldn't notice the tone of the engine change, but I knew I wasn't.

I leveled out at 4,000 feet and finally began to feel in control. Then it happened again—that feeling of freedom I had experienced on my first solo. I started with gentle turns, but as I gained confidence, the turns became steeper until I rolled all the way. After several minutes and a few more rolls I felt okay to land. And land, I did, greasing it in like a pro.

For me, it was all I needed. My nervousness was gone. Once in the air, I was even able to overcome the normal tension on test rides. The confidence that Hunt had shown in me that day and the chance that he took was forever imbedded in my memory. It was a lesson hard to forget. Hunt had shown more confidence in me than I had in myself. He knew that I could fly, and was just cocky enough to let me prove it. It was a scary gamble on his part, and I have since thought about it often. *What would have happened had I cracked up?*

For Hunt, however, luck ran out. We had about 75 hours in the BT and our training at Minter was almost over. We felt good, and well we should. After washouts and accidents, only twenty-five percent of the original starters at Thunderbird were left.

Hunt was flying with Bolken when he spotted McCool. He told Bolken to pull up on McCool's right wing and fly a little formation. Hunt was feeling his usual cocky, fighter-pilot self and indicated to Bolken that he'd take it. He moved in closer, of course, to show Bolken and McCool what *real* flying was like. Then, without any warning, he rolled over the top of McCool. It was obvious to the two cadets his intention was to roll over to a similar position on the other wing, but he misjudged, and whacked McCool's wing off with his prop. Both Bolken and McCool were able to bail out, but Hunt went down with the plane.[3]

---

3   The available accident reports indicate two aircraft from the 324th School Squadron at Minter Field were involved in a tragic mid-air collision on June 18, 1942. The BT-13A piloted by Cadet Magnus G. Bolken received minor damage. Lieutenant Walter M. Hill died when his BT-13A crashed two miles north of Schafter, California. See: https://www.aviationarchaeology.com/, accessed May 7, 2020.

Six

"You mean you're going to LUKE?"
"Yeah … so what's wrong with that?"
"That's the worst, meanest, gawdawfulist, most chickenshit field in the whole country, that's what's wrong. Man, I wouldn't trade places with you for nothin'."[1]

I was with Bledsoe, headed east again, back into the desert, and back once more to Phoenix. I hadn't yet been able to put the funeral and the memories of Hunt and his beautiful young wife into that hidden pocket of my mind where I learned later to put such things. I was not very talkative.

It was four o'clock in the morning and still relatively cool. We had started early, hoping to cover maybe 300 of the 400 miles before the heat became unbearable. I had tried to talk my mother into staying in bed and letting me leave quietly, but of course she didn't. I heard her scurrying around in the kitchen when I got out of bed. Not only did she fix me a big bacon and egg breakfast, but she packed a lunch for the two of us as well.

"You've got a long ride and a big day ahead of you and you need something substantial in your stomach," she said. And she tried to keep the tears from flowing, but couldn't. I didn't tell her about Hunt.

As usual, when faced with the unknown, I was a little nervous, and it didn't help at all to remember that conversation I had with Mel Braxton about Luke.

"I wonder if it's true," I remarked aloud.

"What?"

"That thing about Luke being so tough."

"I don't know," Bledsoe replied. "But my brother, Jeff, says that's the word around. The field's only about a year old, and he claims the brass are mostly concerned about making a good impression."

I knew Bledsoe's brother was an airline pilot. "You think he really knows, Marv? How would he?"

---

[1] Blick made his final flight at Minter Field on June 19, 1942, with 137.05 hours of flight time in total (82.01 solo).

"I don't know, but those airline guys get around. I imagine a lot of them have been urged to join up as instructors. Jeff was approached, I know."

By the time Bledsoe turned off Litchfield road into Luke, our khakis needed to be wrung out, and our moods were not much better. Our first view of the base didn't help either. The barracks were familiar, but the hard-packed dirt of Minter was replaced with soft, fine, silky dust that shimmered in the heat. There were no trees—no shade. It was no oasis, for sure … only a flat, barren spot in the desert. There were unfinished buildings, tractors, piles of lumber, trucks, billows of dust, and a lot activity everywhere.

In March [1941], before the bombing of Pearl Harbor, 1,440 acres of land outside of Phoenix was cleared and the construction started for what was to be Litchfield Park Air Base. It was renamed Luke Field in June by the first commander, Lieutenant Colonel Ennis Whitehead, in honor of Frank Luke, an Arizona native who was the first aviator to win the Congressional Medal of Honor in the First World War. The "Arizona Balloon Buster" became a legend by shooting down four planes and fourteen balloons in seventeen days.

The first class of pre-war cadets started their training in June, living in makeshift tents and flying out of Phoenix Airport until the runway was finished. As the pre-war emergency grew, construction was put on a twenty-four-hour basis and the buildings were filled as soon as they were completed.

The dirt was a problem everywhere, but especially around the runway. The land had been cleared and the slightest breeze would stir up dusty whirlwinds. Planes would land in clouds of dust—dangerous not only for the pilots but the planes as well. They finally sprayed oil on all the surrounding area to keep it down.

As we neared Headquarters, the buildings looked more permanent, and the dust was less disturbed. The building was easy to find. Numerous cadets, in various combinations of dress, were lounging on their baggage outside, immobile and sweating in the sun, gasping at every hint of moving air. Many were familiar, but Balason and Baer were the only ones to acknowledge our arrival. It was too hot to move.

Our orders were to report at 1400 hours. We had only fifteen minutes so we didn't bother with our baggage—we'd pick it up after we signed in. The thermometer near the door read almost 110 degrees, but it was cool inside.

The sergeant took one disgusted look and growled, "I keep hoping someone's gonna come through that door that looks like a cadet, but no … I keep seeing the same old shit." He picked up his cigar from the ashtray and stuck it in the side of his mouth. "You are the sorriest, raunchiest-looking, worst excuses for military men I've ever seen. The lieutenant's gonna have more than a bug up his ass. We have a dress code here and by God you'd better learn it quick! There are *no* goddamned excuses either!"

Bledsoe was about to say something, but then thought better of it. The sergeant checked them off, then said, "Now get the hell outta here!" By the time we were back outside in the heat again, the new arrivals had been formed into ranks and brought to attention. A lieutenant and several upper-class cadet officers were standing nearby. The lieutenant was staring at his watch. The cadet captain looked over at us and yelled, "You three Misters there, fall in."

The lieutenant glanced once more at his watch and nodded to the cadet officer. We were marched to the parade ground about a half mile away. We were happy we had left our bags in the car, but most of the cadets were burdened with B-4s and/or their unwieldy barracks bags.

The cadet captain formed us into ranks, stood us at attention, and then turned to the lieutenant with a salute with, "Ready, Sir." The lieutenant walked over in front of them. He was tall and thin, with dark eyes and hair, looking as if he had just stepped off a page of *Esquire*.

"I'm First Lieutenant Franklin," he said, emphasizing the *First*. "By the looks of you, you haven't yet learned what it takes to be an officer. I wonder what in God's name made you think you could report to duty in such a slovenly condition. Never, ever, have I seen such a sloppy and disorderly group." He paused, as if to let it sink in. "But all that will change, I guarantee. You are now at Luke Field. We make men here … and officers, not slobs! And it starts right now."

He marched officiously down the first row and stopped in front of Balason.

"Where is your baggage, Mister?" He asked.

"I left it in the car, Sir."

"You *what?*"

"I left it in the car, Sir, with the intention of going back for it after I reported in."

The lieutenant turned back to the cadet captain. "Captain. See that all those cadets that don't have their equipment go get it, and then give them an extra lap."

"Yes, Sir."

They saluted and the lieutenant turned and walked away.

"Now then," the cadet captain said. "I am Captain Alder." He pointed to the two cadet officers with him. "These are Lieutenants Grier and Ranckin, who will now lead you on a march around the ramp. After all that traveling you need a little exercise to get the kinks out. You might as well get used to it. You'll know every rock before you're through here. Now pick up your baggage and get started. Lieutenants …"

The trip around the area was a mile. Because of the hot desert sun beating down and the struggle with their equipment, many didn't make it. And they were confined to the post for a month.

After the march, we were given twenty minutes of exhausting calisthenics, and then marched, double time, around the ramp again, considerably without the baggage. Then we were formed up again.

"Lieutenants Grier and Ranckin will now march you to your barracks, where you will have time to get oriented. Those of you who decided ahead of time to get your baggage later will go pick it up and report back here for another go at the ramp."

Yes, Sir, I mumbled to myself, *worst, meanest, godawfullest, most chickenshit...*

Other than the fact that Luke was indeed the worst, meanest, godawfullest, most chickenshit field in the country, and except for spending so much time walking tours in the sun, life for us was much the same as it was at Minter. We flew and studied, and once in a long while, we had a day or two off to go into Phoenix, where Baer could pursue his favorite occupation and others like me could go to a movie and collapse in a hotel room.

Most of us had thought, and hoped, that once we had arrived at our advanced training school our worries would be over. But they weren't. This time the officers were the cause, not the upperclassmen. Most—not all, but most—of the officers were intentionally niggling and officious, and for no other reason than harassment.

The groundpounders or gravelscratchers, as the non-flying officers were called, were hateful enough, but we expected more out of the flying officers—*there, but for the wings, go us.* However, many of them were caught up in it also, strutting around and acting like little martinets. And it was hard to figure out why. Was it the bars that gave them the feeling of power? The wings? Could they be jealous of us for some weird reason? Whatever, that upper-class hazing at Thunderbird was long forgotten. Compared to our life at Luke, it had been meaningful and even pleasurable—a game. We now realized the value of discipline as taught by the hazing there … so different than this cruel and vindictive approach, which seemed to be nothing more than an attempt by the officers to further their own feelings of power over us. They never missed a chance to use any cheap petty power play that entered their minds.

Lieutenant Franklin was the worst, and the one we had the most contact with. He seldom missed a day on the flight line without standing us at attention in the hot sun while chewing us out for some minor infraction of the rules, like a shirt unbuttoned too far, or a plane not lined up correctly. Everyone suffered, no matter who was at fault. Once the whole class was confined to the post for the weekend simply because someone had talked during a formation.

I don't know if it would have been better or not, if we knew then what we learned a long time later. It turned out that Franklin and the rest of the officers were more frightened than we were. The fear started somewhere at the top, adding fuel at each step on the way down to the lowly instructors. We, the cadets, were their release. And it was even worse, because the instructors knew that while we would soon be free, off into the wild blue yonder, they would still be there.

The heat was insufferable. All the buildings, including the barracks, were cooled with window air-conditioning units, and we ran from one cool retreat to another. I was used to the hot and dry California weather, but I'd never before been subjected to 120-degree temperatures. I was sure eggs could be fried on the flagstones—if there were any flagstones and if we had any eggs. Other than the air-conditioned buildings, the only relief was flying. We tried to get as high as possible as quickly and as often as we could. In ground school we learned that on a sunny day the temperature fell 5.4 degrees for every 1,000 feet. That meant if it was 110 degrees on the ground it would be 73 degrees at 5,000 feet or 46 degrees at 10,000. And even better, 19 degrees at 15,000!

Salt tablets were passed out to make up for the salt we lost sweating, but that was the only consideration given to the heat. When the sergeant made the statement about a dress code, he understated it. It was only after a tremendous amount of bitching and near rebellion by the cadets, that the base officers relented and finally allowed us to take our ties off while on the flight line, with only the neck button loosened. That was it—the only place we were allowed that luxury. Sometimes we were subjected to hour-long formations, which required standing at attention in the sun and the 120-degree temperatures, fully dressed in regulation suntans, with ties and caps. Most of the time we'd be just standing there waiting.

Sunburn was unlawful—against regulations—and tours were walked because of it … in the sun of course. My nose had always been vulnerable, so after the first such formation, I cut out a cardboard cover and attached it to my sunglasses. I was ready for the outburst on the first inspection, but fortunately, it never came.

The airplane was an enormous change from the old Vultee Vibrator at Minter, and we loved it. It was the North American AT-6, powered with a 650-horsepower Pratt and Whitney radial engine. We had no trouble adjusting because it was really not all that different. The power and speed, combined with the retractable landing gear made us feel like real fighter pilots. We also had our first exposure to ground and aerial gunnery, as well as the Link Trainer, which was a covered mock-up cockpit for instrument training.

I had been looking forward to the Link, but it was disappointing. The controls were so mushy the resemblance to real flying was almost non-existent. The only person who had any fun with it was the sergeant who sat outside and controlled our flying problems. He delighted in putting us in impossible positions, which almost always caused us to crack up. Bledsoe's reaction was, "I think they must make them that way intentionally, so we'll be so wary of instrument flying we'll stay out of those situations."

My flight this time was with Balason, Carrington, Phillip Adair, Leo Burkett and Rod Sebloux. Burkett was another Californian, but Adair was from Oklahoma and Sebloux from Iowa. Our instructor was a short, rather round, first lieutenant named Qualline.[2] Lieutenant Qualline was quiet and easy going. In contrast to many of the Luke instructors, he preferred to instruct positively. Rather than with constant criticism, he always found something good to say about the flight. Because of that, I had no trouble with my nervousness.

Until it was time to solo …!

---

2 Blick's logbook records Lieutenant E.A. Oualline.

The instructors were obviously not to be trusted with such an important decision. So when Qualline thought one of us was ready, he had to get a second opinion and, to my horror, that second opinion was none other than Lieutenant Franklin.

I felt like I was back at Thunderbird, my confidence completely shaken.

On the walk out to the plane, Franklin asked in a mocking, sarcastic voice, "So you think you're ready to solo, do you?"

I did until now, I thought, but said instead, "Yes, Sir."

It was a complete disaster. He climbed into the back seat and immediately started the engine. I barely had time to get into the cockpit, let alone strap myself in.

"C'mon, for Christsake, let's go! I got other things to do besides sit here and wipe your ass for you."

I sure didn't need that! I was already nervous enough. I taxied out to the runway and there was another airplane there checking mags. I started to pull up behind it, when Franklin suddenly grabbed the controls, goosed the engine, and pulled out in front of the other plane. "I don't have time for this shit," he yelled. "Get your ass out there and into the air!"

"Yes, Sir! But we've always been told to check it out before take-off—"

"Are you trying to contradict my orders? I said I was in a hurry, you asshole. Now get this bunch of crap off the ground!"

My take-off was okay, but still a little reminiscent of my first test flight, and I wondered if I'd ever get used to someone back there watching my every move.

Okay, now I'm off. Hit the brakes to keep the wheels from turning as we go up ... power button to raise the wheels ... throttle back to thirty inches ... prop pitch 2,000 ... check indicators to make sure wheels are up and locked ... keep your head spinning ... needle and ball centered ... speed even. ...

"C'mon, c'mon, get going. Get up there and show me why you think you're so great."

I did what I thought was a pretty good climbing turn and leveled off at 2,000 feet. "Now do a roll!"

A roll! We haven't been allowed to even try them yet!

I did a barrel roll. It was tight, but still not a proper roll. I knew it, but I had no idea what crazy Franklin wanted, and I didn't want to put any negative Gs on him and, besides, I didn't like all that dirt and stuff in my face.

"Jesus Christ," Franklin yelled. "What in the fuck kinda roll was that? I thought you said you could fly! Gimme the stick."

He went through the roll, and with the grit flying through the cockpit I had to admit it was a good one.

"My God this plane is dirty!" He sneered. "Don't you assholes know how to write up a Form One? We got guys down there that are supposed to keep these things clean. Jesus! Now do me a figure eight ... if you think you can, and then see if you can get me back in one piece."

It was a simple maneuver, and I did it well—the turns were smooth and the altitude consistent. I started back to the field.

"You sure as hell'll never make a fighter pilot that way," Franklin yelled. "What the fuck do you think this is, a goddammed bomber? Do another, and get that fuckin' wing up!"

Okay, dammit! My nervousness was beginning to be replaced by fury. In one motion I literally threw the right wing up into an almost vertical position, jammed the throttle forward to hold the speed and hauled back on the stick until I was on the verge of blacking out. I lost a little altitude, but held the turn long enough to complete the first half of the eight, then reversed the turn for the last half.

Oh God! I never should have done that, I thought. *He'll wash me out for sure.* I headed back toward the field. Franklin was strangely silent, and then I had a thought that made me smile. *I must have blacked the bastard out!*

It didn't last. Finally there was a milder, "That's better." But that didn't last either. "Now that I know you can make a tight turn, let's see if you can get me down alive."

The landing went fine until we were about fifty feet off the runway and Franklin got heavy on the controls. I had to fight to override him and as a result we hit the ground too soon and bounced up, then dropped back again hard on one wheel. Franklin was muttering something the whole time, but it was probably just as well that I couldn't make out what he was saying.

I wondered what Franklin told Qualline, but I never found out. It obviously wasn't all bad because I was soloed the next flight, at three hours and fifteen minutes.

Once again, with the relaxed freedom of being alone I was able to concentrate and perfect the required maneuvers easily, and a few more as well, to the extent that I passed the final check ride without the usual trepidation. Thank God it wasn't with Franklin! I smiled, thinking he was probably too frightened to ride with me.

I finished my required flying time—82 hours at Luke—which added up to a total of 225.[3] I think it was someone at Thunderbird who said if a pilot was still alive at 200 hours, he would probably live to become an old pilot.

Even though the flight-line time was over, there was no way to speed up the drudgery of the ground school classes. The instructors all knew our temptations and were overly conscientious about roll-call. As a result, we couldn't leave the base during the day and spent our excess time just existing—loafing around the barracks or the PX, waiting for the weekend and the chance to go into Phoenix. There was a movie at night, but that was a little hard to take every night, especially when it didn't change but a couple of times a week. We were not safe, either, from the machinations of those distressed and tormented souls called officers, who seemed to delight in causing as much discomfort in our lives as possible. They were not about to let down their discipline just because a certain part of our training was

---

3 Blick's logbook records slightly different figures—82.15 hours at Luke for a total of 219.30 by his final flight on August 12, 1942.

over. In fact, Lieutenant Franklin was everywhere, just looking for some infraction of the rules. Like a traffic cop giving out tickets, he obviously felt the brass upstairs were judging his abilities as an officer by the number of cadets walking the ramp.

Weekend passes were issued infrequently, to those of us who were fortunate enough to pass inspections and avoid tours. They were from Friday night to midnight Sunday. I rarely took advantage of them, but once in a while Bledsoe and I would go into town. Bledsoe was married and I was not interested in spending the time on the prowl, as Baer was, so we enjoyed each other's company. My idea of real relaxation was to go to a hotel, take a long luxurious bath, maybe see a movie, and then climb into a double bed between clean sheets!

Baer, however, always had other ideas for me. He was determined to get me to go with him, and of course, get me laid. He couldn't understand how anyone could have priorities different than his. It was on the first weekend after finishing my flying that I decided to go into town again, take what would probably be my last look at Phoenix, and pick up my officer's blouse and pinks (pants) that I had been fitted for earlier. I was thinking I'd leave Saturday, maybe see a movie or two and then come back Sunday, and spend only the one night there. Bledsoe was confined to the base for being one minute late to class, so I had the choice of trying to find someone else, taking the bus, or going in with Baer on Friday night. Mistakenly, I chose Baer. Before going, I made him promise to drop me off at my hotel, and then go his own way. I knew Baer too well and I wanted to do my own thing without an argument. I had no desire to spend my precious relaxation time bar hopping, or whatever it was that he usually did.

It went well until Sunday night. I saw *For Me and My Gal* and couldn't resist *Tarzan's New York Adventure*. I picked up my uniform, and also Bledsoe's, on Saturday, and quietly luxuriated in my peaceful, relaxed freedom. It was about 25 miles from there to Luke and Baer had agreed to pick me up outside the hotel at 2310 hours—ten minutes after eleven. Curfew was midnight.

I checked out and was on the curb at eleven o'clock. I was early, even knowing full well that Baer would probably still be trying to tear himself away from some female body, but I was always early and expected to wait. I had made the appointed time early, purposely, allowing for plenty of leeway to get back to the base.

At eleven-thirty, the butterflies began, and I was pacing. No telling what they would do with us flaunting the rules, now that we had proven we could fly. Knowing the mentality of those officers in charge, I had visions of being set back to the next class as an example. *And to think of having to go through all that again ...!* They might even wash us out and send us off to Bombardier or Navigation School. I could surely learn to drop bombs, but navigation—*forget it!* However, they would probably decide that if we couldn't be on time as a pilot we couldn't be any kind of officer, and break us down all the way to buck privates. Visions of being a foot soldier were back—and after all these nine months of struggle and crap, it was enough to bring up the tears. They would probably treat it as AWOL and throw us into jail or the stockade, or whatever they called it in the Army.

At eleven-thirty-five, I was near collapse. At eleven-forty, I did—I just couldn't take it anymore. My legs were weak and I had to sit down on the curb and try to calm myself. The bastard! The goddamn horny bastard! It was eleven-forty-four and I was just getting up to go back into the hotel to see if I could get another room for the night, when Baer came screeching to a stop in front of me—eyes glazed, and mouth frozen into a silly apologetic grin. I threw my stuff into the back, slammed the door and said, "Go!" But he had already started.

He burned rubber for half a block, obviously hoping to get airborne by the time we got to the corner. His foot went to the floor and stayed there, regardless of curves, intersections or red lights. He didn't say a word, just stared, unblinking, at the road, with that same stupid expression on his face. A trance, I thought, he's in a goddamned trance! Trance or whatever, I knew I'd better just sit there and shut up—that I shouldn't try to warn or advise or even ask how he made out! So I just sat there, eyes glued on the road ahead, fingers digging into my legs like the claws of an eagle, afraid to look at anything else, and hoping that the police were not lurking somewhere ahead. The last time I had looked at the speedometer, it read 90, and we were still accelerating. Normally, when I was riding with other drivers that seemed a little reckless, I stayed calm by telling myself that it wasn't my car—that the driver didn't want to crack his car up and wasn't going to try to do anything foolish that he wasn't sure he could do. I kept saying it to myself now, over and over again, but it didn't work. I even tried closing my eyes, but the lids were stuck open.

At the stroke of midnight, Cinderella style, we pulled up to the gate, and were waved through. I immediately became a dishrag—a dishrag in shock. Baer turned to me with a big grin and said, "How's that for timing?"

We spent much of the time speculating about our futures. The logical approach to our placement would be to put the smaller pilots in fighters because of the smaller cockpits. Also there was some discussion about personalities. Most seemed to think that the bombers would require a calmer, more stable psyche. I knew of no one, however, who wanted to fly the big birds; the lure and reputation of the fighter pilot was too strong. It was worrisome, because we all knew how the Army was so obsessed with the alphabetical approach to everything. And my Chino friend Howard was six-two, and a fighter pilot.[4] I hoped that fighter pilots would be at the beginning of the alphabet.

Unexpectedly, on August 18, fifty of us, including Baer, Bell, Bennett, Betner, Bledsoe and Byers—no Balason—were ordered to Victorville Army Flying School for five days of twin-engine training. It was a random listing and very bad news, we thought. Surely, it was preparation for bombers. Bennett and I rode with Bledsoe.

---

4   Captain Howard L. Galbreath of the 507th Fighter Squadron, 404th Fighter Group, 9th Air Force. Blick mentions in his diary visiting his friend Howard several times while both were in Europe.

Victorville was back into California, but barely, in the Mojave Desert about thirty or so miles northeast of San Bernardino, and we didn't know there was anything there but desert. But there was, even though it wasn't much. It was evidently a new field, still in the process, and we were housed in tar-papered shacks. The planes were trainers, designated AT-9s, and made by Curtis Wright with two Lycoming radial engines.[5]

The transition to twin engines was not stressful. We had to get used to flying with someone in the other seat, but it didn't seem quite the same as having someone you couldn't see, back there looking over your shoulder all the time and, besides, the lieutenants we flew with were gentle and considerate. There were two sets of everything and that was different, especially each time we had to change the throttles. The two engines had to be synchronized and we did that by listening to the sound. It was something I had never thought about, but it made sense. They had to purr together. Landing was wonderful—there was no 'runway'. It was all runway—all hard dry lake bed wherever we happened to land.

We all had no trouble flying our required eight hours in the five days allotted, and were soon back with Franklin and his henchmen. Thank goodness we didn't have much longer to go.

The long-awaited day finally arrived—the graduation ceremony was set for August 27.[6] All that hazing, all of those miserable, humiliating and demeaning incidents and situations, was now behind us. Even so, I was afraid to let myself dwell on it—those wings were not yet in my hand, and until they were I couldn't relax. The road we had just traveled had been too long and too hard to take chances with my emotions. No telling what Franklin might dream up, even at this late date.

It was a disappointing affair, probably because we thought it would be something like West Point with well-known speakers and hats flying through the air afterward. There was a short parade outside, but then we were marched into the theater where a few of the base officers made some polite speeches wishing us luck and telling us what a good class we were. We were then given an envelope with our wings, bars and orders inside, and dismissed.

Finally! Finally, those treasured wings, so long coveted! They were pinned on before we even walked out the door.

I let out a huge sigh of satisfaction and relief when I read that I was ordered to Hamilton Field, California, to fly fighters. Balason and Baer were on the same orders. It was disappointing, though, to learn that Bledsoe was going to Mitchel Field, in

---

5   The Curtiss-Wright AT-9 "Fledgling" (commonly known as the "Jeep") was a twin-engine training aircraft used to bridge the gap between single- and twin-engine aircraft. According to his logbook, Blick flew the AT-9 four times at Victorville, California, for an additional 7 hours 50 minutes' flying time.
6   Year and month of graduation determined "class." There were seven classes graduating ahead of Blick's in 1942. Although there were sometimes monthly gaps, in this case Blick's class 42-H corresponded to August 1942.

New York, also a fighter base. In comparing our orders, we found no clue as to how the assignments were made. There were tall people sent to fighters and short ones, like Carrington, off to bomber bases. It remained a mystery. ...

HEADQUARTERS
ARMY AIR BASE A7
LUKE FIELD, PHOENIX, ARIZONA
August 27, 1942
(SPECIAL ORDERS)   R E S T R I C T E D

(NO.   221)   - E X T R A C T -

1. By direction of the President, each of the following named Aviation Cadets, now at Luke Field, Phoenix, Arizona, upon acceptance of his appointment as Second Lieutenant, Air Corps Reserve, is with his consent, ordered to active duty, effective August 27, 1942, is assigned to Headquarters, Air Force Advanced Flying School, this station, and will report to this Commanding Officer for duty. Each officer will rank from August 27, 1942.

NAME	ENL.ASN.	OFF.ASN.	HOME ADDRESS
*	*	*	*
BLICKENSTAFF, WAYNE K.	19078659	O-728555	Pomona, California
*	*	*	*

By order of Colonel Hoyt:

KENNETH H. HESS
Major, Air Corps
Adjutant.

HEADQUARTERS
ARMY AIR BASE A7
LUKE FIELD, PHOENIX, ARIZONA

August 27, 1942
(SPECIAL ORDERS)   R E S T R I C T E D

(NO.   221)   - E X T R A C T -

17. Pursuant to authority contained in Radiogram, Headquarters or the Army Air Forces. Washington D.C., file AAF AFPMP-Y5779, dated August 26, 1942, to Commanding Officer, Army Air Base, Luke Field, Phoenix, Arizona, the following named Second Lieutenants, Air Corps, are relieved from further assignment and duty at Luke Field, Phoenix, Arizona, and will proceed without delay, on or about August 28, 1942, to stations indicated, reporting upon arrival to the Commanding Officers thereof for further assignment and duty:

     *   *   *   *   *   *

<u>TO: ARMY AIR BASE, FOURTH AIR FORCE, HAMILTON FIELD</u>
      <u>SAN RAFAEL, CALIFORNIA</u>
      (Detached Service for travel by privately owned conveyance: Four (4) days.)

BLICKENSTAFF, WAYNE K.   (O-728555)

*   *   *   *   *

    The QMC will furnish the necessary transportation:
Travel by privately owned conveyance is authorized,
with Detached Service for the period indicated.
    Travel directed is necessary in the military service and when made is chargeable to Procurement Authority: FD 31 P 431-02, 03 A 0425-23.

By order of Colonel HOYT

KENNETH H. HESS
Major, Air Corps
Adjutant.

Seven

We were given four days to report in at Hamilton Field.[1] I decided to ride with Baer, who was also taking Bennett, who was from Glendale, and Balason. Baer wanted to go directly there and spend what extra time we might have in San Francisco rather than Los Angeles.

Our arrival caused a great deal of confusion. We were unexpected and they had no idea what to do with us. They cut some orders to the 81st Fighter Group at March Field, and we had visions of taking another trip back down to March, which was not far from Pomona. But someone decided that wasn't a good idea after all, and why not use us right here at Hamilton. They ended up cutting new orders assigning us to the 328th Fighter Group, which was located there, and put us into the 91st Fighter Squadron.

It was finally official—we were members of a Fighter Squadron.

RESTRICTED

HQ 81ST F GP, AAB MUROC CALIF

SO 68   September 14, 1942

EXTRACT

1. Pur to VOCG IV Ftr Comd, Sept 14, 1942, the following named O, org indicated, WP without delay to the 328th Ftr Gp, Hamilton Field, Calif, for temp duty on matters relative to the IV Ftr Comd, reporting upon arrival to the CO threat:

91ST FTR SQ

2nd Lt Robert H. Adams	0728535	2nd Lt James G. Allen	0728537
2nd Lt John M. Balason*	0728541	2nd Lt Robert F. Beattie	0728546
2nd Lt John H. Behr Jr*	0728551	2nd Lt Robert M. Bennett	0728550
2nd Lt Raymond J. Betner	0726551	2nd Lt Jack T. Bradley	0728561

---

1   Named after First Lieutenant Lloyd Andrews Hamilton of the 17th Aero Squadron, who led a daring low-level bombing attack on a German airfield in Belgium on August 13, 1918. He was killed in action two weeks later. Hamilton Field was a major west coast training base for new fighter groups during World War II, with several Eighth and Ninth Air Force Groups passing through.

2nd Lt Andrew J. Borders	0726558	2nd Lt Lawrence G. Dubois	0790452	
2nd Lt Wayne K. Blickenstaff*	0728555	2nd Lt William A. Higgins	0790235	
2nd Lt Henry R. Jacobus	0790261			

92ND FTR SQ

2nd Lt Allen E. Lowe*	0790275	2nd Lt William J. Maguire*	0728291
2nd Lt Charles R. Mott Jr	0791025	2nd Lt Roland R. McKean*	0790280

93RD FTR SQ

2nd Lt Joseph E. Broadhead	0728560	2nd Lt Paul G. Budesa*	0728566
2nd Lt William R. Burkett*	0728570	2nd Lt Kenneth Caldwell*	0728576
2nd Lt Vic L. Byers*	0728573	2nd Lt Verlin E. Chambers	0728584
2nd Lt James Cannon	0728577	2nd Lt Leslie P. Cles*	0728589
2nd Lt Donald B. Christy	0728588	2nd Lt Henry W. Yellot Jr	0790933
2nd Lt Gordon S. Burlingame*			

The QM will furn the nec rail T.
Priv convey auth. Trav dir nec in mil serv. FD 34 434-02
A 0425-23.

*   *   *   *   *

By order of Lt Colonel WADE

ROBERT H. GRIMES
Capt, Air Corps
Adjutant.[2]

Hamilton Field was about fifteen miles north of San Francisco at San Rafael, which was over the Golden Gate Bridge in Marin Country. After Luke and Minter, we couldn't believe we were on an Army base. It was beautiful—trees, houses, green lawns and paved streets. It looked like the residential area in a small town. I could see then that life might be good in the peacetime Army. And it was such a pleasure to be treated like officers, not like something someone had stepped in.

The 328th Fighter Group flew P-39s, the Bell Airacobra, which was as aesthetically beautiful as any fighter designed, and it had a tricycle landing gear with widespread wheels, which just about eliminated landing accidents—the easiest landing plane I ever encountered. But the first flight was one I have never forgotten. We didn't have to go through being checked out to solo, of course, there was only one seat. We had to have an experienced pilot explain everything, give us a blindfold test for all the instruments and then give us a shove! We were on our own.

I got off the ground okay—no problem with that—but I was unprepared for the speed. By the time I had everything done that I was supposed to do and had my head out of the cockpit, I was so far away from the field I couldn't even see it.

---

2   Those marked with a star would later become members of the 353rd Fighter Group. Blick appears to have been assigned to the 81st Fighter Group at Muroc (on paper at least). Blick's logbook does not record any flying time between his last flight at Luke on August 22 and his first flight at Hamilton on September 29, 1942.

After the initial panic I managed a cautious 180 and headed straight back until, finally, I found the field again.

Our training was mostly formation flying and gunnery—mostly ground gunnery, rather than air to air. We'd dive down on the target, fire, and then pull up into a chandelle and go around for another pass.[3] It was good control practice, but scary, and I had a tendency to pull up too soon (chicken out)! I didn't like to see the ground come up so fast.

The P-39 had 30-caliber guns in the wings, but had a 20mm cannon that was mounted to shoot through the hub of the propeller. I was never sure how it would be in combat, but it was impressive to shoot. It would go *THUNK … THUNK … THUNK* every second or so and each time the plane would feel like it stopped for a fraction of a second. I had the feeling that if it were fired at high altitude the plane might stall.

The more I flew the plane the more disillusioned I became with its performance. It was such a beautiful airplane, and it was really easy to fly, but it was heavy—very heavy—and didn't perform well at all in our practice dogfights. The old AT-6 was much more maneuverable. I had an experience, too, that didn't help any. I came out of a dive, low over the water, not going very fast. When I pulled back on the stick nothing happened, I just kept sinking. I jammed the throttle forward, but still nothing happened—seemingly it was unable to catch the air. I was going to stall right into the water and nothing I did made any difference. But something finally did catch, somehow, and I was able to gain speed and altitude. I mentioned it to several people, but was told that's the way it was sometimes! Great consolation! I never found out the reason, but I was more careful over the water after that.

San Francisco was beautiful and it was a good place to visit, which we did every chance we had. Baer was up to his usual, but I used the time to enjoy the city. I had been there for a few days once before, when the World's Fair was there, so I knew my way around a little, but I hadn't seen it from the air, and that was a fabulous sight. It's a city built on an island, or so it seems, because it is almost entirely surrounded by water. Its tall buildings, reaching skyward from the hills, are not quite high enough to satisfy their urges to be called skyscrapers. It all looked artificial, like something you'd build as a kid.

On two occasions, I flew over the city at night, and that image has remained with me all these years. A painting it was not, but it came close. The blackness of the water and the sparkling city with its bridges was the most beautiful sight I have ever seen from the air.

There was a problem, though, and it probably still exists—the weather. It always seemed foggy and not very pleasant. It helped us with our flying, however. From the air the fog looked like clouds. Our field at San Rafael was usually clear, so we

---

3 A "chandelle" is a steep climbing turn executed to reverse the direction of travel 180 degrees.

never got lost—all we had to do was look at the horizon and head a little north of the 'clouds'.

Compared to what we had been through for the past ten or eleven months, our time at Hamilton Field was relaxing. We flew and had some classes, and best of all we had a little spare time of our own. The classes were mostly navigation and aircraft recognition. We had to assume we were going to the Pacific because they were concentrating mostly on Japanese airplanes.

I had a letter from Bledsoe, which was a surprise. He didn't know where I was, so (leave it to Bledsoe) he wrote to my mother and she gave him my address. He was at Mitchel Field in New York flying out of La Guardia Airport with Republic's new high-altitude fighter, the P-47 Thunderbolt. Before he left home, he had a call from Dick Butler, in San Diego, who was on the same orders, and they drove back together in Bledsoe's old Buick. He did a lot of raving about the P-47 and I couldn't help being a little envious. But I didn't tell him that when I answered.

I also had a letter from Carrington, who got my address from Bledsoe. He was at Geiger Field, Washington, in the 508th Bomb Squadron in the 351st Bomb Group. It was so hard for me to imagine gentle naïve Carrington driving a huge bomber. But he seemed happy as always.

It was nearing November, and there were rumors around that we were going to move out soon. Then I had another letter from Bledsoe.

29 October
Blick,
I just wanted to let you know I was in an accident and am in the hospital. I'm all right—just being observed. We were up flying formation and I was on the flight leader's wing. I was in a good position on the right, and there were two ships on his left—the regular v formation. The flight leader made a tight turn to the right and I was right with him, but I don't know what the stupid element leader was trying to do. For some reason he didn't turn soon enough and came up under me—how he did that I haven't the slightest—and I clipped the tip of his wing off with my prop. He was, of course, under me, in a position he shouldn't have been in, and I couldn't see him. He bailed out, but I brought my plane back. The prop was a mess, but the thing kept running so I took the chance that it would get me home, and it did.

It wasn't my fault, and I think everyone knows it, but the bastard flying that element was a captain, just up for the ride, and he's saying I was in the wrong—naturally! Rank! His wingman saw it all, so at least he'll bear me out.

I'll write more later—just wanted to fill you in.
Keep smilin'
Marv.

[Bledsoe's letter (the original has not been located and it is possible this is Blick's memory of it rather than a transcript) does not correspond with the record of events on October 12, 1942. Bledsoe (then in the 90th Fighter Squadron, 80th Fighter Group flying out of La Guardia, New York) took off on an alert flight and joined with his leader. At 800 feet Lieutenant Donald M. Broady closed too quickly and collided with Bledsoe's aircraft. The tail of Broady's aircraft was severed and it spun in, killing him. Bledsoe was uninjured and was able to make an emergency landing at La Guardia. Broady was Bledsoe's close friend and he had the unpleasant experience of having to tell his wife of the accident and escort her and the remains of his friend back to Los Angeles for the funeral.[4]]

That was a big shock, but there was nothing I could do about it. I had my own problems. We had just received the news that the 328th was moving out, to the Pacific. It was what we were expecting, but there was a twist that we didn't expect. And I didn't know quite what to think about it. They weren't taking anyone with less than fifty hours in the P-39, and that included most of us that were new. There were a few that had flown enough. And Bennett was one of them.

Our orders came in and we were split up—some to Mitchel Field, New York, and the rest to Richmond, Virginia. Baer, Balason and I were still together, on the same orders to Mitchel.

HEADQUARTERS
328th Fighter Group, Army Air Forces
Hamilton Field, California

November, 16, 1942

(SO)
:
(NO 88)   -E X T R A C T-

*   *   *   *   *   *

4. Pur to auth cont in TWX N400G-1, Hq IV FC, dated Nov 15/42, as amended by TWX#N414G-1, Hq IV FC, dated Nov 16/42, the following named Pilots, 2ND LTS, AC, Sdrns as indic opposite their names, are hereby reld fr fur asgmt to this Gp and reasgd to Orgns and Stas indic, and will proceed w/o delay thereto, reporting upon arrival to the CO thereat for further assmt and duties.

TO: New York Air Defense Wing,
Mitchel Field, New York

JOHN H. BEHR JR	0728548	– 326th Fr Sq
WAYNE K. BLICKENSTAFF	0728555	– 326th Fr Sq
JOHN M. BALASON	0728541	– 326th Fr Sq
ROLAND N. McKEAN	0790280	– 329th Fr Sq
PAUL G. BUDESA	0728566	– 329th Fr SQ
ALAN W. LOWE	0790275	– 329th Fr SQ
ROY J. REIGARD	0728726	– 329th Fr Sq

---

4   Marvin Bledsoe, *Fighter Pilot—A True Story*, unpublished, circa 1945, pp. 52–56. See also the accidents reports https://www.aviationarchaeology.com/, accessed May 8, 2020.

The TC will furn the nec Rail T. TDN. TPA. FD 31 P 431-01,. 02, 03, 07, O8 A 0425-23.

   *   *   *   *   *

By order of Major GRANBO:

WILLIAM E. HATCH
1st Lt, Air Corps
Adjutant.[5]

---

5 Blick's logbook indicates his last flight in a P-39-D1 was on October 11, 1942 and his next flight was at Baltimore, Maryland, in a P-40F, December 12, 1942.

Eight

Mitchel Field was obviously a well-known, well-established base, and we found it easily.[1] It was out on Long Island near Hempstead, and the hardest part was just getting through New York City and out to the Island. I did the driving and Baer was in the front seat with the map. We found our way through the Holland Tunnel, up the East River Drive and over the Triborough Bridge, then east on the Northern State Parkway until we saw a Hempstead sign. Simple? Well, it is now, but it wasn't then.

We reported in, but it was too late to do anything about the orders, so we were sent to the BOQ (Bachelor Officer's Quarters) and told to report back at 0900 the next day. We did, on the dot, and the sergeant told us to wait a little while until they could get an official word to cut our new orders. It was very clear we weren't expected, and obvious that no one knew what to do with us. Hurry up and wait!

I began to wonder what would have happened if we had gone off somewhere and never showed at all. Would we ever be missed? We had been anticipating flying those new P-47s ever since leaving Hamilton. We picked up our new orders that afternoon.

(SPECIAL ORDER) RESTRICTED   HEADQUARTERS I FIGHTER COMMAND
                                        MITCHEL FIELD, NEW YORK
NUMBER 314   EXTRACT   30 NOVEMBER, 1942

*   *   *   *   *   *

23. The following assignments are directed:

NAME, GRADE	REPORTED	ASSIGNED TO
ROLAND N. McKEAN 2nd Lt, A.C	This Headquarters, per P.4 S.O. #88 Hq 328th Fighter Group AAF, Hamilton Field California	Philadelphia Air Defense Wing, Philadelphia Pennsylvania

---

1   Named for former New York Mayor John Purroy Mitchel, who became an aviation cadet and fell to his death from an aircraft July 6, 1918. See *New York Times*, July 7, 1918.

November 16, 1942

ROY J. REIGARD		
2nd Lt, A.C.	DO	DO
ALAN W. LOWE		
2nd Lt, A.C.	DO	DO
PAUL G. BUDESA		
2nd Lt, A.C.	DO	DO
JOHN H. BEHR JR		
2nd Lt A.C.	DO	DO
WAYNE K. BLICKENSTAFF		
2nd Lt A.C.	DO	DO
JOHN M. BALASON		
2nd Lt A.C.	DO	DO

The provisions of par. 4c, Bull #27, WD, CS; cIR #261, Wd, cs; Cir #279 WD, cs, apply. TDN TBA, FD31 P 431-01, 02, 03, 07, 08 A 0425-23.

By command of Brigadier General TAYLOR:
R.B.TRAVIS,
Major, Air Corps.
Adjutant.

"Oh shit! Philadelphia! You mean we traveled all this distance for naught—only to go back again to Philadelphia!" Baer was not in a good mood.

"Yeah, it looks that way," I said. "These guys obviously just want to get rid of us. I thought there was a shortage of pilots."

"Well, let's go," Balason sighed. "Not much we can do about it, though, is there?"

"No. You're right, John," I agreed. "But we might just as well spend another night here in the BOQ, and leave in the morning. No one seems to care how quickly we get there."

We had a little trouble finding Wing Headquarters in Philadelphia, but we were pleasantly surprised to find out we were expected, and that new orders were already cut.

(SPECIAL ORDER) RESTRICTED   HEADQUARTERS PHILADELPHIA
            :   AIR DEFENSE WING
NO. 106) E X T R A C T   PHILADELPHIA, PA
                                    DECEMBER, 2, 1942

* * * * *

2. The following named O, having been asgd to Hq Philadelphia Air Defense Wing, pursuant to Par 23, SO 314, Hq I Ftr Comm, Mitchel Fld, N.Y., c.s., are further asgd to Hq 353rd Ftr Gp, AAB, Baltimore, Md., and w/p without delay from Philadelphia, Pa, to AAB, Baltimore, Md., reporting upon arrival to the CO thereat for dy.

2nd Lt ALAN W. LOWE
2nd Lt PAUL G. BUDESA
2nd Lt RONALD M. McKEAN
2nd Lt ROY J. REIGARD
2nd Lt JOHN H. BEHR JR
2nd Lt WAYNE K. BLICKENSTAFF
2nd Lt JOHN M. BALASON

TDN. This is a temp change of sta.
FD 34 P 434-02 A 0425-23.

*   *   *   *   *

By order of Colonel QUESADA:

JESSE M. CHILDRESS JR
1st Lt, Air Corps.

When we found out the orders were to Baltimore, Baer blurted out, "When we arrive there, we will no doubt find new orders to Georgia or Florida, or Arkansas or somewhere."

It was getting ridiculous and a little humorous. "At least we're working our way into warmer weather," I said.

As it turned out, Headquarters for the 353rd Fighter Group was at the Baltimore Municipal Airport, which was ten or fifteen miles south of Baltimore near a little town called Dundalk. After the luxurious quarters at Hamilton Field and those we saw at Mitchel, it was a disturbing and disappointing sight to drive by the one-story tar-paper-covered housing facilities and search out Group Headquarters in the old, weathered cement block building near the tower. The only planes we saw were the airline's DC-3s.

However, we were welcomed respectfully, and given our new assignments—to join the 350th Fighter Squadron right there. No more traveling. We were there at last, and when we returned to the car, the left front tire was flat—almost as if the old car heard the orders!

HEADQUARTERS, 353RD FIGHTER GROUP
Army Air Base, Baltimore, Maryland

December 6, 1942

SPECIAL ORDER)
              :
NO.   40)   E X T R A C T

*   *   *   *   *

5. The following named Officers having been assigned to Hq 353rd Fighter Group, pursuant to par. 7, SO 107, Headquarters Philadelphia Air Defense Wing, Philadelphia, Pa., dated

December 3, 1942, are further assigned to the 350th Fighter Squadron and will report to the CO thereat for duty.

        2nd Lt JOHN M. BALASON
        2nd Lt JOHN H. BEHR JR
        2nd Lt WAYNE K. BLICKENSTAFF

            By order of Major MORRIS

                      Robert G. Gottlieb
                      2nd Lt, Air Corps
                      Adjutant.

Nine

The 353rd Fighter Group had three squadrons, all based at different locations. The 350th was at Baltimore along with Headquarters, the 351st was at Norfolk, Virginia, and the 352nd was at Langley Field, also in Virginia. In Headquarters, along with the non-flying officers, there were three pilots, the commanding officer, the group executive officer, who was second in command, and the group operations officer. In the squadrons, the COs and their operations officers were pilots also. Each squadron was formed with three flights, A, B and C. The flights were not yet all filled, but each was to have eight pilots. Lowe and Budesa went into A Flight, and Baer, Balason, Reigard and I went into C.

After all of our expectations about flying the P-47 Thunderbolt, we were disappointed when we saw our planes. They were Curtiss Wright P-40 Warhawks. The P-40 was the Flying Tiger airplane—the famous one they had decorated with the snarling, shark-like teeth. We told ourselves that if Chennault and his Flying Tigers had done so well with it, it had to be a good plane, but its noisy engine, sputtering as it did, especially on take-off, didn't offer much in the way of confidence and security. And it felt so heavy. It dove like a rock, and for that matter climbed like one too. But the worst feature was the narrow landing gear, and on those short, bumpy runways, every landing was "Glory Be and Hail Mary!" Some difference from the tricycle gear on the P-39! Originally, when we had been transferred to Mitchel we thought we'd be going to England, but now, with the P-40s, the talk was about Africa.

The airport jutted out into the dark, menacing waters of the Chesapeake Bay at Sparrows Point. It was an ideal location for the airline's twin-engine DC-3s, but for the faster fighters, needing half again as much runway length, it was hazardous. And to make matters even worse, there was a large slag pile at the end of the east–west runway, with a tall crane lurking high over it, as if someone had purposely placed it there to keep us honed and sharp, just daring us to hit it. To come in and land on that runway, against the prevailing winds, we had to barely skim over the top of the crane and drop down immediately to hit the end of the runway. A little too long or too fast, it was a sure dunk in the bay.

The north–south runway was even shorter. We felt like the only thing lacking was the tail-hook that the Navy pilots used. As much as we griped, however, we were thankful later on that our training had been so demanding.

Each flight had its own barracks—narrow, tar-papered, one-story affairs, with double rooms on either side of a narrow hallway running the length of the building. Just inside the entrance, was an open ablution area. To the right against the outside wall were three open toilets and on the wall opposite, the urinals. On the left, the sinks with mirrors and open showers. Hardly luxurious. Baer and I were together in the second from the last room on the left and Reigard and Balason were across the hall one room closer to the door.

Dewey Newhart, C Flight Leader, was from our 42-H Class at Luke but, because of the alphabetic separation, I hadn't known him there. After graduation, he was sent to another group—the 31st in New Orleans, I think—but when that group moved overseas, he was sent directly to Richmond to become one of the first original pilots in the 353rd.

Not long after our arrival, the squadron Flight Surgeon showed up—a captain—and he was assigned to our C Flight barracks. His name was Joseph Canipelli, but it only took about a day for us to forget he had a first name. From then and forever after, he was known as Doc. He was a short, pleasant Southerner with a born-in bedside manner and I was intrigued by him immediately. I liked his quiet ease of conversation and especially that he was interested in a few things besides flying and women—something hard to say about Baer and Balason, and many of the others as well.

As the flights grew to full capacity we began to compete: which one had the best formation; which one could get off the ground the quickest; which one could make the fastest and best landing pattern; and which one could sustain the best gunnery scores, etc. The competition was supported, even encouraged, by the brass, because it was excellent training. We were training for combat, and though no one really knew what combat would be like, we did know that the better we were, the better we would be in a tight, tense situation.

We knew, also, that our lives would depend on our helping each other, so our formation was important. We formed the flights into element leaders and wingmen, an element being two airplanes. We hadn't had the time to rate our flying abilities, so the element leaders were picked only because of their experience. We flew in flights of four—two elements. The first element leader was designated the leader of that flight and the second element leader flew behind him and off to one side. Each wingman's job was to stick with his element leader and cover for him.

It was a time of anxiety, and for some, even hysteria. There were constant rumors of submarine sightings and strange, mystical lights at night off the coast. Every day we kept four planes on readiness. Whenever there was an unidentified sighting of any kind, that flight's mission was to take off immediately and investigate.

The four pilots on standby would wait in the ready room, fully dressed and prepared to dash out to the waiting jeep at the harsh blare of the alert horn. They would race to their planes at the end of the runway, which the crew chiefs would have already armed and set running, and then take off as quickly and efficiently as possible and be vectored to their destination by radio.

Our flights made a competitive game out of it, keeping a tally to see who could get in the air the quickest. We never saw anything even slightly resembling a German U-boat, or anything at all suspicious. I had no idea what I'd do if I ever did see something, but the training was exciting—a little boring during the waiting period, but otherwise fun. We usually had two or three alerts during a day, just for practice. For this stand-by readiness, we each received an American Theater Ribbon for participating in the defense of the East Coast of the United States.

Our squadron commander was Captain Wallace Hopkins, who had gone through flight school about a year ahead of the rest of us. He flew occasionally with different flights, but most of the time he was with the group officers, or in the tower watching our training exercises. The squadron operations officer, however—First Lieutenant Stanley Pidduck—was more involved. He instigated all of the squadron flight schedules except the instrument flying exercises in the Link Trainer, which were handled by the individual flights. There were also other projects to keep us busy such as aircraft recognition, which was dreamed up by the squadron intelligence officer. We had full days.

As the squadron grew, our flights became small independent units of sorts, and the competition became even more intense. To the brass, it was akin to a family of highly competitive brothers, and they were sure that when push came to shove, the flights and the squadrons would all pull together as one indefeasible unit against any and all odds. We didn't realize it at the time, but we would always have the rapport and closeness we formed with each other during that period. We were building lifetime friendships.

We were also expanding our education. Except for the few who had been fortunate enough to attend distant colleges, or were rich enough to have traveled, we were products of our narrow, childhood environments. Our tiny, naïve worlds unraveled as our exposure to other lives broadened, but at the same time our real world grew smaller as our awareness increased.

I was fascinated by the dissimilarities in people and their backgrounds, and I was curious enough to try to find out as much as I could about everyone. The various accents intrigued me. I had a good ear, and without making a conscious effort I was soon able to distinguish between the large areas of the country. The change from Georgia to Maryland, for instance, was extreme, but the subtleties in between were harder to pinpoint. To my ear, any odd pronunciation or emphasis was immediately apparent because I was used to the blurred, uninteresting nothingness of the California accent. I liked the easy-going lazy drawl of the Southern states especially. I was a little slow of nature and laid-back myself, so it was no wonder.

Dewey Newhart was heavy set and solid, about five-nine, with a round, rapidly balding head that seemed a little larger than it should be. Although mostly gone topside, he had an abundant growth of dark brown hair on his arms and peeking out from his open collar. He also had a dense, thick and wiry stubble on his face when he skipped shaving. The baldness didn't bother him a bit—he actually seemed to enjoy the uniqueness of it.

In fact, there seemed to be very little that bothered him. I suspected, though, that there was a deeper personality, smoldering somewhere inside. He was a year senior to me, but looked older because of the baldness, and he seemed even more mature because he had a natural attitude of confidence and authority. People listened when he talked, not just because he was C Flight leader, but because he made sense. I noticed that even Hopkins and Pidduck were impressed with his ability to get right to the point.

Dewey was from the show-me state of Missouri (Mizzurah, not Missouree), and he was proud of it. He came from St Joseph, on the Missouri River north of Kansas City. His accent, from the northern part of the state, reflected more of the clipped, flat tones of the Mid-East, than the softer Arkansas drawl. When questioned about it, he said, "During the Civil War, we couldn't make up our minds whether we wanted to go Southern or Northern."

But Dewey didn't inherit any of that indecision. There were few grays in his life—everything was either black or white. It was not that he didn't pay attention to others and their differing viewpoints, he did. He listened to all arguments and ideas, and then made up his own mind. And once that happened, it was set, like welded iron, and there was very little hope of ever changing it. "Okay, then, we'll do this ..." was a favorite expression. And, of course, he was proud of the show-me attitude about wanting proof of everything. He didn't believe in taking chances based on guesswork. Good old horse sense was his wisdom. He was a born and bred skeptic: "Convince me. I'm from Missouri, y'know."

However, when it came to the decision about who was to be an element leader and who would fly wing, he admitted to me that it was a gray area. The TO (Technical Order) for element leader was first lieutenant.

"It's tough," he said. "I know the kind of training we all had at Luke, but I have no idea about the other schools. I can't just take it for granted that we are better pilots. And just because we graduated in 42H doesn't automatically make us better either, than those pilots from 42I or J." He thought for a moment. "So what I'm gonna do is this. We'll just fly everyone everywhere, and see how they do. That's what training is all about anyway. Right?"

"True," I agreed.

"No one says I have to make those decisions now anyway. ..."

Chuck Dinse was the old man of C Flight. At twenty-six he was even older than Doc. He had a degree in engineering from the University of Illinois and was in the process of establishing a career with the Chicago Home Fuel & Utilities Company when the US entry into the war became imminent. It crossed his mind, of course, as it did with every healthy male, that he might be drafted, but he was married and hopeful that he wouldn't be called. Then came that fateful Sunday [Pearl Harbor]. Both he and his wife were so incensed he called his boss to let him know, and signed up immediately.

Dinse was a gentle person, quick to step into a potential altercation with a calming statement, but seldom involving himself in the controversy. As a personality, he was hardly a dynamic force, but his influence was remarkable. There was nothing intimidating about him. At five-nine and a half, and thin, he was just another typical pilot, blending deftly into any group. He had a long face with almost sharp, but regular, features, and fine sandy hair parted on the right. He smoked a pipe almost constantly—at least it was always in his mouth. It was questionable how much it was on and going. Most people clamped a pipe with their teeth so it pointed outward and to one side or the other, the bowl away from the face far enough so the smoke didn't curl up into the nose and eyes. His just hung there, in the middle of his mouth, not quite leaning on his chin, like it would fall out any minute. Most of the time, when he was talking, I found myself concentrating on the pipe, tensed and ready to catch it as it fell. But it never did.

I liked Chuck. I liked his calm and restrained attitude, but because of my own ineptitude, I was mostly impressed by his ability to reach into his memory and pull up factual information. He was an encyclopedia. He could talk about anything. He seemed more aware of what was going on even in the world of art than I, and could, with just as much ease, switch to medicine with Doc or farming with Dewey.

Doc, however, was hesitant, and not so affected.

"I like Chuck," he said. "He's a nice guy, but I just think he's one of those guys who have quick minds and a good memory. I think he's one of those people who can read the headline and the first paragraph, then talk the rest of the story like he knows it all."

"Could be, I suppose, but if true, he's mighty good at it."

"It's an art. People like that are great politicians. They're impressive, and good in business. He's learned the art of small talk. You know, 'How's everything? Great day today, isn't it? How about those Bears? You agree with what FDR is doing with Churchill?' That sort of thing."

"I really don't see anything wrong with that, Doc. I wish I could do it."

"I know. I wish I could, too. Maybe I'm just jealous."

When Dewey made Dinse an element leader with me as his wingman, I found out there wasn't any question about his flying—he was an excellent pilot.

Dewey told me that he thought Chuck had good technical skill, but, "I'm still a little unsure about something and I need your help. He's a little too cautious, I think. But then, I may be reading too much into it. After you've flown together for a while I'd like to know what you think. It's a thin line up there, between recklessness and headwork. We don't know anything about what we'll be facing overseas, but it seems to me that quickness—quick decisions and quick reflex action—might mean the difference between life and death."

I found him a pleasure to fly with—very smooth and considerate. There were no sudden, violent maneuvers that were hard to keep up with. It was almost too easy, and I thought it was great. I could move in close and relax, with never a thought that Dinse would suddenly and without warning turn into me. It was easy for me to submit to the lazy part of my personality. At the same time, however, I knew his flying skills were not being properly tested, and I began to understand what Dewey was talking about. I wondered, too, what it would be like in an urgent combat emergency.

When I didn't become element leader, I was a little pissed, wondering why. I thought the reason was probably because I lacked experience with the P-40, but that didn't make a lot of sense. The thought made it a little easier to accept, though. It was a little hard for me to understand why flying a P-40 would increase a person's flying proficiency any more than flying a P-39. In fact, from what I had heard, the P-40 was probably easier to fly. It bothered me more than I thought it should and I finally had to come to the conclusion that maybe I wasn't quite as good as I believed.

There was a part of me that was happy I was flying wing. I didn't have the responsibility of making decisions and looking out for someone flying off me, who was watching my every movement and making judgments about my flying. As wingman, my only job was to fly close formation and supposedly watch my element leader's (and my) tail.

But the other part—the part that kept telling me I was just as good as he—was eating a few holes here and there in my confidence, and letting little drops of green seep through. It was not a good feeling, and I was not at all happy with myself. My decision, finally, was just to fly the best I could and not worry about it.

When off duty, we were treated like the officers and gentlemen the bars on our shoulders represented. We were not confined to the base, and overnight passes were not a problem. As long as we reported in for our daily duties, we were free to come and go at will.

Baer fell easily into a routine that would deplete the energies of any normal person enough to force him into sick call. When freed from the day's schedule, he would get cleaned up and drive into Baltimore. Then, sometime in the early morning hours, he would return, glassy-eyed with lips rosy from use, and feeling no pain. He'd sit down on the edge of my bed and wake me up out of my deepest sleep. Then, grinning like a clown, he'd start to talk. His story varied slightly from night to night, but it was always long and involved and basically the same—how he got together with this beautiful creature, and how great she was in the sack. It didn't end until he could let me know that, "Jesus, Blick, you just can't conceive how difficult it is to get up and leave that soft, warm, luscious body …" and he'd look around, "… for this!"

I liked Baer, and I tried to be patient with him. He had a kind of confidence that I envied, probably because he was a social person and I wasn't. At the same time, however, there was a strange aura of loneliness about him. He was different and obviously felt out of place—the result of growing up privileged. In his own way he had tried to fit in—to be like everyone else—but whatever he attempted didn't work. In subtle ways, I had tried to tell him to just be himself and to quit trying so hard—that people would accept him for what he was as long as he didn't act like a snob of some kind. But it hadn't worked. He had lived all of his previous life on a different level, in a disparate, almost imaginary, fictitious atmosphere that had no meaning to anyone in this real world.

At first the nightly awakenings were interesting, the stories intriguing, but not for long, and my patience soon ran thin. I knew it was something Baer needed, but I required the sleep just as much, if not more, than he needed to talk. My attempts to turn it off didn't work. It did no good to get mad. He was full of euphoric air, and nothing would deflate him. I tried rolling over and snoring; I tried getting furious; I tried shoving him off the bed, but even that didn't work. He just moved to another position and continued talking. He wouldn't stop until he was finished! I was really perplexed and amazed at how Baer could keep it up night after night, but his recovery was even more baffling. No matter how drunk he was or how late he came in, he was always up and on time for any schedule. I knew what to look for and could see eyes that were a little glazed and bloodshot, but to most people he was wide-awake, alert and ready for the day.

Balason, on the other hand, was an entirely different story. Ever since Baer had taken it upon himself to detach him from his virginity, Balason looked upon Baer as some kind of heroic idol. Baer didn't mind the adoration, and answered by attempting to educate him in some of the more subtle nighttime social skills. It didn't work well, of course—they were just too dissimilar. Baer had been in training since before early puberty, and Balason was a good pilot. Apples and oranges. Balason would go into town with him once in a while, but could never cope with the morning after, or, for that matter, the following day. Not being in the same barracks, Baer could not wake him, and he was late on a number of occasions. It didn't set well with Robert Fortier, his flight leader. He would spend the next week confined to base. But Balason was dogged. By the time he was free, his genitals had once again taken over his reasoning ability, and he would talk Baer into giving him another lesson.

At the beginning of February, the squadron carried out two weeks of gunnery practice at Millville, New Jersey.[1] We dove on ground targets and did our air-to-air gunnery offshore, firing at a large wind-sock-like target towed by another plane. It was an intense time—a little taste of combat—and we enjoyed it. We were too tired to do anything but collapse after the day's activities. Baer cut the tow line twice, losing the target, and there were rumors that the tow plane had some holes in it, but that was not confirmed. It was not unusual to lose the target, once. But twice was enough to get the attention of the brass, and Dewey was concerned.

"I give the target a good lead," Baer said defensively, "just like we've been told. Then I gradually pull the line of fire through the target. It makes more sense to do that than to miss the whole thing by not leading it enough."

He was correct, of course, and there wasn't much that Dewey could say. "You're right. If that had been an enemy plane, you would've hit him. And you can't help it if a stray bullet hits the tow line. But maybe," he said with a smile, "for the sake of everyone else, and especially Hopkins, you could quit leading it so much."

At Baltimore, Baer continued his nightly sojourns as if there had been no interruption. And of course Balason was eager to go along, but he was dragging.

Captain Ben Rimerman, group operations officer, had formed the habit of making the rounds infrequently. He called it "touching base." He didn't consider it an inspection, and he didn't treat it as such, but, when he was around, everyone was sure to be on his best behavior. The enlisted men, especially, were moving and looking busy, even if they weren't. And our intelligence officer, First Lieutenant Rosentreter (Rosie), would hurriedly find something to do, like aircraft recognition, for any of the pilots who happened to be there in the ready room and not doing anything. Rimerman was a congenial person and, even though we didn't see him very often, most everyone liked him. He was never hurried, and stopped to talk and spend some time with the enlisted men as well as the officers. He would usually pick up Hopkins and they would make the tour together. On his first appearance in the squadron after our return from Millville, he found Balason sound asleep in the Link Trainer.

On February 22, Balason, Baer and another pilot from A Flight, received orders transferring them to Camp Kilmer, New Jersey, to join another fighter group rumored to be on its way to North Africa.[2] I was surprised, but at the same time, not surprised. Much as I liked them both, I realized that in the eyes of the brass they were just fuck-ups, and I could understand the transfer. What was hard for me to understand, though, was how they knew about Baer. Was he so transparent?

---

1   Blick's logbook confirms he flew gunnery training flights February 2–13, 1943.
2   Balason actually transferred to the 18th Fighter Squadron, 343rd Fighter Group on the way to the Aleutians. He flew a full tour of operations with them in P-40s before rejoining the 350th Fighter Squadron in England in October 1944. Bill Price, *Close Calls—Two Tours with the 353rd Fighter Group*, Usk, Aviation Usk, 1992, p. 106.

Outwardly, he had always seemed to be in control. Dewey was sharp, though—just maybe sharper than I thought.

I hated to see both of them go, as we had already been through so much together. Baer accepted the transfer as a confirmation of his feelings that he couldn't fit in. It didn't seem to enter his mind that his extra-curricular activities had anything to do with it—that liquor and lack of sleep could possibly dull the edge of his skill. He was more hurt than bitter, though, seemingly accepting the Army way. I could read him well enough to know that he was truly upset about having to leave his friends, but at the same time the thought wouldn't go away that he might be more concerned about finding suitable female companionship in Africa.

Balason, on the other hand, was very upset. He just couldn't understand. "I'm a good pilot, Blick. You know that. Everyone knows that. I'll bet I could take most of these guys in a dogfight." He looked for support, directly into my eyes. "And if I'm good enough for that, I could do it to the Germans, too. So why wouldn't they want to keep me?"

"I don't know, John. Maybe it's only because that other group is going overseas now and needs some good pilots. Could be as simple as that."

"You don't think it's because they're just trying to get rid of us?"

I didn't know what to say. "I really have no idea what goes on upstairs. Who knows?" Balason really was a good pilot, but he just didn't use his head sometimes. "It probably didn't set too well when Rimerman found you asleep in the Link."

Balason's mouth turned up a little, sheepishly. "Yeah ... that wasn't so good was it?"

"At least you'll still be with Baer, John. But you'd better remember that he's a hard guy to keep up with."

"Yeah." He let his head drop. "I think I've learned a lesson."

Everyone in the 353rd had always assumed that our eventual destination would be North Africa. It was a natural assumption because of our P-40s and lightweight, summer uniforms. It was common, rumored knowledge that the P-47 was the plane bound for England as the first US fighter designed specifically for high-altitude escort.

However, around the middle of February, everything changed. A flight of four P-47s landed, and the entire group started the complicated switchover.[3] The planes were brought in first, and then gradually we were issued heavy, cold-weather equipment. When we slipped into those fur-lined jackets we knew the new rumor was true—we *had* to be headed for England. Most of us were happy about it, not because of the war—war was war wherever—but we thought we just might be a little more comfortable. And, in England, they at least spoke the same language—or so we thought.

All were not happy about flying the P-47, though. It was still a brand new airplane, and the rumors were thick and heavy about that "abomination!" We had heard the

---

3 Blick made transition flights in P-47Bs on February 9 and 10 and then switched to the P-47B completely from February 14, 1943.

stories about all the bugs not yet eliminated, and the accidents, and it was hard to ignore them. As rumors do, they continued to surface. We began to hear supposed comments from the pilots in England who had been flying Spitfires. The claim was that the P-47 was suicidal to fly, especially below 20,000 feet. And they nicknamed it the "Juggernaut," shortened later to "Jug." It was filled with bugs—teething problems so-called—including troubles with the radio, but most of all there was the dreaded and deadly *compressibility*—something we knew nothing about.

Along with the airplanes came a technical representative from Republic. He was there mainly to help the crews work on the planes, but at the same time he wanted to let us know that it was the greatest plane built to date, and to assure us that there was nothing to fear. There were some bugs, yes, but they were being worked on and eliminated rapidly. In answer to the questions about compressibility, he could only tell us what they thought was causing it and how to avoid it.

"As you know," he said, "the Thunderbolt is heavy—heavier than any fighter ever built. In a dive, it builds up speed quickly, fast approaching the speed of sound. This is the first time anyone has ever gone so fast and it's an unknown. We don't know exactly what happens, but somehow the faster you go the more the air pressure builds up ahead of the airplane until it becomes almost solid. The controls become immovable, no matter how hard you try, they won't budge.

"Some people have managed to pull out of the dive, but they're not quite sure how they did it. One pilot said that he turned the trim tabs up and just waited … nothing else to do. Then when he slowed down in the denser air the plane pulled out on its own. So right now that's the best we have to offer—use the trim tabs. But … avoid it if you can. If you find yourself in a steep dive, and I'm sure you will at some point, pull out before you get to that speed and you won't have the problem."[4]

We adapted easily. It didn't take long. In two weeks, we were old timers with the plane and wondering why we had ever had any concerns. Everything about it was big, including the cockpit. As small as I am, I always felt cramped in the other planes, and always wondered how taller, bulkier pilots could fit into those tiny cockpits, especially the P-39. No trouble here, though. Plenty of room for anyone.

Actually, it was a little too roomy for Joe Furness. He couldn't seem to master the landing. Then one day he ticked the crane coming in. He reacted by yanking the stick back, which in turn stalled him out too high and the plane dropped with a shattering crash, tail first and nose high at a crazy angle with the wing hitting before the wheels. Fortunately, the widespread wheels saved him, and he was able to swing around in a ground loop off the runway.

Furness was the shortest pilot in the squadron, only five feet, three inches, if that. Someone called him Little Joe and it stuck, but the little changed to Li'l, becoming

---

[4] The 350th Fighter Squadron lost one pilot to a high-speed dive while at Baltimore. On March 1, 1943, Second Lieutenant Meyer Rothblatt died when his aircraft crashed into the Chesapeake Bay.

Li'l Joe. He didn't seem to mind. He was one of those affable, charismatic people, with none of the obnoxious bravado so many small people display, and the whole squadron was concerned about his lack of ability in landing. He was a good pilot and everyone knew it. It was Dewey who finally solved the problem. He mentioned to Pidduck that he thought Joe might be too short to see well out of the cockpit. Pidduck gave him a pillow and told him to try it on the next flight. It worked. There was no further trouble.[5]

There were other difficulties and a few accidents, but with the exception of an incident with a plane that I was scheduled to take up, all were minor, and nothing to be alarmed about.[6] I started the take-off normally, then about halfway down the runway, just when I was ready to lift off, the engine suddenly lost power. There was no time to think—reactions took over and I cut everything back and jammed on the brakes. I stopped off the end of the runway with the wheels about two feet from the water! It all happened so quickly I didn't even have time to break out in a sweat or go into shock. Later, when the crew examined the engine, it was completely frozen—they couldn't budge the prop.[7]

The time was coming—everyone felt it. There was a nervous air of anticipation throughout the squadron ... even with the base personnel. It was a kind of eagerness, tempered by the caution of the unknown. We flew, and flew constantly, almost as if we were attempting to delay the inevitable. We were excited and eager to get involved in the war—to, in some way, revenge the disaster at Pearl Harbor. Yet at the same time the thought of the possible consequences put an anxious knot in our bowels—mine anyway—that we weren't about to admit to.

We had another gunnery session at Millville.[8] What was taken lightly before, as a kind of game, was this time a deadly serious operation. We worked those eight 50-caliber guns hard, both on the ground targets and on the sleeve. We could feel the power, and began to feel as if we, ourselves, were the guns.

We also felt the weight of the plane. Unlike the P-40, when we dove on the target and pulled up after firing, the Jug kept going, mushing along in the same direction until the air pressure on the wings countered the downward speed. We learned quickly to start our pullout early or we would mush right into the ground. We had been warned, so no one did, but it was close. It was easy to concentrate too hard, and too long, on the target and forget to pull out.

---

5   There are two accident reports for Li'l Joe Furness, on March 9 and 24, 1943. See https://www.aviationarchaeology.com/, accessed May 10, 2020.
6   Blick chose not to discuss the loss of Meyer Rothblatt on March 1, or fellow C Flight member, Second Lieutenant Roy J. Reigard, in a mid-air collision on March 24, 1943.
7   Neither Blick's logbook nor accident reports provide any information on this incident.
8   Blick's logbook confirms this as April 12–17, 1943.

Back at Baltimore Dewey made his decisions about the permanent structure of his flight. He added me to his roster of element leaders, promoting us to the rank of first lieutenant.[9] He assigned Dwight Fry as my wingman.

Fry was taller than most, a little over five ten, thin, with sharp features and eagle eyes. I couldn't have been happier with the decision. I had flown with Fry enough to know that he was an excellent pilot, and I liked the idea that eyes like his were back there looking out for me. It didn't take me long to get over the nervousness about someone watching my every move, and I found that I could take comfort in the fact that Fry was there. I'd look back and see that wing tucked comfortably in between my own wing and tail, and see those eyes, always alert and watching.

Headquarters made some changes also. For no reason we could understand, Wallace Hopkins was transferred out and Ben Rimerman took over our squadron. Hopkins and Doc were both from Georgia and had become friends. Needless to say, Doc was upset with that transfer. It was a mystery that stayed unsolved.[10]

We flew, constantly. We flew alerts, flew combat formation, took long navigational trips at 20,000 feet, had dogfights, did aerobatics, practiced instrument flying, and, while the brass looked the other way, we buzzed. We buzzed the water, playing a little chicken to see who could get the closest. And we buzzed the inland hills, taking some delight in scaring the cattle.

To a man, we felt we were ready for overseas duty. We knew it would be different, of course, because none of us had any real combat experience, but we had practiced everything—everything we could think of.

I didn't know about everyone else but I suspected we were all the same—we just didn't talk much about being worried. When I thought about it, I felt it in my stomach. There was that nervousness I always had whenever there was something happening that I didn't quite understand or hadn't experienced. It was a kind of fear, I suspected—the fear of the unknown—but it was nothing to be concerned about. I had been like that all my life, same thing I went through when starting in at a new school.

We all reacted in different ways and it was interesting to watch. Some were more talkative, some were unable to sit still and they paced, and I spent more time alone.

---

9   Blick's logbook confirms his promotion to first lieutenant on April 21, 1943.
10 "Hop's" career did not suffer unduly, and he ended the war as a lieutenant colonel with a distinguished career flying with the 361st Fighter Group out of Bottisham, Cambridgeshire.

Ten

In the latter part of April we were moved to Richmond, where our three squadrons came together and were finally able to train as a whole, complete group until we received our overseas orders.[1]

After Baltimore, Richmond was a dream. The runways were long and smooth—so long we hardly knew what to do. We were used to landing right on the end of the runway, but if we did that we'd have to taxi a mile or so to our parking spaces. We had to learn to land halfway down the runway like everyone else did. It was one of those well-established Army Air Bases. Not at all like the makeshift arrangement we had at Baltimore. Once again, I had the feeling it might be fun to be in the peacetime Air Force.

It was good to finally get a feel what it would be like in combat, flying with the group. It was hard to know what to do—how to train—because we had nothing to go by. It was all so new to everyone. We knew we would be flying a great deal as a group, so we did a lot of formation flying, with each squadron flying three flights, and that put thirty-six planes in the air at the same time. When we were not with the other squadrons, we were usually off buzzing the beautiful Virginia hills. Lots of large green farms with white rail fences—not much like California, for sure. Pretty scary, too, I imagine, for the people and animals. We weren't supposed to do it, but it was mighty good training, and because of that we felt the brass looked the other way.

Richmond was nice, with lots of buildings and a large downtown area where we could enjoy a luxury hotel and clean sheets and long hot showers. We had no idea how long we'd be there so we took advantage of it all whenever we could. We were getting antsy and eager to go. *Let's go—let's get it done!*

Tired of waiting, someone decided to have a C Flight party. Frank Walsh's wife, Marge, came down from Brooklyn, while we were still in Baltimore, and Dinse's wife, Pat, came also, when we moved to Richmond. Fry's wife, Betty, was there too. I thought they probably dreamed up the idea for a party, but I really didn't know.

---

1 The group converged at Richmond, Virginia, April 27, 1943. Blick's logbook records his first flight from there as April 30, and his last prior to movement overseas as May 24, 1943.

The price of admission was two bottles of champagne, and that didn't sound like it came from the girls. The day of the party we all went into town and rented rooms at the same hotel. Pat and Dinse had the largest room so we used it for the party. We filled the bathtub with ice, and then when the people arrived, the bottles went into the ice. It sounds bad, but it really wasn't. No one was obnoxious, and all had an enjoyable time. It was a pleasant change from the more serious atmosphere of the ready room. Good for the girls, too, to see us all together. The only problem, for me anyway, was the next day. I learned that you can get loaded again just by drinking water.

On May 24, we received orders to pack—we were shipping out. I had a local flight scheduled for that day, and I went up anyway, and used the quiet time to try to quell the qualms in my stomach. It was a little like taking the last dip in the pool before they closed it for the summer—I wanted to make the most of it.

We were told to get rid of any excess gear we could—to take the bare minimum—but we were used to traveling light, and it wasn't much of a problem. Everything that we didn't need on the trip went into our footlockers. The rest went into our B-4 bags and, as usual, they turned out to be heavy and hard to cope with. I wrote to my mother and tried to be as upbeat as I could, but I knew what her reaction would be. Even though it was expected, it would still be a shock. They gave us an APO number (Army Post Office), which I gave to her to use. We had no idea where we were going and I told her I'd let her know when we were settled.

A convoy of GI trucks took us into Richmond where we were loaded on to a troop train to Camp Kilmer, New Jersey.[2] Kilmer was a mammoth staging area, processing thousands of troops for overseas duty. It was located near New Brunswick, not more than fifteen miles from Perth Amboy and Raritan Bay, and the Atlantic. ...

It was organized confusion at its best. I have wondered many times since then, how they ever managed to get everyone and everything separated and together. In our 350th Squadron alone, there were 27 pilots, 9 other officers, and 256 enlisted men. Multiplied by three with an added 6 pilots, 17 other officers and 50 enlisted men of Headquarters, we had a minor miracle. And that was only the beginning. There were thousands of others.

On June 1 we were loaded into trucks again for the short ride to the Bay, where we boarded the enormous English masterpiece, the *Queen Mary*. It was a long, terribly complicated process. Fortunately, it was early, but the sun was out, and it made its impression. Decked out in our winter issue, we were far from comfortable. We waited in the sun ... and we waited—the Army way. The ship was loaded D deck first, from the bottom up; the GIs went first. "Jammed" was a better expression than loaded—jammed like hogs on the way to slaughter. The officers had first-class

---

2 Named for Alfred Joyce Kilmer, famed for his poem "Trees" of 1913 and killed in action July 30, 1918.

staterooms, our rank determining how many were in the room. Initially a single or double, my room was filled with five bunk beds, two to a bunk, so nine other first lieutenants.

We didn't complain, and with good reason. The *Queen Mary* was originally designed to carry a record 2,300-plus passengers, and our loading was almost 16,000! There were GIs in and on every available space, including the decks. The ship was "double loaded," which meant that the GIs below, and the ones on deck, swapped places every day. They would sleep in their bedrolls on the deck one night, and the next cramped somewhere deep in the ship's pungent bowels, like the swimming pools. Each swimming pool was filled with four- or five-deep bunk beds, with only enough space to squeeze between them sideways. Even though it was uncomfortable on the deck, they were mighty happy when it was their turn to be out there under the stars.

I was fascinated by the ship, and I explored it as much as I could, but other than the galleys and the main lounge, there wasn't much to see. To prepare for the war effort the ship had been stripped of all its past luxury. There were glimpses, however—things like the warmth of the wood decor—and it was easy to imagine what it must have been like. The lounge was immense, with comfortable chairs and tables, now looking a little soiled and tarnished. I tried to spend time there reading, but there were just too many people and too much confusion. Eventually, I gave up and spent most of the time in our stateroom, stretched out on my bunk with some Perry Mason books I had found in one of the little PX-type stores scattered about.

Eating was a problem. They served two meals a day—continuously, by area. And the lines were long. After my first English breakfast of something that resembled a limp piece of raw fish and a limp slice of tomato, I gave up on that meal, except for a cracker or something I could scrounge up at the PX once in a while. I concentrated on the "dinner" meal, which was any time from about two o'clock until four o'clock, and which gave me the distinct and lasting impression that the English were lousy cooks!

After a couple of days out, I was bored and feeling grungy, so I decided a bath was in order. The bath was saltwater, which I really didn't mind, in fact, I rather liked it. Coming from the California beaches, I was used to saltwater—not in the bathtub, however. I used a bar of soap that looked like the soap my grandmother used to make. It was supposed to be saltwater soap, but when I tried it, all it did was put sort of a gooey kind of film over me, and no matter how hard I tried, it didn't come off—at least it didn't feel like it. I wasn't really sure. It was a foolish idea to start with, I thought. Why try to be the only clean one on the ship?

The *Queen Mary* was the fastest ship on the high seas. Because it could outrun any German submarine, it needed no convoy for protection. Even so, we zigzagged across, taking no chances that a sub could pick up our path and lie in wait. When traveling in a straight line, the ship could make the crossing in four days, but with the irregular course, it took five. Although there were rumors of sightings, the trip was uneventful. On June 6, we rounded the tip of Northern Ireland, entered the Firth of Clyde, and disembarked at Gourock, Scotland.

It was nearly seven o'clock by the time we were all loaded into trains on the way to our various destinations. We had no idea where we were, only that we were in Scotland and headed south to England. As with all troop trains, our speed was leisurely. I didn't mind, though, because it gave me an opportunity to absorb the scenery and, of course, the longer it took, the longer it was until we had to face the reality of the war!

I was fascinated with the small, winsome villages along the way. The buildings reminded me of something I might have put together as a kid—my impression was one of building blocks stacked together at crazy angles, with deep sloping roofs and strange-looking, many-fluted chimneys. There were various combinations of materials: bricks, stones, something looking like stucco, and thick, rugged wooden beams. And, then, on the roads, bricks and cobblestones. To me, they were such wonderful textures—pictures right out of a book of fairytales.

In every village, people stood in the streets waving to us—women and children and the older people of the home front. And whenever the train stopped, there were smiling women in light, blue-gray overseas caps and uniforms with Red Cross shoulder patches, holding out doughnuts and cups of tea and juice for us. It was heartwarming, and I have always retained that picture in my mind, and the looks of hope and trust on all those faces.

Between villages, the countryside was a patchwork quilt, laid out on rolling hills. And the green! Everywhere the green. It was a kind of deep, grayed-down green, not the bright, lawn-like yellow-green I was used to seeing. It was the green of shade, of moisture, and it was everywhere. It was beautiful, but coming from the varied and arid California landscape, I couldn't help wondering if it might get a little monotonous after a while.

It was midnight, and still light enough to read a paper. Not quite the land of the midnight sun, but almost! Later, we would find out we were only about 500 or 600 miles below the Arctic Circle. It was hard to believe.

It was eleven the next morning when the train made its final stop, at Grimsby, on the northeast coast of England. It was on the south bank of the Humber, across from Hull, a major British port. Again, the Red Cross was at the station to greet us with sandwiches and drinks. From there it was a short ride, by convoy on the wrong side of roads much too narrow for our large American trucks, to Goxhill, our new home. Goxhill was an old English RAF field that had previously housed the American 78th Fighter Group, which had moved to Duxford, about forty-five miles north of London. Instead of the usual American-style barracks, our quarters looked more like cement bunkers—one such building designated for each flight. In a similar, but smaller building, relatively convenient to all, were the baths and toilets.

For the first time, we were exposed to the nightly blackout. The English had learned the hard way that any light on the ground was an announcement to the German bombers that there was life below and, consequently, a target. Any light was positively forbidden, not even a match. Every doorway was covered with black, light-absorbent baffles, forming a short, right-angled, maze-like tunnel. Because light rays travel in straight lines, not a glimmer showed outside the baffle as the door was opened. That night, Dewey hooked up his radio and found a station playing familiar music; almost familiar, but not quite. The tunes sounded like something we should know, but were not entirely recognizable. It was a German station playing their answers to Tommy Dorsey and Glenn Miller. Then, after the music, came the sexy voice of "Axis Sally," welcoming the 353rd to Goxhill, and promising to come visit us soon![3]

Once again, we were put on hold. Our planes were not there because the three fighter groups already in combat, the 4th, 78th and 56th Groups, were not yet up to their full complement, and new planes were allocated to them first. There were, however, a few older planes on the field that were flyable, and gradually newer ones began to trickle in around the middle of the month.

We flew as much as we could to become familiar with the landscape and any new and different English regulations.[4] In many ways, the English seemed smarter—perhaps because of the necessity of the war. All of their fields were the same, with three intersecting runways, enclosed by a circular taxi strip with revetments for the planes. This meant that wherever a pilot was in England, the flight procedures were exactly the same, and the runways identical. In the States, it was just the opposite—confusion! Every airport was different.

Early in July, when we finally had enough planes in combat readiness, a few of our higher-ranking pilots were sent to the other groups to fly several missions, to get their feet wet. Major Morris, 353rd Group CO, and Captain Christian, 351st CO, went to the 56th Group. Captain Duncan, group executive officer, and Captain Bailey, 352nd CO, joined the 78th Group, and Captain Rimerman, 350th CO, and Stan Pidduck flew with the 4th Group. Dewey was temporarily in command of the 350th.

The bulk of the 4th Fighter Group was the original RAF Eagle squadron—Americans in the RAF. They were transferred to the 4th Group in September 1942 and flew their first mission in October. They were, by far, the most experienced combat pilots. Much of their experience, however, had been in the sleek RAF Spitfires, and they didn't like the Thunderbolts. They complained that flying the P-47 was like flying a dive-bomber, rather than a fighter.

---

3   "Axis Sally" was American citizen Mildred Gillars, who was convicted of treason in 1949 and imprisoned until 1961. The "welcome" story is common to many 353rd Fighter Group veterans and other 8th Air Force Groups, but I have not been able to verify the veracity of the broadcast.
4   Blick's logbook records his first flight from Goxhill on June 16, 1943.

The 78th Group was the second group to arrive in England, but it was a P-38 Lightning group. Their P-38s, and many of the pilots, were soon sent to North Africa because of heavy losses there and problems getting replacements. The group was then replenished with experienced P-47 pilots and planes. The 56th Group was the first group to arrive fully equipped with P-47s. Both the 78th and the 56th flew their first mission in the middle of April, 1943.

During July, we received regular shipments of new airplanes. New planes from the factory were always plagued with bugs that had to be worked out, eliminated if possible, and there were technical changes to be made—practical changes that were a result of flight experiences. Most of us, finally, had our own planes, and we were allowed to name them. I couldn't think of anything very creative, but eventually painted a nude girl (front on one side of the plane and back on the other) and labeled it "Hell's Belles." At this point, I can't really remember which came first, but I also named it "Soubrette," which was a name I had seen in a dictionary and seemed to go well with the nude girl.[5]

On August 4 we were moved to Metfield in East Anglia, the part of England jutting out into the North Sea between the Wash and the mouth of the Thames River. The field was twelve miles inland and about halfway between Norwich and Ipswich, only a few miles from Halesworth and the 56th Group. We were, at long last, prepared to face the enemy.

---

5 No picture of "Hell's Belles" has been located. The only confirmed photograph of Blick's aircraft named "Soubrette" is his seventh LH-U (42-26416). The appendices provide a full discussion of all Blick's aircraft.

Eleven

As a combat fighter, the Thunderbolt showed promise, but its escort ability was questionable. Due to its voracious thirst—the powerful 2,000 HP engine used 100 gallons of fuel an hour, and its range was limited to about 170 miles—we had to return home long before the bombers reached their target. The German Luftwaffe used that to their advantage by waiting for the fighter protection to leave before attacking the bombers. We soon learned how to extend our range by thinning out the mixture, thus using as little as 60 gallons an hour, but it wasn't enough. The bombers continued to suffer heavy losses.

Beginning in the third week of August, General Ira C. Eaker's Eighth Bomber Command put into effect a plan named STARKEY, designed to confuse the Germans. In an attempt to halt German troop movements to Russia and Italy they concentrated on attacking the Pas-de-Calais coastline, just across the Channel, to indicate to the Germans an invasion was imminent. The bombings were mostly directed at airfields and were relatively easy missions for the new groups and replacement crews arriving by the thousands in the ETO.

To add to the hoped-for confusion, on the 17th, General Eaker launched two missions deep inside the Reich. Two-thirds of his force went to the Schweinfurt ball bearing factories—a high-priority target—and one-third on a long-range shuttle mission to the Messerschmitt factory in Regensburg, surprising the Germans by retreating southward over the Alps to bases in Tunisia.

On August 9, now Lieutenant Colonel Morris took our squadron to Halesworth to fly a mission with the 56th Group. It was not a long mission, only a sweep of the mainland coast, but it gave a little insight into procedures.[1]

---

1   The 351st went to Debden to fly with the 4th Fighter Group and the 352nd went to Duxford to fly with the 78th Fighter Group. This was Blick's first operational flight, a Rodeo (fighter sweep) over enemy territory. He flew as Captain Pidduck's wing with his logbook recording 1 hour 48 minutes' flight time. 56th Fighter Group records indicate landfall at Knokke at 1645 hours, 25,000 feet. The group landed at 1739 hours. See David R. McLaren, *Beware the Thunderbolt—The 56th Fighter Group in World War II*, Atglen, Schiffer, 1994, p. 28.

As always, when something new or unusual was about to happen, I was up early. My interior alarm was somehow timed to sound off before the mechanical one on the clock. My usual jittery stomach was awake also.

The briefing room was a bare room, arranged with folding chairs facing a huge map of Europe that covered most of the wall. Push-pinned to it, a red string stretched out from Halesworth, across the North Sea to the Dutch coast [at Knokke], then northeast to [Rotterdam and the Hague] and back across the water to Halesworth, an arrival time posted at each point. It had all been set up earlier by group intelligence.

When we were all seated, Colonel Zemke came in, picked up a pointer and stepped up on the raised platform in front of the map. He pointed out the headings and the route we were to fly, explaining that it was a [fighter sweep].

"We won't be going in far, but that doesn't mean we won't run into any enemy aircraft. They can be anywhere, at any time, so keep your eyes peeled. Remember, good formation means good protection. And radio silence is important. I don't want to hear any unnecessary talk. As Yardstick, I'll be talking to Colgate, our control."[2] He hesitated, looking around as if he wanted to say more, but didn't know quite what. Then he said, "And remember, watch your ass. It's the plane you don't see that shoots you down."

The colonel stepped aside and handed the pointer to the group intelligence officer, who indicated the known locations of airfields in the area and where he thought we might encounter flak.[3] He also warned us about Goering's group of yellow-nosed FW190s that loved to pounce on unsuspecting planes. That information was not news. From the moment we landed in England, we had heard about those yellow-nosed fighters and how good they were—the pride of the Luftwaffe. They were not to be taken lightly!

When the intelligence officer finished, the weather officer delivered his briefing. He told us the clouds overhead would clear, and the visibility would be unlimited as we approached the mainland. The wind at their altitude, not much. Forty miles an hour.

Once again Colonel Zemke took over to give us our start-engine time, then looking at his watch, began a countdown to synchronize our watches ... to the second.

---

2   "Yardstick" is the call-sign for the 56th Fighter Group leader. Blick wrote "Nuthouse" in his original. This call-sign actually referred to Microwave Early Warning (MEW) control based on the Continent from November 1944. At the time of this mission, the 65th Fighter Wing "Colgate" controlled operations, later to be replaced by 66th Fighter Wing "Oilskin" from November 18, 1943. See Roger A. Freeman, *The Mighty Eighth War Manual*, New York, Jane's Publishing Inc, 1985, pp. 80–83.
3   "Flak" is an abbreviation of the German word *Flugabwehrkanone*—literally "aircraft defense cannon" and refers to guns of all calibers used against attacking aircraft.

Colonel Morris led Pipeful with A Flight.[4] B Flight was in the Blue position on his left, and Pidduck, with our C Flight was in Red position, on the right. I was flying [Pidduck's] wing and Fortier and Furness were flying the 3 and 4 positions. Each squadron flew an extra plane as a spare, to fill in for anyone who might have trouble.[5]

It was a gray day, as it was most of the time, but the clouds underneath gradually diminished, allowing the dark, threatening teal waters of the North Sea to spread out ahead. At 25,000 feet, when Yardstick leveled off, the visibility was excellent, and on the distant horizon there was a vague change of color, from the cool of water to the warmth of land. We could see the Dutch coastline. I had no feeling of motion. My wing hung there as if held up by an invisible force, about halfway between Pidduck's wingtip and tail. The only sound was the purr of the engine. Nothing to do but wait. It was hypnotic—just sitting there staring at Pidduck. As we neared the coast, I felt the tension in my stomach escalate. Was it fear? I wasn't sure. I felt alone, on my own, but of course I wasn't. I wondered if everyone else felt the same. ...

Landfall! We were over enemy territory! This is it, I thought. After all this time, all those months and months of preparation, I finally made it. The reality that I was actually there was hard for me to accept. I was there, yet nothing was different, nothing had changed; I was still in the plane, flying as always. And yet, all of a sudden, everything had changed. It was too much to grasp. We had crossed the line—I was in the ring. And I had on the gloves. I hoped!

We flew inland for a few more minutes, then started a gradual turn to the left. I tried to be aware of our location, where we were and where we were going, but flying as a wingman, my job was to protect my leader, Pidduck, who was leading the flight. It was too hard, looking behind all the time and into the sun, where those Germans always hid. I'd try to look, to quickly glance around, but each time my formation flying would go to hell. I was constantly correcting, with a suspicion that from an outside viewpoint I must have looked like a bird with a damaged wing. There had to be a better answer.

---

4   "Pipeful" was the call-sign of the 350th Fighter Squadron. "Roughman" and "Wakeford" referred to the 351st and 352nd Fighter Squadrons respectively. A squadron was divided into "flights" of four aircraft with White Flight leading, followed by Red, Blue, Yellow and sometimes Green and Black, depending on how many aircraft were on the mission. Each pilot was numbered in the flight so that White One referred to the squadron leader and Red Three the element lead of Red Flight. This facilitated efficient communication in the air; for example, "Pipeful White Three, break right!" is a clear instruction for that specific pilot to take evasive action.

5   The original of this chapter was clearly a hangover from Blick's fictional work. In his version, Blick described the mission as flown on August 14 and led by Colonel Morris. The account is clearly of the first squadron mission on August 9 led by Colonel Zemke. With the aim of maintaining the chronology and accuracy, I have substituted a similar (but less imaginative) account of the August 9 mission provided to me by Blick in 1998 from this point in the chapter.

Zemke flew north to Rotterdam, which I caught a glimpse of once out of the corner of my eye, then turned back toward the coast, just north of The Hague. As we were about to make landfall out, someone yelled in the radio, "Flak ahead!"

"I see it," Zemke was calm.

He made a slight change in the course, to the right, and continued on. The bursts continued to blossom all around, but low. Instead of climbing, he then dove down a little to pick up speed. This, of course, put him on the level of the flak, but by then the Germans had corrected for altitude and the bursts were above him, and behind because of the change of speed. That was fine for him, I thought—good evasive action—but that put the flak on the level of the other two squadrons! However, the German gunners seemed to be after the lead squadron, and they continued to make corrections.

I was hardly aware of the explosions, only that I had to fly through the black smoke still hanging in the air.

Still alert to the possibility of those deadly yellow-nosed fighters streaking out of the sun with guns blazing, I kept my attention directed there, but a thought crept into my mind. Why hadn't I been bothered by the flak? In fact, the more I thought about it the more I realized it hadn't frightened me at all. Something real, perhaps? Something I could actually see? Maybe. Maybe that's what the nervousness was all about. Those fighters, up there in the sun—that I couldn't see. What was it Zemke had said? *It's the plane you can't see that shoots you down!* The fear of the unknown. I had to find some way to make those German pilots just people, no different than us. Intellectually I could understand, but how was I to control the emotions?

Out over the water, Yardstick reported in to Colgate again. Then, letting down gradually, he set a new course toward Halesworth. I relaxed. It was over ... a brand new experience, for sure!

The clouds had broken over East Anglia and the landing was without incident. That night I wrote a letter to my mother. I wanted to keep her up on what we were doing, but it was hard because I really didn't know what to say, or how to say it. We weren't supposed to say anything about the missions—at least what they were all about—and that was understandable. However, judging from what we heard, it wouldn't matter because the Germans seemed to know everything we did anyway.

I told her it was our first mission, and I started to go into my feeling about what a lousy job I had done, placing more emphasis on flying good formation than on looking for the Germans up there waiting to pounce on us and shoot us down. I ruled that out quickly because it would just make her worry all the more. So I just left it with the fact that it was our first mission—what we had been training for all this time—and went on to other things like our living arrangements, and how we were eating well. At least that would eliminate part of the worry.

Twelve

We had our first feel of escort on the August 14 [mission] when we met a dispersed and wounded group of bombers heading home over the North Sea. The next day we picked up another group as they were coming out over the Calais area.

Our first real escort mission was on the 16th, to Elbeuf, northwest of Paris. We ran into a number of FW190s, and during the encounters, Colonel Morris was last seen in a steep dive chasing one of the 190s. Six missions into the war and we were without a group commander! Major Loren McCollom, group executive officer of the 56th Group was immediately ordered to take over Colonel Morris's command.

On the night of Colonel Morris's fatal mission, I had dinner with Dwight Fry and Dub [William W. Odom].

"You were on that mission, Dub. What happened to Morris?" Fry asked.

"Dunno. I don't think anyone does. Frank [Walsh] and I were with Dewey, and when those fighters went after the bombers, Morris took off toward them. We followed, but he was up ahead with the 352nd. We lost him when Fortier saw a couple of FW190s and took off after them. Frank and I started after one, but he saw us comin', and the bastard went streakin' down flat ass, so I said to hell with it. By that time we were all scattered with no e/a in sight, so we came home. I didn't even fire my guns!"

"I'm surprised the guys in the 352nd didn't see him," I said.

"It was busy up there. Herfurth was flying his wing and he says that when Morris dove down on that plane, there was another 190 that started in after him, so he went after it. He lost it, and then when he pulled back up, Morris was nowhere to be found."

"Compressibility?"

Dub was hesitant. "Could be. But it wouldn't surprise me if he got in a tangle with that German pilot and was shot down."

I wondered how serious Dub was. I was never quite sure with him. "Really?"

"Yeah. Either of you ever fly with him?" We both shook our heads. "I have … I know that he was supposed to be some kind of a hot-shot pilot, but I wasn't impressed … at all. I know, I know, I shouldn't be saying that, now that he ain't no longer with us, but they keep telling us not to tangle with those guys down there on the deck."

"Were they Goering's group?"

"If they were they hadn't painted their noses yet … at least the ones we saw."

We were quiet then, and thoughtful. I was thinking about Morris. None of our pilots had had a chance to know him at all. He had seemed very aloof—untouchable—and it was hard to give him the credit he probably deserved. After all, he was a colonel and the group CO. He got there somehow. He surely wouldn't have the rank and responsibility if he didn't deserve it. I didn't know about the flying, but I had heard that Morris seemed a little conservative, whatever that meant. I didn't think a group CO should be some character that fancied himself as the greatest hot pilot that ever flew. Maybe we were all just a little too quick to criticize.

[Reflecting on Morris in 1998 Blick wrote: "Morris was a mystery. We didn't really know him at all. The vision that stayed in my mind all these years is of a tall, straight, stiff, wooden robot who talked the words that he knew he was supposed to say. I have no idea what he felt about going into combat. The talk was that he had proven himself over and over again as a good pilot, but we didn't see that. In fact, I don't remember flying with him at all—maybe I did [Blick flew in the same squadron as Morris on August 9 and in the same flight on August 15, 1943]. But I got the impression he was a little indecisive in the air, which may or may not have accounted for his demise. It wasn't so much that he was disliked as a CO, it was more that he was unknown." An unfounded and ugly rumour circulated for many years among the group, that Morris had been shot down by one of his own men. This somehow got attached to Blick (who did not even fly the mission). Blick recounted: "It started after that third mission. I claimed a probable (denied) as I thought the pilot had bailed out. It did not show on the film. I was the first in our squadron to contact an enemy and since Colonel Morris was lost, an unthinking person joked that I probably mistook the 109 for a Jug and shot down Colonel Morris! It was quite a burden to carry, and each time I associated with my crew I felt uncomfortable. I had discussions with Colonel McCollom and he wanted me to name anyone who made these statements for punitive action, but he was shot down before any action was taken. (No one blamed me for his loss!) I did have two more destroyed, which I didn't get on film or have a witness and didn't make a claim due to fear of ridicule and embarrassment if denied. … It's like, 'Other than that, Mrs Lincoln, how did you like the play?' I relish the other memories of that time and try to look at the positive!"[1]]

Fry broke the silence. "I wonder what McCollom is like."

---

1 Blickenstaff to Cross, 1998. Blickenstaff to Donald Corrigan, December 26, 1992.

"Yeah," Dub said. "I guess we all do. Coming from the 56th he oughta be good." He smiled. "Don't think it would take much to be better."

"He seems like a real nice guy. And he's got the experience—thirty-eight missions already, so the rumor goes."

I started to get up. "Well, we'll find out soon enough … I don't know about you guys, but I'm hitting the sack. I'm up tomorrow."

"Yeah, me too," Fry said.

"Not me" [said Dub]. "I'm sleepin' in. You sure you don't want to go over to the club for a bit?"

"Nope." We started to leave.

"Try to have a little respect for those of us still sleeping in the morning."

"Sure."

[Blick wrote of Loren G. McCollom in 1998: "We were all delighted that McCollom was sent over from the 56th to take over the group. Not only was he experienced, he was friendly and likeable, seemed to know what he was doing—an all-around nice guy. And besides, he looked *like a fighter pilot should!* I'm sure we were all thinking, 'Now here's a guy who can really lead us.' He immediately inspired that kind of confidence. Of course it helped that he had been in the 56th. How could he not be good, coming from the 56th?"[2]]

Our mission was to pick up the bombers as they were leaving the target area near Brussels, and escort them home. Major McCollom was leading the group and Rimerman our squadron.[3] It was the first time using one of the new seventy-five-gallon belly tanks. The extra gas allowed us to extend our range another 100 miles or more, depending, of course, on what we encountered.

Range was a constant and worrisome problem. The Air Technical Section of the Eighth Fighter Command had been experimenting for months with jettisonable auxiliary tanks. The first useable effort was an impractical and unwieldy 200-gallon belly tank. Not only did those tanks cause excess drag, they refused to draw gas over 20,000 feet, forcing the pilots to drop them, while only partially empty, over the water. That meant they had to climb quickly to a safer, more reasonable altitude just before making landfall. The new pressurized seventy-five-gallon tanks allowed us to climb to any altitude and keep the tanks until they were empty. They were also streamlined and made only a slight difference in the airspeed.

My fourth mission [was on August 19, 1943—an escort to the Gilze-Rijen area]. I was beginning to feel less apprehensive. Because I hadn't yet seen an enemy aircraft, there was a feeling of complacency—that perhaps those yellow noses weren't always up there in the sun or hiding behind every cloud waiting to pounce. My nervous

---

2 Blickenstaff to Cross, 1998.
3 The group flew two missions on August 17, 1943, both escorts led by Major McCollom with Major Rimerman leading the 350th Fighter Squadron. Blick did not fly either mission. See 350th FS Records, AFHRA, Maxwell, Alabama.

stomach still reminded me of the risk—the challenge—but once I got into the air and formed up with the group, the twinges were not so prevalent. At landfall-in, I was still uneasy, though. It was that old "I dare you to step over the line" thing we used to go through as kids. Whatever the rationale I used to ease my mind, the fact remained that we were flying over enemy territory and there was nowhere to hide.

I was flying as element leader, and I was more comfortable knowing that [Walter L.] Angelo was back there, watching out for me. With that thought, I looked back and gave him a thumbs-up sign. I knew I wouldn't be as open to criticism for my formation flying; it wasn't as critical that I stay locked into a formation so close I was afraid to relax. For the first time, I began to look around.

We leveled off at 30,000 feet over billows of broken clouds that swelled to about 15,000 feet. I remembered how much fun I'd had, playing tag in and around such clouds, back there—so long ago—when all the flying wasn't quite so serious. Through the holes I made out the long coastline, reaching for the Walcheren Islands to the north and to the south past Belgium into France. Then, out of the silence, came the now familiar, "Landfall in on time" from Slybird … and the twinge in my stomach.[4]

We continued inland, and I noticed the other two squadrons gradually easing in closer.

"Pipeful White Two here, Slybird. Bogies ahead at one o'clock."

"Roger, Pipeful White Two."

McCollom made a slight turn to the right, and I searched the horizon for some sign of the enemy. I could see only the blue of the sky and the blurred line of contact with the earth.

That would be Hurst, I thought. What the hell kind of eyes does he have? *I can't see a thing!* A few minutes later, I finally saw some tiny, gnat-like spots just above the horizon. At first, I thought they were only specks in my eyes, but then, when they didn't go away, I knew they had to be the bogies—and then came the rush of adrenaline.

"Pipeful White Two here, Slybird." Hurst again. "Bogies are bombers, Slybird."

"Roger, Pipeful. I see them."

I couldn't believe it. I could just barely make out the spots and Hurst was identifying them as bombers! *Jesus!* Closing in, I finally saw the smoke-darkened area hovering around the bombers, and the new explosions interspersed among them. Then, as the bombers left the target area behind and turned toward home, an excited voice screamed into the radio.

"Slybird! Slybird! Many bandits high nine o'clock!"

"Slybird here. I see them."

In order to close the distance between us and the bombers a little faster, McCollom had let down to nearly 26,000 feet, but then he saw the FW190s high above, and pushed the throttle forward and climbed. But it was no use. The 190s dove toward

---

4 'Slybird' was the codename for the Group leader on the mission until April 23, 1944, when it changed to 'Jonah' to indicate the Group leader. Freeman, *War Manual*, p.83.

the bombers before we could head them off. I saw one 190 burst into flames as they went right through the bomber formation and disappeared below.

"Slybird here. Bombers are withdrawing. Stay alert."

Two or three minutes later, we were at 28,000 feet, still above the bombers, when Hurst noticed a group of ME109s to the right and behind the bombers, turning toward us. McCollom pushed his throttle forward and led us right down into them, opening fire almost immediately.

Confusion was instant. The 109s dispersed and I took out after one. I followed as it rolled over and headed down, but when the heavy Thunderbolt's speed increased so rapidly, I gave up for fear of going into the dreaded compressibility. I shot back up to altitude. Angelo was no longer with me. Everyone was scattered, but the bombers were mostly intact.

"Slybird here. I'm circling at the rear of the bombers with two other planes. I'll complete the turn and then head out."

There were several responses. I finally determined which three planes were Slybird's and headed toward them. Others did also. We stayed with the bombers all the way to the coast, and were, by then, back in a reasonable formation. A little flak was thrown up at us as we went out, but it was more like a parting gesture of some kind and not worrisome. My adrenaline was still flowing freely. I realized that what I had just been through could hardly be called an encounter, but that's what it was, and I had survived. And it was exciting, no doubt about that!

Out over the water, and settling down again, I relived the experience, wondering if I had done the right thing. Had I broken off too soon? What if I had followed that 109 on down? How much of a threat really, was compressibility? I didn't know, and I didn't want to find out, but how would I ever know when it was going to happen if I never went through it? In my mind there was only one conclusion—I was of more use to the group alive than dead.

After the [de]briefing, I had dinner with Doc.

"Pretty good show, wasn't it," Doc said, not really as a question.

"Yeah. It was good to hear about Walsh and Fry. I was worried when they didn't show up."

"They both came out alone on the deck just about out of gas. Fry landed at another field to refuel and was late getting here."

I was still thinking about my performance and Doc noticed that I was not as talkative as usual.

"What's bothering you?" he asked.

"Nothing much, Doc. Just wondering about a couple of things."

"For instance?"

I didn't know if I should even get into it. "I had a chance today to contribute to the cause, but I think I fouled it up." I stopped, then mumbled, "I don't know … but it's bothering me."

Doc started to grin, but then realized I was serious. "You don't think you contributed to the cause? That's pretty silly you know."

"Yeah I know … I know I'm contributing … but … it's not really that, Doc. It's just that I don't know if I did the right thing or not."

He waited. He knew not to urge—that I'd get to it on my own if he waited long enough. Doc was good about that. We had talked enough for him to know me well.

"I chickened out … I think. I was on the tail of a 109 and he rolled over and dove, practically straight down. I followed, but my plane took off downward like a shot. In a couple of seconds I was going so fast I was afraid of compressibility and broke off."

"That's it?"

"Yeah."

"Good God, Blick! What do you mean, you chickened out? You know damn well what happens in that situation—you go right into the ground!" He rolled his eyes. "Chickened out! … Jesus Christ!"

"Yeah, I know. That's why I broke off. But maybe that wouldn't have happened. What if it didn't? I could have been down there dogfighting the 109 … maybe shooting him down."

Doc shrugged hopelessly and thought for a minute. "Let me ask you a stupid question, Blick."

"Go ahead."

"What was your mission today?"

I wondered where he was going. "Escort."

"And what are you supposed to do in an escort mission?"

"Protect the bombers." Still no clue.

"That 109 you were chasing—did he ever get back to the bombers?"

"No."

"Then you did your job, right?"

"Yeah. You're right."

Doc let it sink in for a bit. "You know what your problem is?"

"What?"

"You're thinking about yourself and shooting down enemy planes, rather than about the job you're supposed to be doing. That's what's bothering you. You think your job is to come back here and paint swastikas on your airplane, instead of keeping the Germans from shooting down our bombers."

"Maybe you're right, Doc, but that German will be back up again."

"True, but he would be anyway, even if you shot him down, in another plane—unless, of course, he was killed." He hesitated, thinking … "I doubt if you're really out to actually kill people anyway. …"

"I suppose …"

Thirteen

Weather over the Continent was dubious at best, and cloud cover hampered the accuracy of the bombing. The British had experimented with various navigational aids for blind bombing, which helped, but not substantially. The latest, a radar scanner called H2S, which gave a crude impression of the terrain below, could be fitted easily under the nose of a B-17. Although the British were hesitant, they finally consented to its use on the American daylight bombers. Radar was in its infancy and secret, and they did not want it falling into enemy hands.

Because the H2S device was limited, it was installed on the lead bombers, who became known as the Pathfinders. A Pathfinder would seek out the target, then release a smoke marker for the following bombers to drop on. The first trial Pathfinder mission was on September 23, over the port of Emden. Although there was a great deal of confusion, the bombing pattern was much improved.[1]

The results of their initial efforts showed substantial promise, but they also left considerable room for improvement. The major problem was the wind, which carried the marker's smoke off target, disrupting the aim of the following bombers. They needed more Pathfinder aircraft with trained crews—at least one in each group formation.

The weather was not good and there was little hope for improvement, so it seemed like a good time to get away from it all for a while. I asked Fry if he wanted to go to London with me. Of course, he said yes and we got the okay from Dewey. It was generally accepted that we needed whatever relaxation time we could get to counter the build-up of tensions, so the yes from Dewey was almost automatic.[2]

---

1   H2S or "Stinkey" was an airborne ground-scanning radar used by the 482nd Group in late 1943. The Americans later developed and used H2X "Mickey" in the last eighteen months of the war as a blind bombing and navigational device. Freeman, *War Manual*, p. 240.
2   The exact date of Blick's trip to London is unknown—his diary mentions he was in London for New Year's Eve 1943, but does not detail any previous trips there. The squadron was rotating by flights through RAF bases near London at the time and this may have occasioned the trip into the capital.

I knew Doc would like to go, too, and found him in the dispensary. "Hey Doc, Fry and I are off to London for a couple of days. Why don't you come along?"

"You got a leave?"

"Yeah. Great, huh?"

Doc glanced up at the dreary clouds. "The weather wouldn't have anything to do with it, would it?"

"Well .... could be," I smiled. "It doesn't look like there'll be much activity around here. And Dewey didn't seem to mind. He says Pidduck is leaving it up to the flight leaders."

"Okay, I'd like that." He turned to go. "I have to ask Ben, y'know ... and get ready."

Doc had Sergeant Feron, one of his medics, drive us to the train station in the tiny village of Harleston.[3] Quaint, was a better description.

"I've never seen a gate across train tracks before," I remarked.

"Makes sense," Doc said.

"Yeah. I guess."

After a short wait, the stationmaster came out of his small cubicle, looking at his pocket watch. He walked out to the gate and moved it around to a new position, blocking off the road.

"I wonder what happens if the train is late, like they usually are in the States," Fry commented.

Doc smiled. "I guess the cars would just pile up."

Fry looked around. "What cars?"

"Or," I speculated, "maybe they're never late."

"There's an even better question," Fry said. "What happens if the train comes early, and the stationmaster's taking a pee break, or doesn't get out there soon enough to move the gate?"

The compartments were large enough to squeeze in possibly ten people, but eight would fit better. We found one that was empty. I went in first and took the seat on the window side facing forward—I wanted to look out. The train started to roll, so smoothly we hardly noticed.

Fry was first to remark about it. "Look at that. I didn't even feel it—no jerks or huffs and puffs, just a quiet, gentle start. Even electrical trolleys, back home, aren't that smooth. How do they do that, anyway?"

Doc said, "I don't know, but I did read, once, that they are smoother riding than ours because they lay the tracks differently. I could be wrong, but I think it's that we lay both rails down evenly, and the English alternate, so the wheels on each side of the train hit the connections at different times. That causes a slight rolling motion from side to side, rather than the leapfrogging motion we have."

"They look a little smaller than ours, too," I said. "Are they?"

---

3   There is no Sergeant Feron listed in 350th Squadron records.

"I don't know … maybe. Could be because they're just laid out differently, with these compartments the way they are."

"Yeah, could be."

With the stops, it was about a three-hour ride to London. Doc and I spent most of that time enjoying the English countryside, with only an occasional comment. We were comfortable with each other and savored those silences with the understanding allowed by good friends.

Predictably, Fry fell asleep almost as soon as he found a comfortable position. He was one of those high-energy people with a metabolism that ran full speed most of the time. Once in a while he had to stop and re-energize. Dub [Odom] said once that he had two speeds—fast and stop. I was somewhat envious of the type, but at the same time, I really had no desire to be one of them. Fry's constant motion made me a little nervous. There were times I could barely control a strong desire to shove him into a chair and yell at him to settle down.

That flow of adrenaline, or whatever it was, certainly didn't hurt his flying ability, though—he was a very skillful pilot and wingman. He was alert, and his reactions were immediate. In fact, everything about him was quick. When he turned to look at something, he didn't just turn, his head jumped from one position to another—a little like a bird, or a cat. He even smoked a cigarette with that same driving force, throwing the butt away in half the time it took most people.

I had no qualms about flying with him on my wing. He was like a sidecar on a motorcycle—always there, always looking. But, in a way, it worried me a little. I was afraid I might be becoming too dependent on him, and I for sure didn't want that. It was too easy to fall into a kind of lethargy—a disaster in the making. It was too early, though, for conjecture. We hadn't, as yet, been really tested. I was just glad to have those eyes back there watching my butt.

I looked over at him, slouched in the corner, legs stretched out and feet up on the opposite seat, and I was struck once again with the realization of how young we all were. Asleep, with his short, tousled, burnt-umber hair, Fry looked like a teenager who should still be in school. Yet here he was, involved in a war, risking his life for something we all knew very little about.

The train stopped at the Liverpool Street Station.

"Anybody got any ideas about what we're supposed to do now?" I asked.

"Not me," Fry said. "I haven't the slightest. You're the one that's supposed to lead me around."

"That's in the air, stoop, not in strange cities."

Doc was smiling. "It's a good thing you've got me along. I asked Feron. I found out a long time ago that if you ever need to know anything about anything, you ask a GI! First of all we have to find a cab. A cabby, don't y'know!"

And I had to laugh. "That's pretty funny—a lazy, Southern drawl with an English accent."

"Okay, so I'm not an actor. We still have to get a cab. Feron said to go to the Red Cross club—that they would help us find our way around. And he said the best one is Rainbow Corner, not far from Piccadilly Circus."

"Piccadilly!" Fry blurted. "I know about that. It's the London red-light district, right?"

"I suppose ..." Doc said, "but it's where all the theaters are. It's like Times Square in New York."

"If you say so. I don't know anything about New York."

"You know ... the Broadway plays."

"Oh. ..."

"But before we do that," Doc suggested, "we should go get a hotel room."

"And did Feron tell you what hotel we go to, too?" I asked.

"Yeah. He mentioned a couple, but there's one called Claridge's I'd like to see. Every time I read about London they mention it. It's *the* one in London — where the elite go. It's called the resort of Kings and Princes."

"Then that's for us," I said. "Right, Dwight?"

"Right."

We had no trouble finding a cab; a few were lined up outside the station. We picked one, and it was impressive. It looked like something out of early Henry Ford, even down to the long horn—red-rubber bulb and all—mounted just outside the open doorway on the driver's side. The car was patterned after the old horse-drawn carriages, with the driver covered, but sitting outside the closed-off compartment behind. The driver nodded when Doc told him "Claridge's," and we stepped up and into the cab.

Before we were even comfortably settled, the driver beeped the horn and swung the car around sharply into the oncoming traffic, almost as if the wheels were turned at a 90-degree angle. It was our first ride in a London cab, and it was a ride to remember. The fact that we were driving on the wrong side of the road didn't make it any easier. The cabbies obviously had their own rules and adhered to them steadfastly, but they were beyond my understanding. It was some kind of game they played, reminding me of the old dodge-em cars I used to ride on the boardwalk at Long Beach. When one car was only inches ahead of the other, the driver seemed to have the right to do anything he jolly well pleased, even turn directly into the other car, and it was up to that driver, then, to either slam on the brakes or sustain a collision. Formation flying on the streets of London! Doc tried to sit back and play it cool, but his confident smile became a worried grimace at every confrontation. Why the crunch never occurred defied any reasonable explanation. The constant cacophony of the beeping horns could have been their signals, but even so, I was sure those drivers were blessed with some kind of extra-sensory perception.

Claridge's Hotel was everything we anticipated from Doc's information. The entrance hall was imposing, with its marble floor, the magnificent staircase and the chandeliers overhead, that still sparkled. I was reminded of the one-time elegance and luxury of the *Queen Mary*.

Our reception was warm and gracious. The long war years of hardship had taken their ample toll, but the women and older men still available, did their best to preserve the quiet dignity that had always welcomed their fashionable visitors. It was an impossible job, but they tried, and we three Americans were appreciative

Doc looked around in awe. "Imagine what this was like ten years ago," he said. "I can almost hear the Hungarian quartet as the liveried footmen serve their guests."

"Poetic. ..." Fry said.

Later, after our necessary ablutions, we returned to the desk where we were given directions to the Rainbow Corner. It was not far, and rather than chance another ride in a cab, we walked. We went out on Brook, down past Berkeley Square (pronounced Barclay), to Piccadilly and headed east. In just a few short blocks we were in the heart of Piccadilly Circus. Fry was hungry, but was overruled when he suggested eating. Doc and I thought it would be better to go to the club first and get some information about restaurants.

It was cold and damp, and we were glad we had worn our heavy shortcoats. It wasn't raining, quite, but the moisture was beginning to bead up on our shoulders and caps. We would learn later that umbrellas and raincoats were standard apparel for the city ... actually, for anywhere in England.

Except for the need to glance right instead of left before stepping off a curb, the city looked and felt familiar, much like the heart of any other large city. The war seemed remote. The cabs and the people were there, maybe not quite crowding the streets and sidewalks, but they were there, hustling about, tending to business.

It didn't take long, however, to notice differences in the details. The huge advertisements, almost entirely covering the buildings, were strange—Greys Cigarettes, Guinness Is Good For You—Gives You Strength, Votrix, Schweppes Tonic Water, Player's, Gordon's Gin—and then, at one of the corners, people were patiently standing in line near a sign that read START QUEUE HERE. A bus pulled up—our first look at a London double-decker. On its sides, between the upper and lower levels, were two familiar ads—Coca-Cola and Wrigley.

"Did you notice how quiet and orderly the people were, getting on that bus?" Doc remarked. "Not much like home, for sure."

Although outwardly the city seemed untouched by the war, we began to notice little things, like the headlights on the cabs and the street signals, which were painted black with little slits for the light to peek through. And the ever-present, ugly reminders on all the entrances to the buildings—the maze-like black baffles of blackout.

I observed, too, that most of the people were older, and those who were not, were women. The strain of long years of severe austerity had taken its toll, but there was a feeling of determination there—I could sense it—in their carriage and attitude. They would never give up. And my heart went out to them.

The Red Cross canteen was designed to make the soldiers comfortable. It was large, well lit, warm and cozy. We were greeted cordially by an older woman with graying hair pulled up in a bun and dressed in the familiar Red Cross uniform, who told us, in a pleasant mid-western accent, to make ourselves at home.

There were refreshments, magazines, newspapers, a radio, a phonograph, comfortable chairs. "Feel free," she said. "If you have questions, we'll try to answer them. Or if you just want to talk, we'll do that, too."

After we had looked around for a bit, I said, "Y'know, I don't know about you guys, but I think I'd just as soon eat something here and maybe hang around a while, then go back to the hotel. I'd like to get up fairly early in the morning and see some of the city."

Doc agreed. "It's true. We've had a long day just getting here, and bed sounds good."

Fry looked disappointed. "Okay," he said hesitatingly. "If that's what you guys want. I'm sure not going off by myself!"

The menu was not elaborate, mostly sandwiches and a few simple desserts. I saw the word waffle and wasted no time making up my mind. I couldn't remember when I last had waffles. I felt a little foolish when I went back the third time, but the bronze-haired girl with the nice smile, who made them, reassured me quickly that I wasn't alone. "We're trying to give you boys a taste of home," she said.

After we ate, Doc picked up a copy of *The Times*—the leading London daily newspaper—from one of the tables and settled into a comfortable leather chair, looking very much like he belonged there. The lounging area was designed for comfort, off to one side of the room in front of a small fireplace. There was a large coffee table surrounded by a couple of sofas, with end tables and lamps, and several comfortable chairs, all mixtures, designed for comfort, not looks. Along with *The Times*, there were some copies of the satirical English magazine *Punch*, and to make home seem a little closer, some old copies of *The Saturday Evening Post*, *Life* and *Collier's*. There was also a stack of *Stars and Stripes*, the American-published newspaper for servicemen.

The cartoons on the covers of *Punch* caught my attention so I picked one up and sat down on a sofa. Fry glanced at a *Stars and Stripes* for about half a minute, then bounced up and started to wander.

I thumbed through a few pages, but lost my concentration and finally put the magazine down on my lap. I lit up a cigarette and just sat there, a little spacey, watching the people and listening to the music. Fry was talking with one of the girls and there were three couples dancing, mostly just swaying in one place to the rhythm of Glenn Miller's *Moonlight Serenade*. The music transported me back to the night I went to see Tommy Dorsey at the Palladium in LA. The band was there but Tommy Dorsey was missing for some reason, and it was up to a young, skinny singer named Sinatra to give some life to the band. I remembered that I had told everyone I knew that when Sinatra first started with the Dorsey band, no one could ever replace Jack Leonard. I had to smile at the thought. Sinatra seemed to do all right, even if he didn't sound like Jack Leonard.

I liked it there. I liked just sitting there thinking about something besides flying and the war. We were a long way from home, but home seemed a little closer here. All it took was a little imagination and I could almost believe I really *was* home. And it wasn't hard to figure out that's what the Red Cross centers were all about—taking our minds off what we were doing for a minute or two.

I was dozing. "First time in London?" Startled, I looked around. The bronze-haired girl who had served me the waffles sat beside me.

"Yeah," I said, after my wits had come back. "It's the first." Again I noticed her beautiful smile. She was a little older than I had thought, though. Twenty-five, maybe?

"I thought so," she said.

"Are we that obvious? How'd you know?"

Her eyes were clear and translucent, marbled with varied sepias and greens, like those prized agates I used to have in my marble-shooting days. "I didn't really," she replied. "It's just the way you were looking around. It was your first time here at the club, and I knew if you hadn't been here, you probably hadn't been to London."

"You remember everyone that comes in here?"

She laughed. "No, of course not." But then she added, "But how could I forget you!"

"Okay, okay," I grinned. "I humbly accept the flattery." It worked, though. It caught my attention. I turned toward her, throwing one knee up on the cushion, and leaned back on the arm of the sofa. I liked her.

"I'm Blick," I announced, offering my hand

She shook it and said she was Marylou, but then, "That's not your real name."

I had to laugh. "Well no, not exactly," I said. "My name is Wayne, but everyone calls me Blick. My last name is Blickenstaff."

"Okay … makes sense."

"So, Marylou … you're not English, so how come you're here and where are you from?"

"Just like that you want to know my life story?"

"Sure, why not?"

"Guess."

It was a chance to test out my ear for accents. "Well, let's see … there's a touch of the South, but not too much—a little mid-western maybe. How about Tennessee?"

"Close," she answered, "It's Kentucky. You're pretty good. How about you?"

"You can't tell?"

"No. Nothing there I can recognize."

"That's the clue, you know. It's California. California is such a mishmash of everything, it's nothing."

"That's true," she said. "I should have known. I went out there one time with my parents, when I was just out of high school—to San Francisco. You from there?"

"No, farther south. I was stationed there for a while, though, after I graduated from flight school, at Hamilton Field across the Golden Gate … but I'm from LA. Well … not exactly from LA, but about thirty miles east of there."

I hesitated, then ventured, "I know how I got here, but how about you?"

"It's simple. …" She glanced over at her counter, then got up hurriedly. There were a couple of GIs there. "I have to take care of business. Be right back."

I watched with admiration. She walked so easily and gracefully, head barely bouncing. Her walk didn't match up with her perky personality. Perky went with bouncy and she wasn't bouncy. It was a crazy thought anyway!

She looked up at me once, while making the sandwiches, and smiled when she saw me watching, which I did until she finished with the GIs and returned

"Now then," she said, as she sat back down. "Where were we?"

"You were about to tell me why you're here, so far away from home, taking care of us GIs."

"That's right. I started to tell you there isn't much of a story—it's not very complicated. Could I have one of your cigarettes?" I offered my pack. She took one and I lit it with my Zippo. She leaned back, inhaling the smoke.

"Thanks," she said finally. "I had a younger brother in the Air Corps. He was at Pearl." She choked a little, and her eyes filled.

I reached for her hand. "I'm sorry." I felt awful about opening it up. "What a terrible shock."

"Thanks. I'm getting used to it now—most of the time. But once in a while it sneaks up on me, always at the wrong time." She smiled a little. "Johnny—that was his name—was so eager, so alive … and so in love with flying and the Air Corps that I wanted to do something to help avenge his death. He always had such good things to say about the Red Cross, and when I learned how much they needed people, I joined. It was that simple." The gesture she made flowed from the tip of her fingers to the shrug of her shoulder.

I had to ask. "Pardon the interruption, but were you a ballet dancer?"

She gave me an odd look, but then laughed. "How did you ever think of that?"

"The way you move."

"Thank you, but no, I wasn't … I'm not. Not professionally, that is. I had a lot of classes, though, from the time I was very small, all the way through high school. And we used to put on shows all the time—strictly amateur stuff."

"I knew it," I said, satisfied.

"You're very observant, you know."

"I don't know about that, but I'm trying. I'm studying to be an illustrator, so I'm supposed to be observant. But I interrupted. It's a long way from Kentucky to England."

"An artist? Imagine that!" She let that ride, and went on. "It wasn't hard. I volunteered for overseas duty and took the first thing that came along. It was to England, directly to London, and I've been here ever since. Took me about six months from when I joined." She sat for a minute, smoking. "So ... now that you know all about me, tell me about being an artist."

I did. More than I had ever intended. I obviously needed to talk and she seemed interested. Every time I was ready to stop, she'd come up with another statement or question that needed some kind of explanation. It was a good session, and we both seemed to enjoy it. When we were ready to leave she handed us a give-away map with places of interest, things to do, movies, plays, where to eat, etc., that had been prepared by the Red Cross just for people like us. I thanked her and told her she had made my London trip memorable already.

Outside it was black. Not just dark ... black!

"My God!" Doc exclaimed. "How the hell we gonna get back to the hotel?"

Gradually our eyes began to pick up some tiny lights here and there. The clouds had broken, allowing some stars to show, and that helped to outline the blacker on black of the buildings. And soon we could make out little slits of light serving as headlights on the cars—the only obvious purpose being to let people know they were there. They certainly couldn't throw out enough light to help the drivers see where they were going!

"I suppose we could try to get a cab," I said.

"Yeah?" Doc scoffed. "You go find one. Go ahead. Walk right out there and hail one. You think he'll see you?"

"You've got a point."

Fry was more optimistic. "Let's walk. We can make it. It's getting a little easier to see, and it's pretty simple. We just go down to Piccadilly and continue on until we see Berkeley. And there should be people around to ask if we get in trouble ... if we can see them!"

"Yeah," I agreed. "We don't have a lot of choices. ..."

It was a nightmare, stumbling around blind with open eyes, until we began to see well enough to make out different values of dark and form them into shapes. We actually began to walk without stretching out our arms like sleepwalkers.

About halfway to Piccadilly, a low, wailing sound started in the distance, and grew and grew, rising in tone and volume and bouncing off the buildings until it seemed to come from everywhere. It was like nothing I had ever heard—an eerie, siren sound bordering on the supernatural, spreading into the remote hollows of London, and into the depths of my head, sobbing and resounding against my eardrums. To this day I can still hear it.

"Holy Christ!" Doc yelled. "We're in the middle of a goddamn air raid!"

"I thought they were over."

"So did I."

"Obviously we were wrong!"

In the distance, past the buildings, we saw searchlights stab into the sky, and felt a rush of activity—electricity—beside us. Forms rushed by, and out of the darkness a voice said, without panic, "Take shelter!"

We just stood there looking up at the searchlights and listening to the sound of anti-aircraft fire, which was getting closer all the time. We saw what looked like an airplane caught in the lights, but we weren't sure.

Then came the bombs. The first boom was in the distance, but each successive one was closer, heading directly toward us, until we saw each lightning-like flash and felt each shock. Finally realizing that it was no longer something to stand and watch like the fireworks on the Fourth, and that it was too late to find a shelter, we instinctively located a doorway and huddled there, with arms over our heads like kids waiting for the next blow by an irate parent.

Then it was over, as suddenly as it had started. The noises stopped, it was dark again, and then came the long-drawn-out, high-pitched 'all-clear'. And once again we were able to breathe.

Doc said "I guess I don't have to tell you, we were pretty stupid!"

"Yeah," I agreed. "Dumb Americans!"

As Fry had suggested, the walk back to the hotel was no problem. By the time we got back to Piccadilly, our eyes were accustomed to the darkness well enough to orient ourselves. The only trouble was finding the turn on to Berkeley, but a passing shape was kind enough to give us proper directions.

In the morning, we went downstairs for breakfast, and afterward Doc and Fry acquiesced to my desire to walk around and see a bit of the city, without again risking our lives in a cab.

The walk was considerably longer than we had anticipated. Following the guide we picked up at the canteen, we retraced our steps to Piccadilly Circus, where we expected to see some indication of the bombing, but didn't. The people were carrying on as usual—the bombing obviously a way of life.

While walking by the theaters with their placards and posters of the current plays, and late American movies that were being shown, I still had trouble coming to grips with it all—it was very dreamlike. I knew better, but for some reason, I was expecting a city torn and ripped apart by the war, with hungry people struggling to stay alive. Instead, I saw a large metropolitan area, looking much the same as New York or any other sizeable city, and filled with normal, active people involved in ordinary activities. The pain and heartache had to be there, but they obviously had learned to set it aside and get on with the business at hand.

"Let's come back again and take in a show or two," I proposed, pointing at the Strand. "I don't know about you guys, but I'd like to see *Arsenic and Old Lace*."

"I would, too," Doc agreed.

"We could go today," Fry suggested.

"No, we ought to do what we're doing—see a little bit of the city," Doc said. "We have to head back this afternoon anyway."

"Yeah, I know. One night's not long enough."

"Well ... it would be, though," I said, "if we knew what we were doing—if we planned it ahead of time. If we see the city this time, next time we'll know our way around a little better."

"True."

We walked south along Regent Street, then turned left on Pall Mall and into Trafalgar Square, where we saw Nelson's Column, which supported the statue of Lord Nelson.

"Who's Nelson?" Fry asked.

"You got me," I shrugged. "Doc?"

"I don't know either," Doc said. "I guess we don't know much about English history. It's a familiar name, and I'm sure we learned about him in school, but I can't remember. ..."

We were headed toward the National Gallery, and I was glad to hear Doc say, "Let's go in and take a look."

"I was going to suggest it myself."

"Yeah, I knew you would. Dwight?"

"It's okay by me."

As we went up the steps past the Greek columns, I mentioned, "I *have* heard about the National Gallery, though. It's supposed to be one of the greatest art museums in the world, especially for all those early guys."

"You'd think, with the war and all the bombings, they'd stash everything away somewhere, like underground, and close up shop," Fry commented.

"Yeah, good point. Maybe they have."

Inside, in the hallway leading to the different wings, I was prepared to see a few paintings on the walls, but none were there. "Looks like you're right, Dwight."

"Yeah."

In the center of the area, propped up on an easel, there was an apologetic notice from the director of the museum, Kenneth Clark, informing us that because of the war, the paintings had been removed to a safe place until the end of hostilities. There was no mention, of course, where they were.

The notice went on to say that concert pianist Myra Hess would give lunchtime performances of classical music daily. Admission was one shilling, donated to the Musician's Benevolent Fund. After the war I read a story about Myra Hess. When she heard about the paintings being removed from the gallery, she worried that it would be detrimental to the cultural lives of the London people, so she offered to give daily lunchtime recitals of classical music. Director Clark was enthusiastic and convinced the government to accept the offer. She played daily at lunchtime, for six and a half years—1,698 concerts.

From the gallery we went south on Whitehall toward the Thames, passing the familiar Downing Street, until we stood, gaping, before the magnificent Gothic twin towers of Westminster Abbey.

"It says here that work on this was started in 1245," Doc read. "Can you believe it?"

Fry said. "We should be able to look inside. Let's go see."

We didn't know what the various rooms were, but we were properly impressed by the immensity of it all, and the beauty of the detailed workmanship. French High Gothic architecture, the brochure said. To walk in under those awesome, high, arched ceilings was a religious experience in itself, I decided.

We found a bench near a grassy, park-like area by the river and sat quietly for a while, resting our feet and watching the boats. Afterwards, we headed north again to St James's Park and Buckingham Palace.

"Is this where the King lives?" Fry asked.

"That's right." Doc was reading the brochure again. "When they're in London, which they aren't much of the time."

"Big, isn't it?"

"600 rooms! And it sits on 40 acres. I wish we could go in and see them."

"Is this where they do the changing of the guard?" I asked. "I'd like to see that."

"It sounds like they only do that when the Royal Family is in town. Be nice to see, but I doubt they'd let us, nowadays."

We continued on, with a tour through Green Park, ending up once again on Piccadilly. From there, it was back to Claridge's, and one last taste of luxury before returning to the wars—a pleasant and leisurely early dinner at the restaurant.

[Blick does not discuss a tragic loss experienced by B Flight of the 350th Fighter Squadron in September. Heading down to Biggin Hill, Captain Irvin E. Venell and Lieutenant Harold W. Long lost their lives after crashing in poor visibility. Blick only wrote "This weather-related incident was hard to take for all of us … and especially for B Flight. It was another example of how treacherous the weather is. We can (and did) look at it in hindsight and say that they should have turned around and returned to base, which we were always told to do, but on a flight like that, the decision is hard to make, and it's easy to wait just a little too long. It was a tremendous loss to B Flight. Long was an excellent pilot, and Venell was a flight leader with exceptional leadership qualities. It was always harder to lose people when they weren't in combat. Seemed such a waste."[4]]

---

4 Blickenstaff to Cross, 1998. See Graham Cross, *Jonah's Feet Are Dry—The Experience of the 353rd Fighter Group in World War II*, Ipswich, Thunderbolt, 2001, pp. 408–9.

Fourteen

In October, the air battles took on an intensity previously unknown. As the Americans accelerated their bombing attacks, the Nazis, who had shown little interest in the blind, radar bombing, soon realized the urgency of the situation and pulled fighters off other fronts, increasing their numbers from 300 to 800.

On October 14, with the ball bearing factories at Schweinfurt again the target, Bomber Command had hoped to send 360 B-17s and 60 B-24s to Schweinfurt, but because of the weather, less than 300 were airborne. The Germans were out in force, with up to 200 fighters ready and waiting. At the end of the day, 60 bombers were missing; 5 crashed in England, 12 others were totaled because of battle damage, and 121 needed repairs. There were 600 men missing, 5 dead and 43 wounded.

Although the mission was considered highly successful—a stunning blow to the enemy—the losses were twice that considered allowable by the Eighth Air Force.

Morale was at an all-time low at the bomber bases.

I eased away from Dewey a little so I could look around. I was flying Blue Three with Fry on my wing, behind Dewey and Walsh. Major Rimerman was leading the squadron and had positioned himself off to the right of Major Duncan, who was Slybird for the mission, and flying with the 351st. In the distance on the left, I could see the loose formation of the 352nd.

Our mission [on October 14, 1943] was to escort a group of B-17s as far as Düren, a small town just inside the German border. The bombers were going on to Schweinfurt. It was not a mission the bomber crews hungered for—they had suffered heavy losses the last time, and there was no reason to assume it wouldn't be worse on this occasion. They would be battling the Luftwaffe all the way from Düren to the target and back.

The bomber group was ten minutes late because of the weather, and we had to use precious fuel waiting over the Channel. When finally we spotted the B-17s, we took our positions, Slybird weaving above and ahead of the bombers, Bill Bailey and the 352nd off to the left, and we were on the right. We took it for granted it would stay that way until we were forced to withdraw at Düren, but the Luftwaffe had it planned otherwise. Near landfall in, over Walcheren Island, about twenty ME109s and FW190s came streaking down out of the sun to attack the 352nd in a highly unusual and surprising move—obviously an attempt to disrupt the escort instead of the usual attack on the bombers. It was meant to be a surprise, and it was.

The radio was suddenly frenzied with a constant barrage of calls, some a little histrionic, and then through it all, the clear, imperturbable voice of Glenn Duncan.

"Slybird here, Wakeford. Do you need help?"

"Not yet Slybird. We have about twenty bandits here, but we're okay."

"Roger, Wakeford. We'll stick with our big friends."

Contrary to his statement, Duncan took two of his flights and went back to see for himself, and be of help if necessary, and to make sure the rear boxes of the bombers were protected. At that point, however, the Germans were not interested in the bombers. In fact, they had their hands full with the 352nd and soon ran, obviously in over their heads. Later, at the debriefing, the 352nd was credited with four 109s and three damaged. They lost no one in the skirmish.

Duncan and the rest of us continued on course with the bombers. The 352nd encounter was a reminder to be wary … to keep eyes peeled. I was nervous and looked back at Fry, who returned my thumbs-up signal, and I felt more at ease.

Near Düren the radio crackled.

"Pipeful Leader! Bandits attacking the bombers—ten o'clock low."

A hesitation [from Rimerman], then, "I see them. We'll take one crack at them then we'll have to leave." Rimerman rolled gracefully off to the left and his flight followed.

I looked, and finally saw them at the tail end of the rear bomber box, looking like flies around a cow's nose on a warm summer day.

Dewey was also excited. "We're going down, too, Blue Flight. Stick with me."

I had a monstrous adrenaline rush as I followed Dewey downward toward the bombers, right into a clutter of FW190s and chaos. Thank goodness for that—it stopped me thinking about my queasy stomach. Before we could get there, the bomber that was being attacked by the German fighters, slid off to the right in flames. *Ten men gone,* flashed through my mind. Dewey pulled up on the tail of one of the 190s and I saw strikes. The canopy popped off and pieces from the right wing and tail flew back toward Dewey. He swerved to dodge them. The 190 snap-rolled suddenly and went careening down, smoking. I started after another, but Dewey's number two, Walsh, beat me to it, and I saw strikes as he fired. The radio had gone berserk—a blather of sound, confusing and impossible to understand.

Dewey saw another 190, low about three o'clock, and went after it. With Walsh gone, I followed. Dewey would need cover. I took a quick glance back to see if Fry was still there, but saw, instead, two 190s with flashing wings, right on my tail. Shocked, my reaction was immediate. There was no time to think—I jammed full left rudder and put the plane in a vertical bank with the stick in my lap. The plane shuddered, almost stalled, and for a second I blacked out, but the 190s weren't able to turn with me and went on by. When my vision cleared, I found myself almost in a position to fire, but the 190s were turning, hard, and the deflection was too great. They were taking no chances, though, and both rolled over and headed for the clouds below.

Still acting on impulse, and taken with my success, I followed, but when the Germans disappeared in the clouds, I gave up, and zoomed back up to about 12,000 feet. All of a sudden I was alone. Dewey was nowhere in sight. Fry was gone. I couldn't see the bombers. The radio continued to sound off sporadically, but had calmed considerably. Slybird, wherever he was, said he was circling once, before heading home. Rimerman's words had been to "take one crack and then leave," so I turned toward home, guessing at a compass heading of 310 degrees.

I had climbed to about 14,000 feet when I saw a group of planes off to the left coming toward me. Spitfires, I thought, coming in to meet the bombers. As they closed, the lead planes turned toward me, and I saw the shape of the wings. It was a squadron of 109s! Alone, and low on fuel, I dove for the safety of the clouds.

On instruments, I set the compass again on 310 degrees and started to let down slowly. I came out of the overcast at about 2,000 feet and continued down to the deck. I had no idea where I was, but I knew it was best to get down where I wasn't so easily seen. Under less strenuous circumstances, I would have enjoyed buzzing all the little farms and villages and scooting up and down the hills. I was still running on adrenaline, though, and at the moment didn't appreciate the aesthetics of it all.

The landscape flattened out as I approached the coastline, making me easier to be seen, and more vulnerable. By then the Germans surely knew I was coming. I had tried to vary my heading before I got there, just to add a little confusion, but I knew that it was chancy, regardless. As I neared the beach, I hugged the ground, closer than I had ever been except for landing, so close I felt I would touch any second. I skimmed over the beach and as I went out over the water there was a loud thunk ... I had hit a breaker! My reaction was to immediately yank the stick back but logic demanded I stay there, and I did. Out of my peripheral vision, I saw spurts in the water like heavy rain on a puddle. It took an instant to register. "Holy shit!" I yelled aloud. "They're shooting at me!"

There was nothing I could do but continue on, and get out of there as fast as possible ... and hope! No gas or not, I jammed the throttle full forward. I was soon out of range ... and with a huge sigh of relief I cut the throttle back again.

The gas didn't look good, and I leaned the mixture out as far as I dared, then cut the throttle back to the bare minimum. It was all I could do to keep from pushing the throttle forward to get there faster, but I knew that the slow speed would take me farther because it used less gas. Too late now, but I wished I had stayed up at altitude where I could still keep my speed up by descending slowly.

After watching the needle on the gas gauge creep slowly downward for what seemed like hours, it was almost on empty when I finally saw the coastline. I was south, but with a slight correction I was soon able to make out the barrage balloons at Lowestoft. I had no choice but to boost the power and climb over them. I wasn't sure just how far I could trust the accuracy of the fuel indicator. Supposedly, there was a little built-in leeway. I called the tower and told them I was low on gas and coming straight in.

Duncan came back with most of the 351st Squadron intact, and with some of the other two squadrons. Many others were low on fuel and landed at other fields, and some were damaged. One, Robert Geurtz, in the 352nd, landed on one wheel, the other blown out by enemy fire. Our Robert Peters in A Flight was killed in a crash landing near Brentwood. Rimerman, Newman and Walsh claimed one destroyed, and Dwight Fry, my wingman, did not return.

After the debriefing, I was at the tower, outside leaning on the rail and smoking a cigarette when Doc found me. "You all right?" He asked.

"Yeah."

Doc turned around sideways, one elbow on the railing. "He's not coming, Blick."

"Well … maybe."

"No. He's not coming."

I took a long drag, letting the smoke out slowly. "I keep hoping, Doc."

"I know, but he's not coming." Doc pulled out his tobacco pouch and started filling his pipe. "You've got to let it go, Blick. Sooner or later you have to, and the sooner the better."

"Yeah, I know." I turned to look directly into Doc's eyes. "It's my fault, you know. I should have been looking. Those two guys probably shot Fry down and then came after me."

"He was supposed to be watching—wasn't that his job?"

"Yeah, sure. And he was probably back there yelling like crazy, but there was so damn much confusion on the radio, I couldn't make out anything!"

I threw the cigarette butt over the rail and continued. "I was so intent on what was ahead—Walsh was gone and I thought Dewey needed help—I didn't even think about what might be happening behind me!" I looked away. "That's being a good combat pilot …? Bullshit!"

"You can't do two things at once, Blick. You had to make a decision. Life is full of them, and you can't go around telling yourself you're wrong every time you have to make a decision!" He let that sink in a little. "We may never know what happened to Dwight, but you just can't blame yourself for everything that happens like that! You did your job and did it well. Learn from your experience—that's the only way to get better."

"You're probably right, but it isn't every day you lose your wingman. … Just give me a little time, Doc."

The next day a teletype came from General Kepner: "THREE FIVE THREE FIGHTER GROUP IS TO BE ESPECIALLY COMMENDED FOR THE SUPERIOR SUPPORT AFFORDED THE BOMBERS AND THE DESTRUCITON WREAKED ON THE GERMAN AIR FORCE."

Fifteen

The onset of winter brought an increase in weather problems. Storm conditions, too intense even for the bombers, averaged, at the least, two a week. During those days of bomber inactivity, the idea of using fighter-bomber tactics was born.

The shackles on the Thunderbolt had been designed for either 500- or 1,000-pound bombs, but there was no data on procedure. The job of execution fell to the 353rd Group Major Glenn Duncan, group executive officer, and Captain Walter Beckham of the 351st, who had some previous dive-bombing experience in P-39s and P-40s.

On October 22, we were scheduled to escort B-26s to Cambrai. According to the weather officer, the overcast was around 600 feet, nothing too unusual.

I sat on the strip, waiting for Pidduck and Jack Winder to pull out on to the runway and take off. McCollom was leading the group and Rimerman the 350th, with Lowe, a quiet, shy person, but a good pilot, on his wing. Pidduck had Red Flight with Winder as wingman, and Pinky Lorance and I flew his element.

It was the group's 38th mission and my 20th. The visibility on the runway was okay, but I looked up at the overcast and wondered how many times, out of those twenty days, we had taken off and climbed up through clouds. I should have counted. If nothing else, it certainly was good instrument training.

As soon as Pidduck pulled out and started down the runway, I followed, a little sooner than usual. I wanted to form up with Pidduck before we hit the clouds if I could. It was so much better, and easier, to go into the clouds already in formation, than it was to try to form up later. We never knew how thick the clouds would really be, even though the weather people always seemed so sure of themselves. Pidduck obviously was thinking along the same lines because he waited just below the clouds until I pulled up on his left wing. Pinky was on his right.

The clouds were sometimes so thick I could barely make out the shape of Pidduck's plane. The mist would suddenly become completely opaque and he would disappear. There would be a moment of panic, but then he would gradually fade back in. I tried to keep one eye on my own instruments just in case I was forced to use them, but it was nearly impossible while still flying close enough to see Pidduck's plane.

As we climbed, however, the visibility cleared a little and I was even able to see Pinky, hanging in there on Pidduck's other wing. I wondered if Pidduck had any idea where Rimerman was. It wasn't worrisome, though; we were used to forming the squadron above the clouds.

Pidduck made one slow circle, climbing to 5,000 feet, and then straightened out on the planned 170-degree heading out over the Channel.

McCollom broke radio silence. "Slybird here. I'm at 8,000 feet on a heading of One Seven Oh. Still in the overcast."

It was the signal for everyone to state their positions and it was obvious we were scattered. Unless we could get out of the clouds, there was no way we were ever going to get together. Pidduck looked back at me and rocked his head and shoulders forward a few times, signaling he was increasing his speed a little. We were 3,000 feet below Slybird.

At 10,000 feet the visibility seemed to be a little better. But it could have been my imagination. At 15,000 feet, Hurst, with Yellow Flight, pulled up behind me, and another flight tacked on to Pinky. It was a flight from the 352nd. The light was better, but it was eerie, as if we were caught in the eye of a hurricane. It came from everywhere, yet nowhere. In contrast to the forbidding gray below, it was warm and inviting above. I wanted to reach up and grab it, but just had to sit there and wait. The flights that had joined us were the only signs of movement I had seen for what seemed like hours. We were all just hanging there, suspended in space, with no up or down. It was like flying in a dream. We were completely isolated, going nowhere and coming from nowhere. Wherever I looked it was the same. The only stability was looking at the other planes and the instruments! Without instruments it would have been disaster. But, of course, without instruments we wouldn't have been there in the first place!

At 20,000 feet, we could finally tell which way was up. The sun was attempting, unsuccessfully, to burn its hole through the murkiness. Even the grayness below had disappeared. Shouldn't be long now, I thought. But what will we do once we get out? There won't be any bombers there. How stupid! At 25,000 feet I could almost make out the shape of the sun—but not quite. It was like being on the bottom of a huge swimming pool. At 30,000 feet the sun was beginning to look like a hazy ball of light. We were almost out!

Suddenly and startling, the piercing sound of the radio: "Oh my God, I stalled! I'm on my back!" There was quick heavy breathing. "What'll I do? Air speed 400 … Oh God! Now it's 60 … I can't see." Terrified breathing! "Instruments don't work … can't control! Oh Jesus—!"

We could all hear the terror and panic in his voice, but there was nothing anyone could do. We couldn't even shout words of encouragement—his hand was evidently frozen on the transmission button. All we could do was listen. He was panting …

"I can't see …!" The pitch was higher, and began to tremble. "It's dark! Nothing works! Five hundred miles an hour … can't control … Jesus …! My G—"

And then silence.

Then … the controlled voice of McCollom. "This is Slybird. Relax … and pay attention to what you're doing. We should be out soon."

I wondered …

At 35,000 feet the sun was still a hazy ball of light. My plane was struggling. In order to keep up, I had gradually been easing the throttle forward, but the plane was borderline stalling. The stick was mushy, responding a little like an old Link Trainer. Any violent maneuver would be disaster.

The flight from the 352nd had disappeared.

"Pipeful Yellow here. I can't keep up, Stan. I have to leave."

"Stick with me, Pipeful Yellow." The angle of Pidduck's plane leveled a little. "I'm going to leave, too. Turning back to a heading of three five oh."

"Roger, Pipeful Red. Wilco."

"Pipeful Leader, this is Pipeful Red. I'm going home." Pidduck tried calling Rimerman, but there was no answer. "Pipeful Leader, Pipeful Red here. Do you receive?" Again, no answer.

Pidduck's turn was a slow one. He dropped the nose to pick up speed first. Too easy to spin out with any quick maneuver in that thin, mushy air. By the time he found the heading, our speed was up and we were descending rapidly. He wanted to make sure he let down over the water.

The mission was a complete fiasco, botched from the word go. The weather prediction was all wrong. The mission should never have been scheduled to start with. The B-26s aborted early but the word never got to Slybird. About a third of the 353rd pilots were smart enough to turn around when they realized they'd never find the bombers. [Alan W.] Lowe spun off Rimerman's wing and Rimerman came home alone. Walter B. Stone, a long, lanky redhead and one of our new replacements, also spun out. Neither were heard from again. Cles, one of the original pilots from the 352nd, spun out, but managed to right himself at the last minute and return home on the deck.

The dive-bombing idea was conceived more as a means to get the Luftwaffe in the air, rather than to do any significant damage. Except for the escort missions, the German fighters stayed on the ground, avoiding any contact with us. This forced our P-47 pilots to go down and get them. Fighter Command ruled that out, however, because it was felt that the Thunderbolt could be outmaneuvered by the German 190s and 109s at low altitudes.

To practice, Captain Walter Beckham took four other pilots of the 351st to a tiny little islet off the coast of Wales. Only 150 feet by 50 feet, it was a formidable target. It took time, but after two and a half months of practice, the pilots became quite accomplished. Their best efforts were achieved by starting from 10,000 feet at a 60-degree angle, then pulling out at about 4,000 feet.

On November 25, we gathered in the briefing room. The string on the map stretched to an airfield at St Omer, France, not too far inland. Colonel McCollom did the briefing.

"This will be our first dive-bombing mission. In fact, it will be the first dive-bombing mission in the ETO." He smiled. "As you can see on the map, our target is just inside the French coastline." He pointed. "It's the Fort Rouge airfield at St Omer. You all know that Major Duncan and Captain Beckham have been experimenting with bombs for two months and have had some good results. Now's our chance to make it pay off. We'll go in about 15,000 feet, make a diving turn and release at about 4,000 or 5,000. I'll go first, so follow my lead. I'm taking four flights from the 351st. The rest of you will be our close support … the 350th on my left and the 352nd on my right. The 78th Group will also be there as escort.

"We're not expecting the Luftwaffe to be in the air, but I want to make it clear that the flak is likely to be very heavy. The Germans will wonder what we're doing, going in so low, but they will be ready, you can count on that. We've been making mincemeat out of the Pas-de-Calais area, but it hasn't stopped them. Our intelligence sources tell us they have been steadily increasing their gun positions. They're obviously preparing for an invasion. We want to surprise them as best we can—so get in there and out quickly. Any questions?"

I flew White Flight, to the left of Rimerman, who was leading the squadron. I saw the black puffs in the distance even before we made landfall, and it was soon right on our level. Rimerman weaved a little and varied his altitude. I wondered if it did any good, but it was the thing to do. The German gunners were good. But they should be—they'd had enough experience.

It was black around us by the time we got to the airfield, the smoke from the explosions spreading. It was the first time I had actually heard the crackling bursts, and seen the flame inside. I knew, then, it was close! I thought of the bombers, who had to face it on most missions. Could they ever get used to it?

I was in a good position to watch McCollom and his dive-bombers. As planned, they went in on a path south of the field, as if they were going on inland, and then rolled over to the left and angled downward. McCollom led the way through bursts of flak; his flight stretched out in tandem right on his tail.

Suddenly McCollom's plane was a ball of flame! I watched in horror as the plane dropped to the ground and shattered into burning bits. I thought I saw a parachute, but I wasn't sure. There was always the hope. …

With their enthusiasm dampened, the rest of his squadron continued the bombing as planned, but they found out later the mission was not considered successful. The results were poor, causing very little worthwhile damage.

Fred LeFebre, who was flying behind McCollom, saw the whole thing. He reported, "The flak looked like it hit the main fuel tank and exploded. The fire took the skin right off the plane and I could see the colonel sitting there in the cockpit. Through the flames I saw him reach up and throw the canopy back, then climb out. It didn't look like he was on fire. I didn't have time to see if his parachute opened, but the guys back of me said it did."

Another CO gone! He would be missed ... everyone liked him. He was mild mannered, soft spoken and friendly, yet, as a leader, forceful and inspirational.[1]

Only forty-six missions and two COs shot away. *That had to be some kind of a record!*

---

1 Lieutenant Col Loren G. McCollom survived to become a prisoner of war.

Sixteen

At the beginning of 1944, there were ten P-47 groups and two P-38 groups in England. Fighter Command was able to put 550 fighters in the air, nearly achieving a one-to-one escort for the bombers. The Luftwaffe, however, had increased its numbers on the Western Front to 1,500. But the German pilots were reluctant to engage the American fighters unless they were on an escort mission. The Allies felt it necessary to achieve air superiority if the planned invasion were to be successful. General Arnold sent a pressing New Year's message to the Eighth Air Force insisting, "… Destroy the Enemy Air Force wherever you find them, in air, on the ground, and in the factories."

To replace Colonel McCollom, General Kepner chose to go inside the group. He liked Major Glenn Duncan's aggressive nature and turned our group over to him.

Duncan appointed Rimerman as his executive officer, thus necessitating changes in the 350th. Stan Pidduck was promoted to squadron CO, and Dewey was chosen to be his operations officer. That left the flight leader spot open in C Flight, which Stan and Dewey filled with Chuck Dinse.

Duncan was tall for a fighter pilot—five-ten or -eleven—with a lean, wiry body and regular features. His hair was a light sepia, and so fine it was constantly in motion as he moved. He was an enigma to most of us. We all knew of his eager determination, his hatred for the Nazis, and his awesome ability to handle the airplane. And we knew, too, of his leadership in the air, but as a person he was quiet and withdrawn, seemingly shy and bashful—difficult to know. Those of us who had flown with him found him erratic in his movements, impulsive, and in general hard to fly with. We were upset, also, because he seemed to think it necessary to always go farther inland than the mission required, past our scheduled point of withdrawal, which was determined by our fuel capacity. Something drove him, but what it was, no one knew. It came off as pure inconsideration. Being the leader, his throttle could be set at a constant speed, and he used the minimum amount of fuel, but the pilots flying behind had to adjust their speed continually in order to keep the formation intact. The tail-end-Charlies were invariably sweating out the gas on the way home, even without any enemy activity.

[I pressed Blick on his thoughts about Colonel Duncan several times over the years. In 2011, he wrote "My feeling about it all now, is that Rimerman was a leader, and Duncan wasn't. He wasn't easy to fly with—very erratic, where Rimerman was smooth. To be a leader I think you have to be concerned about the people you are leading. And Duncan had always been the kind of guy who did what he wanted to do—what he was good at—and expected his pilots to follow. But very few could, simply because no one could match his flying ability. When he first started leading the group, he was impossible—we all thought he was a nut. All he seemed to want to do was hunt down the Germans and to heck with those of us trying to follow. Time and again we would return on fumes. ... We followed him because we had to—that was our job. But later on, we liked to be there with him because there was always the chance of running into some excitement. He was a magnet—somehow he always seemed to draw excitement to him, and his outward hatred for the enemy was catching. He was a really strange guy. ... [Later, I] realized he actually did care about his pilots."[1]]

During the winter months of 1943/44, weather was a major factor in the air war. In December, we ran only eleven missions. In January also, there were only eleven, but in February, we managed fourteen.

That first disastrous dive-bombing mission was deemed unsuccessful, but Fighter Command considered it a good start on a practical idea. Consequently, whenever we could get off the ground, we continued to sandwich airfield bombing runs in between our escort missions. With practice, we gradually became more expert. The McCollom tragedy was always there, however ... always fresh in minds, and it was hard to weigh the results against the flak danger and feel we were contributing much to the war effort.

On December 1, we flew the 353rd's fiftieth mission. It was escort, the target Leverkusen, inside Germany near Cologne. At turn-around time the 350th was bounced by a squadron of ME109s. It was a fast and furious melee and I, leading Yellow Flight, finally had the chance to fire my guns. It was a long deflection shot, but I saw strikes and claimed a damaged.

[Blick's Encounter Report:

A. Combat
B. 1 December, 1943.
C. 350th Fighter Squadron
D. 1215 approximately
E. Vicinity of Target
F. Low cumulus about 12,000 feet, visibility excellent
G. Me 109
H. One Me 109 damaged
I. Blue and Yellow Flights encountered 30 plus Me 109s at 30,000 feet in the vicinity of the target, escorting Me 210s and 110s with rockets. I was leading Yellow Flight when

---
1   Blickenstaff to Cross, 2011.

Lt. Zolner (my no 4) called a break. I decided the only thing to do was take one crack and get out, as we were passed our withdrawal time. I got on the tail of a Me 109 and was closing when he started a turn to the right. The turn tightened up and I was almost stalling, giving him a couple of rings deflection and a short burst in which I saw strikes on his right wing. He rolled over and went down and I pulled up.

Later as I was coming out at about 8,000 feet between 8/10 cloud cover above and solid overcast below I saw an Me 109 going down from about 10,000 feet. As I was watching it, the left wing fell off and then the whole thing fell apart in small pieces. I saw no chute or flames or no one shooting at it. That was approximately 1230 hours.

I claim one Me 109 damaged.

Wayne K. Blickenstaff
1st Lt., Air Corps.]

Again, I was on the deck heading home. This time, however, I was in even worse shape. I had used up needed gas, and was sure I wouldn't make it back. There was nothing I could do, though, but grit my teeth and hope. At the Channel, it was decision time. I decided I'd rather be wet than be a prisoner, so I continued on, hoping the British air-sea rescue operation was alert.

According to my tense and tightened nerve endings, the crossing took at least three times as long as it usually did. I had been flying on fumes—the needle on the fuel gauge down below the empty mark—for several minutes before I finally saw the English coastline. I landed at the first base I saw.

The flak had been bad on the way out, but I didn't realize I had been hit until I saw a hole the size of a watermelon in the bottom of the fuselage. Good old P-47!

My wingman, [Joseph] Rosenberg, crash-landed on a farm, but was uninjured except for a cut on his nose, so he was okay. John Devane, flying my number three, also had battle damage. [Robert N.] Ireland claimed a FW190 probable [and Charles O. Durant a ME110 damaged.]

Between December 1 and 22, the group flew one dive-bombing mission to the Gilze-Rijen airfield, and six escort missions, without seeing any enemy aircraft. It was Christmas and I was homesick. I wrote to my mother:

England, Dec. 25, 1943
Dear Mom,
It's Christmas! And I'm about as far away from home as I can get. The weather is wet, dreary, and downright miserable, but that seems to be normal here. I used to like the cool and damp weather, but no more. We walk around on dirt that feels like a sponge most of the time. With every step, the water oozes out from around your shoes. I'm surprised the island hasn't just melted away and sunk, long before this! The only way to get warm is to huddle around the stove in the ready room, and then you have to keep turning, like you were on a spit of some kind, because the part that's away from the stove freezes.

But I really shouldn't complain, and I'm not all that much. I know that we're so much better off than those poor guys slogging their way through the mud. We get our dirty work over in a hurry and then we can come back to baths, good food and clean clothes and beds.

It hasn't really been such a long time, but it seems like we've been here forever, and it doesn't help that it's Christmas. I'm probably overly melancholy at the moment, but it's hard not to think back on how happy an occasion this day has always been, with all the lights, the presents under the tree, and especially how all the faces light up when people say Merry Christmas. I never will forget, ever, that Christmas, back when I was twelve, when I got my bike. It was probably the greatest surprise I ever had, probably because I was still thinking Santa was bringing the toys and I didn't really expect such a big one. But then, too, I remember the last Christmas we had, when we were in LA by ourselves, just you and me, and how quiet and pleasant that was. That was a good time, even if it didn't last long.

I wish there was some way I could help you not worry, but I know you will. I just want you to know that we're doing all right (even with the lousy weather), and that I love you and wish I could be there.
Wayne

On December 30, on an escort mission to Ludwigshafen, Red Flight was caught up in the weather and separated from the rest of the squadron. They ran into ten aggressive 109s and had a quick and furious fight, and our squadron lost another of our experienced pilots, William Odom, who was leading the flight.[2] Dick Stearns, his number three, claimed a probable, but was all shot up and lucky to make it back.

[Blick wrote: "The loss of Dub [Odom] was hard to take. Doc (Canipelli) and he were good friends. Both being Southerners they found common ground immediately. Dub was about five-eight, as most of us were, but slight. His white hair and clear, albino-like skin made him look fragile and delicate, but it was only an illusion. I always felt that under that skin there were wires and rubber bands. He stood out in a crowd, not just because of his light hair, but because of his good looks. Without his too-wide nose he could have been considered pretty. He was normally quiet, and I found him a little hard to talk to. With his ever-present cigarette going, he'd settle back, fasten his eyes on yours and listen eagerly, but when it came to talking about himself he didn't volunteer much. He took his time when he talked, and gave thoughtful answers to questions. He seemed always just a little far away—somewhere else—like he was maybe thinking of home and wishing he was there.[3]]

On January 5, 1944, Duncan destroyed the only enemy aircraft in the sky—his sixth. On the 7th, Rimerman led the group with the 350th on an escort mission to Ludwigshafen. About withdrawal time, the bombers called to tell us they were being attacked just south of Paris. Dewey, flying Blue Flight, went down into them. Walsh, his element leader, fired, but made no claims. Hart, one of our newer replacements, was flying my wing and crash-landed at East Church out of gas. He was okay, but it upset me because Duncan went in too far again, as was his habit, leaving us with too little gas for the unexpected conflict! Pinky Lorance, who had

---

2   Squadron records indicate fifteen Me109s in the region of Charleville/St Hubert; 350th FS Records, AFHRA, Maxwell, Alabama.
3   Blickenstaff to Cross, 1998.

been flying spare, went inland as far as the gas in his belly tank would let him, then turned around to go home. He spotted a wounded B-17 struggling with two engines feathered and, with two other P-47s escorted it out to the Channel and back to England.

The bombers continued to pound the Pas-de-Calais coast. It was a mass of craters, looking much like the surface of the moon.

On January 24, we flew a long escort mission to Frankfurt. Duncan led the group with our squadron and I flew his second element. The bombers were recalled because of the weather and Duncan took us deep into Germany on a sweep. I could hardly control my anger. I was fairly confident I'd have enough gas because I was right up front with Duncan, but I worried about the rest of the group.

The trip was uneventful until we were on the way out. When we were about half the distance to the coastline, Duncan spotted a flight of ME110 bombers flying about 6,000 feet heading inland. There was no hesitation—gas be damned! In no time at all he was lined up behind one and firing. I was right behind him, firing also, but the plane I picked was too quick for me. I had too much speed and, in an attempt to follow, I racked it up into a turn so tight I almost blacked out. I fired but there were no hits. Duncan saw the pilot bail out of the plane he hit, and then he went on to shoot another one down.

[Blick's Encounter Report:

A. Engagement
B. 24 January, 1944
C. 350th Fighter Squadron
D. 1305 approximately
E. Vicinity of Termonde
F. Visibility good at 4,000 feet
G. Me 110
H. Nil
I. I was flying white 3 in Col. Duncan's flight at 16,000 feet. We bounced a flight of 4 Me 110s flying at 6,000 feet. They did a slow break and turned eastward. I fired at one, opening at 300 yards, giving a short burst, but could not get the proper deflection and still see him. I broke off the engagement.
I make no claim.

Wayne K. Blickenstaff
1st Lt., Air Corps.]

Already short on gas, we had no time to spare. Duncan, Dewey and John Zolner went out on the deck. They were so low, Zolner hit a tree but the plane made it home anyway. They landed at Manston, barely making it over the Dover cliffs. Somewhere along the way, I picked up Willy Price and Ken Chetwood of B Flight and went out at 10,000 feet.

Dewey shot down a 109 over an airfield just as it was landing, but then was chased by another that almost got him. Duncan claimed two 110s; Dewey, a 110 and a 109; Li'l Joe, a 110; Dinse shared a 110 with Stearns and Zolner damaged a 190.

[Blick commented: "I was not the only one angry with Duncan. We just couldn't rationalize his recklessness (with our lives) with his ability to find and destroy the enemy. He certainly put his life on the line, also, and we couldn't fault him for that—never did he ask anything of us that he wouldn't do himself. But somehow, he just didn't seem to realize that everyone wasn't the pilot he was—that some of us just might not be able to handle those tight situations he led us into, or the fuel problems on the way home. And what made us furious was that each time he carried us inland farther, it was a signal to Wing that we could go that far, and we'd find the next mission scheduled to go in to that point before withdrawing. All we could do was lean the mixture more and more until the engine decided there just wasn't enough gas there to feed it. ..."[4]]

On February 3 the weather was questionable, but after an hour's delay, our group took off on a long trek over water to Wilhelmshaven. Dewey led our squadron and I had Red Flight. Wilford Hurst had Blue. Except for the haze on the distant horizon, the visibility was excellent.

We were flying at 31,000 feet over the target area when we ran into twelve 109s coming toward us about 1,000 feet above us. I pulled up and had a long head-on shot at one, but missed. At a 400- or 500-mile per hour closing speed, I couldn't get my nose up high enough to hit him before I had to dump the stick to avoid collision. By the time I turned back, all had disappeared—turned tail and dove for the deck. Dewey got one, and went after another, but unfortunately Hurst was under him going after the same 109. He was slightly ahead of Dewey, and neither saw the other. Dewey went down on top of Hurst and chewed his tail off. Hurst's plane dropped like a rock. No one saw his chute. [Captain Wilford F. Hurst was killed in action. Blick wrote: "Hurst's loss was a major blow to B Flight and to the squadron. He was an excellent, level-headed pilot with eyes like a hawk. He was always the first to point out bogies. ..."[5]]

Dewey's plane continued to fly, but how, was a mystery! All of his instruments were out, and the engine was vibrating like a car with only one good spark plug. He was able to dead-reckon his way home and land, but when the plane rolled to a stop on the runway, he shut it off and jumped out, too afraid to sit there any longer.

Dewey's plane was an example to everyone of the incredible punishment the P-47 could take and still stay in the air. Who could have believed that even those

---

4 Blickenstaff to Cross, 1998.
5 Blickenstaff to Cross, 1998.

2,000 horses would be powerful enough to drive its propeller through that tough fuselage and still continue to run?

[Blick's Encounter Report:

A. Engagement
B. 3 February, 1944
C. 350th Fighter Squadron
D. Approximately 1050
E. Vicinity of Wilhelmshaven
F. Broken cirrus from 18,000 feet to 24,000 feet with 10/10 overcast approximately 10,000 feet.
G. Me 109
H. No claim
I. I was leading Red Flight following close behind Capt. Newhart who was leading Pipeful Squadron. We sighted 12 Me 109s being vectored into the rear of the bombers after they had turned off the target. These Me 109s were approximately 32,000 feet and 1,000 feet above us and when they saw us, like scared rabbits, they all dropped their belly tanks. I turned my flight around trying to pull up behind them but as we were still climbing, they pulled away until we were up to their level. We then started to gain on them and when they saw they couldn't out run us, turned back. Capt. Newhart had taken his flight around behind them so while I took a short head on shot he was shooting from the rear. The Hun I was shooting at broke and split S'd down along with the rest.

It is my opinion that these Germans were very leery of the P-47. They tried to get away and when they saw they couldn't—hit the deck. Also—the belly tanks were fitted to the fuselage and looked from a short distance like the scoop on the P-51.

I make no claim.

Wayne K. Blickenstaff
1st Lt., Air Corps.]

[Walter C.] Beckham claimed two 109s, making him the leading ace in the ETO. He was a small, quiet man with an uncanny ability to spot enemy aircraft, and had been promoted to CO of the 351st when Shannon Christian was transferred to Wing Headquarters. As a whole, however, the group didn't fare well on the mission, trading three for three. Two pilots from the 351st were also missing.[6]

Despite the loss of Hurst, there was some good news for the 350th, and especially for C Flight. Dwight Fry was in London! It was February 3, 1944, only four months after he went down. A few days later, Fry was back to see everyone before starting on a speaking tour to the other groups. It was policy that once a pilot made it back after being shot down, he was out of the war. He was on his way home, back to Richmond, Virginia.

In our quarters that night, he told his story. He was flying my wing that day and, as we started down, following Dewey, two 109s came after him. He turned

---

6 First Lieutenant David C. Kenney and Second Lieutenant Lloyd A. Thornell were both killed in action.

into them and they split up. He was able to draw a good bead on one, and with a lucky shot, hit it. The German pilot bailed out immediately. The other pilot made a tight turn on to Fry's tail, shooting. Fry shoved everything forward and dove for the trees. The 109 stayed with him and continued firing. Fry threw all caution to the wind and pulled up sharply into an Immelmann, but still couldn't shake the German—he was obviously one of their elite.[7] Fry had been skidding, and the bullets were missing, but in an attempt to outrun the 109, he centered the ball and was hit immediately. The plane lost power and was no longer a match for the 109. Fry held the disaster off for a bit by hugging the treetops, where the German was reluctant to fly. But then Fry made the fatal mistake of reversing his turn, allowing the German to riddle him across the cockpit. The instrument panel disintegrated before his eyes and his Mae West was cut in two. There was no other choice but to zoom up and bail out. When he left the cockpit, his ankle hit the tail, breaking three bones in his foot, and he was tangled in the shroud lines of his parachute that didn't open until he was fifty feet above the ground.

His luck held, though. Within an hour, the Underground had him doctored and in bed. After a month, when he was able, he spent a little time seeing Belgium and touring Paris, then the French Resistance helped him "walk out" through Spain. He was healthy—none the worse for wear—and feeling thankful and very, very, lucky.

The winter weather's inactivity weighed heavily on Duncan's broad shoulders and he took to heart General Arnold's words about seeking out the Luftwaffe "… wherever you find them." Before a scheduled escort mission to Schweinfurt on February 22, he asked Hank Bjorkman at group intelligence for the location of a couple of airfields en route. Then, on the way to the target, he took his squadron down on the deck to strafe one of those fields, northeast of Bonn, deep inside Germany. Beckham followed him down with the 351st. Dewey, who was leading our squadron, was told to cover.

It was a risky, unheard of attempt to damage Luftwaffe planes and, as I told Doc later, just dumb and terribly inconsiderate on the pilots flying with him. I couldn't help but feel that something deeper was driving Duncan—that it was only a move to try to satisfy his own hunger for action, without any regard at all for his pilots. Most of the pilots just wondered about his sanity.

Five pilots were lost on that mission, including Beckham, who was hit by flak and bailed out. The squadron returned on the deck. Duncan's windshield was covered solid with black oil—a wonder he made it back at all. They claimed only seven planes destroyed—not a very good swap. Major Walter C. Beckham was the leading ace with eighteen planes to his credit.

---

7   Taking its name from the World War I German fighter pilot Max Immelmann, in the historical use it is a sharp rudder turn off a vertical zoom to rapidly reverse the direction of flight.

Seventeen

With our inability to get the Luftwaffe in the air except during the bombing runs, Colonel Duncan was chafing at the bit. The sight of all those airplanes, just sitting on the various airfields ready for the taking, rankled him and triggered a plan in his mind. With our new paddle-props, which increased our turning ability and our rate of climb, he believed the P-47 was no longer inferior to the German ME109 and FW190 at low altitudes. The plan, which he presented to General William Kepner, was to organize a group of pilots, trained to go in low, as a surprise, and strafe those planes. General Kepner went for the idea.

The group was formed using sixteen pilots, all volunteers from the 353rd and four other groups. In honor of General Kepner, they were known as "Bill's Buzz Boys."

At the same time, Colonel Duncan and Major Rimerman were still experimenting with bombs. The newer planes had wing shackles for drop tanks, but useable also as bomb racks. They tried carrying a 1,000-pound bomb under each wing, along with a 108-gallon belly tank, but it was unwieldy and their practice attempts at dive-bombing were inaccurate. They proved, only, that the idea was feasible.

March and April 1944 were decisive months in the battle for air supremacy. Hardly a day passed without action for the American fighters. The Luftwaffe, however, showed no signs of fatigue.

In the briefing room, I found Doc and Bill Tanner. "No breakfast, huh Doc?" I asked.

"No. It's too early. I can always get something later."

"Are we really going to get off today?"

"Looks like it, doesn't it?"

Duncan picked up the pointer and stepped up on to the platform in front of the map. "The mission today is really a repeat of yesterday and the day before. It's Berlin again. Just to recap for a minute, the first mission to Berlin was a complete washout. The weather was so bad the bombers aborted and we didn't see a thing. We did learn something, however. Using the new 108-gallon tanks, we were able to go all the way.

"Yesterday was the same, but a couple of the bomber groups didn't hear the recall and went all the way to the target. We managed to get eleven planes in the air, but after climbing up to 25,000 feet in the soup, we never found the bombers, and again saw no action. In a way, it was successful, because they bombed Berlin for the first time; but it was a fouled-up mission and there were unnecessary losses. The fighter groups claimed eight destroyed but lost twenty-four!

"So today, let's see if we can do it right." He drew attention to an area southwest of Berlin. "In an attempt to confuse the Germans, our bombers are heading toward Leipzig." He pointed. "We will rendezvous with them here, not too far from Leipzig, and carry them through their run to Berlin and out again, as far as we can. We're still short of planes. The 350th is in the process of getting their new planes operational. They can only fly Lieutenant Dawson and Lieutenant Ireland [with the 351st]. I'll be flying with the 352nd."

I was in the ready room, fighting drowsiness while attempting to write a letter, when Doc came rushing in.

"C'mon, let's get over to the tower. They're coming back all shot up."

I looked at my watch. It was 1.40 p.m.

"It sounds like they were in a big fight and Ireland got all shot up. Duncan is talking him home."

Several planes landed before we got to the tower. The fire truck and the ambulances were in position, ready to go. In the tower, the air was electric. We could hear the radio and the clear, distinct voice of Duncan. "You still okay, Rob?"

"Yes." His voice was tired and quivery with the vibration of the plane. "It's still running. ..."

"We're almost there. You've come a long way. Just hang on a little longer. Concentrate on staying with me. Tower, we'll be there in a couple of minutes. Ireland is hurt and has no instruments. We're coming straight in."

"Roger, Slybird. We're ready."

"Okay Rob, still with me?"

"Yes."

"There's the field. Just stay with me now. I'll take you right to the runway."

"Roger, Slybird."

"There they are," someone said. The outside observation platform was crowded. We watched the two planes in the distance as they made a slight turn to line up with the runway. Then, as Duncan said, "Okay Rob, you're all lined up. Just go on in," we watched Duncan pull away, off to the side.

Then the shock of the unexpected! Abruptly and without any warning, Ireland's plane flipped over and dove straight into the ground in a bomb-burst of flame and black smoke. We observers couldn't speak or move—we just stood there, gasping in silent horror.

Finally, a voice said, "Oh ... my ... God!"

It was later, in the debriefing, when we gradually began to piece together what had happened. About five minutes after withdrawal, Duncan's squadron ran into a bunch of 109s. Ireland and Dawson were right in the middle of a huge free-for-all, and both planes were damaged, but Ireland had trouble with his controls, something wrong with the aileron, he thought. Smoke filled the cockpit and he could barely see out because of oil or something on the windshield. He was ready to jump, but Duncan heard him and rushed to his aid, convincing him he could make it home. With his calm, steady, confident voice, he nursed Ireland all the way out of Germany and across that huge expanse of icy-green water to the airfield.[1] There, coming in to land, Ireland automatically hit the flap lever as usual, but only one flap went down, flipping the plane over.

The emergency crews were into the flames immediately and somehow got him out and to the hospital, but he was in a coma. Doc didn't think he'd live. Duncan landed, changed clothes, talked to no one, and disappeared.

The bombing had been excellent and the mission was considered a success even though the losses were heavy—69 bombers and 11 fighters. The Luftwaffe lost 175 planes, the bombers claiming 93 and the fighters 82. Duncan added two more to his record.

Doc caught up with me in Operations the following day and spoke somberly. "Ireland died this morning."

I just nodded. I couldn't think of anything to say. "You didn't have any hope for him. ..."

"No. He was too far gone."

"He never knew what happened, anyway."

"No." We walked over to a couple of chairs. "But Duncan does."

I looked at him, wondering. "What does that mean?"

"You don't know? You don't know why he took off like that?"

"Well, yeah ... I suppose. I didn't really think much about it."

"How would you feel if you talked someone in, all the way from Germany, promising him everything would be okay, and then forgot to warn him about the flaps?"

"I see what you mean. I'd think I killed him."

"That's right, Blick. Duncan's sitting somewhere out there berating himself for not telling Ireland about the flaps. Thinking that he should have let him jump, and if he had, Ireland would be alive today. Most people would be drunk, but he's not a drinker, so he's just sitting somewhere trying to pull himself together."

I reached into my pocket and pulled a cigarette out of the pack. I offered it to Doc, then pulled out another and lit them both. "Y'know, Doc. I'm beginning to change my opinion of Duncan I think. That whole thing yesterday was so unlike

---

1 Control tower records for the 353rd indicate Duncan picked Ireland up as he returned to Metfield approximately ten to fifteen minutes before the crash.

anything I figured him for. I know he's a fantastic pilot, but he always seemed so egocentric ... and so reckless—just out there to please himself without any regard for anyone else. Now I'm not so sure. What the hell drives him anyway?"

"He hates the Nazi system with a passion, but I don't think that's all of it." Doc inhaled and was silent for a minute. "He's a complicated guy, in a way a little like you. I think his feelings run deeply, but he has a lot of trouble expressing them—doesn't even know how. His expression is in his flying. It makes him mad, I think. It's a little like the guy who's so frustrated he crashes his fist into a wall, causing more damage to his fist than the wall." He stopped to see if I grasped what he was trying to say. "Then yesterday, when he didn't think to tell Ireland about the flaps, he blamed himself. That's probably what most people would do, but he just couldn't handle it—no way to express himself. He's got to isolate himself and try to will himself back into a workable pilot and leader again. It'll take him a few days. I'd be willing to bet it'll be years before he can even mention this."

[Blick commented: "That was the mission that changed my mind about Duncan. His effort in attempting to save Ireland, and then his terrible punishment to himself for not thinking about telling Ireland about the flaps, made me realise that he was not the inconsiderate nut that I thought, that he was in fact a sensitive caring person with a tremendous sense of responsibility as well as his driving hatred for the Nazis."[2]]

I was thinking about Ireland. If there was ever a character, he was it. He was an excellent pilot, and highly intelligent and likeable, but with his wild eyes and unruly hair sticking out in all directions, he was pretty far off the wall. I thought of him as one of those people who walked a finely drawn line between genius and just plain crazy. On the days we were forced inside, we played a lot of bridge. I liked him as a partner because there were always surprises—you never knew what was coming next.

"What are you smiling about?" Doc asked.

"I was just thinking about Ireland. ... Crazy guy. One day in one of our bridge games, he was doing his usual blabbering up a storm. Then out of the blue he said, 'Y'know, when I was born, my parents threw away the baby and kept the afterbirth!'"

It was March 1944 and I had flown forty-three missions—no wonder we were beginning to feel like old hands around the new replacements who continued to arrive. Duncan and Rimerman decided there were enough pilots to add another flight in each of the squadrons—D Flight. In the 350th I was designated D Flight leader and promoted to captain.[3] The change was not great, but we began to fly four flights rather than three. In my new D Flight I had Walsh, Li'l Joe Furness and five of the newer pilots, Hart, Mueller, Main, [Paslay] and Moretto. It was a good group.

---

2 Blickenstaff to Cross, 1998.
3 Blick's combat diary confirms the formation of D Flight on March 2, 1944, but the paperwork did not catch up until March 7, 1944. Blick was not promoted to captain until April 4, 1944. See 350th FS Records, AFHRA, Maxwell, Alabama.

[Blick does not discuss a tough loss for the new flight on March 8, 1944. He wrote "D Flight lost [First Lieutenant John] Zolner on the 8th [he was interned and returned to the UK September 18, 1944]. I was banking on him for a lot of help with the flight. He was flying my airplane [P-47D-5-RE 42-8557 LH-U] on an escort mission to Berlin. They ran into some action, he shot down one, but was hit in the main gas tank. He had only enough gas to get to Holland. Rimerman and Stearns saw him bail out and get picked up by some people in a black car, but they didn't know if it was friend or foe! Hart shot down one that day, so D Flight got two and lost one. ..."4]

---

4   Blickenstaff to Cross, 1998.

Eighteen

Bill's Buzz Boys flew their eighth and final mission on April 12. Their total claims were fourteen aircraft destroyed, six probably destroyed, fourteen damaged on the ground and a probable in the air. Also, seventeen locomotives destroyed, fifteen probables, and three damaged, along with numerous boats, hangars, flak positions and other targets of opportunity.

A message later that day from General Kepner stated: "Upon completion of today's mission the flying unit known as Bill's Buzz Boys will be dissolved and pilots and planes returned to their proper station. The Commanding General expresses his sincere appreciation to each pilot and to those supervisory personnel contributing to the successful development of new fighter tactics."

In the month from March 16 to April 14, the 353rd flew seventeen missions. We destroyed five enemy aircraft, but four pilots were lost and one went down in the Channel. He was later picked up by air-sea rescue.

On April 14, our group was relocated to AAF Station F-157 at Raydon.

Raydon was farther south in East Anglia, twelve miles inland, up the Stour River from Felixstowe. It was about halfway between Ipswich and Colchester, and once again less than three miles from Boxted, the new home of the 56th Group. For the first time we were housed in Nissen huts, one for each flight. Doc chose to be in with D Flight, and Dewey felt more at home with us also.

The tour of duty for the bomber crews was originally established at twenty-five missions, but it was changed, later, to thirty-five. For the fighters, however, the tour was [200] combat hours instead of missions. As the number of fighter groups increased, so did the required combat hours. It seemed to us that the number was increased every time we were about to finish.[1]

---

1 The combat tour for fighter pilots was 200 hours and increased to 300 on May 15, 1944, for those with less than 180 hours. It reduced to 270 hours for the first tour on September 15, 1944, (180 hours for the second tour) and rose again to 300 on February 11, 1945 (200 hours for the second tour).

Even so, by mid-April, Devane, Dawson, Pinky, Fortier and some of the other older, more experienced pilots were approaching the end of their tours. Combined with losses sustained in combat—pilots like Zolner—we were faced with the growing problem of replacements. There was a constant influx of new pilots, supposedly combat trained—but nowhere near ready for missions. The theories they were taught in the States were not the reality—it was the college graduate finally forced out into the real world. I had to smile when I remembered being told, while still in Baltimore, that the old-time one-on-one dogfight of World War I was a thing of the past—that it was now all a matter of teamwork, helping each other! Out of necessity, I began to log more and more training time, and it was cutting into my mission time.

Typically, the newer pilots were ready and eager, full of élan, and of course, always somewhat cocky. It may not have been the right psychological approach, but I formed the habit of working on the pilot that seemed a little too full of himself, for his own good. I usually tried to take him for a ride and try to prove, somehow, that experience could win out over younger, and possibly better, technical ability.

It was a touchy situation because of the fine line drawn between enough confidence and too much. To be a combat pilot, a certain amount of ego was necessary, and I certainly didn't want to destroy that; I just wanted to take the edge off a little. I wanted to make a point that flying in a combat situation required more than just the ability to handle the airplane.

I couldn't help but remember, though, how much I had hated those check rides, and how I had come close to flunking each one simply because I couldn't seem to perform well while someone was watching. So there I was doing the same thing to other pilots! There just wasn't any other way, if you wanted to find out how well someone handled the airplane. I kept telling myself it was different—in actual combat your life might depend on something you did or didn't do.

I never seemed to be able to fly with everyone, so I tried to choose someone the other pilots respected, and who was social enough to do some talking. I felt the right person could be very helpful in terms of my own image—and, also, I really didn't like to tell people to do something I couldn't do myself.

The planned mission had been scrubbed and Dewey had just finished a meeting with the squadron.[2] The last thing he said was, "Get out there and clean up your landing pattern." I let everyone disperse and caught Geoffred Moretto's eye. He was one of the new pilots I had decided to go up with. He was tall, with an umber brush of close-cropped hair and bright, alert eyes. He was not skinny, but at first glance his prominent cheekbones gave him that appearance. And to me he seemed a little too cocky.

"Like to go up for a little ride, Fred?" I asked.

---

2 Blick's diary for this day, April 19, 1944, indicates that he led the squadron on a successful mission and then flew with Moretto.

His eyes lit up. "*Yes, Sir!* I'd like that."

By the time we had our gear together and the planes were readied, the clouds were burning away. The ceiling was about 1,000 feet, but there were holes and blue sky. I took off with Moretto hugging my wing, and headed straight into the clouds. We were out about 6,000 feet and I climbed on up to 10,000. Moretto was glued to my wing the whole way—close and steady.

At that point I had been taking it easy, interested only in how well Moretto could stick with me as a wingman. Avoiding the clouds, I did a slow diving turn to the right—into him—down to about 5,000 feet, and then pulled up and rolled to the left. Moretto's position on my wing never varied. I rolled again, this time a little quicker, and dove straight down to build up speed for a loop. Again, Moretto was with me the whole way.

I looked around and gave him the thumbs-up sign and said, "Okay, Fred, now let's do some serious flying. Get back in a trail position and stick with me."

I gave him just enough time to get in position, then flipped into a vertical bank to the left, and heaved back on the stick, pulling streamers off the wings and about five Gs on the meter. I started down, but instead of continuing, I reversed the turn, pulling streamers again, and drew up sharply into an Immelmann, rolling out at the top at about 12,000 feet. I smiled, cocky myself! It was a maneuver that usually lost the more inexperienced pilots. My smile didn't last long. A glance in the mirror showed Moretto still there … and it was a little frightening. Had he been a German pilot, I'd be dead!

With no hesitation, I rolled again, then put down half flaps to slow a little and allow an even tighter turn. I couldn't believe it, but Moretto stayed right with me—he was right there on my tail the whole time. This was no ordinary pilot, I thought. He knew what he was doing and was prepared for anything.

A little desperate, I hit the flaps, jammed the throttle full forward and dove, pulling out at about 200 feet. I saw that I had put some distance between us then and knew that Moretto would be running full throttle to catch up, so I chopped the throttle back and did another tight turn, hoping Moretto would slide right past me. Once again, though, he seemed to anticipate my every move.

Nothing worked! Usually by then, our positioning would be reversed and I would be sitting back there in the firing position. Supposing it was a real German … I'd have to do something. What would it be? I could think of nothing to do but dive for the deck. Again, I lowered my flaps a little and pulled it around into a tight turn, right on the trees. We did a complete 360 and I seemed to gain a little. Encouraged, then, I did a dumb, stupid thing—I lowered the flaps a little more.

I was concentrating so hard on the turn I didn't realize how much I had slowed. Without any warning whatsoever, the plane stalled and flipped over. Usually there was a little warning shudder before the stall, but this time the warning and the stall were simultaneous. We were already so close to the ground there was no time for any thought, and no margin of error—I was dependent completely on reaction and adrenaline. I jammed the throttle full forward and gained just barely enough speed to straighten up and miss the trees; I was already prepared for the shock.

When I finally recovered and realized I wasn't dead, I saw Moretto ahead of me in perfect position for firing! I was finally there, I thought, state of shock and all. *What a way to demonstrate my superior combat ability!*

Moretto tried a few turns, which were easy to follow and I decided we'd had enough—*I'd* had enough! I said, "Okay, Fred, get back on my wing and we'll go home."

I went through the peel-off and landing procedure we had talked about in the meeting and Moretto was right with me. He was good, no doubt about it.

"How'd it go?" Doc asked me later.

"Okay ... he's good."

Doc was staring at me, a worried look on his face.

"You don't look too hot," he said.

"I'm okay," I said, avoiding his eyes.

"You're white as a sheet. ..."

"I'm okay."

"And you're shaking."

"I'm okay, dammit."

"What the hell do you mean, you're okay ... you're shaking—you never shake!"

"So? I'm shaking ... too much coffee."

"Don't give me that bullshit, Blick. You don't shake ... all you do is slow down! What happened?"

"Okay, okay ... I almost spun in! I told you, the guy's good. I couldn't lose him."

Doc wouldn't let up. "So what were you doing?"

I finally looked at him, chagrined. "We were right on the ground in a tight turn and I stalled ... and flipped over!" I grinned a little, embarrassed. "I thought sure I'd had it. It was pure luck that I missed the trees."

Rather than sympathy, which I was really wanting and thought I'd get, Doc gave me a look of disgust.

"Goddamn dumb showoff!" He said.

"Got rid of him, though," I said weakly. "He probably thinks I'm the greatest pilot who ever lived!"

"Yeah ... now! What would he have thought if he'd watched you auger in?"

With that, Doc disappeared for a minute and came back with a couple of pills.

"Here," he said, "take these."

"Oh for Christsake, Doc, I'm okay. I don't need sleeping pills. What do you want me to do, go sleep it off?"

Doc smiled. "Probably the best thing for you—but these aren't sleeping pills."

"You've got a damn pill for everything. What're these?"

"Only a mild sedative. They won't hurt you … just calm your nerves down a bit."
I grew thoughtful. "You know something Doc?"
"What's that?"
"I'm getting too old for this crap!"
"Yeah, that's right. What are you now? Twenty-four?"

Nineteen

In May 1944, as the impending invasion drew nearer, Bomber Command combined their ongoing pounding of the already pock-marked Pas-de-Calais coast with heavy, strategic attacks on the oil industry, deep in the heart of Germany.

Because of the success of Bill's Buzz Boys, Fighter Command began to send some groups to take care of their escort responsibilities and others on separate missions to strafe airfields. By the end of April, General Kepner's pilots claimed 621 German planes wiped out in one month. In May, with the continuing attacks on airfields, he launched large-scale strafing assaults on the overall German transportation system, called targets of opportunity, which included trains, stations, rail installations, bridges, barges, etc.

The weather eased slightly, allowing us to fly twenty escort and four low-level strafing and dive-bombing missions. There were nine airplanes lost and seven pilots missing.

With the loss of pilots, due to both enemy action and completed tours, major changes had to happen. Three pilots in our squadron finished in April, and in early May four more, including Walsh and Stan Pidduck. Stan was transferred to Wing Headquarters and Dewey took his job as squadron CO. I was promoted to squadron operations officer [May 1, 1944] and Li'l Joe Furness was given D Flight. Dewey talked Walsh into getting an extension, and I made him my assistant. Willy Price finished [also May 1, 1944] and signed up for another tour, then went home on leave.

Dewey was promoted to major, and as a consequence was forced to move out of the D Flight hut and into the "Wheelhouse." When we moved to Raydon, the group acquired a typical two-story English house for the field grade officers—major and above. How we did that I don't know. It was a short distance off the base. The Army way has always been to separate the chiefs from the Indians, with the idea that too much familiarity breeds loss of discipline. Field grade officers were the chiefs. I always wondered if the same class difference existed between colonels and generals. Maybe the generals were the *big* chiefs.

Dewey didn't like it a bit, but being Dewey he didn't complain. He had been close to us—Doc and the rest of the squadron—especially C and D Flights, ever since Baltimore. He liked Duncan and Rimerman and the other group officers, but he found it difficult to be anything but businesslike with them.

With Mueller gone—transferred to air-sea rescue because his plane lost power on take-off and he landed in someone's farm—and Bergeron and McDonald missing, and now Dewey gone, the D Flight hut looked strangely barren.[1] There were replacements, but not enough fast enough. As a consequence, I was constantly struggling to keep enough planes in the air. I refused to shave my training program and put pilots up before they were ready.

But then the unforeseen happened. *I received a call from Marvin Bledsoe.*

"Marv!" I almost shouted. "My God! Where the hell are you?"

Bledsoe was laughing. "Here!" he said. "Right here in England."

"How ... why?" I was bewildered and stammering. "Where ...?"

"Take it easy, Blick, you'll bust something."

"Yeah, I know, but—"

"I talked them into letting me fly combat. I'll tell you all about it if you can get me out of this hole."

I finally calmed down a little, and asked where he was.

"We're in a reception center somewhere, but don't ask me where it is. I do know, though, that we came in at Liverpool and that there's a field somewhere around here called Atcham."

"I should be able to find that."

"Blick. Do you think you could get me in your group?"

"I'd sure like to. I don't know how those things work, but I'll damn well find out. We can sure use you."

Dewey okayed my trip to see Bledsoe, but the weather conspired against me and I couldn't leave for three days. Atcham was about an hour away, a little north and west across the island.[2] Finding him was easy. A sergeant at the field was only too happy for the diversion and drove me to the center. Unwittingly I had timed my arrival so we could have lunch. Bledsoe looked good—no different.

We hugged. "It's so great to see you Marv. I've really missed you."

"Yeah. I can't tell you how good it is to be here—all the hell I've been through."

"I've been wondering. I didn't have the slightest idea where you were. You just disappeared."

---

1   Mueller made seven air-sea rescue flights before making his escape following completion of his tour. He returned to the squadron for a second tour, flying his first mission on September 1, 1944. On October 24, 1944, he hit wires while strafing and became a POW for the duration. First Lieutenant Arthur C. Bergeron was killed in action by flak on May 29, 1944. Second Lieutenant Joseph C. McDonald was hit by flak flying Blick's aircraft on the same day and was captured, but later repatriated due to wounds received.
2   Blick's logbook and diary indicate he made the three-hour cross-country flight to Atcham to see Bledsoe on May 21, 1944.

"Let's go eat, Blick. We've got a lot of catch-up to do."

"Yeah, for sure." We walked. "How did you know where I was?"

Bledsoe still had that wonderful spontaneous smile. "How else? I called your mother again! She told me you were in England and what group you were in. The rest was easy."

Bledsoe motioned toward one of the larger huts.

I continued. "We have a classmate from Luke, but I doubt if you know him. Dewey Newhart?"

He shook his head. "No. We hardly knew anyone that wasn't a 'B', right?"

"Yeah, I didn't know him either until Baltimore. He was there when I got there. You'll like him. He's a really nice guy, and a great pilot." I grinned. "You'd better, anyway. He'll be your CO if we can get you into our squadron."

We went into the officers' mess, filled our plates and sat down at one of the tables. I was hungry and sampled the beans.

"Okay … now tell me."

"It's a long story, but to condense it …" He took a bite of bread. "Mmm, this bread is good. So far it's the only thing about England I like! When I left Mitchel, I was sent to a replacement pool and one of the colonels liked me well enough to assign me to a general as his aide. It sounded like a good, cushy job, but I couldn't take it and finally got out, only to be sent to Santa Ana and then to Merced, a basic training school, to be an instructor." He smiled and took another bite. "They thought I was overqualified and should be in an advanced school. So to make a long story short, I wound up again at Luke."

"Oh my God!" I exclaimed. "No wonder you said you've been through hell."

"Yeah, but you don't know the half of it. Being a cadet there was miserable, but a cadet's life is a pleasure compared to that of an instructor. I was a first lieutenant and I thought I'd be okay, but it didn't make any difference. You just can't imagine what they have to go through. I tried, from the day I got there, to get out and into combat!" Bledsoe was angry again just thinking about it. "All they wanted to do was to get their quota out and the paper work done right. Paper work … God! We were inundated with it. We couldn't spend nearly the time with the students that we should."

He was silent for a long time. I could feel him stewing.

"I don't need to go into all the details," he said finally. "There were hundreds of them. I eventually was put on their blacklist when I flunked some students and refused to change their grades. Then, when there was a call for volunteers for overseas duty, I was the first to put my name on the list." His smile again. "Hell, I would have signed up for submarine duty at that point—anything to get away from there." He continued. "I sound like I was so eager to get out I couldn't think about anything else, and I guess that's true, but Blick, it's just killing me—what's going on there. I think about it all the time. Those pilots they're turning out don't know their ass from any other hole, especially about instruments. They're gonna kill themselves or someone else! And I walked away from it."

There wasn't much I could say. "Nothing you could do about it, Marv. You might as well concentrate on something else. I know now why we have to do as much training as we do, on our replacements."

Bledsoe got up. "You want some coffee?"

"Yeah, that would be good."

I watched him go. He had just exposed a different side of himself—a side he had always kept hidden. His crusader inclinations came out in his more unguarded times, but I had never before seen him so forceful. I had to get him in our squadron. His instructor experience would be invaluable with the younger replacements.

When Bledsoe returned with the coffee, I asked, "Do you know any of the other instructors who would be good for us?"

His eyes lit up. "You think you can get me in your outfit?"

"Truthfully, I don't really know, but I don't see why not, and I'll sure try. We need pilots, and I don't see why we can't have our choice if we have one. What about others?"

"Let me try. I know a couple, but let me feel them out. They're probably all good instructors, but I don't know about this combat flying."

I sipped my coffee. "See if you can get back to me right away. We'll need the names as soon as possible so we can submit them."

My thoughts went back again to our cadet days. "I wonder what ever happened to Carrington. Last I heard he was on his way to some base in Texas, flying B-17s."

"He's over here somewhere. At least he was. I had a letter from him while I was at Luke." Bledsoe grimaced. "It was a God-awful letter. Hard to believe, but he was co-pilot on his very first mission, and they ran into flak. There was a burst in the cockpit and his pilot's head was blown right off. The plane was such a mess there was no way to get rid of the corpse and he had to fly all the way home with his headless pilot sitting right there next to him."

"My God! What an initiation! I wonder if he's still around. He might be through with his tour, though, by now. Do you remember what group he was in?"

Bledsoe shook his head. "No. If I kept the letter it's at home."

"I may still have mine. I'll have to look it up. I'd like to see him again. What a shock that must have been! He always seemed so naïve … and dependent. I'll bet he grew up in a hurry!"

Twenty

The strafing missions produced dramatic results, but we soon learned that low-level buzzing across airfields with guns blazing was not as much fun as we first thought. The Luftwaffe quickly increased their anti-aircraft defenses and soon their gunners were the ones having fun. The first planes across the field drew little gunfire, but once the surprise was over, the following planes had to fly through a wall of flak looking much like a fountain of sparkling water. In the April missions alone, the fighter groups lost a total of 109 planes.

In the first few days of June 1944, the 353rd flew eight missions with no action. The weather was conspiring against us again, but there was a growing anticipation, something in the air that lifted our spirits. It was like the tiny, microscopic amoeba, doubling and doubling again until it encompassed the whole of England. No one knew, but all guessed, and worked with renewed vigor and determination.

Two days later, Bledsoe was back on the phone with the names of three instructors, all first lieutenants. One of them, named Vernon Rafferty, he knew well enough to recommend highly, but the other two, James Ruscitto and Milton Graham, were guesswork.

I found Dewey. "I just got the call from Bledsoe," I said.

"What'd he say?"

"He gave me three other names. One is a friend of his, but the other two he wasn't sure about, but they seemed okay. All have a lot of hours and are good instructors."

Dewey rubbed his head. "Do you think this is a good idea, Blick?"

"Yeah, I do ... I really do. I know Bledsoe very well, and I know he's really good, so I'm certain there won't be a problem there. As for the other guys, I trust Bledsoe's judgment. If he says the guy is good, he's good. And regardless of all that, we won't be taking as much chance with them as we would be with what they'd send us."

Dewey thought for a minute. "Okay. I'll go see if I can put the pressure on Ben."

Doc and I were on our way to a briefing, trudging along in spongy soil that hadn't had a chance to dry out in weeks. It was still dark and, as usual, the drone of the bombers surrounded us, grumbling with the effort as they struggled up through the clouds to their assigned altitude.

"Look at that stuff, Doc," I gestured ahead. "I hope it's just the darkness, but I can't see a thing. How are we supposed to take off in this crap?"

Doc took a good look up and felt the mist on his face. "You can't," he said. "You're not going anywhere."

"This is so damn typical. We get up at this ungodly hour, get briefed, then sit around and wait and wait until they finally scrub the mission!"

Doc looked over at me. "You're in a great mood this morning!"

"Yeah, I suppose … it's just this crummy weather. It's funny … I can remember when I was a kid, I liked this damp, cool, misty stuff. But I never had it day in and day out before. I was used to the sun, and the fog felt good."

Doc broke into a grin. "Just think of it this way, Blick. You can get out of it and into the sun. All you have to do is fly up through it, and the rest of us poor slobs have to stay here and drip!"

"True. But I don't know which is worse—sitting here comfortably in the soup, or sitting there in the sun, all cooped up and strapped in, unable to move."

"You've got a point. You want to switch?"

I opened the door and waited. "Well … now that you put it that way, I guess not." I felt a little better.

We went in and sat down. "Look at that," I remarked. "All the way to Berlin again. It's getting to be a habit."

Rimerman stepped up on the platform. "We haven't heard anything to the contrary," he stated, "so we have to assume the mission is a go. I don't have to tell you to be careful on take-off. It's still dark, and you may have noticed, it's foggy!" The ends of his mouth took a slight turn upward, and an appreciative murmur went through the room.

To most of the pilots, Ben Rimerman was a little scary until they began to know him a bit more, and he was a hard guy to get to know. I still felt a little uncomfortable with him, even though I was beginning to understand him, and I didn't think the reason was just because of the difference in rank. He was quiet, sometimes maddeningly so, making silences so uncomfortable that the conversation often became forced and stupid. It took me a long time to realize that it was due to extreme shyness and an inability to make small talk.

The impression Rimerman evoked was that of a strict, rule-book type of person, but that was somewhat contradictory. When push came to shove he would bend the rules as readily as anyone, especially in the air. He was smooth—a superb pilot, extremely concerned about those of us flying with him. He never made a jerky, hard-to-follow movement. Even a quick turn, indicating great urgency, was made with a flowing, effortless, ballet-like flair. There was no slipping and sliding all over the sky, just perfect control at all times.

Physically, he was only about an inch taller than I was, and stocky. Impressions, however, belied the reality. Because of his large, circular head he seemed cherubic and pudgy, but a thirty-one-inch waistline said otherwise. His face just didn't fit with the body. His hair was thin, which added to the ball-like appearance, and set in the middle of his face were two small intense eyes capable of boring right through a person if necessary. His mouth stretched across that circle in a straight line, looking almost cartoon-like, but it could open up into a large friendly grin and disarm even the most suspicious.

All this was attached to a short, bullish neck that he could shove forward into a stubborn position that, in effect, said, "When I want your opinion, I'll give it to you!" At that point there was no argument.

He turned to look at the map, and continued. "The weather's bad here, but [the weather officer] assures me that it's only overhead—that it'll break up out over the Channel." He looked around the room and grinned his half-smile. "Of course we've heard that before, but there's not much we can do but count on it. So we'll take off and form up out over the Channel. The 56th will probably be doing the same thing, so I'm going to make a right turn and climb on course until we get above this stuff. Then I'll do a slow 360 to the left, and we can get together there."

Rimerman returned to the map. "As you can see, we're going to Berlin again.[1] This time we're taking the bombers in, and if everything goes okay, we're strafing these two airfields on the way home ... here"—he pointed to one just west and a little north of Berlin—"and here." He indicated another farther to the west on the way back. "If you get separated and don't find the fields, we have the okay to find our own targets." He stood there for a good thirty seconds just drilling those eyes into the group, and they waited expectantly for the other shoe to drop. Then he said quietly, "Lately we seem to have forgotten about radio silence. Let's try to be a little quieter."

I had White Flight with one of the newer pilots, Fred Moretto, on my wing. John F. Starr and Bayard C. Auchincloss were flying my second element. As we took off, I thought I could see a little light filtering down through the fog, but I wasn't sure, and I wasn't about to take my eyes off the instruments. Moretto was glued to my wing and I made a slow turn to the right, hoping, as always, that the other planes ahead were doing the same. In the dark, and especially in the fog or clouds with no lights to be seen, there was always a feeling of isolation, but the knowledge that all those planes were there in the clouds at the same time induced the thought that it was nothing but pure luck if you managed to get out without hitting someone. In fact, we were not always lucky. Just a few missions before, two bombers had collided in just this kind of situation.

---

1   Blick has used some artistic license here. From his subsequent description, he is clearly writing about the first mission for the group on May 30, 1944. The target that day was Magdeburg and Lieutenant Colonel Christian of the 351st Fighter Squadron led the mission. I have chosen to leave the excellent pen portrait of Rimerman in place to give the reader an impression of his "typical" briefing style.

I straightened out on a heading of 87 degrees and set my rate of climb at 500 feet per minute, then just sat there, concentrating on the instruments and waiting. I didn't need to look for Moretto, I knew he'd still be there. He was an excellent pilot, one of those wingmen you couldn't lose no matter what. He reminded me of Hart, who had flown my wing on so many missions. Hart was as good a wingman as I had encountered, and although I was happy for him when he finished his missions, I hated to see him leave and talked him into signing up for a second tour.[2] He would be back.

Ten minutes later we were at 6,000 feet and still in the clouds. It was considerably lighter overhead, though, and I could see Moretto clearly, but the view beyond was like trying to see through a frosted shower door. I could tell the tops of the clouds were close, and it was a struggle to resist the temptation to haul back on the stick. It was another 2,000 feet before we rose out of the last of the scud, which for the last few minutes had rushed by in great gobs of translucent steam, giving us, finally, a sense of motion and speed. I breathed my usual sigh of relief as we emerged into the clear, spirited beauty of the sun, which was already two inches above the horizon.

I looked ahead and off to the left and couldn't believe my eyes. Sixteen airplanes that had to be [Shannon] Christian's! I looked over at Moretto, who nodded, indicating he had seen them also. Sometimes things worked out the way they were supposed to, I thought, and turned to cut inside and take my position.

Starr and Auchincloss were out shortly, also, and they pulled up in position about the same time. Christian made two large, lazy circles before the group was all together, and then he continued toward our rendezvous with the bombers. We were at 23,000 feet over Meppel when we spotted our big friends low at one o'clock. Christian stayed above them with the 351st, while the 350th and 352nd took their positions on each side of the bombers.

With the squadrons throttled back and weaving, sometimes ranging far out, the trip was uneventful all the way to Magdeburg. As always, however, there was heavy flak over the target. We watched, safely outside, while the bombers plowed right into it and dropped their bombs. No matter how hard I tried, I couldn't numb myself to the sight of those wounded and limping bombers struggling out of that black hole, and the thought of those ten people inside each.

It had been a long mission. I logged five hours and twenty-five minutes, my longest mission to date. After a mix-up with the Luftwaffe, the 352nd barely made it back [due to lack of fuel]. Five airplanes had to land at other fields. Poindexter got two 190s, but his wingman, Edwards, was shot down.

Another mission was scheduled for the afternoon—dive-bombing on a bridge in France. Everyone was tired, but I was short of pilots and had to schedule many repeats, including myself. I led the squadron again.

---

2   First Lieutenant Robert S. Hart completed his first tour of 200 hours on May 7, 1944.

I didn't want to fly Dewey because he only needed one more mission to finish his tour, and I wanted him around. He had put in for a second tour, and would be back, but he would be gone for a couple of long months. I didn't mind the added responsibility of taking over the squadron while he was gone, but the lack of experienced pilots was becoming more critical by the day. I didn't like the idea of talking anyone into coming back for another tour—one was bad enough—but we needed pilots. By signing up for a second tour, pilots were given the opportunity to have a month's leave to the States if they wanted it. That meant the time away would be at least two months, which was a mighty long time in this environment. So far, Hart and Winder were gone, Dewey and Walsh were almost finished, and Li'l Joe would be off soon. That was just in D Flight. Dinse [was close to] finishing and wouldn't be back—probably the smartest of all.[3] It was still a mystery when the invasion would take place, but we all knew it was near, and that made it even more imperative that we had experienced pilots.

I needed Bledsoe!

The target was a bridge across the Somme River, just northwest of Amiens, not too far from Herman Goering's old Abbeville yellow noses that we had been so afraid of during our first missions. The bridge was vital to the German troop movements south toward Paris and Rouen. We encountered some flak along the coastal area, but nothing near the target. We made two passes, and it went well. I saw many strikes, two of which were mine, but we'd have to see the results later to find out what actual damage we had caused. One of the 351st pilots, whose name I have now forgotten, was lost.[4]

At the end of the day, I totaled up my hours. I had flown eight hours and thirty-five minutes.

---

3 Captain Charles W. Dinse completed his tour with 203.05 operational hours on June 14, 1944.
4 First Lieutenant Harry Hunter's aircraft was hit by ground fire and he was forced to bail out west of Amiens. German forces captured him and he saw out the remainder of the war as a POW, spending some of that time in Buchenwald Concentration Camp. See Graham Cross, *Slybirds—A Photographic Odyssey of the 353rd Fighter Group*, Hitchin, Fighting high Ltd, 2017, p. 179.

Twenty-one

All through the tense, exciting and never-to-be-forgotten night of June 5, 1944, ground crews, carrying brushes and cans of paint, worked steadily, painting wide, black and white stripes around the wings, fuselages and tail sections of all the fighters. Overhead, the constant drone of huge flights of bombers and troop carriers, on their way toward Normandy, left no doubt about the approaching invasion. Although it was highly secret, it was the main topic of conversation in the native pubs.

We were briefed from 10.30 that night until 2.00 a.m., when we were released for breakfast and take-off at 3.00 a.m. Our mission was to patrol our assigned zones above 8,000 feet and prevent enemy aircraft from reaching the assault areas. The Ninth Air Force was given the task of cover for the ships and close support for the invading forces.

Dewey, Doc, Walsh and I were together in the mess hall. Because he was a major, Dewey was required to eat at the "Wheel" table with the other field grade officers, but this was a special occasion, and he thought he might be forgiven this one infringement on military policy.

"Blick," Dewey began, with a mouthful of scrambled (powdered) eggs. I looked up, waiting until Dewey had swallowed. "This is gonna be a helluva busy day. ..."

I smiled. "Really?" We all laughed.

"Okay, okay!" Dewey said. "So I just made an intellectual statement! It's still going to be busy, right? And guess who's going to be busiest?"

I waited, knowing full well what was coming.

"We have to be organized ... better than we have ever been before." He took another bite. "You heard Duncan," he went on. "Except for this first mission, we're going out by squadrons so we can keep a continuous cover of planes over there all day long. That means someone has to be here all the time, scheduling and keeping track of the planes and whatever else is going on."

"And that means me, right?" I said. I said it as a statement, not a question.[1]

---

1 Blick, in his capacity of squadron operations officer, did not fly on D-Day. He flew two missions on June 4 and two on June 7, 1944.

"Right."

Walsh broke in. "Who's flying the first one, Blick?"

"You are, for one. I put a schedule up for this first mission."

Dewey continued. "I don't need to go into it all over again, but Duncan is flying with us on the first one. ..." He looked at his watch. "That's almost now. And the 352nd will go along, leaving Rimerman to go out with the 351st two hours later."

I started to get up, then sat back down and looked at Dewey. "I scheduled you, tentatively, for the [second] mission, Dewey. You don't have to go, you know. I just sort of thought you might want to ... even though you've finished."

Dewey threw up his hands and rolled his eyes a little. "Oh hell ... I forgot!" he blurted. "I have some information you guys will love to hear." He let it hang for an instant. "All leaves have been canceled 'till further notice!"

Reprieve! I thought ... and then felt guilty for thinking it. I felt bad for them, but I needed pilots![2]

Dewey was right. I hardly had time to eat until late that night, checking planes and pilots and planning the flights. But I wasn't the only one. Much to their credit, the ground crews kept every plane they had in commission the whole day.

The group flew seven missions. The first one took off at 3.30 a.m. and the last one returned to the field at [nearly] 11.00 p.m., thankful for the long English twilight.

The first mission, with Duncan leading the two squadrons, was uneventful. The cloud cover was about nine-tenths, and they saw no enemy aircraft. We were to learn later that, because of our campaign against the German airfields, only 155 German airplanes were able to challenge the landings that day.

Due to the weather, our planes were loaded with bombs for the rest of the missions, and we were turned loose under the overcast on targets of opportunity, namely locomotives, trains and whatever other transportation we would see. On the fourth mission, Dewey and his group [tried to] shut down a railroad tunnel near Bréval.

On the penultimate mission of the day, Bailey, with the 352nd, left six trucks of a convoy burning, and [just missed] an ammunition train [with their remaining bombs]. "It looked like the grand finale of a Fourth of July celebration," someone said.

One of the 352nd's newer pilots, Flying Officer Green, got a little too close to his own bomb and was blown up by it, but the pilots with him saw a parachute open. He had been with the group less than two weeks.

On June 7 we [the group] ran nine missions—strafing and bombing missions on targets of opportunity. I scheduled myself on two of them. On the initial one—the first of the day for the 350th—I led with White Flight. The weather was so bad we never made it to the assigned area. We had been briefed to go in at 2,000 feet,

---

2   As Blick notes in his diary for June 6, 1944, Newhart had applied and been given a fifty-hour extension.

but the ceiling was only about 500 and we stayed just below, making it almost impossible to tell where we were.

We found out quickly, however, where we shouldn't be—right on top of some heavy gun emplacements! As soon as we realized we were being shot at, we scattered in all directions. I found myself frustrated and alone. I had stayed below the clouds, right on the deck, and when I pulled up just under the scud, where I could relax a little and look around, no one was in sight. The others had obviously scooted up into the clouds. *Damn! It was all my fault*, I thought. I should have been more careful. I wondered what Dewey did.

With no idea at all where I was, I flew in large S's, heading generally south, for about ten minutes, looking for something to unload my bombs on. I found nothing. But then, as I turned to leave, I saw a railroad. It was something, anyway, so I cut it in two and headed home.

The squadron straggled back in ones and twos. Walsh didn't show. I went over to the tower and waited with Doc, optimistically reacting to every little sound on the radio. But there was nothing from Walsh. After half an hour of silent waiting, we finally looked at each other, and without a word turned to go. Walsh was missing! *He could have been home by now if we hadn't talked him into getting an extension!*

Rimerman led my second mission. Our target was a railroad tunnel south of Beauvais. We found and destroyed some locomotives and caved in the entrance to a railroad tunnel. On the way home we saw a motor convoy and left it disorganized and burning.

Duncan, flying with the 351st on the sixth mission, again demonstrated his uncanny ability to locate action. He found what must have been the only aircraft in the air taking off from the Beauvais airfield. As the squadron attacked, they were jumped by enemy aircraft and in the ensuing battle, Duncan added another to his growing list of victories [Duncan claimed a JU52 and half an ME109]. Along with numerous other ground targets, the squadron destroyed nine planes in the air and one on the ground.

That night, I sat down to write a letter to Walsh's wife, Marge. It was too soon, but I'd wait to send it. I knew also that I didn't have to do it … that someone from intelligence would write an official note. But I knew Marge and felt she deserved more than that. I sat there staring at the paper for a long time, not knowing how to start.

Francis Walsh was one of the original C Flight pilots at Baltimore. He was one class behind me, but he was already there when I arrived with Balason and Baer. As soon as Marge heard where he was, she found a place to stay in nearby Dundalk. All of C Flight knew her well.

They were a picture of opposites. He had dark, wavy hair and reddish, freckled skin, with a heavy beard all the way down his neck to his collar. The skin of his neck was even redder and was bumpy, the bumps making shaving a daily, miserable and sometimes painful ordeal. It took him twice as long to shave because he'd nick the tops of the bumps if he tried to rush, and wind up with dabs of toilet paper all over his neck. Most men would have given up long before and let the beard grow, but Walsh was determined, and accepted it as part of his daily living.

Marge, on the other hand, was tall and blonde, taller than he was, with fair skin that tanned easily. So full of life, she always had a joyful greeting for everyone and a wonderful perky smile. I liked the way her hair bounced around her shoulders as she walked.

Both Walsh and Marge were from Brooklyn and I never tired of listening to their accents—so different from Doc's and the California nothings I had grown up with. I smiled just thinking about it.

Walsh's ambition was to be a fireman. The first time I heard that, I couldn't believe being a fireman could even be an ambition. For kids, yes, but a grown man? The more he talked about it, though, the more I began to understand. Except for the risk, it was a good job—secure—and one that paid well enough to support a house and raise a family. So what else would anyone want?

He was brought up in a deeply religious Catholic family, and I learned the hard way to abide by the old saying about never arguing politics or religion. I never quite knew what to think about God. I had always felt of myself as being some kind of agnostic and when I asked, "How do you know there's a God?" my question was not meant in any derogatory way, it was simply a matter of curiosity. Walsh's answer was simple. "There just is," he said. At the time I wasn't smart enough to leave it there so I kept pressing and received, always, the same answer until finally Walsh just walked away.

"That'll teach you," Doc said with a big grin.

I still held the pen in readiness, but I hadn't written a word. I looked at the blank paper and all I could see was the face of a little baby girl, born while we were at Metfield.

Twenty-two

On June 6, the Germans had only eighty operational fighters in France. With the news of the landings, they immediately committed most of their troops, including the Luftwaffe, to the new front, and by June 10 they had arrived at new bases surrounding the Normandy area. Their forces were still numerically less than the Allies, but they were determined to make themselves known, aggressively bombing the Allied troop positions.

By June 9, our group had flown more operational hours and put in more claims than any of the other fighter groups. We had destroyed thirty-five airplanes and delivered over half of the total bombs dropped. The weather continued to hamper our operations but, regardless of the dangerous conditions, we flew missions on twenty of the last twenty-one days of the month. During that period we flew thirty-three missions; fourteen were bombing and strafing, and twelve were combinations. Nineteen planes were destroyed in the air and seventeen on the ground. Other claims were twenty-four locomotives, thirty-eight rail cars, seventy-eight motor vehicles and numerous cars, tanks and barges damaged. Our successes were not without pain, however. We lost fourteen planes and thirteen pilots.

On the 8th, we had three missions, and we flew once again as a complete group. Bill Bailey led the first, Rimerman the second and Duncan the final one.

At last, I had the call I was waiting for from Marv Bledsoe. He and the other three instructors had all been assigned to the 350th and were to arrive in Colchester, by train, at 5.20 in the afternoon. With the last mission in the air and the scheduling finished for the day, I drove into town to pick them up. As operations officer, I had my own jeep.

On the way back as we approached the field, the mission was returning. I drove directly to the tower to watch them come in. At the time, I thought it would be a good initiation for the new instructors into the world of combat, but later, in hindsight, I wasn't so sure. Duncan, as usual, had been able to drum up some excitement, and was all shot up again. He had flown the whole way back on instruments, and landed using his trim tabs because he had no elevator control![1] For a moment, I

---

1   Duncan's aircraft, LH-X VII (a/c 42-25971), received CAT AC battle damage to the horizontal stabilizer, June 8, 1944.

toyed with the idea of telling my passengers that sort of thing happened all the time, but thought better of it. I was sure they didn't need me to tell them it was a far cry from the safety (and boredom) of instructing. With D-Day only three days behind us, it was a tough time to be a replacement.

The next day I took Bledsoe up for a flight.[2] It was mostly for looks. I wanted to get him flying missions as quickly as possible, and I needed some sort of strength behind my statement to Dewey that he was ready.

It was another soupy day with a 500 foot, or so, ceiling that looked solid, but so much the better, I thought—it'll make it easier to prove to Dewey how well Bledsoe can fly. We took off together and Bledsoe was there, stuck tight to my wing. I stayed under the clouds and headed out toward the coastline. I wanted to see if there was any room over the water, before going up into the clouds. There was at least 400 feet, and I lifted my nose up into the clouds. At 4,000 feet we were out on top.

I looked over at Marv. "Just thought I'd show you what the sun looks like. You probably haven't seen it for a while."

I did a few fast, sharp turns, fairly violent, then dropped back down into the clouds. Bledsoe was locked on to my wing the whole time. It was more important, with so much bad weather, that I find out how Marv did in the clouds. All it took was a couple of climbing and diving turns to find out what I needed to know. Marv didn't vary his position a foot.

I started down on a heading that would take us back to Raydon and, looking back at Bledsoe, I motioned for him to stack the formation up, which he did without any verbal instruction. It was standard procedure for letting down in an overcast.

"There's almost always some room to let down over the water, Marv. You'll need to use it a lot."

Back on the ground, Bledsoe grinned and asked, "Well, did I pass the test?"

"That wasn't any test, Marv," I said. "I just wanted to make it *look* like one!"

That night I rounded up Dewey and Doc and said I'd spring for drinks at the officers' club. Knowing Dewey, who had never touched alcohol in any form, would refuse, I talked him into going anyway to have a coke. Dewey was intuitive enough to know that I had more on my mind than just socializing, and once we all had our drinks and were seated, he didn't waste time with small talk.

"Okay, Blick," he said. "What's the bitch?"

I smiled. Just like Dewey, I thought. Let's get right into it! "No bitch, Dewey ... this time! Just a pitch!" I went on. "You all probably know what I'm going to say anyway." I took out a cigarette, stalling a little. I wasn't quite sure how to approach it. "You all know that I went through cadet training with Bledsoe and he is an exceptional pilot. We need pilots right now, and I want to use Bledsoe. I went up with him today and he's technically better than most of the pilots we've got, plus

---

2   Blick's logbook confirms this flight with Bledsoe took place on June 9, 1944.

he's older and so much smarter." I took a sip of my drink and lit the cigarette I'd been tapping on the table. "I know, I know ..." I held my palm up, "he's a good friend of mine and maybe I'm a little prejudiced, so I'll go by what you guys think."

"Doc. What do you think?" Dewey asked.

Doc looked at Dewey, then me, then at his drink, thinking. "You guys are the pilots—"

I broke in. "Now don't start that stuff, Doc. You can't just wheedle out of it. We're asking for an opinion."

"You didn't give me a chance to finish. I was going to say that I can't say anything about his flying ability. For that I have to go by what you're saying." He leaned back in the chair, one hand on the glass. "But tell me, has he ever dive-bombed? Has he ever had to fly home with a beaten up airplane and the gas gauge on empty? Has he ever had a guy on his ass firing real bullets? I haven't the slightest idea how he would react, and I doubt you guys do either."

"You're right there, Doc," Dewey agreed, "we sort of eased into it. No one picked us up and dropped us right into the middle of all the flak. It's a little different out there right now ... for sure." He looked at me. "You really think he'll be okay, Blick?"

"I don't know about being okay, if that means coming out alive, but I'm convinced he's as ready as any replacement we've ever had." Dewey was mulling it all over and I went on. "As for Rafferty and the other two, we don't really know anything about them, but they all have a lot of hours, and I'd like to get them started too, as quick as we can."

Doc took a drink, then said, "It's right, Dewey, in the sense that you all had to learn as you go, and I have to agree that all that flying experience means a lot, even if it was in an AT-6. Most of the kids who come in don't have nearly the maturity that these instructors have."

"Okay. I'm convinced. So here's what we'll do," Dewey said. "You can take Bledsoe up with you on the next mission—break him in. Keep him close. But, like you said, take it easy with the others until you're really sure. Okay?"

"Good," I smiled. "Thanks." I told Dewey that, if at all possible, I'd like Bledsoe and his buddy, Rafferty put into D Flight. I wanted Marv, especially, in my hut.[3]

For the first mission on the 10th, I led the squadron and left the new pilots with Dewey.[4] It was another dive-bombing mission, on targets in the Bernay area.

---

[3] Bledsoe flew his first mission on June 10, 1944. James O. Ruscitto, Vernon G. Rafferty and Milton H. Graham flew the next day (June 11, 1944). Ruscitto and Rafferty proved a success. Graham was a disappointment, flying only four missions before transferring to the 50th Control Squadron.

[4] The mission reports for the first mission by the 350th on June 10 held by the AFHRA, Maxwell, Alabama and those held by NARA are incorrect. The control tower log confirms Blick led the mission with Lieutenant Coffey as his wingman. Lieutenant Chetwood led Red Flight. To confuse things, Blick lists the mission as taking place on June 9 in his war diary. This appears incorrect and it seems that it was a bad day for record keeping all round!

The overcast was solid, and rather than take the chance on finding a hole over the Continent, I went in under it. My flight shot up a truck convoy, but in the process became separated from the rest of the squadron. The combination of bad visibility and a low ceiling, made it almost impossible to keep more than a flight together, so it was up to the individual flights to search out their own targets. We had to fly in and out of the scud just below the clouds in order to stay high enough to get a reasonable bombing angle when and if we did see something. The air was always bumpy there—reminding me of those days in the rough air over the desert at Thunderbird.

With my flight, I flew around for about twenty minutes looking for something to unleash our bombs on when, finally, we saw a railroad bridge. We all dropped on it, but we just couldn't get a good run and all missed. Then, as we were forming up again, I spotted a train puffing along without a care in the world, a perfect opportunity to make up for our inept bombing effort.

"Seldom here, let's get it," I said quickly.[5]

I rolled over and, concentrating on the engine, let go with my eight fifties, then dragged my sight along the cars as far as I could until I had to pull up. Our attack was a surprise, but there were German gunners aboard, ready for just such an emergency, and it took but an instant for them to return fire.

Ken Chetwood, [leading Red Flight], was struck.

"Blick! I'm hit!" There was panic in his voice. "This is Ken."

"How bad, Ken?"

"There's smoke, and the oil pressure is dropping."

"Hang on. We're heading toward the beachhead." I looked around but didn't see him. "Ken, where are you?"

"I don't know. I pulled up into the clouds and when I came back down no one was around."

"Ok, just stick on zero. It's not far."

There was silence for a minute. Then, "It's getting worse, Blick, I can't see. I'm gonna bail!"

"Not yet Ken, wait! Can you see the instruments?"

"Yeah ... just."

"Run that thing as long as you can, Ken. Not far to go now."

"It's bad ... I can hardly see." The transmission was getting mushy. "I think the engine's on fire."

"Keep it going, Ken. Are you holding your altitude?"

"Roger, but I can see the fire now." I could barely understand him. "It can't last much longer."

"Just a little more, Ken. We'll be there soon."

---

5   The 350th call-sign changed from "Pipeful" to "Seldom" on April 23, 1944. The 351st became "Lawyer" and the 352nd "Jockey." See Freeman, *War Manual*, p. 83.

There was some weak garble and then nothing. I tried again, and again, but finally gave up, sure that Chetwood was down somewhere, hopefully far enough across the lines to be out of danger. It would be close, though, I thought, and there was the wind, which could blow him back into enemy hands. I refused to allow myself to dwell on it and forced my mind into thinking about Bledsoe instead.[6]

It had not been a good mission. We found out, later, in the briefing, that Martin Coffey, one of the newer pilots, who had been with us only five weeks, had waited too long to pull out and mushed into the trees.[7]

"I'm more upset about Coffey than I am about Chetwood," I told Doc later. "I know it's not really my fault, but I feel like it is."

"Why, for God's sake?" I knew Doc felt he had to ask just to get me talking. Not only did we have a special communication together, but it was his job as flight surgeon to keep our morale up. It was difficult. Being a medical doctor was nothing by comparison. In fact, most of the time I was attempting to boost Doc's morale! He was the one always depressed because of the lack of medical challenge. We were good for each other.

"We've been so busy, and we're so short of pilots we can't give them the right kind of training. There's no excuse for Coffey's mushing into the ground." I was emphatic.

"You don't think it was his fault? Doc asked. "You don't think he should have known better?"

I knew what Doc was doing, but went on anyway. "Yeah … sure he should have known better. Everyone knows how heavy this plane is and how it keeps right on going after you pull up, but he should have been trained for this kind of situation—they don't get that in the States." The more I talked the more upset I became. "Bledsoe'll tell you that!"

"Blick!" Doc shot out in an attempt to calm me down. "Blick, listen. These guys are individuals—grown up individuals. Most of them are only a year or two younger than you are, some just as old. They have to get their experience just like you guys did. Some are not going to make the right judgments, just as some of you didn't. Some will kill themselves, just as some of you did. You've come pretty close yourself, or don't you remember that?" He let that sink in a little. "You can't, Blick … just can't take all of them on your shoulders, and baby them along."

I was quiet, and reached into my left shirt pocket for a cigarette.

Before I lit it, Doc asked, "Can I borrow one of those?"

I reached in and pulled out another and handed it to him, then lit it for him. "As usual, you're right Doc," I said, "but I just can't help thinking that it didn't have to happen, and that we are somehow responsible."

---

6   Blick's war diary confirms that First Lieutenant Kenneth Chetwood made it back to Raydon on June 13, 1944.
7   Coffey was Blick's wingman so he would have been aware, even if he did not see it happen, that he had been lost.

Doc managed a smile, but it was a sardonic one. "If you want my opinion," he said, "none of this shit should be happening!"

My second mission of the day was to shut down a long, railroad tunnel southwest of Paris. Duncan was leading the group and Dewey the 350th. I had Blue Flight with Bledsoe on my wing [flying his first mission]. I knew Bledsoe was nervous. How could he not be? It was my seventy-seventh mission and I still had those butterflies.

"You'll be okay, Marv," I reassured him on the way out to the planes. "Just remember to stick with me ... and keep your eyes open. Things do have a tendency to happen quickly up there."

"Yeah, I sure will."

"And stay off the radio unless you've got something important to say. We have a lot of trouble with some of the younger kids—they think with their mouths."

"Okay."

"And don't worry about the bombs," I went on. "They don't really affect the flying that much—a little heavy on the take-off, that's all. But the main thing ..." I emphasized, "is to give yourself plenty of room to pull out after you drop them. It's easy to concentrate so hard on the target you wait too long. Just the other day we had a guy mush right into the trees."

The weather was good over the Continent and we went in at 15,000 feet, dodging some insignificant flak over a few cities along the way. I wondered what Bledsoe was thinking about it, but with his mask and goggles, I couldn't read him. He just hung there on my wing, not moving.

Gradually, we nosed down as we neared the target, and leveled out about 5,000 feet. Ahead, Jonah and his squadron made their run on the tunnel.

Then Dewey announced, "Okay, Seldom. We'll go down in elements. Make those bombs count."

"Here we go, Marv," I said, "all set?"

I rolled over and dove, and Bledsoe followed about fifty yards behind. My bombs exploded off to the left of the tunnel. As I pulled out of the dive there were streamers. I didn't see what Bledsoe did, but he told me later he did just what I had warned him about—waited too long. He panicked and only released one bomb. When he pulled up there was smoke and debris at the mouth of the tunnel, and he didn't know if he'd hit it or not.

"Great shot Marv," I yelled. "That's putting it where it belongs." I paused until Bledsoe was back in formation, then said, "Wait until Red Flight finishes, Marv, then go down and drop that other one."

"Okay."

The second time around Bledsoe was not so nervous about getting the whole pattern and procedure right—he was all alone and could take his time. He centered the ball and put his sights right in the middle of that big hole. When he pulled out, there was nothing—nothing at all! He'd missed completely, I thought. Or had he forgotten to arm it? My dismay lasted but a second. As we watched, a huge cloud of smoke and dirt spewed out of the tunnel. He had skipped the bomb right into it and it had exploded inside. What luck!

"Hey!" It was Duncan. "Who did that?"

"It was Bledsoe, Jonah," I answered. And everyone heard. Bledsoe had proved a point.

The same day, pilots of the 78th Group were jumped by over twenty enemy aircraft while they were on a bombing mission. Ten pilots were lost.[8]

---

8 Seven pilots were lost in the action (four KIA, two POWs, one evaded) and a further three pilots were KIA in other actions. See Garry L. Fry, *Eagles of Duxford—The 78th Fighter Group in World War II*, St Paul, Phalanx Publishing, 1991, p. 137.

Twenty-three

The fighter groups continued to fly two, three and four missions daily, weather permitting. Because of the short summer nights, the pilots were awakened early, many times at three or four o'clock in the morning.

From D-Day, it took only eight days to establish the Ninth Air Force solidly in Normandy. This allowed the Eighth fighters to roam farther inland. The bombers, meanwhile, were unrelenting in their crippling assaults on the German oil industry.

Since the night before D-Day, I had been putting in sixteen- to eighteen-hour days, even when I wasn't flying. The little catnaps I could sneak in once in a while weren't really very satisfying. After the last mission on the 11th, I put the schedule up for the morning flight, along with all the contingency plans I could think of that might be necessary. Then I announced, emphatically, to our operations clerk and everyone else, that in the morning, come hell or high water, I was sleeping in and I didn't want to be awakened. I was so in the habit of getting up, I wasn't sure it would work, but I was tired and wanted to try. I felt I deserved it.

I awoke the next morning when the hut came alive, but I willed my eyes to stay closed and my brain to stay mostly asleep. I was restless for a while, but when things quieted down my mind relaxed and the tired body took over. I dropped deeply into silent and dreamless pleasure.

"Blick ... BLICK!"

A hand was shaking me, and I jumped, startled, and tried to focus. It was Doc. "What?"

"You'd better get up, Blick. Dewey is missing!"

"Oh shit! ... Oh God, NO!" I rolled out from under the covers, fully awake. "Geez-uss Kerist!" I reached for my pants. "Shit!" I yanked them on. "Shit! Oh shit ... SHIT! ... How?"

"The squadron was bounced by forty-some planes."

I jammed my feet into my shoes and struggled with the laces.

"They hit him and he got as far as the coast where he ran into more. The last anybody heard he was calling for help."

"The one time I sleep in …! Shit!"

Doc hesitated before going on. "There's more, Blick," he said finally.

I stopped dead and locked on to his eyes. "More? … Oh God … No!"

"Also, Bedford, Main, Moretto, Phelan and Peters … and if Ruscitto [flying his second mission] hadn't blown away a guy on Brown's tail he wouldn't be here either."

I sat back down on my bed and leaned over, holding my head. My heart was pounding against the walls of my chest. "My God! … Oh my God! That's just about all the experience we have left in the squadron!" I looked up at Doc through blurred vision. "What the hell do we do now?"

I have never forgotten the sickness of that morning. My first thought had been of the squadron, but what began to grow inside was something I find hard to describe, even now, when it is so long past. It was suddenly a lonely and terrible emptiness, to be sure, but there was more. It was anger … yes, there was the awful festering anger … of uselessness and hopelessness, and of course the emergence of raw, bitter feelings of payback—vengeance! I couldn't explain all this. How could I ever justify to myself that all of this death and destruction—this evil—was worth it? How could I ever convince myself that Dewey's and all the other deaths were a good thing—that they were fighting to protect our country, and our families? That we were all warriors and we had to expect this kind of thing? That it was part of the game? I had lost a part of me … not like losing a finger or a leg, but something deep inside, like a chunk out of my heart. It was something that, for sure, would never grow back … and it never has.

And where was I … ? Sleeping!

Duncan was furious. He called up Wing Headquarters and demanded permission to go back in and "clean them out!" He got the okay.

Rimerman led the group with the 351st, I took the 350th and Poindexter the 352nd. Everyone in the 350th wanted to fly, but as much as I could, I didn't fly the pilots that were on the first mission. Tanner insisted, so I gave him Red Flight, and Li'l Joe had Blue.

Rimerman positioned the squadrons at different altitudes, determined to find the Luftwaffe. Rimerman went in at about 5,000 feet, Poindexter at 10,000, and we went in at 15,000.

Tanner was the first to spot them … dead ahead about 2,000 feet above us.

"Jonah, bogies 12 o'clock—"

He couldn't even get it all out before we were right in the middle of them. We met head-on—at a closing rate of about 600 miles an hour. It was an immediate melee of tremendous proportion—forty-plus Germans and our sixteen P-47s; to an observer at a distance, a bevy of bats spitting out venom. It was, at once, everyone for himself. The dogfight of World War I to the third power. At least we were prepared—not like Dewey.

As we met the 109s and 190s, I picked the first plane I saw and pulled up, firing. It was no use, we met too quickly and I barely skimmed by underneath. All in one motion, I jammed full left rudder and threw the stick to the side and yanked it back into a vertical bank … and dimmed out for an instant. But by the time I had turned, the 109 pilot had turned also, to the right, and we were once again headed straight into each other. I repeated my maneuver, this time completing my roll, and then reversed my turn. I obviously confused the German pilot, which I was trying to do, and wound up on his tail. But the German was smart. Before I was able to get into position to fire, the 109 split-essed for the ground. I followed, right down to the deck, throttle jammed all the way forward. I was close, but the German started some wild evasive skidding action and my tracers were missing. We were in a tight turn and I was just about to get my nose far enough in the lead when the pilot decided to give it all up and shot up into a cloud and disappeared. I hung around for a while, waiting, but never saw the 109 again.

In a way, Dewey and the others were avenged, but it was hard for me to see it that way. The squadron destroyed four. Tanner and Li'l Joe each had two and Li'l Joe's wingman Starr, damaged one. It was a substantial rout, with the group getting nine destroyed and several probables, but in my mind, it would take a whole lot more than that.

The next day, another early morning mission was scheduled, and with the losses of the previous day there was nothing else I could do but fly the ex-instructors. There were barely enough planes to put up four flights.

It hadn't dawned on me until then that there was no longer anyone in the squadron to ask but me. I was the one in charge. I had always checked everything with Dewey, preferring to let someone else take the gaff if the decision turned out to be wrong. But suddenly it was different, and I wasn't sure I liked it. I knew the rest of the squadron would be just waiting, wondering if I could even make a decision!

I certainly understood. All my life I have never been what you'd call an aggressive person. I don't know why—I never really thought about it from a shrink's standpoint—maybe it had something to do with my older brother, but I really think it was just an overabundance of shyness. I didn't like to call attention to myself. Why make waves if I didn't have to? From an outsider's standpoint, I suppose I was the picture of indecisiveness, and that bothered me a little because I didn't see myself that way. But when I thought about it I could see how that could happen. Actually, I liked not having to make the decisions, as long as they worked. And with my little input once in a while, Dewey's usually did. There was no need for me to make noises about anything.

I have never shied away from accepting responsibility; it's just that I don't seek it. My job, as operations officer, was to help Dewey run his squadron, and that's what I did. We talked about everything and I wasn't about to try to intrude into his area. As close as we had worked together, I had no qualms about being able to take over his job. It was just that it didn't come off that way to others. I had the problem, then, of asserting myself, and letting it become known that I was not just a yes-man follower.

The problem was solved for me, and I had to admit that I was disappointed. It was obvious that Duncan and Rimerman weren't sure enough of me yet, and so they transferred Major Kenneth Gallup, who was a more experienced pilot, in from Group [Headquarters] to take over the squadron. I continued my [squadron] operations job. As it worked out, I ran the squadron from there. Ken was a good looking guy—he looked a lot like someone Hollywood would pick to portray a pilot—and he was a good pilot. It was easy to see why Duncan picked him, but he was a hard person to know, and he seemed to prefer it that way. We hardly saw him except for mission times. He was a friend of Duncan's, and he spent his time with the field grade officers, rather than mingling with the pilots of his squadron. I'm not sure I was right, but I always had the feeling that he was tired and worn out, and the last thing he wanted to be doing was flying missions—so different from our Bill Tanner, for instance, who wanted to fly every mission.

[Major (later Lieutenant Colonel) Kenneth W. Gallup was born in Hope, New Mexico on August 24, 1918. He was a flight school friend of Colonel Duncan's and had served in the Panama Canal Zone at the same time as he did. Blick wrote of him: "He was a little of a mystery to all of us. I never did know him very well, but he was always nice enough and I liked him. He was a loner and didn't really associate with any of us. As I remember, he was built well, about five-nine or -ten, and slim but not skinny—his proportions were good. He had dark hair and fair skin. I always had the impression he was older than the rest of us. He was a good combat pilot—easy to fly with, and never seemed to get upset with anything much—very easy going, just not sociable."[1]]

Before he arrived, I had, of course, been thinking about who I would make my operations officer when I took over the squadron. Logically it should be Tanner, but he just wanted to fly, without all that other responsibility bullshit. I settled on Willy Price.

Willy had proven himself over and over again to be an energetic and aggressive flight leader, and he seemed to get along well with everyone. In the air he was a hawk, but a little contradictory on the ground, wandering around with his hands in his pockets and waddling, toes pointed outward like a relaxed, flat-footed cop pacing his beat. That, combined with his youngish good looks, and eyes that sparkled with dry humor, gave the impression that he didn't care much for Army wherewithal. The brass wondered if he should be in a leadership position, but after

---

1   Blickenstaff to Cross, 1998.

all this time knowing him so well, I knew it was all just a cover, and that he took all his responsibilities seriously and could be trusted completely.

Willy was from Pittsburgh and took a lot of ribbing about it. *No one* ever came from Pittsburgh. He spoke with the clear, clipped, flat accent of the mid-eastern states, which made his humor even more enjoyable, especially to those who were from the more relaxed and laid-back parts of the country. He was about five-eight with dark hair and clear brown eyes.

I had to start using the ex-instructors, and on the next mission I led the squadron with Bledsoe as wingman and Rafferty as number four, and gave Li'l Joe Red Flight with Graham on his wing. I told Gallup what I was doing and he didn't seem to mind. In fact, he didn't seem to care what I did.

Rafferty was a nice guy, and as a pilot verified everything Bledsoe had said. He was about my height, but a little rounder. He looked soft, but I suspected there was a lot more muscle there than appeared. His hair was light brown and thinning, which helped give the impression that he was older and more serious than his years, He settled into the squadron easily.

I told Tanner and Li'l Joe what I was doing—that we needed to break the instructors in as quickly as possible and they agreed.

The mission was to destroy a bridge at Tours, south of the beachhead deep into France. I was a little concerned ... with good reason. The old-timer, Bledsoe, had two missions under his belt, Rafferty the same. It was no way to indoctrinate new pilots!

The success of the mission was questionable. There were bombs all around the bridge and I saw several hits, including one of mine, but it was hard to tell how much damage they did. The flak was intense and we couldn't hang around to wait for the smoke to clear.

As we left the scene, Rafferty called, "Seldom White Leader, this is White Four. I've been hit."

Oh God! He seemed calm enough, I thought, but there was a slight tremor in his voice. "How bad, Vern?"

"It's bad! I think ... I don't know. There's a hole in my canopy and the plane is running a little rough, but I'm okay. I think I'm losing oil."

"That's what's important. ... Pull up in front and I'll take a look."

I eased my plane back behind Rafferty's, then gradually went under and to the other side, looking it over carefully. "You're all banged up, Vern. There are a lot of holes, but nothing that looks vital." I returned to my normal position. "But the whole side of the plane is covered with oil. Let's see how it goes, then we'll take another look at it when we reach the beachhead."

"Okay."

A little later, there was a panic call from a pilot in the 352nd.

"Jockey Leader, Jockey Leader ..." his voice was shrill "... this is Jockey Yellow Four. I'm in trouble!"

"Jones, this is Jockey. What's the trouble?" That was Bill Bailey.

"I've been hit! I'm losing gas, Jockey."

"Where are you?"

"I'm alone."

"Where?"

"I'm at 5,000 feet heading north."

I automatically started to search the sky. Abel Garey, my White Three, called. "Seldom White Three here. There's a plane down there about eleven o'clock, Seldom White."

"I see him. White Two, you go on with the rest of the flight, I'm going down to check."

"Roger."

"Vern, watch your oil. If you don't think you can make it, land on the beachhead."

"Roger, Blick."

The communication between Bailey and Jones continued. Bailey was doing his best to calm him. It helped a little, but Jones was frightened.

I broke in. "Jockey, this is Seldom White. I think we've spotted Jones. I'm going to check."

"Roger, Seldom."

The plane was Jones's.

"Jockey, Seldom here. We have Jones, and we'll stay with him."

"Roger, Seldom, thanks."

I pulled up close, on Jones's right wing. There was a hole in the bottom of the fuselage and liquid pouring out. I was pretty sure it was gas.

"Tom," I said, as calmly as I could. "How's your gas?"

I heard the button go down, and a couple of quick breaths. "It's less than a quarter …" deep breath, "… but going down fast."

"Everything else okay?"

The button again, quickly, but he took a few seconds to breathe. "Yes … I think so. …" The button stayed down, with more quick breathing. "It's running a little rough … it seems okay, though … yes."

"Okay, then, Tom, lean your mixture out and pull the throttle back, as much as you can and still keep your altitude."

"Roger, Seldom."

I could see him working at it and I reset my own throttle.

"Okay, Seldom."

"Okay, we'll stretch it out as far as we can, Tom. It isn't too far to the beachhead. Just stay on this heading. We'll be right here."

"Roger."

The gas continued to pour out and I hoped it looked like more than it really was. We kept going for about four or five minutes, then I asked again, "How's the gas now, Tom?"

"Low … almost empty."

"You're going to make it. We're close. Look up ahead … we can see the water. Start letting down slowly to keep up your speed, and ease up on the throttle again … just a little."

"Roger."

We were down to about 1,000 feet when I saw an airfield. It *had* to be friendly! "There's a field, Tom. Go straight in—not enough gas to go around."

"Roger, Seldom."

I made a call to Rafferty. "Vern, how are you doing?"

"I'm okay, Blick."

"Maybe you'd better land here too."

"I think I'll try for home. The oil pressure has stabilized and the plane seems to be running okay."

"Okay, Vern. It's your call."

As we neared the field, it became clear that it was an RAF emergency strip put down in a hurry. There were several Spitfires scattered around. I learned later that it was probably the only one on the beachhead—there for just such an emergency.

"The runway will be short, Tom. Don't overshoot! Remember, you can't go around."

"Okay, thanks Seldom." He was calmer.

We circled the field, watching Jones. He made a perfect approach. With wheels and flaps down he eased it on to the ground right on the end of the runway.

But then suddenly, and for no apparent reason, the plane exploded into flames!

"Oh my God!" I yelled aloud. Then, without a thought, I dove for the runway. On the radio I blurted out, "I'm gonna go see what happened!"

"Roger, Blick. Good luck."

As I neared the end of the runway I saw that it was as basic as a runway could get—narrow and covered with those metal, lattice-like things they could unroll quickly on any reasonably level surface. Reasonable was the key word—I rode it to the end like I was on a roller coaster. And it was made for the short landing run of Spitfires. I used it all, standing on the brakes the whole way. The initial impulsive reaction quickly gave way to reality, and I wondered why I had landed at all, but even more important, how the hell would I ever get off again!

I taxied up to a makeshift hangar and was met by an English sergeant in a jeep, who saluted, smiling. "He got out, Sir," he said.

"He *did*?" I couldn't believe it. "How? From the air it didn't look like he had a chance!"

"They got to him just in time."

"Is he all right? Can I see him?"

"I don't know how badly he is burned," the sergeant said. "He was taken directly to our hospital. I can take you there and you can see for yourself."

"Good. I'd appreciate it very much." I looked around. "I just can't believe you got him out ... and that he's already in the hospital. You really work fast!"

"We try, Sir. We're used to it, don't you know."

"Yes, I guess so."

The sergeant smiled again. "And it's only a field hospital, not very elaborate."

The ride was only a mile or two, but it gave me a chance to look around. The scenery was not as green as the English countryside. There were some hedgerows but the land was mostly open fields, with few trees. It looked more like home. There was even some dust, and I suddenly realized that was a rarity in England. The few houses we passed were well-worn mortared rock and brick, with interesting shapes of cement outlined with dark wooden beams. Everything showed the stress of the occupation.

The sergeant drove up to a once-white, pock-marked church. Inside, the pews had been removed and replaced with rows of cots, which were mostly occupied. Several nurses were in attendance. I spotted Jones, still in his flight suit, lying on one of the cots at the far end of the room. He smiled when he saw me. "Hi Captain."

I started to put out my hand, but noticed that his were bandaged. "You don't know how good it is to see you, Tom. Are you all right?"

"Yeah, I think so. I have a few burns, but they're not serious."

"What happened out there? I was watching and you were doing fine, then all of a sudden it looked like the plane exploded."

Jones looked puzzled. "That's right. I don't know what happened. I was practically on the runway and finally was able to breathe easy again, when, for no good reason, it caught fire—maybe a spark when I cut back the throttle. I don't know."

I looked around. "Not very luxurious accommodations," I remarked, smiling, and sat down on the bed.

"They're great," Jones said. "I'm just happy I can take advantage of them."

"Yeah ... I guess so." I thought for a minute. "You'll be all right here won't you, until we can get you back?"

"Sure."

"Right now I'm not sure how that'll happen, but we'll get you picked up at some point." I reached into my pocket and handed him my pack of cigarettes. "These won't last long, but they're all I have with me."

"I have some, too. I'll just take it easy." He made a face. "If I have to, I can bum some English ones!"

"I don't envy you that," I said. Then I stood up. "I'm going to go. I should get back. Everyone's going to be wondering about you. Is there anything you want me to tell anyone? Bailey's going to be mighty relieved to hear that you're okay. ..."

"No, Captain. I'll be all right. But thank you for all you've done. I wouldn't have made it without you."

At the field I gave them all the information I could about Jones and thanked them for their remarkable rescue. The same sergeant dropped me off at my plane with a "Good luck, Sir," and a salute.

I taxied out and positioned the plane as close to the end of the runway as I could get. I looked down its length and cringed. *Now let's just see how good you are, Blickenstaff.*

I lowered the flaps all the way, then held the plane with the brakes and pushed the throttle forward. Clouds of dust billowed out behind and the plane began to tremble and bounce around, straining like it knew it was supposed to be in the air and wondering why it wasn't. I held it as long as I could ... then let it go. Suddenly released, it leaped forward and picked up speed, bounding down the runway, up, down, from side to side, like a jackrabbit. On every bump, I thought I might become airborne, but it settled back down each time—no matter how hard I tried to lift it. Then at the very end, when there was no more room, I yanked with all my strength, and it lifted, balancing precariously on the thin line of a stall. It thought it was almost time, just wasn't quite sure. Thank goodness there were no tall trees around, I thought—or even a fence, for that matter!

But I was off okay, and on course, headed for home. It was only then that I allowed myself the luxury of thinking about what had happened—that I had actually walked on French soil. And I was sure I was the first P-47 that had landed on—and taken off from—the beachhead.

As soon as I was within range I called the Raydon tower to tell them I was on my way and to relay the message to Bailey that Jones was okay. I landed only about an hour later than the rest of the group, and was greeted with the good news that Chetwood was back. He had bellied in a couple of miles inside the lines and was not hurt.

There was also news that Edwin Peters was in a RAF hospital south of London with his left leg gone from the knee down. His story was one of incredible courage and determination. When over the Channel, he had bailed out and hit the tail with his leg. Then, with a remarkable presence of mind, he removed his belt and pulled it tight around his leg, making a tourniquet to stop the bleeding. His troubles weren't over, though. In the confusing entry into the water with shoulder straps and tangled parachute lines, he lost his dingy and had to struggle to stay alive for an hour and a quarter before air-sea rescue could get to him.

He said he wanted to come back to the group and run the snack bar!

[With the extended discussion of the June 12 disaster, Blick did not mention that he fired his guns again on June 30. Blick's Encounter Report:

A. Combat
B. 30 June, 1944
C. 350th Fighter Squadron

D. 2125
E. Compiegne, Noyon, Soissons.
F. 8/10 cumulus, visibility 8 to 10 miles
G. Me109
H. 1 Me109 probably destroyed, and 1 Me109 damaged
I. On June 30th, we were to dive bomb a bridge near Romilly on the Seine, and afterwards strafe targets of opportunity. Major Gallup was leading the Squadron and Group, and I had Red flight, consisting of Lts Tuttle, Benjamin, and F/O Yocum. Major Gallup became separated from us when we went down to shoot up a convoy, and we (by this time, I had the rest of the Squadron and a couple of other flights following me) headed northeast looking for him. We saw the truck convoy he had been shooting at and I was about to go down on it when I saw approximately 10 109s about 12 o'clock to us at 5,000 ft. This was south and I believe a little west of Chalons.

Our first attack was a head on pass during which I saw strikes on the one I had singled out. After this first pass at least half must have made a bee line for home because by the time we turned I could only see about 5 e/a. Some, however, were inclined to be fairly aggressive and it took at least two more head on passes before I was able to get on the tail of one. As soon as I started firing, this one split 's'd from about 5,000 ft and then pulled straight into the clouds. I saw strikes as we were going down, and also heavy strikes on the left wing and cockpit just as he entered the clouds.
I claim one Me109 probably destroyed and one Me109 damaged.

1440 Rounds

Wayne K. Blickenstaff
Capt., Air Corps]

[There was a further shocking loss for the squadron that Blick does not mention in his account. On June 28, 1944, First Lieutenant John F. Starr crashed while attempting to land and lost his life. Blick wrote: "The 350th had the best landing pattern of the three squadrons, and we were proud of it. We picked it up from Duncan, of course. We came low over the field (180 degrees from the direction of landing), to the right of the runway, then when we got to the end of the runway, or just a little beyond, we'd cut the throttle, hit the flaps and wheels, and pull up and around 180 degrees in a tight turn, which would slow the airplane to the right speed for landing. The flight leader would, of course, make the tightest and quickest turn—the others following at just a little distance. We'd get on the ground very quickly that way—no dragging it all out. I felt a little responsible for Starr's death, but Doc convinced me I shouldn't feel that way. Our landing pattern had been getting sloppy and I was pressuring them to tighten it up. Unfortunately, Starr tried too hard, extending himself a little beyond what he was capable of doing. He stalled at the top of his turn, rolled over and went straight in just beyond the end of the runway. He … just peeled off too tightly."[2]]

---

2 Blickenstaff to Cross, 1998.

Twenty-four

In July, we flew twenty-nine missions in twenty-three days. Most were bomber escort missions or sweeps. During the latter part of the month, we flew two missions in support of an Allied plan, using the heavy concentration of all available aircraft, to break through the German defenses in the Saint-Lô area. The American armies raced through the broken lines, moving south and then east, around the main bulk of the enemy's strength.
And Glenn Duncan was down!

We were stunned! It just couldn't happen! *But it did!* The bullets finally found his Achilles heel, and there was nothing he, nor anyone, could do about it. He had returned so many times in planes looking like broken sieves, most of us began to think he had some kind of special communication with the big man upstairs.

I had flown on the mission, but I didn't see what happened. I heard it all, however. In fact, the whole group heard, because Dunc, in his usual calm and very clear, distinct voice, gave a running account all the way to the ground, worthy of any commentator on the nightly BBC news.

Afterward, in the briefing, we pieced it all together. It was July 7, and it was a long mission deep into Germany, scheduled for four and a half hours. The target was Leipzig, and our job was to escort the bombers all the way to Steinhuder Lake.

As always, when we left the bombers, Duncan started looking for some action, and spotted a number of planes on an airdrome northeast of the lake. He was flying with the 351st and took them with him. He destroyed an HE111, but north of the field he ran into a screen of intense light flak, and took a hit that severed his oil line. He pulled up with his engine smoking and headed toward home.

We heard, "Jonah here. I've been hit and I'm losing oil," and from that point on, his thumb was on the send button and the airwaves were open. He obviously didn't want the radio busy with all kinds of suggestions and consoling attempts to help—he wanted to do the talking himself. And talk he did. ...

He watched the oil pressure go down to zero. He explained that he was going to wait until the last minute, then find a field and belly it in. He told how "amazing this plane is that it can run for so long with no oil." He calmly talked about how it was blowing cylinders, and we could all hear how rough the engine was running. … And then we heard it stop! The 351st pilots surrounded him, angry that there was nothing for them to do but watch and listen.

On the way down to a tiny field, he told Bailey, who was leading the 352nd, to take care of things until he could return in about three weeks. Then he remarked, "Sure do wish one of you fellas would come down and pick me up so I could fight again!"

The squadron circled the field and watched him make a perfect belly landing—fourteen minutes after he had been hit. They were prepared to shoot anything that moved. Everyone in the group heard the landing, and then, "I'm on the ground!" He climbed out of the cockpit, then reached back in and said, "Goodbye, Fellas, I'll be back in three or four weeks." Then he tossed an incendiary bomb into the plane, jumped down, waved at the planes overhead, and ran into the woods.

The rest of his flight looked for a place to land, thinking they could pick him up, but could find none. They finally went back and shot into the fire, just to help things along, then flew around the area as long as they dared, wanting to give him as much time as possible to get away. Sadly then, they turned toward home.

Glenn Duncan's relationship with our group had been a strange and contradictory one. Originally full of reservations and doubts, we were filled also with an almost unequivocal admiration for him, not only for his uncanny flying ability, but also for his eagerness and determination to seek out and destroy the enemy. It was a slow start, but his reputation had grown throughout the whole European theater to that of an authentic hero.

The following day, Ben Rimerman was appointed group commander, with Bill Bailey as group operations officer. With that announcement, there was a teletype from General Kepner:

FROM COMFICOM EIGHT 08/0920B
TO COMMANDING OFFICER, 353RD FIGHTER GROUP
BT
CONFIDENTIAL 8/FC/29A I DESIRE TO EXPRESS MY VERY GREAT REGRET AT THE TEMPORARY LOSS OF COLONEL GLENN DUNCAN PD HIS SPLENDID HELP ON EVERY MISSION WILL BE MISSED CMA HOWEVER HE HAS LEFT A SPLENDID ORGANIZATION IN THE 353RD FIGHTER GROUP THAT I AM CONFIDENT WILL CARRY ON CMA AS THEY KNOW HE WOULD HAVE PD THE GALLANTRY OF COLONEL DUNCAN WAS WELL SHOWN IN HIS FINAL BRAVE MESSAGE QUOTE I WILL BE BACK IN THREE OR FOUR WEEKS UNQUOTE "NEVER QUITTING" COULD WELL BE THE MOTTO FOR THE ENTIRE VIII FIGHTER COMMAND AND INDEED ALL FIGHTERS OF THE ARMY AIR FORCES EVERYWHERE PD COLONEL DUNCAN'S RECORD TYPIFIES A FIGHTER PILOT'S CREED PD HE WAS OUTSTANDING AS A TWO FISTED FIGHTER LEADER AND A GROUP COMMANDING OFFICER PD

SIGNED KEPNER

"I don't know Doc ..." I said.

Doc looked over at me. "What?"

"I'm ready to finish up and get outta here."

It was seven o'clock in the morning and, after sending the group off on another long escort mission to Munich, we were lounging in the ready room smoking and sipping coffee.

"You tired?" Doc asked, a little too quickly. I had never admitted it before.

I saw his concern. "Now don't get that eager, psychiatrist look in your eye," I said. "I'm not ready for one of your flak homes yet. I'm just talking about a simple leave."

The proper term was rest home. A major part of a flight surgeon's job was to keep a psychological eye on his people—watching for signs of combat fatigue—a mental and emotional weariness brought on by the stress of the missions and the war. The idea, of course, was to catch the symptoms and do something about them before the illness would lead to a pilot's death. There were several old inn-like English homes scattered about, out of the war zone, mostly in the western and southern part of England, where pilots could be sent at a flight surgeon's request. For about a week, usually, a person could enjoy leisure-like living away from anything remotely resembling the war. It was something everyone wanted to do, and the doctors had to be on their toes to be sure a pilot really needed it.

"So?" Doc smiled. "I've never seen anyone yet that knew when he needed to go? What makes you think you're any different?"

"You don't think I do?"

"No."

"That's bullshit and you know it." I took a long drag on my cigarette, and let the smoke drift out. "I'm tired, yeah, but not *that* tired." I hesitated for a long minute, studying the end of my cigarette "Y'know Doc, I really don't know what to do. I'd like to leave, but I can't ... yet. There's nobody left. We're still waiting on Hart, Winder and the others to come back from the States. Price is gone too, now." I stopped again, thinking.

"What about Bledsoe and the other instructors?" Doc asked. "Can't you use them?"

"Yeah, Doc ... but I'm in enough trouble as it is. I've already pushed them ahead of some of our pilots with more combat experience! Guys like Garey and Hargus and Paslay, who have been here longer. Can you imagine what'll happen if I let them start leading flights?"

Doc got up. "You want some more coffee?"

"Yeah. Might as well."

Doc had scrounged, coerced and succeeded in installing a snack bar for the pilots. Somehow, he had convinced the Wheels that we needed it, and managed to find one of his medics that could cook and handle it. It started as an experiment and was an immediate hit. There wasn't much there to start with except little snacks like spam on that extraordinary dark English bread, but as time went on, Mac, the corporal who ran it, became more creative and would sometimes bake tarts and fill them with chocolate pudding or canned fruit, or any other delicacy he could come up with. And of course there were juices and coffee. As always, there were the finicky and unappreciative who spent most of their time bitching about the spam, but that just meant more for those who liked it. In general, though, it was a very popular place, especially after missions and during the long waiting hours.

"I know it's a problem, Blick …" Doc said when they sat back down again, "but your first thought has to be what's best for the squadron."

"I know … but is it good for the squadron to have a bunch of disgruntled pilots?"

"Well now." He sounded like an old-timer twice his age. "You know you can't please everyone, and those guys are here to do a job, regardless of whether they're happy or not, right?"

"Yeah, I suppose." I pulled up a straight-back chair and put my feet up on it. "It would sure be a lot easier if they're happy, though."

Doc knew what the problem really was—I was highly sensitive and overly concerned with people's feelings—and Doc appreciated it, but he also knew that discipline in the service was not based on people's feelings. They were in the middle of a war. "You're right, of course," he said, "but tell me a fact, Blick. Would you rather have the guys think of you as a leader who's strong and decisive, or someone who's wimpy and afraid to hurt a few feelings?"

"Well, of course. When you put it like that …"

I reached into my shirt pocket and pulled out the whole package of cigarettes this time, along with the Zippo. With an expert shake, one cigarette popped up and I offered it to Doc. I took one myself and then lit them both. I knew Doc was right, but it was not an easy thing for me to do. And it was true, I was getting tired. My next mission would be my ninety-sixth, so I suppose I had reason to be. But it really wasn't the flying as much as it was keeping the organization functioning. I was running out of experienced people. I had to start letting Bledsoe and the others lead. Maybe they weren't experienced in combat, but they sure knew the flying.

[Willy Price published his own account of his time with the squadron that was critical of Blick's leadership in advancing the instructors over those with combat experience and emphasizing flying discipline over (as Price saw it) aggression. Blick responded: "It bothered me when I read it, but the more I thought about it I realized it was probably because he, himself, felt more aggressive. He was finally in a position that allowed him to be, and consequently he felt everyone else was too. And some of it may be true—aggressiveness does rub off on people. But he didn't realize what was happening to the squadron. When I returned to the squadron it was in terrible shape, with lack of discipline on the ground and in the air. The formation flying and landing pattern we had always been so proud of had disintegrated. The number of accidents had gone sky high. Right away, I had to start in on a training program again. I don't think it set too well with the younger pilots, but it was necessary.[1]

Fortunately, we didn't see much enemy activity in the latter part of July, and that helped my problem. Also, the weather didn't cooperate much better than it did in the dead of winter, and that helped because it was good training. On the 11th, 12th and 13th we had escort missions to Munich, but saw nothing but friendly planes and clouds. In fact, on the 13th they let everyone get halfway to Munich, far enough in to encounter flak, and then scrubbed the mission.

On the 19th, we flew two groups, A and B. The mission was as escort to Frankfurt. Bailey went out first with A Group and Gallup led our squadron. I decided to take B Group and went out with sixteen planes an hour later. We were with our bombers all the way to the target, and saw all kinds of friends but no enemy aircraft. That mission was my ninety-seventh and the next one would push my hours over the 300-hour tour requirement.

One other bit of news came down through the grapevine—as most news did—that our group would be fully equipped with P-51 Mustangs in a month! We didn't really know if that was good or bad. We loved our huge, safe, lumbering old P-47s, and the parting would not be easy.

I spent the rest of the month repositioning some of the people when I could, giving them a little more responsibility. Chetwood was the only one I had left with enough combat experience to lead the squadron. There were others, though—many excellent pilots with plenty of potential, including the ex-instructors—but it would take time to build the squadron back again. And, I wasn't going to be there. Willy would have to do it … if he'd ever get back. I had to give Chetwood a little rest, so, on the 20th, I scheduled Abel Garey, who had been with us since January, to lead the squadron on an escort mission led by 352's now Captain Poindexter.

The rest of the time I spent wondering why Willy was taking so long!

---

1   Blickenstaff to Cross, 1998. See William J. Price, *Close Calls—Two Tours with the 350th Squadron, 353rd Fighter Group, Eighth Air Force, in WWII*, Usk, Aviation Usk, 1992, pp. 57, 69 and 97. For an extended discussion of the controversy within the 350th at this time see Cross, *Jonah's Feet*, pp. 279–281.

Twenty-five

In August, the Allied forces swept across France, liberating Paris and sending large German forces fleeing to the northeast. The 353rd flew thirty-nine missions. Twenty-five were bombing and strafing missions aimed at the enemy's transportation system. We destroyed 240 locomotives and over 700 rail cars along with numerous other essential targets. In addition, we destroyed 83 German aircraft on the ground and 29 in the air, and 17 pilots and planes were lost.

At long last, on August 4, Hart, Winder and Willy Price finally made it back, looking good and well rested. Also on that day, the group had some air-to-air action again.

Gallup led the group with our squadron on an escort mission to Hamburg, and they were bounced by about thirty-plus 109s from above. In a fierce battle, Gallup shot down two and his wingman, Olger Aal, downed one. But Denny Yocum, flying Gallup's second element, was shot down by another bunch of 109s coming in from three o'clock. Middleton, who was leading Red Flight, also was credited with one, along with Thomas Creekmur, who ran one of the 109s into the ground without firing a shot. Following in Duncan's footsteps, Gallup was all shot up and barely made it back. The final score was twelve destroyed, which was a record for the group at that point.

It was always hard on us to lose people, but we had grown used to it and were able to file people away in the depths of our minds, away from the reality of the moment, so we could stay hardened enough to go on and do what we were there to do. The loss of Denny Yocum, however, was especially hard on all of us. He was young—just a kid. Not that the rest of us were much older, but he was so typically a kid, living and reacting with his emotions rather than his head. Bledsoe, who was older than the rest of us, couldn't help feeling like a father. Technically, Yocum was a very good pilot, but a little off the wall emotionally. He had a hatred for the Germans not unlike Duncan's, but it was not contained, and he didn't seem to know why. He came off as being something that he thought he was supposed to be rather than being real. He was eager, tremendously aggressive, and seemingly unafraid of anything, almost as if he wanted to die in order to prove something to the world.

Now that I'm older, I realize how typically teenage Yocum was. He was given a uniform, placed in an unusual, elite kind of position, and suddenly his life became more symbolic than real. In reality, the job was an adult job. Physically he was ready, but his mind hadn't matured yet. We see it happening all around us, especially in times of war, and it is tragic.

With Willy back and ready to take over, I scheduled myself for my last mission, on August 7. It was a dive-bombing and strafing mission in the Amiens area of France. It was considered successful, with many targets of opportunity wiped out, including Bledsoe's four aircraft destroyed on the ground and my locomotive. I was happy I made it through the mission!

The next day brought another tough blow for the squadron, and especially for me. Bob Hart was strafing an oil truck. As he flew over it, the truck exploded, knocking him over on his back and he went straight in. In my desperate need for experienced pilots, I had talked him into coming back … to his death! It was his first mission since his return. At that point, I didn't really know how much more I could take.

[Blick said of Hart: "He was one of those really nice guys—tall, conservative, staid—and an excellent pilot. He was one of those pilots you couldn't lose even if you tried, when he was flying your wing. His death hit me hard because I felt I had a lot to do with his return for a second tour."[1]]

However, on August 10, I left for home with Lieutenant Colonel Bill Bailey, who had also just finished. While we were still in England, or Ireland, I don't remember where exactly, waiting for our flight, we heard that the orders for my promotion had come through. So Bailey pinned on my leaves and I went on home as a major.[2]

It was a long journey, and it was a long time ago, so long ago that my memory has faded almost to the point of being nothing at all. I do remember, however, that we flew in a four-engine military transport plane—designated a C-54, I believe. We took the northern route, refueling at bases in Iceland and Greenland. I also remember feeling a little queasy in the stomach some of the time, like I might get airsick, a feeling I had never had before. The reason, I thought, was the change of perspective. Rather than looking out the front and concentrating on flying, we sat in bucket seats along the sides of the plane and faced inward. Without windows, there was no way to orient myself and the normal movement of the airplane didn't set too well with my innards.

I'm not sure where we landed in the States—it could have been Bangor, Maine—but somewhere I rode a troop train, and I remember it as not being very

---

1 Blickenstaff to Cross, 1998.
2 Blick's promotion to major was effective on August 9, 1944; 350th FS Records, AFHRA, Maxwell, Alabama. A photograph taken at the time shows Blick was still at Raydon.

pleasant. I had the orders to ride it all the way to California, but instead I hopped off at the first opportunity and flew home on a regular civilian airline.

The homecoming was, of course, very special and very enjoyable. Truthfully, it was coming in out of the cold, and the first thing I did was to get rid of my heavy clothes. It didn't take long to feel once again like a Californian. I've never been one to rush around on a vacation trying to see and do everything. I've always felt like that sort of thing makes the time go faster, and when I'm having a good time I want to slow it down, and enjoy it, so that's mainly what I did. Ralph, my brother and my exact opposite, couldn't understand that. He was all set to keep me going every minute, until I borrowed his car and went off by myself.

I've mentioned before that two of my good school friends were pilots: Howard Galbreath, who was in the Ninth Air Force, and Richard Wright, who was in the Navy, and they had both been home on leave at different times, along with quite a few others my age. So it wasn't as if I was unusual, a lone hero of some kind returning from the war. People were wonderful to me, but I was not all that exceptional, and I was happy about that.

My brother was four years my senior and hadn't yet been drafted. He and his wife were living in our old house in Chino and he was a member of the Chino Volunteer Fire Department. He took me to a meeting one night and it went all right, meaning I didn't have to make a speech. I didn't mind answering questions—that was easy. A veteran of World War I who I had known all of my life, needed to tell us all about his wartime experiences, and that helped take the emphasis off me.

And then there was Charlie Wallace, my father's good friend, who was the Chino jeweler. I knew him very well, and he wanted to take me to lunch at the local Rotary club. Well, I couldn't very well refuse, but I was not at all eager. He said they would ask me to say a few words, and offered to help me with them. Foolishly I refused, thinking that it was not going to be all that hard. And of course I couldn't have been more wrong—it was pure disaster. However, thank goodness I was not supposed to be a speaker, and if they didn't know it before, they found out in a hurry. Other than that, the lunch was good.

I borrowed Ralph's car when he didn't need it, to ride around and visit all of my old hangouts in Chino and Pomona, and especially in Los Angeles. Most of the people I knew were in the military but a very good friend in LA, Don Leeper, was 4F because of a punctured ear drum, and I looked him up right away.

Don had a girlfriend living in an apartment in West LA with two other girls, not necessarily Rosie the Riveter types, but all working for the war effort, which most people did in those days. His girlfriend was named Betty, and so was one of the others, whose last name was Evans. The third girl was Avenell, but she seemed to be busy elsewhere most of the time.

We double dated with the two Bettys several times, and we got along very well together, all of us. With all the girl talk I had been subjected to in the last two or three years I thought I might have finally found a girl I could consider a girlfriend. It was one of those romantic things—we were at war and we were each at that age when we thought it was time to have a real relationship. When my leave had ended and it was time to go, there was a mutual feeling that we would continue the relationship through letters and see what happened.

Leaving was not one of my happier times. I wasn't prepared for the flow of tears, expected as it was. My mother and I went to visit my aunt, who was also one of my mother's best friends, and the storm let loose. Evidently she had been worried about me the whole time I was in England, and had been so relieved to see me home. But then to think I was going back again was more than she could cope with.

It takes something like that to break through the crust of a hardened and thoughtless mind. With the exception of my mother, I never really thought much about others who knew me and might worry. I, of course, knew that nothing would happen to me. Their fears were real, however, and they were not spared the news—they knew all about the dead and wounded.

Twenty-six

Range was a continuing problem. The P-51 Mustang Fighter Groups, the 339th, 355th, and 357th along with the 4th Group, which had been switched over, had proven the Mustang's worth as a combat airplane. With only six 50-caliber guns, it lacked the firepower of the Thunderbolt, but more than made up for it in range. The Mustang, carrying two 108-gallon wing tanks, allowed the pilots to penetrate as far as Berlin, fly around for a half-hour, and return safely.

As the Germans pulled their combat zones back, the Eighth Fighter Command deemed it necessary to stretch its coverage, and started the slow process of converting all of the P-47 groups to P-51s—all but one. Because of the 56th Group's brilliant record, Fighter Command bowed to their wishes and allowed them to keep their beloved Thunderbolts.

My orders were to go to Atlantic City and await transportation back to England. While there, I was to be given thorough physical and psychological examinations to make sure I was ready to go back into combat. There were a few others there from the 353rd and several from a couple of other groups, but, except for Jim Poindexter from the 352nd, I don't remember who the others were.

We were given rooms in one of the luxury hotels along the boardwalk. I wasn't sure if it was because I wore the gold leaves of a major or not, but I had a fine, clean room by myself with all of the lavish amenities. Every evening they prepared a large, buffet-style table full of food, and as a creative gesture for us, a masterfully carved centerpiece of an eagle sculpted in ice. We were treated as royalty and we made the most of it, knowing it wouldn't last long. Other than seeing the doctors, there wasn't much for us to do, but eat and drink … and wait.

My first appointment was with the psychologist, and it went something like this:
The sign on the door read MAJOR ERIK SCHWARZ. Conditioned by Hollywood I had pictured a small, heavyset man with thick, rimless glasses and disappearing hair combed sideways, but the man who said, "Come in Wayne. Good to see you," without a trace of an accent, in no way resembled my preconceived image. He looked to be about thirty—tall, thin and neatly dressed in his uniform,

which carried the medical caduceus on each lapel. He motioned me to the one, lonely chair in front of the desk and I sat down while he continued to read what I assumed were my records.

"Be right with you," he said.

He may have been only trying to relax me, but he succeeded very nicely in making me even more nervous by continuing to read in silence. I was sure a hidden camera was filming my every reaction, so I made sure my movements were even slower and more controlled than normal. I thought of trying to outwit him by moving the chair out of camera range, but resisted the temptation—*better to play the game his way!*

The room was simple, almost stark. A desk, two chairs, a bookcase filled with formidable-looking volumes, two sickly-looking plants of a genus I didn't recognize, and a framed diploma on the wall that I couldn't read except for the hand-lettered word "Psychology." There was no couch.

About the time I thought I should get up and come in again, he set aside what I saw was only a magazine with a partly nude girl on the cover, and picked up the top folder on his desk. After glancing at it for about three seconds, he said finally, "Well, I see you've got quite a record here, almost a hundred missions."

I nodded, but it didn't matter; I was nodding only to myself. He didn't bother to look up.

"How do you feel about that?" he asked.

How do I feel about that? What the hell was that supposed to mean? Was I supposed to say I'm happy? ... sad? ... terrified? ... a hero? Maybe if I just ignored the question he'd forget it. ...

He put down the folder and stared right at me—obviously his best act.

Not being trained in the art of intimidation, I lowered my eyes and started mumbling. "Well," I said even slower than usual, "It seems to me that I've—"

"Just as I thought," he interrupted. "Don't like to talk about it, eh? Don't blame you." He smiled. "Tell me, what are the girls like over there?"

He was still staring. I began to concentrate on his eyes to see if he ever blinked. "There are ... a—" I started, but he cut me off again.

"When do you masturbate?" he asked.

WHAT! Not do you, but when? My God, what was I supposed to do with that?

"Well ... I suppose you might say—"

"Good," he said, still not blinking. "Now tell me about your mother."

MY MOTHER! Oh please! For God's sake, not that! Now he's going to blame everything I do on my mother. He probably blames the whole goddam war on Hitler's mother!

"Well ..." I started slowly ... "I really don't see—"

"Right," he said, still staring. His eyes began to turn glassy—heavy concentration on something other than my psychological wellness, probably the girly magazine. I began thinking that I should be the one sitting behind the desk and he should be sitting in the chair. The conclusions on the record would be somewhat different.

He finally lowered his eyes and started writing. "How do you feel about going back," he asked. "Do you want to?"

"No ... I—"

"Who the hell would," he remarked, and smiled as he continued to write. "Well, thanks very much Wayne," he said finally, and stood up to offer his hand. "You seem pretty normal to me."

Obviously the interview was over. As I turned to leave I saw him sit down and reach for the magazine.

I had mixed feelings about the physical examination the following day. I had always been a little bit of a health nut and I for sure didn't want the doctor to find anything wrong with me, anything big, that is, like a heart condition or leukemia or something like that, but on the other hand, it would be nice to have an excuse not to go back.

While swept up in the excitement of danger, common perils and wartime camaraderie, it was easy to say I'd take my leave and come back for a second tour. The reality of it, though, was a little more difficult. After several weeks in the States, with the memories of the dark, dreary days and all of the tensions fading away, I wondered why I had made such a stupid decision. The idea of going back to all of that again turned out to be one of the hardest things I've ever had to face. It didn't make it any easier either to spend our waiting time in one of Atlantic City's finest hotels.

We all felt the same way, and the big thing was to try to outwit the doctors so they would make a pronouncement of unfit for further combat, either physically or mentally it didn't matter! The favorite drink at the time was rum and Coca-Cola, and a few people discovered that if they drank enough they couldn't pass the physical because of too much sugar in the urine.

But I was too afraid, or too shy, or maybe just too honest or something, to try anything like that, so I went to my appointment with the attitude of whatever will be, will be.

The uniformed nurse took me into an all-white, sterile-looking room and handed me a bottle. She pointed to another room, which I assumed was a bathroom. "You can fill this up in there while you are waiting on the doctor."

"But I just—"

"That's okay," she said, "It doesn't have to be full."

Well, as happens sometimes, I stood there for what seemed like five minutes before it started. And then, of course, the bottle was so small it filled immediately and I had to cut it off and try to keep from dribbling while transferring the whole operation to the john.

When the nurse came back I handed her the bottle and she held it up and smiled. "See ..." she said. She opened another door. "Now you can go in there and strip to the waist. The doctor will be here shortly." I went in and she closed the door after me. I took my shirt off, and sat on the edge of the examining table and waited for the doctor. It was not the doctor who came, however, it was another nurse with blood pressure equipment. She made no comment—no hello, no smile—just went right to work. After sticking a thermometer in my mouth, and making sure it was under my tongue, she took my blood pressure and wrote the results down on a pad. I struggled to see what she wrote, but couldn't. She was very adept at hiding it. Then she searched for my pulse and finally found it, checking it with her watch. Normally I can feel my heartbeat increase with nervousness, but this time, when it might have been to my advantage, the beat even seemed slower than normal! She recorded that information also, and with still no smile or comment, left.

The doctor came in smiling, and shook my hand. "I'm Doctor Josephs," he said. He was older, with a full head of gray hair, a little unruly, as if he had been scratching his head. His body was thin, and with his generous growth of hair he looked a little top-heavy. At least he was congenial.

"Going back overseas again, are you?" he enquired as he listened to my chest with his stethoscope.

I answered "yes," but it wasn't really a question. He then asked how I felt, still listening to my chest, and I began to wonder if he heard something unusual.

"Fine," I said.

"Good. You can get dressed now."

"That's it?"

"Yes," he nodded. "You can leave now."

"If anything comes up we'll let you know," he added.

I didn't hear of anyone that wasn't okay to return. The doctors were not stupid and they were very much aware of the tricks the pilots tried. With the people who attempted the sugar-in-the-urine approach, the doctor just said, "Lay off the booze for a couple of days and then come back."

The nervous twitch or meaningless blather didn't work with the psychologist either. And it was understandable. We were trained to fight Germans, not doctors.

My trip back to England was reminiscent of the first one. But only in the sense that we were once again on the *Queen Mary*. It was a very different trip as a major. I was in a stateroom with only three others—all majors.

Twenty-seven

On October 2, the 353rd Group started operations with the new P-51 Mustangs. In combination with forty-two P-47s, Colonel Ben Rimerman took twelve P-51s on an escort mission to Koblenz. The first complete Mustang mission was flown the following day and the gradual changeover continued throughout the month.

The Luftwaffe changed its strategy somewhat by concentrating on one bomber group at a time with a massive head-on attack using 100 or more fighters—a hit and run operation that left tremendous destruction in its wake and little opportunity for our fighter groups to do their job of protection.

Twenty-three missions were flown by our group on seventeen days, twenty-one of them escort. Six P-51s were lost, mostly because of problems with the new airplanes; one because of a leaky oil line; two because of loss of coolant; one lost its propeller; one was shot down by our own B-24s after letting down right into them because of no oxygen; and one for unknown reasons.

Strafing claims were high, but there was only one air-to-air claim for the month. That victory, however, was significant because it was the second ME262, the German jet, to be downed by the Eighth Air Force.[1] Although the jet was a new, major weapon, the Germans couldn't produce them fast enough to stop the onslaught of the American bombers. They also used so much fuel their usefulness in the air was cut short.

Back again in cold, damp and sunless England, I found my return to be even tougher than I had imagined. Somehow I needed to get the adrenaline flowing again, and channeled in the right direction. It was not so simple. It had been straightforward enough to get my mind back into the civilian mode, but not so the other way around. Too easy to remember all of those things I had found so easy to forget. I couldn't help feeling I had never been away.

---

1   Blick is referring to First Lieutenant Carl Mueller's victory on October 6, 1944. Mueller did not submit a claim so was not awarded the credit. There is strong evidence to suggest that his was the first successful "whole" victory by the Eighth Air Force against the Me262. See Cross, *Slybirds*, p. 198.

The group had acquired twenty-one new pilots—eight for the 350th Squadron. It wasn't enough—it was never enough! Casualties, resulting from all of the train busting and airdrome strafing, were high. Four pilots had been killed, seven were missing, and many had returned shot up and then hospitalized or NYR (not yet returned). The result: the number of available pilots was not much different than when I left—only the names had changed.

As expected, I returned as CO of the 350th, with Willy Price as my operations officer. I was really upset because Bledsoe was gone, and because Willy had ignored my request that he should not fly him so much. I had been counting on him for help when I returned. But he was long gone—he must have flown every mission! I had to admit to myself, though, that I was happy for him. He made it through his tour and was on his way home to his wife and small daughter, whose name "Little Princess" he had painted on his plane.[2]

I arrived on October 21. On the 24th the group flew its second mission since my return and we lost two more pilots from our squadron. On the 25th, a pilot in the 351st was shot down by our own bombers.[3] Combined with the fact that Rafferty was finishing his tour, the problem of losses and lack of available experienced pilots made it urgent that I become operational again as soon as possible. I did, however, talk Rafferty into hanging around for another couple of weeks. We were supposed to be getting another bunch of replacements and I wanted him to be in charge of their training.[4]

My mind had been so completely detached from anything related to flying, I felt the need to adjust backward, back to the feel of the air again. We still had a P-47 on the field and I took it up for an hour or so. And it didn't take long—once in the air, the thrill rushed back and I was a bird again.[5]

The next day I started my transition to the Mustang. As usual with all of my new experiences, I had minor anxieties on take-off, but once airborne, they smoothed over quickly.

The plane was a dream to fly—highly responsive to the controls, fast and extremely maneuverable. Being used to the P-47, which had been designed as a high-altitude fighter, I was surprised and delighted to discover the P-51 was equally good at altitude. It's in-line, liquid-cooled engine was noisy, though, which made it seem more vulnerable and less dependable than the P-47's beautiful purring air-cooled, radial

---

2   Marvin Bledsoe completed his tour of 270 hours with his last mission flown October 3, 1944. James O. Ruscitto, who joined the squadron with him, was brought down by flak on September 18, 1944, and evaded back to the UK.

3   Losses on October 24, 1944, were Captain Carl W. Mueller, who hit wires while strafing and became a POW, and First Lieutenant Robert W. Hedler, killed in action by flak. Second Lieutenant Bernard J. French of the 351st was killed in action on October 25, 1944.

4   The other pilot from the group of instructors, Captain Vernon G. Rafferty, completed his tour on October 26, 1944.

5   Blick's logbook confirms he took a P-47 up for forty-five minutes on October 25, 1944.

engine. I knew, however, that it was only a matter of getting used to the different sound. To me, the comparison was like the difference between a Ford and a Cadillac.

The P-47 was *safe!* For over a year I had watched it return home, still able to fly with incredible battle damage, and I liked that—of course I liked that! I still had a touch of those butterflies down there in my stomach before every mission, and I wondered about the P-51. Was it dependable? With its liquid-cooled engine, all it would take would be one bullet in that coolant line.

I was pleased, though. After taking it through every maneuver I could think of, I came to the conclusion that the advantages probably offset the disadvantages. The loss of firepower didn't bother me. A hit (or miss) with six guns instead of eight probably wouldn't make much difference.

On the 27th my new plane was ready. This time I was not at all creative, and named it *The Betty E,* after my new-found girlfriend. At the time it seemed to be the thing to do, but it was a mistake. The relationship ended, and even after all of these years the name is still there, haunting me, following me around like an unwanted tattoo.[6]

In the evening of the 27th I received a call I laughed at, thinking it was some kind of a joke. I went along with it for a bit, but soon realized it was, in fact, for real. It was from John Balason, who had arrived with eleven other new replacements for our squadron: Agnew, Caton, Cowen, Duke, Dyer, Elkins, Jung, Miller, Orzelek, Prescott and Robison.[7] Well … it was about time! But Balason …?

Out walked Bledsoe and in walked Balason! It wasn't quite the same, though, for sure. I knew Balason to be an excellent pilot, but the life here was different. Sometimes just being a good pilot was not good enough. It had been a long time since I had seen him and I didn't know where he had been all that time. I had hopes that he had learned to make use of his head a little better. He was still a second lieutenant, though, and that was a bad sign.

He was at the officers' club and I rushed over to see him. He was immediately apologetic when he saw my leaves, and with a sheepish grin said, "They didn't like it up there much when I got bored from lack of excitement and buzzed the field upside down!"

I smiled. "That figures. Up there … where?"

"The Aleutians."

"The Aleutians! I thought you went to Africa!"

"I did … but came back."

That did it. I needed to hear the whole story, so I bought him a drink and we sat down at one of the tables.

---

6 Blick's logbook confirms he received "MY NEW U" on October 27, 1944. Between October 26 and November 2, 1944, he logged ten hours' P-51 transition time before going operational.

7 These were part of a replacement influx of thirty-one pilots received by the group on October 25, 1944.

He explained that after Rimerman caught him in the Link at Baltimore, he was shipped off with Baer and a few others to ferry P-40s to Africa. They were sent first to Langley Field where they practiced short take-offs, and then they were jammed on to an aircraft carrier for the long ride overseas. In true Army fashion, when it came time to take off the carrier, they couldn't find Balason's name on the list. And of course, no one knew what to do with him so he stayed on board and made the long trip back. Eventually he was reassigned to a tour of duty in the Aleutians.

"What about Baer?" I asked.

"He took off. I've never heard from him, so I have no idea where he is."

Even though I recognized that Balason was not the brightest about rules and regulations, I knew what kind of pilot he was and I was happy to have him. I was thankful I had another pilot whose flying ability was not open to question. There was the worry, of course, about his stability, in the sense of deferring to our experience and heeding our orders. It was not the Aleutians any longer—he had joined the big league.

A few days later I had a visit from Rimerman. It didn't surprise me. I had been anticipating it because I knew he'd never forget the Baltimore episode. I was sure he would always consider Balason some kind of a fuck-up, and if our need for replacements hadn't been so crucial, he probably would have refused to take him. And it didn't help a bit that Balason was still a second lieutenant. I wasn't about to tell him, either, about the buzzing in the Aleutians. I just made up a story that promotions hadn't been available.

"How's Balason doing?" he asked.

I didn't know what he expected to hear, but I said, "Okay. He has flown one mission and aborted."[8]

"That doesn't sound too good to me."

"I know ... but the abort was legitimate. I checked the plane. The oxygen wasn't working. I thought he played it smart not to try to go on." When Rimerman didn't reply I continued. "He's a good pilot, Ben, and he's eager. But, as I said before, he's got to realize this is a lot different than what he's used to, and a lot depends on his ability to think and follow orders. I'm hopeful that he'll eventually come to the conclusion that he can't win the war alone."

"If you say so," Rimerman grinned.

My first mission after returning was escort to a small target between Haasburg and Berlin.[9] I wanted to get used to the plane, so I took Red Flight with Willy leading the squadron. I was shocked when I walked into the briefing room and saw the mission stretched out on the map. The string looked about twice as long as what I

---

8   Balason flew his first mission on November 2, 1944, and returned early for unknown reasons (he was given 1:30 operational hours, but no sortie credit).
9   Blick led Red Flight on November 4, 1944, giving withdrawal support to 2nd Division B-24s attacking Misburg (Field Order 1286A).

remembered. I was already a little jumpy, and that didn't help any. It was one thing to go to Berlin and back again, in and out on a relatively straight line, but quite another to escort the bombers in, watch the bombing, and then escort them back.

There were over 400 fighters for 300 bombers. That was unusual—an indication that intelligence was expecting a large turnout of German fighters. We didn't see any, though, except for a few contrails high above us from the German jets. But that was a scary sight. Scary because we were flying at 30,000 feet, and those contrails were at least 10,000 feet above us. It was a new, and unknown, threat. So far four jets had been shot down, but they were destroyed only because of some lucky incident.

The Germans could sit up there waiting, out of reach, then dive down through a formation of bombers at a speed unheard of before, take a bomber with them, and then zoom right back up to safety. There seemed to be nothing our fighters could do about it—no one had yet been able to come up with a tactic to combat that maneuver. Intelligence had very little to go on. All they knew was that the jets had no range. They consumed so much fuel their air time was limited to one or two passes. But that fact didn't ease the tension for the bomber crews.

Fortunately, the jets were scarce.

However, once again I was impressed with the P-51s performance, and any doubts I had disappeared along with my churning stomach. One thing was not so good, though. I was used to the P-47's warm, comfortable cockpit, and the P-51's was anything but. Not only was it smaller, it was cold—*really cold!* I hadn't had such a cold ride since I started flying. How in the hell, I thought, could such brilliant designers work out everything so carefully with such a wonderful, beautiful airplane yet forget something so basic as the pilot's warmth?

It was my 100th mission and longest to date. I logged five hours, with a new determination to do two things—dress warmly and build up the calluses on my butt.

Rafferty had been doing a good job with the new replacements. I filled him in on Balason—how we had been together all the way to Baltimore, and what had happened there. I told him, too, that I'd like to get him started flying missions soon. He confirmed what I had told him already about Balason's flying ability, and said he thought he'd be okay to go now.

"You know him better than anyone, Blick," he said. "You'll have to be the judge when it comes to combat."

"Yeah, I know. And that's the tricky part. We'll just have to see how he uses his head."

[The mission for November 16] was target and withdrawal escort from Aachen, in the general direction of Koblenz and Frankfurt. I cornered Balason after the briefing. "You saw where you are flying today?"

Balason nodded, with that familiar, partial, complacent, Mona Lisa-like smile that was always so hard to read. I was never quite sure if he was really smiling or just embarrassed. There was always that feeling that he was just pretending to listen so everyone would be happy, but planning all along to do his own thing with the intention of showing everyone how good he was.

"Now listen John," I said. "Try to concentrate on what you're doing, and don't do anything stupid. [Your leader is] a great guy to fly with—you'll see. He's probably the smoothest pilot you'll ever know.[10] I've told him how well you fly, so just stick with him. The main thing is to just keep your head out of your ass and you'll be okay. He likes close formation, but not so close you start wobbling his wing around. You don't have to show off how close you can get … just be steady. He wants to be able to trim his ship and leave it alone to make it easy for the rest of the group. Okay?"

Again, the nod.

"Okay … have fun." I turned up my collar and stepped outside to watch the take-off. The weather was lousy, but … so what else was new!

The planes were already on the move out to the runway. Although not new anymore, it was still a stirring sight—all three squadrons going forth to do battle.

[Balason's leader] had the green light and started down the runway. Balason was in perfect position, as I knew he would be. But they looked a little slow. [The leader] must be taking it easy because of Balason, I thought.

What *was* he doing? I felt a knife slice into my belly—a rush of nerves. *He's using too much runway … if he doesn't haul back soon, they'll both be in the trees!*

There he goes … finally! And oh my God, there goes Balason … shooting right by him, up into the clouds! What the hell is he doing! "Oh shit!" I said aloud. What now? Damn stupid fool! Balason's deep in it now! … And I am too!

As the next element took off, [the leader] made a tight turn under the overcast and dropped his wheels again. He's coming back, I thought. Now he's got an airplane to complain about as well as a lousy wingman!

The pilot sandwiched himself in between elements and landed. When he was out of the way, the rest of the group took off and disappeared into the mist. I drove out to meet him as he pulled into the revetment.

"I couldn't get any power," he said. "Damn near augured us both in!" He sort of humped his shoulders a little and grinned, embarrassed. "I finally managed to wave Balason on. He was sticking in there like I was flypaper. I thought I'd never get rid of him. He must have thought I was some idiot of a pilot!"

I smiled inwardly. All that worry about how Balason would perform, and the pilot was worried about what Balason thought of *him*!

The weather was still bad when the group returned. Doc was there, as usual, sweating everyone out. When the flights emerged from the crud, intact, it was obvious they hadn't run into any noteworthy opposition.

---

10 Records are possibly inaccurate for the mission of November 16, 1944. They list Balason as a flight leader (impossible for a pilot flying his fifth mission unless Blick was trying him out as an experienced pilot). The flight that day had two experienced pilots, Ferrell and Schilt (both of whom logged over five hours). Balason logged 4:30 hours.

Wayne K. Blickenstaff was born in Pomona, California, to Perry H. and Hazel L. Blickenstaff on June 25, 1920. Blick's father was a practicing veterinarian in the Chino district. The photo shows Blick with his parents and his older brother Ralph L. Blickenstaff, born in 1916. Sadly, the family would be met with tragedy when Perry died at the young age of forty-three in 1936. (Perry Blickenstaff)

Blick on his graduation day from Pomona High School in 1938. (Perry Blickenstaff)

While at high school, Blick, his brother Ralph and another gymnast formed a three-man balancing team. Blick maintained his agility well into later life and could still walk downstairs on his hands in his early fifties. (Perry Blickenstaff)

Blick as a newly minted "Mister" or aviation cadet at Thunderbird Field, Glendale, Arizona. He conducted his primary training here from February to April 1942. (Perry Blickenstaff)

Blick's young age is fully apparent in this photo taken during his basic training. He graduated as a pilot and second lieutenant in Class 42-H on August 27, 1942, aged twenty-two. (Perry Blickenstaff)

After graduation as a fully fledged pilot in 1942, Blick took the opportunity to visit his mother, Hazel, before his military duties took him overseas. (Perry Blickenstaff)

Some of the original members of C Flight of the 350th Fighter Squadron, likely at Baltimore prior to overseas movement. Left to right are Second Lieutenant Dwight A. Fry, Second Lieutenant Francis T. Walsh, First Lieutenant Wayne K. Blickenstaff, First Lieutenant William W. Odom, First Lieutenant Dewey E. Newhart and First Lieutenant Tom Lorance. (Cross)

Mrs Marge Walsh was snapped with Dewey Newhart, the leader of C Flight, and who looks to have caught too much sun on a squadron trip to the beach. Blick knew Marge Walsh well and had the difficult task of writing a letter to the young mother when her husband was lost on June 7, 1944. (Cross)

The legendary commander of the 353rd Fighter Group, Colonel Glenn E. Duncan. Blick initially struggled to understand his aggressiveness and apparent "recklessness" on missions but later came to appreciate his leadership. (Cross)

An early shot of Blick in the cockpit of a P-47 Thunderbolt (not his), taken as part of a series of public relations photos while the group was based at Goxhill in the county of Lincolnshire, England. (Cross)

Top: Letters to and from home were vital for morale. Here Blick snatches the chance to write some letters home to family while at Goxhill in the summer of 1943. (Canipelli)

Left: In the summer of 1943, the Eighth Fighter Command ordered Thunderbolt pilots not to fly lower than 18,000 feet while on bomber escort missions over Europe because of the relatively poor performance of the aircraft at lower altitudes. Blick used his artistic talents at Metfield to illustrate the dangers of being "sucked down", but a visiting commander told him to remove it for fear it would undermine overall confidence in the aircraft. (Canipelli)

An atmospheric shot taken during a final "pep" talk in the 350th 'Ready Room' in late summer 1943. The tension in the faces is evident. Left to right (facing camera) are Second Lieutenant Robert N. Ireland, First Lieutenant Wayne K. Blickenstaff, Major Ben Rimerman (giving the briefing) and First Lieutenant Edward M. Rosentreter (350th intelligence officer). (Cross)

Some of C Flight of the 350th heading out to the planes after briefing at Metfield, 1943. Left to right are First Lieutenant William W. "Dub" Odom, First Lieutenant Wayne K. Blickenstaff, Second Lieutenant Francis T. Walsh, First Lieutenant Tom "Pinky" Lorance with Second Lieutenant Walter L. Angelo and Captain Dewey E. Newhart seated on the hood of the Dodge command car. (Cross)

The vital work of the ground crews kept the pilots and planes in the air. In front of First Lieutenant Dewey E. Newhart's plane *Mud 'n Mules* at Metfield are (left to right) Newhart, his crew chief Staff Sergeant Layton E. Baker, Staff Sergeant George Davis, Staff Sergeant Samuel S. Woods, Staff Sergeant Edmund N. Nelson, and two unknowns. (Cross)

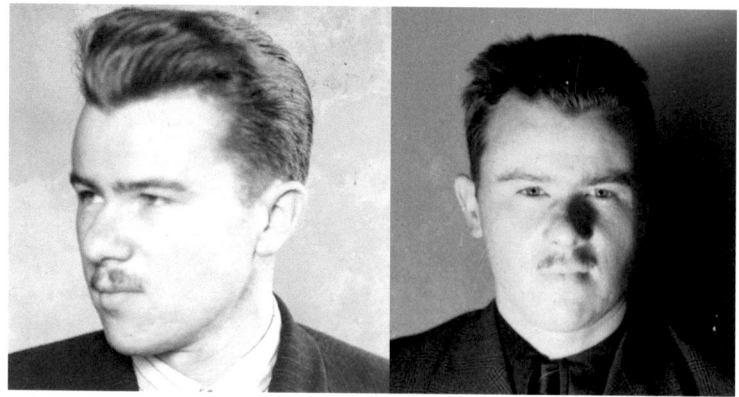

Blick wore civilian clothes for these "escape and evasion photos" taken at Metfield. The idea was that the photos could be passed to members of the Resistance, should the pilot be brought down in enemy territory, and used for forged documents to help with their evasion back to the United Kingdom. (Cross)

A photo showing damage to Blick's second Thunderbolt (P-47D-2-RE LH-U 42-7988) on November 3, 1943. The incident remains a mystery as no records could be found to detail the event. Blick was not flying the mission that day. (Cross)

Blick's third Thunderbolt hit trouble on December 1, 1943 (not December 4 as recorded on the photo) when German flak found its target. The rugged Thunderbolt got Blick back to Metfield, but he recorded in his understated diary entry that there was "a hole the size of a watermelon in the bottom of the plane. Flak seems to be pretty good!!" (Cross)

Photos of the ladies Blick painted on the port and starboard sides of his third Thunderbolt (P-47D-6-RE LH-U 42-74647). Blick used his artistic talent to decorate his aircraft until the regular loss of his aircraft made it difficult to continue. (Cross/Canipelli)

C Flight member First Lieutenant William W. "Dub" Odom was from Ashburn, Georgia. Dub was lost to enemy fighters on December 30, 1943, on his thirty-fifth mission. (Cross)

Blick's first wingman, First Lieutenant Dwight A. Fry, was shot down by enemy fighters on his nineteenth mission, October 14, 1943. Fry managed to evade via the Comet Line and was back in London by the end of January 1944. He made a trip up to Metfield to see his comrades in early February and was photographed here with Major Henry B. "Hank" Bjorkman, group intelligence officer. (Cross)

Blick proudly wears the Distinguished Flying Cross and Air Medal awarded to him at Metfield, March 23, 1944. (Perry Blickenstaff)

Blick's fourth Thunderbolt (P-47D-5-RE LH-U 42-8557) did not last very long. It was hit by flak while flown by First Lieutenant John "Zeke" Zolner from Ravena, New York, on March 8, 1943. Zolner eventually made it back to the group on September 18, 1944, after a period of internment in Switzerland. Note the different-styled lady artwork painted by Blick. (Cross)

The 353rd moved from Metfield in the north of the county of Suffolk to Raydon airfield (seen here) in the south near the border with the county of Essex in April 1944. Raydon is roughly equidistant between the towns of Ipswich and Colchester. (Zielinski)

The full complement of the 350th Fighter Squadron at Raydon, early May 1944. Back row (left to right) Main, MacDonald, Durant, Starr, Bergeron, Auchincloss, Brooks, Rowan, Hargus, Winder, Murray, Paslay. Middle row (left to right) Devine, Garey, Fortier, Dinse, Price, Furness, Moretto, Blickenstaff, Hart, Sullivan. Front row (left to right) Newhart, "Mike," Pidduck. (Cross)

At some point before his promotion to captain on April 4, 1944, Blick took a trip to Scotland. Left to right are Captain Joseph "Doc" Canipelli (350th flight surgeon), First Lieutenant Wayne K. Blickenstaff, Second Lieutenant Francis T. Walsh and Captain Charles W. "Chuck" Dinse. Dinse was happy about a new bottle of "Vat 69" whisky he had acquired and concealed under his trench coat. (Canipelli)

Blick, center, with Captain Charles W. Dinse to his left and First Lieutenant Robert S. Hart to his right in front of Dinse's Thunderbolt *Fatty Patty* (LH-T). Dinse became leader of C Flight (after Newhart was elevated to squadron operations officer) and completed his tour on June 14, 1944. Hart was Blick's second wingman as a replacement for Dwight Fry and completed his tour on May 7, 1944. Blick asked Hart if he wanted to sign up for a second tour but, sadly, he was killed on his first mission after returning from leave when an explosion hit his aircraft while strafing, August 8, 1944. (Canipelli)

April 14, 1944, saw No. 1426 Enemy Aircraft Flight (unofficially known as the RAFwaffe) visit Raydon to familiarise the pilots with the types of enemy aircraft they might encounter. Blick could not resist the opportunity to jump into the cockpit of FW190A-5 PN999 to check out the controls even if he was not allowed to fly it. (Cross)

Blick using the eternal language of the fighter pilot to describe an encounter with the enemy to Sergeant Eichnor at Raydon. Behind them is Blick's seventh Thunderbolt (P-47D-25-RE LH-U 42-26416 Soubrette). Blick had stopped painting the artwork on his aircraft by this stage and Phil Rossi painted this example. (Cross)

Captain (later Major) Dewey E. Newhart from St Joseph, Missouri, was the original commander of C Flight and moved up to squadron operations officer and then commanding officer in May 1944. Newhart finished his tour and volunteered for an extension during the D-Day period. He was lost to enemy aircraft when the squadron was caught at low level in the disastrous June 12, 1944, along with five others from the squadron. (Cross)

First Lieutenant (later Captain) Francis T. Walsh from Brooklyn, New York, was an original member of C Flight and Blick made him his assistant when he became operations officer in the squadron. Walsh completed his tour but stayed on for an extension during the D-Day period. He was lost over the Channel flying his 75th mission on June 7, 1944. (Cross)

The charismatic Captain Marvin V. Bledsoe from Los Angeles, California, was a flight training friend of Blick's from class 42-H who went on to become an experienced flight instructor. As the 350th Squadron began running out of experienced pilots in mid-1944, Blick took the opportunity to bring Bledsoe into the squadron along with several other instructors. Bledsoe eventually wrote his own account of the war, published as *Thunderbolt— Memoirs of a World War II Fighter Pilot* in 1982. (Cross)

Captain Vernon G. Rafferty from Eau Claire, Wisconsin, was another of the instructors Blick brought into the squadron to rebuild experience and flight discipline in the depleted squadron during the summer of 1944. (Cross)

Blick flew the last mission of his first tour on August 7, 1944, and was promoted to major two days later. Lieutenant Colonel William B. Bailey was on hand to congratulate him and officially hand him his gold oak leaves before Blick left for a well-deserved rest back home in the United States. (Cross)

Stills from Blick's gun camera film showing his attacks on ground targets in France, June 7, 1944. (Perry Blickenstaff)

With so many pilots lost flying his aircraft and to try and avoid the apparent bad luck, Blick ordered that nobody else should fly LH-U. This was impossible to enforce while he was home on leave and led to the destruction of *Soubrette* on September 19, 1944. As Captain John B. Rose landed the aircraft at RAF Rochester he skidded on some wet turf and crashed into a canteen building. Soubrette was written off but, luckily, Rose emerged without injury to himself or anyone else. (Cross)

The flight surgeon was one of the key members of a squadron, responsible for managing the stress levels of the pilots and keeping the tightly wound organization functioning. Blick (right) felt that "Doc" Canipelli (center) helped him through his wartime experience and was one of the reasons why he survived. Left is Captain William F. Price from Pittsburgh, Pennsylvania, who commanded the squadron while Blick was on leave during the late summer of 1944. (Cross)

Blick's ninth aircraft (P-51K-1-NT LH-U *Betty E* 44-11353) at Raydon, probably December 1944, before the three rows of checkers were extended to eight as identification markings on the aircraft nose. (Cather)

Blick flew his third Thunderbolt from Metfield between some point in November 1943 and late February 1944. It is shown here with white quick identification markings on the nose and tail and a representation of the artwork painted by Blick himself. (Artwork © 2022 Vincent Dhorne)

Blick flew his seventh Thunderbolt from Raydon between mid-June 1944 to when he completed his first tour in early August 1944. The aircraft was one of several camouflage P-47s used by the group and is shown here with full invasion markings in force until early July 1944. The nose art was by the prolific group artist Phil Rossi. (Artwork © 2022 Vincent Dhorne)

Blick flew his first Mustang and eighth aircraft from Raydon between late October and November 27, 1944. Named after his then girlfriend back home, he scored his first four victories in the aircraft. Battle damage received in his November 27 action resulted in the aircraft visiting Station Engineering and it subsequently joined the 352nd Fighter Squadron. (Artwork © 2022 Vincent Dhorne)

Captain William F. Tanner from Canastota, New York, was the "hot pilot" of the 350th Fighter Squadron and remained with them throughout the war. Blick saw Tanner as a natural fighter pilot with a look that said, "Don't mess with me, Buddy." Tanner flew two tours and amassed an incredible record of 137 missions and 514:50 operational hours. He was also an ace with 5.5 aerial victories. (Cross)

First Lieutenant John M. Balason from San Diego, California, was another of Blick's friends from class 42-H. He had been transferred from the 350th while they were still in the United States to fly P-40s into North Africa. A mix-up with his orders eventually saw him fly a tour of operations in the Aleutians and then join the 350th again in late October 1944. He was brought down by ground fire on the mission on February 22, 1945, and became a prisoner of war for the duration. (Cross)

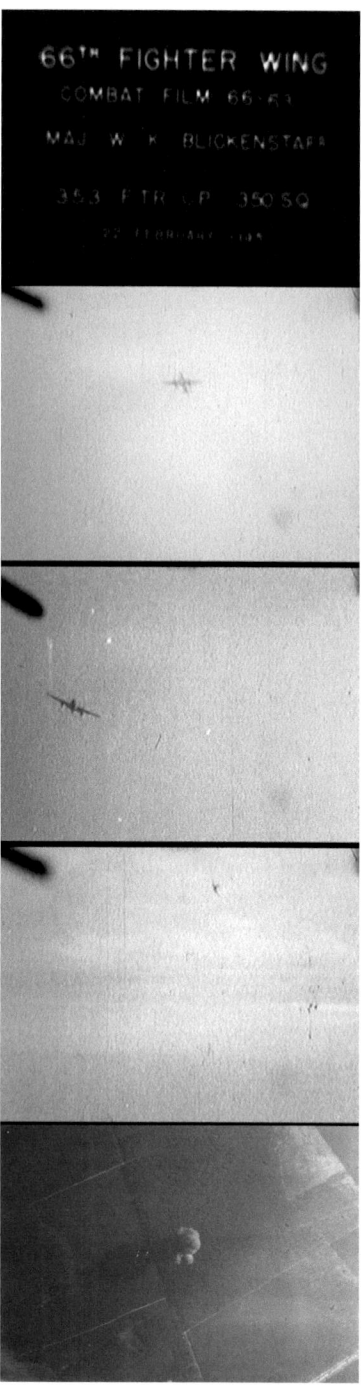

Blick's ME262 victory of February 22, 1945, captured by his gun camera. Blick also had a K-25 side-mounted camera fitted and snapped the final demise of the German jet in the last picture after the pilot had bailed out. (Perry Blickenstaff/Canipelli)

Left: With drop tanks fitted and guns taped to keep moisture from getting in, Blick is helped by his ground crew into *Betty E* (44-11353) for a mission in late 1944 or early 1945. (Cross)

Below: *Betty E* (44-11353) was hit by flak on the mission of February 28, 1945, causing one of the undercarriage legs to fail. Not wishing to bail out, Blick chose to make a "one-wheeled" landing at Raydon. (Cross)

Safely down and with comparatively little damage done from Blick's "one-wheeled" landing on February 28, 1945. *Betty E* was repaired and back flying again on March 13, 1945. (Canipelli)

A purposeful Blick strides out of the Operations building to lead the second mission of the day on March 24, 1945, in support of Allied forces crossing the Rhine. The sign near the door advises "Bicycles will not be parked against building." (Cross)

Blick's tenth and last aircraft (P-51D-25-NA LH-U *Betty E* 44-72374) at Raydon in the summer of 1945. The "firing butts" are visible in the background to locate the photograph. (Canipelli)

The 350th loved table tennis and had fierce battles in their "Ready Room" throughout the war to pass the time. Top dog was said to be Ed Rosentreter, squadron intelligence officer. Left to right in this shot taken at Metfield are Lorance, Blickenstaff, Price, Walsh, Newhart, Stearns and Angelo. (Cross)

Blick flew his ninth aircraft from early December 1944 until battle damage sustained on March 24, 1945, sent it into the hangar and reassignment to another pilot. He was flying this aircraft for his five victories on March 24, 1945, and likely also for his Me262 victory on February 22, 1945. He was also flying this aircraft for his one-wheeled landing on February 28, 1945. (Artwork © 2022 Vincent Dhorne)

Blick flew his tenth and final aircraft from Raydon between March 27, 1945, and his return home in July 1945. From the available photographic evidence, it appears to be the only one of his Mustangs to carry crew names and victory markings. (Artwork © 2022 Vincent Dhorne)

Blick catching some much-needed shut-eye in the 350th "Ready Room" at Metfield, 1943 or early 1944. (Canipelli)

Major Stanley R. Pidduck takes a drink from the fountain located in the 350th Fighter Squadron "Ready Room" at Metfield, "Compliments from the 350th Tin Benders." Pidduck was commander of the squadron until May 1, 1944, and was affectionately known as "Pappy" because he was a few years older than most of the pilots. (Perry Blickenstaff)

The operational status boards in the 350th Fighter Squadron "Ready Room" at Raydon. Two of the "Raydon Ladies" are visible and were painted by several of the squadron to "brighten" things up a little. (Cross)

The front door of the "Wheelhouse" in the village of Great Wenham that still exists today as the Manor House. Blick had to gain entry to his room at the back of the house one night after a party in the Auger Inn when his roommate decided he needed the room to be more private. (Cross)

In the spring of 1945, Blick and "Doc" Canipelli took a trip to Paris. There is no specific mention in Blick's diary or logbook, but it seems likely that it was either April 19 when he "took Doc for a ride in the two-seater" or May 11 when he logged a flight in the Group AT-16 aircraft. (Cross)

The reunion party held on May 17, 1945, to celebrate the safe return of Lieutenant Colonel Loren G. McCollom, the group's second commanding officer, who had become a prisoner of war on November 25, 1943, after being hit by flak during the group's first dive-bombing mission. McCollom is noticeably thin after over a year in captivity, while Colonels Duncan and Bailey (to McCollom's left) are sporting tans from a trip to the south of France. Blick is standing on the left, glass in hand, and wearing a cut-down "Eisenhower" jacket. "Doc" Canipelli, 350th flight surgeon, is kneeling on the right. The officers' club bar was known as the "Auger Inn," a gallows humor reference to pilots "auguring" in when they crashed. (Cross)

June 1, 1945, saw Blick in attendance to Brigadier General Murray C. Woodbury (left, facing) of the 66th Fighter Wing based at Sawston Hall for an inspection visit. Next to Woodbury dining in the officers' mess is Colonel Glenn E. Duncan. Opposite Woodbury is Lieutenant Colonel Charles Bruett (353rd ground executive officer) with Blick opposite Colonel Duncan. (Cross)

Blick caught sunbathing in preparation for a return to California on a rare day of English sunshine in the early summer of 1945. His chosen spot is behind the 350th Fighter Squadron "Ready Room" with the large building of the base motor pool in the background. (Cross)

Pilots ready to leave Raydon for home in the group's Noorduyn UC-64 Norseman. Left to right, standing, are unknown, Captain Donald L. Barber, Captain Harrison B. Tordoff, Lieutenant Colonel Wilbert H. Junttila, Captain Horace Q. Waggoner and unknown. Kneeling left to right are Lieutenant Colonel Vic L. Byers and Lieutenant Colonel Wayne K. Blickenstaff. (Cross)

Veterans ready to catch the flight home in July 1945. Left to right are Lieutenant Colonel Vic L. Byers (351st Fighter Squadron commander), Lieutenant Colonel Joe L. Thury (339th Fighter Group), Lieutenant Colonel Wilbert H. Junttila (352nd Fighter Squadron commander) and Lieutenant Colonel Wayne K. Blickenstaff (353rd Fighter Group operations officer). (Cross)

Colonel Ben Rimerman commanded the 350th Fighter Squadron from May 1943 until becoming 353rd Fighter Group air executive officer on November 25, 1943. He then commanded the group from July 7, 1944, when Colonel Glenn E. Duncan was brought down by flak. Sadly, he died in an aircraft accident, along with Captain William J. Maguire of the 351st Fighter Squadron, flying to a party at Raydon on August 11, 1945. Blick initially found Rimerman difficult to get to know but came to understand him well while residing in the "Wheelhouse." He is standing in front of his aircraft *Diane* (believed to be P-51D-25-NA LH-V 44-72958). (Cross)

Blick's mother, Hazel, clearly pleased to have her son safely home in 1945. Blick's older brother, Ralph (right), enlisted in the US Army in April 1945 and served until 1946. (Perry Blickenstaff)

Blick in his studio at the Famous Artists School doing what he loved, mid- to late 1960s. Famous Artists was an art correspondence school founded in Westport, Connecticut, in 1948 by members of the New York Society of Illustrators—principally Albert Dorne and Norman Rockwell. Blick joined the school as an instructor in 1965 and remained there until 1975. (Perry Blickenstaff)

"It doesn't look like they need our help, does it?" I said and turned back out of the moisture, mumbling "Crummy weather." It was hardly even a statement, and certainly needed no reply, but Doc said, obligingly, "Yeah." His pipe hardly moved.

The ready room began to fill with pilots in various stages of disentangling themselves from their straps, buckles and zippers. The bitching was hard to ignore. Obviously the weather was terrible everywhere.

"Where's Balason?" I asked of everyone in general, and no one in particular—mostly myself. There was no answer.

I found Tanner, [the squadron and] White Flight leader. "Where's Balason?"

"I don't know. He never showed up."

I still hadn't seen him, and cornered [the leader of] Yellow Flight.[11]

"Where's Balason?" I asked.

"I don't know," he said. "Was he supposed to be with me?"

"He was supposed to be with *someone,* dammit! So where the hell is he?"

"Well, don't get mad at me, Blick, I don't know. I never saw him."

I tried another. "Where's Balason?"

"Never saw him, Blick. I tacked on to Tanner, but I never did see Balason."

I went back to Doc, who asked the same question. "Where's Balason?"

"No one knows. What do you suppose happened to him? Wouldn't you know it. … If anyone could take a perfectly normal milk run and fuck it up, he'd be the one. You'd think by now someone would know if he's down somewhere. … Last thing I told him was not to do anything stupid!"

"He'll show, Blick—don't sweat it."

"You're sure?"

"No …"

The pilots were finished with their debriefing and the ready room had thinned out. The mission was successful, but only because they had found the bombers and stayed with them. The return flight was so miserable they were relieved just to be home again. It was the kind of weather that sometimes left us scattered all over East Anglia.

Doc and I were about to leave when I got a call from the tower. I looked at Doc. "This must be it."

It was. Balason was on his way.

"Thanks very much," I said, and turned to Doc. "He's coming in. Where do you suppose he's been?"

"I guess we'll find out," Doc smiled.

"Yeah … let's go get him."

---

11 Blick originally wrote Haynes, but he did not fly the mission, so it is possible that it was either Ferrell or Schilt.

Balason climbed into the jeep with all his gear, looking more sheepish than ever. I was determined to keep my cool and let him explain before I said anything. Instead, I immediately blurted out, "Where the hell have you been?"

"You'll never believe this," he said.

"Try me."

"You told me to stick with my leader, and I did." He smiled. "When we took so long to take off I thought he was just testing me, and I hung in there. But then he started making all those funny motions and I didn't know what he meant, but finally I realized he wanted me to go on, and I goosed it and went right on up into the clouds. I guess he'd been too busy to use the radio before. He told me to join up with another flight and told Tanner to take over the squadron."

I pulled up to the ready room and parked, but just sat there waiting for him to go on.

"And that's what I did, Blick. The clouds were thicker than I expected but when I finally broke out there were a bunch of planes off to the right and I latched on to them … and flew the whole mission with them." There was that little half smile again. "It did seem kinda weird that I didn't understand any of the conversation that was going on. Nothing that was said seemed to relate to anything, but I just thought it was because I was new and not really broken in yet. I didn't recognize anything, even the field when we landed, and when I got out no one looked familiar. I finally asked one of the pilots where we were. He said Manston, because of the weather."

Manston was an emergency RAF field. They called it the "Lame Duck Landing Strip."

"When the guy asked me what group I was with, I realized I had flown the whole mission with another group—the 55th, I think he said!"

"Oh my God!" I looked at Doc. He just shrugged and smiled. I couldn't believe it. "You mean you couldn't tell the difference between their markings and ours?"

Balason couldn't look at me. "Well, we both have checkered noses, and I guess I never paid that much attention to the colors or the letters of the other squadrons. …"

It was incredible, I thought. "That's just great! You've been here all this time and still don't even know what our planes look like!"

"Well I know we're LH, but I never really looked at the 51st or the 52nd."

Only Balason … I thought. *Only he could do that.* By the time we were back in the ready room I had cooled a little and could begin to see the humor in it. "Well … I guess no harm has been done. At least you did what you were supposed to do. And I can always get Rosentreter to give you a course in aircraft recognition."

Twenty-eight

As the end of the year approached, the weather worsened, restricting air operations. We flew only seventeen days in October and seventeen in November. The Germans used the time to their advantage, renewing their efforts to halt the advance of the Allied troops.

It was early, and as always, cold and dark. We were so used to the fog, rain, low clouds and generally piss-poor weather we didn't even bother to mention it anymore. My knees were beginning to look like English knees—a couple a bloomin' roses—from standing in front of a fire. We heard the sound of our own planes being readied on the line, but the mournful drone of the bombers overhead was absent—a sure sign the mission was something other than escort. I was scheduled to lead the squadron with Ed Duke, one of the newer pilots, on my wing.[1]

In the briefing room, there was that same incredibly long line stretched out across the map. I thought I should be used to it by then, but I wasn't—always that nervous twinge in my stomach, and I wondered if others felt the same. Hopefully, I was able to control my outward appearance well enough so everyone would see my calm, cool, nerves of steel.

Wilbert Junttila, another Luke classmate and CO of the 352nd Squadron, was leading the group as Jonah. He was a Nordic-looking, heavy-set, big-boned blond. He was about five-nine or -ten, and husky, with a roundness that eliminated most of the muscle definition of a thinner man. His head was a hair too small for his body, making him appear taller than he was. He went by the nickname "Weep," and I never knew why. I didn't think it had anything to do with crying.

He stood with pointer in hand, waiting, hitching his pants up a little every once in a while, to keep his belt from slipping off hip bones that were difficult to find—a clue, I was sure, to his future physical appearance.

---

1 The mission was November 27, 1944, and Noah Cowen was the scheduled wingman, but Blick's Encounter Report confirms Duke flew this position on the day.

Weep didn't talk much, but when he did, he didn't stutter and stammer around; he just said what was necessary and that was it. I always had the feeling he didn't care much about the business of combat. But then, who did?

"No bombers today," he said. "We've got our own show. We're going all the way in here to strafe a bunch of oil tanks." The pointer went to the tiny dot on the map that no one could see, just south of Berlin.

I only half listened. It was the usual explanation, mostly for the benefit of the newer pilots. I was always happy to have someone else responsible for the navigation, and I was glad Weep had the group this time, especially for this kind of a mission. On such a long haul, a small change in wind speed or direction could throw us miles off course by the time we reached the target area, and it was up to Jonah to make the proper corrections along the way in order to find the target. At 20,000 feet, which was our scheduled altitude, the whole German countryside looked the same—just one huge patchwork quilt. I wasn't a very good navigator in the best of conditions, but so much of the time there was cloud cover, and after 500 miles of trying to orient ourselves by peeking down through holes, we were supposed to find oil tanks?

There was a big plus, though, for the leader of a strafing mission. The first pass over the target was usually a surprise to the Germans, but they were ready for the following squadrons. On second thought, maybe having the responsibility of finding the target was the better deal.

The clouds were not thick, and we formed up easily. I pulled my squadron into position on Weep's left and slightly above, trimming the ship for an easy 300 feet a minute climb.

After the dark, depressing, early morning weather we had just climbed through, the brilliance of the sun on the white clouds, and the deep blue of the sky, never failed to thrill me. It was so calm and serene it was hard to believe we were on our way to cause death and destruction. Rather than a White Knight going off to do battle with the Black Hats, I was a dove, lazily enjoying my natural habitat.

That serenity was a danger, however—something I had to battle with at that same point on every mission. There was nothing to do. The warmth of the sun through the canopy, in combination with the hypnotic drone of the engine, invariably dulled my senses and made me sleepy. It was a constant struggle with my dogged eyelids. Even with the plane trimmed as perfectly as possible it would still slowly drift off course, making it mandatory that my eyes be open. I could explain away minor turns as corrections in course, but a long curve and altitude change? No way!

Fortunately, as we approached the Continent, the lassitude gave way to my normal tension. Also, I was shocked into sudden alertness by the loud crackle of the radio, "Seldom spare leaving."

It was another twenty-five minutes before the silence was shattered again, this time by Nuthouse, our ground control. "Nuthouse to Jonah. Large group of bandits ahead. Change course to zero-eight-zero. Acknowledge."

"Roger, Nuthouse. Changing course to zero-eight-zero. Jonah out."

Needless to say, I had an automatic adrenaline rush. I started to examine the sky ahead. It had taken me a long time, but I had finally learned how to look. The normal approach was to scan the sky in a kind of sweeping motion, but in that manner the tiny specks were too easily passed over. I had to learn to search the sky in small patches, looking carefully at each patch before moving on to another.

I saw what appeared to be the group Nuthouse was vectoring us toward. "Seldom here, Jonah," I said, as calmly as I could. "Bogies at eleven thirty, a little high."

"Roger, Seldom."

I inched the throttle forward and started to climb. As I approached, I saw a huge group of enemy planes—easily 200—heading south. They were flying in two bunches, looking more like a gaggle of gnats than a structured formation.

"Lawyer Leader, take the ones on the right. Seldom and I will go after those on the left."

"Roger, Jonah."

They were all fighters, and I was now fully and completely awake. I had never seen so many all at once.

I had gained enough altitude and speed to pull up behind them easily. So far there was no indication the Germans were aware of what was about to happen. There were huge, billowy contrails flowing out behind all the planes. A beautiful sight, yes, under less strenuous circumstances, but they were a hindrance now, making it difficult to move into the ideal firing position. I closed in on one of the planes, half in and half out of the cloud. With such a perfect target, my reasoning told me to wait for the perfect shot, but my emotions and the excitement of the moment said to hell with that, and I couldn't resist pulling the trigger. I fired three short bursts and watched in disbelief as pieces began to fall off the plane. One final burst and the whole plane disintegrated right in my face. The pieces came hurtling back right at me, as if it was some sort of last-ditch revenge. I ducked—but that did no good of course. I popped the stick forward, missing the debris by inches.

The excitement was building—the thrill of finally, after all this time, actually shooting down a plane! Already I was hungry for more! I pulled back up to the main group—Duke was still with me—this time attempting to position myself to the side of the contrail. Why there was no effort to counter-attack I couldn't imagine, except to think that the Germans might think we were part of their group. I fired again, with the same result. Pieces again, but this time the plane fell off to the right, allowing me to rake the cockpit area. I was so close I could see the tremendous power of those bullets as they ripped into the metal of the fuselage. The plane started to smoke and then flipped completely over, heading straight down with the engine blazing and leaving a trail of black smoke—a stark contrast to the white horizontal stripes of the contrails.

Obviously surprised, the Germans finally came out of their stupor. Suddenly, planes were all over the sky with smoke and flames everywhere. Up ahead, the main group just continued on, robot-like, with no seeming awareness of the disastrous activity going on behind them.

Radio silence was a thing of the past. The air was filled with an impossible mishmash of overlapping, blurted, explosive exclamations, which went something like this:

"Jockey Blue Three break left!"

"I've got one behind you, Bob!"

"Jesus Christ, did you see that!"

"My God, he's on your tail—break!"

"Whee-oo!"

"Look at that, Seldom Red!"

"Ten o'clock—quick, Blue Three!"

"Where are you, Yellow Three?"

"They're above you, Lawyer Red!"

"White four—lookout—behind you!"

"Fire dammit. Shit!—my guns don't work!"

"I'm going down after him—cover me!"

"Let's go!"

I tried again to close in on the tail of another FW190 at the rear of the main group, but then noticed an easier target about nine o'clock below. I slid off and down, but misjudged my closing speed. I yanked the throttle back and tried everything, even the flaps, to keep from overrunning him. Nothing worked. As a last resort, just as I was about to chew the tail off the 190, I pulled up into a barrel roll around him. I was halfway around when the German pilot saw me and split-essed full speed downward. It was a smart maneuver because I thought he was heading right on down to the deck for home, and turned back toward the main gaggle—a foolish assumption. The German zoomed right back up and started firing a long right-angle burst before I even realized he was there. I felt the hits all over my cowling.

"Oh shit!" I blurted aloud. "I've had it."

But everything still worked, and I instinctively hit the stick and rudder and turned into the 190 … then with another roll, I ended up once more on his tail. By then, I had lost my excessive speed and was able to turn with the German pilot. In fact, I gained a little in the turn. I pulled the trigger, dragging the gunsight right through the German's line of flight. I saw the strikes creep up the tail and fuselage. The pilot rolled again, but by doing so he decreased the deflection, which allowed me to hit him with a good long burst into the cockpit. I watched until I saw the plane go into the ground.

I looked around. Hard to believe, but Duke was still there. Once again, I headed back in the direction of the main group.

Duke suddenly warned, "Seldom Leader, break left!"

I yanked the stick, then noticed another 190 on Duke's tail. "Duke! You've got one behind you, too. Break right!"

The German followed Duke, allowing me to make a complete 360 and pull in behind him. I fired immediately, and saw strikes. The plane rolled and headed straight down. This time I followed all the way through the roll, firing the whole time, finally seeing pieces beginning to fall off as it continued down, on fire and smoking.

I had been too engrossed in the conflict to notice that it was becoming increasingly more difficult to see—my windshield was covered with oil.

"Let's go home, Duke," I said, and as Duke pulled up on my wing, I could see the smile in his eyes. It was a pleasure to give him the old thumbs-up sign.

[Blick's Encounter Report:

- A. Combat
- B. 27 November 1944.
- C. 350th Fighter Squadron
- D. 1245 Approximately
- E. Between Steinhuder Lake and Brunswick.
- F. Good
- G. FW 190
- H. Four (4) FW 190s destroyed in the air.
- I. I was leading Seldom Squadron on the 27 Nov., 1944, briefed to strafe an oil supply depot at Annaburg. At approx. 1255, in the vicinity of Steinhuder Lake, 'Nuthouse' control informed us that there were bogies at 10:00. This was almost immediately verified by contrails in that direction. We promptly turned toward them and observed 3 gaggles of at least 75 each. We met the lead gaggle on a 10:00 pass and recognized them as FW190s, white noses predominating. Being to the left of Jonah, the opportunity of the 1st bounce was ours, so that we were able to position ourselves behind the gaggle by a left turn. As the gaggle proceeded in a southerly direction, I pulled in behind one and gave him 3 or 4 short bursts with the result that pieces began flying off the E/A. In the meantime I closed rather rapidly, gave him one final burst, and he seemed to disintegrate. To avoid flying through the pieces, I popped the stick forward as he began to fall off to the right.

  I pulled back into the same gaggle onto the tail of another. A few bursts at an estimated range of 500 yards caused pieces to fly off him. The E/A started a slow turn to the right. After closing a little more, I gave him a good burst and observed strikes all over the cockpit and he went down with the engine afire and smoking badly.

  The enemy formation persisted in a southerly direction and I again caught up to it and got on the tail of another E/A. While attempting to close sufficiently for a good burst, I noticed another E/A about 9:00 and slightly low to me. I was having difficulty overtaking the E/A ahead, so I chopped back and slid over behind the E/A at 9:00 o'clock. However, I began to overrun him, so I started a barrel roll around him in an attempt to stay behind. When a quarter of the way around in my roll, the E/A made a sharp turn to the left and away from me. Before I could take advantage of this opportunity, the E/A split S'd, and thinking that he was evading to the deck, I turned to select another from the mass gaggle. He pulled back up into me, firing a long 90 [-degree] deflection burst which hit my cowling as I turned to meet this pass. As he continued to pull up, I quickly rolled over and ended up on his tail again. As I had by now lost excessive speed, I was able to turn easily with the E/A, and hit him with several bursts of rather large deflection. I then followed the E/A as he rolled over and started down, clobbering him in the cockpit with a good burst. Not being too certain that the E/A would not pull out, I watched him as he continued down. I saw him go straight in, so I zoomed back up.

The main gaggle continued merrily on its way, ignoring the flights that were going for its rear. I again started after them with my wing man following. Lt. Duke, my wing man, had done an excellent job as he was with me during the entire show. We had chased the gaggle for about a minute when Lt. Duke warned me to break left. As I broke to the left, I looked back and saw an FW190 on Lt. Duke's tail. Lt. Duke elected to break to the right and the 190 followed him. This enabled me to complete my turn so that I was able to pull up behind the E/A. Immediately after observing strikes on the 190, he rolled over and split S'd. I followed through getting strikes in the middle of the airplane. Pieces began to fly off the 190 and it continued down, smoking badly.

Since the main gaggle was by now too far distant to overtake, we headed out. Some of my oil lines had been broken by that lucky 90 [-degree] deflection shot, causing me to land at Denain/Prouvy with five lbs. oil pressure.

All of the combat took place between 20,000 and 30,000 feet. As I recall, the majority of my hits were, surprisingly, directly in the cockpit area. Full credit for this is given to the K-14 gunsight.

I claim four (4) FW190s destroyed in the air.

Wayne K. Blickenstaff
Major, Air Corps.

[Blick wrote of the "ace-maker" K-14 gunsight: "The K-14 sight was a masterpiece. I could never figure out distances and leads like the directions said we were supposed to do, but I just aimed ahead of the plane and dragged the cross hairs through the line of flight. Couldn't miss that way unless the guy was really slipping, and most of the time you weren't worrying about that in a dogfight."[2]]

I put the plane into a slow rate of descent to keep up speed and conserve fuel. I was hoping to make landfall out at about 10,000 feet. I was concerned about my oil. The plane was obviously leaking oil badly, because the pressure was gradually sinking. It was a long haul across the water and I had to make a decision whether to land on the mainland or chance the crossing. The North Sea was the angriest-looking water I had ever seen and I had no desire to ditch in it. My conservative nature told me it was better to land.

"I've got a pretty bad oil leak, Duke," I said finally. "You go on home and tell them I'm okay and that I'll be back as soon as I can. I'm going back to that field we saw on the way out and see if they can do something with the plane. You'll be okay ... just continue on this course."

I saw him nod in agreement. "Okay," he said. "Good luck."

I turned back and started letting down. I had seen some P-47s there and thought it was probably a Ninth Air Force base.

---

2   Blickenstaff to Cross, 1998.

It was the right decision. When I landed, the windshield was almost completely covered and the oil pressure was down to five pounds.

A tech-sergeant met me as I climbed out of the cockpit. "Looks like you've been havin' fun, Major," he said.

"Yeah. A little. Do you think you could take a look at this thing and get me back across the Channel any time soon?"

"I'll try," he replied. "Why don't you go over to Operations and wait? I'll let you know what I find."

About three-quarters of an hour later, the sergeant came into the Operations room to report that my oil lines and throttle linkage were all shot up and it would take several days to repair them.

"But there's a B-26 on the field that's leaving for Ireland soon," he told me. "Maybe you could hitch a ride."

The B-26 was a fast, light, twin-engine bomber called the Marauder. The pilot was happy to drop me off at Raydon, and I arrived back at the field only about three hours after the rest of the group.

Everyone was pleased, but surprised to see me walk out of the B-26. Duke had filled them in on the victories. The group's total was twenty-two—the largest number of enemy aircraft destroyed in the air for the group to date, and I made the record book as the only pilot in the group to shoot down four in one engagement. It was, as the British would say, "A bloody good show."

[Blick received the Silver Star for actions on November 27, 1944 (issued May 8, 1945). The citation read: "For Gallantry in action while leading a Squadron of P-51s on a fighter mission 27 November 1944. Over Germany, Major Blickenstaff observed three (3) large formations of enemy aircraft. With utter disregard for their numerical superiority, he selected a group of approximately seventy-five (75) planes and led his Squadron in a daring attack. As the battle mounted in fury, Major Blickenstaff found himself alone with his wing man, surrounded by hostile fighters. Undaunted and with his vision partially obscured by spraying oil, he exhibited such remarkable fighting prowess that the enemy fled in disorder. The combat skill, courage, and dogmatic aggressiveness Major Blickenstaff demonstrated in destroying four (4) enemy aircraft on this occasion reflected highest credit upon himself and the Armed Forces of the United States. By Command of Lieutenant General Doolittle."]

[On medals, Blick subsequently wrote: "When I enlisted in the Air Corps and eventually was sent overseas, like it or not I expected to do a job, just like any other soldier. I didn't take the medals lightly, but I was never able to understand why we were given Air Medals and Distinguished Flying Crosses for *just doing our job!* It's great, sure, to be able to show them off, now, but why give us a medal just because we did what we were supposed to do? I really do think that all of us (GIs included) should have something to show for our service, but to single us out …? Our dedication, loyalty, risk, performance, whatever, was really no different than anyone else's. We just happened to be a little more conspicuous. I feel differently about my Silver Star, though. It was given to me for something a little unusual—special.[3]]

Being a major, and a "field grade" officer, had its advantages. There were many special privileges, including separate meals and billeting, use of a staff car anytime, and a jeep of my own. I was not dishonest enough to say I didn't like it—steak instead of hot dogs—but I didn't like the way it disconnected me from the pilots I had shared so much with.

I was not surprised when Rimerman called me in to inform me I was moving to the Wheelhouse. I remembered when it happened to Dewey. I bumbled around a little, with some weak objections, but I knew the statement was not just a suggestion. It was an order. Rimerman just smiled, in his usual grinning way, and said nothing. There could be no argument.

Hardest to tell about the move, of course, was Doc. I decided to wait until after dinner that night.

"Let's go for a walk, Doc," I said, when we had finished. "I've got something to tell you."

The light was failing a little earlier now, and the descending cloud cover overhead made it seem even darker. It hadn't rained for at least two days, and the ground didn't feel so much like we were walking along the edge of swamp. We took the long way back to the hut. Doc had been very quiet through dinner, and my antenna had been vibrating.

"Ben called me in and told me I have to move to the Wheelhouse," I said finally. I didn't know how to say it other than to come right out with it.

"Yeah, I know." Doc always seemed to know everything. "Or, I should say I knew it was coming soon—not exactly when."

"I told him I'd rather stay where I am, but he wouldn't listen."

"We both know he wouldn't make any exceptions to that policy."

"Yeah, I know, Doc, but that doesn't make it any easier. I don't really know any of those guys very well." I hesitated ... thoughtful. "But, it really won't change anything much—just the sleeping part."

We walked for a while in silence. I had a feeling the move wasn't the only thing bothering him. "What's the matter, Doc?" I asked. "You've been quiet all evening."

"Nothing." He hesitated ... but then went on. "I guess I'm just bored ... and depressed."

"Depressed ...? About what?"

He thought for a long time ... and I waited. "It's mostly this whole damn scene. It catches up with me once in a while. I sit around here, day after crummy day, doing the same damn thing ... watching you guys having your fun flyin', sweatin' you out, listening to you bitch, wet-nursin' you along. Before long I'll be blowing your

---

3   Blickenstaff to Cross, 1998.

snotty noses and hand-feeding you … and there's not a chance in hell of anything ever changing. I've been a captain, and sitting in this same goddam position, for three years now, and I'll still be sitting here when the war ends. You'll probably be a goddamn general by then!" He had to smile a little at that. "Do you realize how many guys I've played nursemaid to, watching them come and go? Nobody pays the slightest attention to old Doc … and I'm supposed to always be here, ready for anyone who needs his nose wiped or his pecker looked at or a shoulder to cry on. Half the time I don't even know what the hell I'm here for—the squadron bitching post, mostly!"

No wonder my antenna was vibrating. It suddenly hit me that Doc was talking mostly about me! He was feeling used! And with good reason. He had diapered me through all kinds of situations from second lieutenant to major … and now the move to the Wheelhouse! Although Doc was only three years older, he had been like a father to me, all through this, and had I ever told him thank you? *My God!* I thought, *how do I tell him now?… Whatever I say will sound like insincere garble!*

"I'm sorry, Doc," I finally replied. "What do I say?" I watched my shoes. "I guess I just always took it for granted that you knew how much I appreciate you, and what you've done for me. Dammit, Doc, I never could have coped with this whole situation without you. No way to count the number of times you've pulled me through some crisis." I stopped, chagrined, and looked at Doc. "But it's true, I've never talked about it. I guess I just felt you could see inside and realize how I felt."

"I do know how you feel, Blick," Doc said then. "But for Christ's sake, I'm just a human being, y'know. It's nice to hear a compliment once in a while … everyone needs to feel useful."

"Yeah … you're so right. I just got so swept up with what's going on and what's happening to me that I forgot. But—and please believe me—I don't *mean* to hurt."

"I do know and understand all that. But you asked … and it does catch up with me once in a while when I begin to feel sorry for myself. This whole goddam business is so depressing sometimes I just can't control it."

"You're certainly allowed … if anyone is. In fact, I don't really know how you stay as sane as you do."

We walked on toward the hut, and I noticed that Doc's head was a little higher.

With the move to the Wheelhouse, I looked forward to one thing—the possibility of finally getting warm. The Nissen hut's single coal stove was a worthy experiment, but it didn't prove out very well. It was simple in construction, looking like a large ball with the top and the bottom chopped off. Attached to the top, was a long flue pipe going straight up and out the roof. The fire never went out. When we were to be gone, or sleeping, we banked the coals so it could be started again easily. The air space in the hut was much too large for the stove, and of course there wasn't any insulation. In our attempts to warm it, we'd pile on the coal until the stove was red hot and glowing three-quarters of the way up the flue. It would finally get warm nearby, but that warmth seldom reached the far ends of the hut.

At night, I piled everything I had on top of me, including my heavy winter flying equipment, but still the dampness would seep in. And there was nothing under the cot but cold air. My California metabolism just wasn't able to cope with it.

There were so many memories in that hut, though … and so many ghosts. It seemed there were always newly emptied beds. The worst was that terrible awakening on the day Dewey was lost—half the hut! I refused to allow myself to dwell on that.

I knew the move would not affect my friendship with Doc, but there was something about that close-quartered communication that contributed considerably to our sanity. …

[The "Wheelhouse"] was an almost square, two-story brick house with two chimneys, each with two flues at the top. The bricks were the light, varicolored kind, and the trim was white, now dirty and peeling due to the long war years of neglect. From the outside, everything about the house was symmetrical. The red, wooden door was positioned exactly in the center with a large-paned bay window on either side. Directly above the door and the bays, were three identical windows evenly spaced from each side of the house. The roof was slanted toward the front door with another overhanging roof covering the lower windows and door. A hedgerow separated the house from the road. It was not unusual—in fact a very typical, small, English-countryside house.[4]

For me, however, it was far from typical. In my mind, I visualized the hallowed ground where policies and decisions were made; the chess games with lives; the warm and comfortable *good* life—a place to escape from wartime terrors and tensions.

Should I knock or just walk in?

I pulled the jeep into what was once a gravel driveway, now mostly overgrown with grass, got out, grabbed my B-4 bag and walked up the worn path to the door. I hesitated, but only for a second, then reached for the doorknob. I walked right in—after all, I was one of them now.

I was welcomed by Tom, a sergeant whose full-time job was to take care of the house and its occupants. We started up the stairs directly in front of the door. I noticed a living room off to the left and my eyes went directly to the fireplace on the far wall. The room looked comfortable.

Tom motioned to a door on the right. "That's Colonel Rimerman's room," he indicated. "He's not here much, though. Just to sleep."

There was a bathroom straight ahead at the top of the stairs, and four doors, two on each side of the hall. Tom opened the door on the left, closest to the bathroom.

"This is your room, Major," he said. "You're in with Major LeFebre."

"Great," I said. Fred LeFebre was CO of the 351st.

---

4   The "Wheelhouse" as it was known, because the "Big Wheels" resided there, still exists in Wenham today as the "Manor House."

Without ever giving it any thought, I had just assumed I'd have a room to myself, but of course the house was much too small for that. I really liked Fred, though, so I couldn't have done better had I picked my roommate myself.

The room was not spacious, but seemed adequate. My bed was near the window, overlooking the backyard. Fred's was along the opposite wall, with a large desk in between. There was a small, but ample closet, and a chest with six drawers—plenty of space.

"You saw the living room downstairs?" Tom asked, and I nodded. "There's a kitchen in the back, which no one uses much, another john just below this one, and a shower out back—a recent addition. Just make yourself at home and let me know if there's anything you need. I'll be around. If you want a fire, just light it—it's ready to go.

"Thanks Tom, I'll make out."

There wasn't much to do except put some clothes in the empty drawers and hang up the others. The only other equipment I had was my footlocker and a bag of dirty clothes, which would arrive later.

The whole house felt cold and damp. With no one around, there was no reason for it to be otherwise. The shower Tom had mentioned was actually out the back door but in a little room of its own tacked on to the house by some ingenious soul—an American innovation. The English were tub-oriented.

My hopes for warmth and the good life were completely shattered the first night. English central heating was reserved for the chosen few, obviously. The warmth of the entire house was dependent on a little blurb of coal in the tiny fireplace downstairs. It didn't take long to find out why the house was used only for sleeping. Better to spend off hours in the officers' club with a drink in hand.

That first evening, I lit the fire, got out my letter-writing material and prepared to spend a comfortable night writing letters. The coal burned and I saw the flames, but I could feel no heat. I slowly inched my way forward until I was almost burning my feet, but still my backside was freezing—it was warmer in the Nissen hut! The only way to get even a little warm was to rotate continuously like a roast on an open spit. I was better off in bed.

The sun, when it came out, warmed the upstairs a little during the day, and I finally had to admit that even with the lack of warmth it was more comfortable living. The semi-personalized bathroom and the shower helped tremendously. Except for Doc and a couple of the others, the amicable closeness of the hut began to fade.

Twenty-nine

December was another bad-weather month. The group flew twenty-two missions, all escort except for one fighter sweep to the Koblenz area. There were only three encounters with the enemy in the air, resulting in nineteen destroyed and three losses. This raised the group's total to 286 air-to-air victories; 398 in total.

Significant in the month was the major counter-attack opened by the Germans through the Ardennes area on the 16th, later to become known as the Battle of the Bulge. The Germans pushed some sixty miles into the Allied lines and were threatening to go even farther because the weather was so severe the Allies could offer no help from the air.

The clouds hung motionless over the field, oozing drizzle like a super-saturated sponge and leaving no sign of a horizon. As I sat waiting at the end of the runway, I realized I had been listening to the sound of bombers ever since I'd awakened. Usually by the time we were ready to take off, the noise overhead was long gone.

We had been briefed for an escort mission to Giessen, about thirty-five miles north of Frankfurt.[1] With the hope of being more effective against the new jet menace, we had varied our tactics slightly. To cover more area around the bombers, we split up into two groups, A and B, using one group as close protection for the bombers and the other to sweep the area ahead, looking for enemy aircraft. I was leading A Group and Weep was leading B Group with two flights of the 351st tacked on to each group. I had Duke on my wing again.[2]

The fuzzy green light from the tower lit up and we were off ... into the clouds and on instruments almost immediately. Duke was in close, adjusting to my every movement. The clouds were so dense I could barely see Duke's cockpit. Once again, we were taking off in the direction of the 56th—right into their traffic pattern—and, as usual, I was nervous. It was bad enough when the visibility was good. I hoped their take-off time was different.

---

1   Blick is describing the mission of December 11, 1944.
2   The mission plan says Balason was flying Blick's wing with Lieutenant Duke flying wing to Captain Allison.

Even while in the clouds I had to begin my turn, or the rest of the group would be so widely scattered when they came out, we'd never get together. I started a very cautious, gentle turn to the left. *Suddenly there was a huge gray shape like a whale in murky water, streaking by, missing my wing by inches!* And then it was gone, not even giving me a chance to cry out, *"My God—that was a B-17!"* There wasn't time to react or even time to be shocked—that would come later. I had to concentrate on my instruments.

The clouds lasted forever, or so it seemed, and I became edgier by the minute—more and more upset at our so-called weather authority, who had promised us that the stuff wouldn't be thick. Finally, the light overhead began to filter down … and then we were out.

As always, I went through a strange moment of disorientation when I broke out on a slant, and I had to make the transition from instruments to contact flying. I had the feeling I was level and the clouds were tilted—vertigo! Duke was still there, and so close I could recognize the relief on his face. I wondered if he had seen the bomber. Behind Duke, I saw the next element emerging, and beyond them, the 56th Group was almost formed.

Because of the thickness of the cloud layer, I made one more 360 to give our two groups more time to get into position. Once we were on course, we were nearly formed and I was able to relax.

When I finally looked around I could hardly believe my eyes. Every space in the sky was swarming with some kind of airplane—no wonder I had heard the roaring engines all morning. Everywhere I looked there were bombers and fighters at various altitudes in the gradual process of getting together or already off on their eastern heading. After the feeling of complete isolation while in the clouds, and then the sudden realization that all those planes were milling around in there together, it was the moment for a prayer of thanks.

We were scheduled to rendezvous with our bombers shortly after landfall in, but that was a problem. Not only had we lost about four minutes in forming up, but recognition would be difficult with so many bombers in the air. Each bomb group had its own set of markings, but those markings were not easy to see from a distance, and going from one group to another took time. With an arbitrary guess, I changed my heading four degrees and increased my airspeed by four miles an hour. The extra circle had allowed Weep to get his group together and I could see them a little below at four o'clock.

Again, the warmth of the sun and the purr of the engine began to have its usual effect, but the excitement of the take-off and the whole forming-up process hadn't worn off completely. Also, there was the problem of locating the bomber group. The cloud cover below was breaking up, and without the white background to silhouette them, identification would be even more difficult. There were three formations ahead at about the right altitude. I chose to try the one in the middle.

It wasn't our group, so I drifted off to the right, and smiled as I saw the familiar squares. Lucky!

"These are ours, Weep," I said.

"Roger, Jonah."

Twenty-five minutes later, the bombers turned right, on their second leg to Giessen. There was no sign of the enemy. With so many airplanes in the sky, heading in various directions, I couldn't help but imagine what tension and apprehension was created on the ground with the speculation of where the bombs would fall.

As we closed in on the general Frankfurt area, bursts of flak began to appear, and by the time the bombers neared Giessen there was a huge inky cloud hanging over the city—at their exact altitude—and growing larger by the second! A dark and dirty, science-fiction monster devouring the sky.

At that point there was nothing for us to do but hang around outside the flak area and watch the bombers fly straight into that black hole. After the bombs were released, the bomber pilots could take any evasive action they felt necessary, but until the bombing run was completed, their paths had to be absolutely straight and level over the target—the planes were flown by the bombardier!

I sat there with my group and watched pieces breaking off, wings and engines blown away and tumbling down, smoking planes heading downward in slow-motion spirals, whole airplanes disintegrating in one explosive flash of flame—and only a few parachutes! *Ten men, each at the beginning of his adult life, in every one of those planes.*

We saw the flares of the lead bombardiers and the patterns of the explosions on the ground ... and hoped they were hitting the target.

The weather was beautiful. With the clear, bright, deep blue of the sky overhead, airbrushed with a pale tint of green off toward the horizon, and a few puffs of white scattered about, it was the picture of peace and tranquility. Yet, the scene we watched was filled with unimaginable horror, both in the air and on the ground. We were witnesses to the ultimate incongruity—a surreal dream sequence.

I had a new gadget—a K-25 camera—mounted inside my cockpit just behind me, pointing out to the left and downward. It was triggered with a toggle switch installed near my left hand. If I flicked it on and off, it would take single pictures, but if I held it on, it would click pictures automatically, about one every second. I used it mainly to photograph the bombing results—a useful tool for group intelligence.

When the bombers had finished their run, nothing remained of their once-organized formation. The planes came out of the hellhole individually, at various levels, many with engines smoking and props feathered, unable to hold their altitude. Those that could, made an attempt to form up again for the long trip home. No one knew what to expect on the way out, but they understood that a wounded, individual bomber was a sitting duck—perfect prey for any enemy predators.

Our job was to get as many bombers home—or at least to friendly territory—as we could.

"Jonah here," I said. "Blue Flight, you and Yellow Flight stick with the main group, and take them home. I'll hang around here for a bit with Red Flight. If you get in trouble let me know."

"Roger, Jonah."[3]

The smoke had cleared somewhat and I turned to make another 360 around the area, looking for stragglers in trouble. I also used the opportunity to get more pictures of the bombing results. Visually it looked good, but it was hard to tell. A thump and a little black cloud told me I was getting too close to the target area. The Germans obviously decided they might as well try to get the fighters as well. There was another big burst off to the right just ahead. Not only did I feel and hear it, I saw the flame inside, so I knew it was close. I dumped the stick and dove out of the area in a hurry. Once again I was impressed with the accuracy of the gunners—how could they come so close when they couldn't even see such tiny specks in the sky?

"Red Flight here, Jonah. There are a couple of big friends low at four o'clock."

"Roger, Red Flight. Stick with them. I'll go on."

On a general heading toward home, we searched the skies above and below but saw nothing until Balason, who was flying Black Three, picked up a struggling B-17 very low at eleven o'clock. With his wingman, he went down to investigate.

"Don't get too close," I said. "Just let them know we're friendly … and covering them."

Closer inspection revealed how shot up the bomber was. Half the tail was gone, two engines were out, and the plane was gradually losing altitude. Rather than bail out, they were trying desperately to limp back over the front lines. It seemed to me that they were almost there … if they could just hold out a little longer. We watched and waited, circling and weaving.

"Just hold it a little longer," someone said.

They did … and then with a sigh of relief, I saw some of our own GI trucks on the ground. They must have seen them also, because the plane veered off to the right toward an open field.

"They're going to belly it in," I said.

"There they go."

The plane cut into the field, leaving a straight path of smoke and dust behind, before coming to a halt at the edge of the clearing.

"Made it. Great job!"

I circled once again and we saw the crew pile out and wave.

"I only count seven," I stated. "Anybody see more?"

"No."

"Let's go home," I declared, rocking my wings in answer to their waves.

---

3 As "Jonah" Group Leader, Blick probably specified the squadron he is speaking to in this exchange. He was also flying as Seldom Leader for the mission.

The evening teletype stated that 1,532 bombers were put up that day, striking at various transportation targets. Thirty planes were lost or NYR. Included in those that were lost were two that collided in the clouds that morning a few miles from Raydon. I made a conservative estimate that there were at least 750 fighters, which brought the total of American planes in the sky to 2,282!

I've mentioned Howard Galbreath before. He was a childhood friend. We had played together, gone to school together, and worked together all of our formative years. After high school we were separated, but our friendship had survived.

He was always thin, and he grew into a tall, lanky man, reminding me of the early pictures of Howard Hughes. He had joined the Air Corps a year before Pearl Harbor, and the stories he told of his flying adventures, along with his uniform, helped convince me that I should also try to join. He was now a major in the 404th Fighter Bomber Group, which was part of the Ninth Air Force. They had arrived in England shortly before the invasion, and were moved to the Continent as soon as the facilities were available.

We had talked on the phone twice while he was still in England, but we never found the right opportunity to get together.[4] I had learned that the 404th Group was stationed at St Trond, a field in northern France, and waited for the right opportunity to stop and see him. That right opportunity was an escort mission to Frankfurt, and Duke was again scheduled to fly my wing.[5] After the briefing, I caught him alone.

"It looks like we're flying together again, Duke. I have a question for you."

"Okay."

"Now please ..." I said, "if you don't feel right about this, say so. This is no order—I'm just asking. I have an old friend I'd like to see, in the Ninth Air Force, that I haven't seen for years. He's stationed at a field in France, not too far off our course today." I offered Ed a cigarette. "I'm wondering if you'd go along with faking something wrong with your airplane on the way out so I could take you in there to check it out?"

Duke was obviously surprised, but I saw a little mischief creep into his eyes. "Sure," he said. "That would be fun ... let's do it!"

Knowing Duke, I had been sure he'd agree or I wouldn't have asked. I also knew he would keep his mouth shut. "Okay. It doesn't have to be much—could be a rough engine, electrical problem, oil pressure ... almost anything that might be a little worrisome over the Channel."

"I'll think of something," he said.

---

4   This is clearly some artistic license from Blick. His war diary confirms that he visited his friend Howard Galbreath at Winkton on April 20, 1944, and that Galbreath visited Raydon on June 16, August 6 and August 8, 1944. Clearly, they were good friends.

5   Mission of December 18, 1944.

Our rendezvous with the bombers was uneventful, but as we flew toward the target area we saw what looked to be a solid wall of clouds from the ground up to around 30,000 or 40,000 feet. It was a mammoth front, and as we approached I felt like I was in one of those tiny ships I had seen pictures of, in Alaska or somewhere, approaching a glacier. Whatever its height, we were not about to go over it. There was nothing to do but fly right into it. I moved the squadron in a little closer. It was the kind of weather occurrence that made a person wonder how bright the generals really were, sitting back there in their comfortable offices.

Bitching about the weather came with the job, especially in England—I didn't know about elsewhere in the world. We all knew, even then, that the generals had nothing to do with it—they were just going by the reports from the weather people, whose predictions were based on the general weather pattern, which traveled from west to east. However, we knew from our many experiences that Mother Nature was playful, and liked to vary her routine. In reality, the predictions those generals received were just so-called "educated" guesswork.

Even though the clouds could conceivably break up before we reached the target, it didn't look like it—it looked like they were there permanently, and it was my guess we'd never see Frankfurt.

The bombers continued on course, but they had to be wondering the same thing—what possible use could they be in that mess? As they got closer to the wall, another large bomber formation was emerging off to the right ... obviously aborting the mission. Smart, I thought. Why didn't our bombers make the same decision *before* they went in? Did they have to see for themselves? And what about us, were we supposed to follow the bombers in? Or go home without them? It wasn't my decision. LeFebre was Jonah and it was up to him.

As if on cue, LeFebre said, "Jonah here. Close it up good and let's go in and see what it looks like. If we lose them, we might as well go home."

Inside the clouds, there was a hazy glow everywhere, like looking through misty, off-white glasses, and the bombers were still visible. The farther we penetrated, however, the darker it became, until everything but my flight disappeared.

I continued muttering to myself, "Say it Fred. Dammit, let's get outta here. What the hell good are we doing like this!"

I was about to press the button when Fred spoke: "Jonah here. I'm aborting the mission. I'll make a slow right turn to a heading of two-seven-zero."

"This is Seldom, Jonah. Roger ... will follow."

"Jockey here, Jonah. Me too."

With a huge sigh of relief I started the turn and glanced back to see if everyone was following. I could barely make out Red Flight. I completed the turn, but it seemed to take forever before the overhead glow came back and we could see each other again. Then, all of a sudden, we were out—just like that—as if someone had opened the shower door.

I saw Jonah up ahead, and what was probably Jockey off to the right, a little low. I looked back, again, at the towering wall of cloud, sliced off like piece of angel food cake. Unbelievable!

I made my decision to land at St Trond. The course we were on would take us a little north of the field, but I had counted on that. Another fifteen minutes would do it.

I had neglected to work out hand signals with Duke, but when the time came I went through some strange motions, which Duke interpreted correctly.

"Seldom White Two to Seldom Leader," he said. "My oil pressure is dropping. I think I've sprung a leak."

"How bad is it, Duke?" I asked. "Do you think you can make it across the Channel?"

"I don't know. It's dropping steadily. I'm not sure I should take the chance."

"Okay. Hang on a minute. Let's see if we can find you a field. I'll go with you."

I called Tanner, who was flying Blue Flight. "Seldom Blue. You take everyone home. I'm going in with Duke."

"Okay Blick, Blue Flight here. Good luck ... out."

At St Trond, after we had landed and were walking toward Operations, Duke said, "I really did have an oil leak ... or something. I didn't have to fake it."

"You're kidding," I said, shocked. "If I'd known that, I wouldn't have been so lackadaisical about the whole thing. Why didn't you tell me?"

"I did."

I laughed. "Yeah, I guess you did. Now let's see if we can find Howard."

We walked into Operations.

"Trouble, Major?" the sergeant asked.

"A little," I told him. "We've got an oil problem. Do you know where I can find Major Galbreath?"

"You mean *Colonel* Galbreath. Just a minute."

He picked up the phone. "What's your name, Sir?"

"Blickenstaff,"

"Sir," he spoke into the phone. "There's a Major Blickenstaff here to see you."

The sergeant hung up the phone and said, "He'll be right here, Major. Just make yourselves comfortable. It'll only be a few minutes.

Howard loped through the doorway, ducking a little, with a big grin on his face. He still walked slightly off-center. One hip was a little higher than the other as a result of a broken pelvis when we were kids. He had been hit by a car right in front of my house. The driver was so upset he stopped, picked Howard up, ran up and put him down in my mother's flower bed, and then ran back to the car and took off. No one ever saw him again.

"Hi Colonel," I grinned as we shook hands. "Congratulations."

"Thanks. What in hell you doin' here?" he asked. "You're supposed to be up there fightin' the big war, not down here with us ground troops."

"We were, but Duke, here, developed an oil leak … and besides, we thought maybe we could talk you into parting with some champagne. Ed, this is Colonel Galbreath … we've known each other since we were about three years old."

"Good to meet you, Sir," Duke smiled. "Is it true that you have champagne?"

"We just might be able to scrounge up a little. Let's go find out." On the way out he turned to the sergeant. "See if you can get someone to fix that oil leak, Frank."

We climbed into Howard's jeep and he drove about a mile to some old stone buildings. The winter weather and neglect showed, but the beauty of the landscaping was still there.

"This is where we live," Howard pointed out. "It used to be a German rest camp, with all the trimmings … steam heat, pretty Belgian maids waiting on tables—a real country club. You going to spend the night?"

"We weren't planning on it, but it wouldn't take much to talk us into it. I don't know, though … we should get word back to the base. You think you could do that?"

"I don't know," Howard said. "Let's talk about it at lunch. You hungry?"

"Sure, why not." I glanced at my watch and it was only eleven o'clock. We could stay quite a while and still get back before dark.

Howard wasn't kidding about the Belgian waitresses. We got the full treatment—a five-course meal including some French wine. What a way to fight the war, I thought. But I had no idea how temporary it was.

"I've been thinking," I said. "It's early, and we should probably get back. I don't think I can make a very good case for staying overnight, unless you can't get that oil leak fixed for some reason."

"Why don't you let Duke take your plane now and you can stay?"

"Well … that's an idea. You want to do that, Duke?"

"Sure. It sounds okay to me."

I thought Duke would probably be bored, anyway, just sitting around for a few hours listening to us rehash old times.

After lunch we walked over to Howard's quarters. It was in the middle of a spread, looking a little like Thunderbird, only much more luxurious. The walls were stone, with heavy wooden doors and thick wooden ceiling beams and window frames. There was a bedroom, a bathroom, and a small sitting room with a fireplace, a leather couch and a couple of comfortable chairs—even a rug on the floor and a small, round, hardwood coffee table. A little envy crept into my psyche.

Howard picked up the phone and asked for Operations. "Any word on that oil leak, Frank?" I could tell by his expression that he was pleased with the answer. He hung up. "They're not going to get it fixed tonight, so I guess you're stuck."

We sat there most of the afternoon and talked, in-between phone calls. Planes were taking off and landing constantly.

"Our missions are short," Howard explained. "We get calls from the lines about something that's bothering them, like a gun position they can't seem to knock out.

Then we get some of our air cover over there as quickly as possible to strafe or bomb the area. It works well as long as the weather is good. When it isn't, though, we can't help much."

"Don't you have trouble strafing your own people? That's what I'd be afraid of."

"We had problems like that at first, but not anymore much … we're getting a lot better. We work on a grid system, and we've now learned to stay in the right grid." He smiled. "At least, most of the time! The biggest problem we get now is when someone somewhere along the line gets the grid all fouled up."

About three-thirty Duke left for the field, and a half-hour later, Howard got another phone call. "You'll never guess what's happened now," he said, as he hung up. "Duke taxied into the tail of one of our P-47s. Your plane seems okay, but they want to check it out anyway."[6]

"That does it," I replied. "I guess you've got us for the night."

"I'm not complaining."

That night after dinner, with a very sheepish and apologetic Duke, Howard broke out a bottle of champagne. As we started on it, he received another phone call. When he hung up, he said, "You guys go ahead. I don't know what's going on, but they've called an emergency meeting. I'll be back as soon as I can."

He returned in about an hour and a half, looking grim and worried—very different from the boyhood pal I knew.

"Two things," he announced. "First of all, the Germans have broken through our lines and are heading in this direction. We're going to have to pull out of here it looks like—probably tomorrow sometime! The second thing is the weather. It's socking in solid all around us. You'll be lucky to get out of here in the morning. Better get up *real* early. Your planes are okay to go."

"Anything we can do?"

"No … not now anyway. Get some sleep and get out as quick as you can. You can sack out in the next room there. Someone will wake you up, and I'll see you for breakfast."

I didn't sleep well because I felt, or rather sensed, the flurry of activity going on around us. It reminded me of the nervousness hanging in the air after the news broke about the bombing of Pearl Harbor—nothing I could quite pin down, just an uneasy excitement.

The next morning, Howard said, "Our field is the only one around that isn't zero-zero, and it's not very good either—and getting worse by the minute. You'd better get out of here while you can. Forget breakfast. You don't have time."

He dropped us off at our planes, shook our hands and wished us "Good luck."

"Same to you, Howard. And thanks for the champagne." He had given us four bottles to take back. "I hope this breakthrough is not as serious as it seems right now."

---

6 No accident report could be located to confirm the details of this incident.

"We'll be okay," he assured us. "We just have to pull back a little."

We had no way of knowing at the time that the breakthrough was very serious, and would go down in the history books as the Battle of the Bulge.

We took off on instruments and broke out about 2,500 feet. It was solid—we could see no openings anywhere, and I thought about that mammoth wall of cloud that we had seen the day before. This must be related to it. I considered what it might be like over England—usually it was worse! But I told myself we'd make it somehow … as always.

"I'm going to let down over the Channel, Duke. There's usually a little space between the water and the clouds. Maybe we can weave our way through the smokestacks and barrage balloons and find the field."

"Okay. I'll be with you." I knew he would.

The clouds were dark and dense and I could barely make out Duke's plane. It was time for caution, and my let-down was slow and easy. The altimeter said fifty feet—it was worry time. I motioned to Duke.

"Stack it up now," I told him. "And be ready to pull up quickly at any time. I'm going on down a little lower."

I felt my wing shudder a little as Duke moved to a position slightly above me. We were down to twenty feet … and still no water. I continued to inch the plane down until the altimeter read zero! There was no water in sight even then. I couldn't believe there was no airspace. I'd have to go up through it all again. The gauge could be wrong. Altimeters were based on barometric pressure and they weren't always accurate. I continued easing down, ever so slightly—an inch at a time, fully prepared to yank the stick back instantly on contact, when either the prop or the scoop at the bottom of the plane hit water. I had run into waves before, with the P-47, but it didn't have that big scoop, and I, for sure, didn't know what that would do when it hit.

The altimeter read ten feet below zero and still no water. I began to feel the stupidity of it all, but the recklessness of it was a challenge, and I was even more determined to find out where the damned water was. I almost looked forward to hitting the water so I could test my reflexes!

At fifteen feet below, my peripheral vision picked up some wisps of cloud going by and I unglued my eyes from the altimeter long enough to take a quick glance downward. *The water was there after all!* We were about ten feet above the surface. Not much working space, but I felt there might be more as we headed toward land.

But there wasn't. Instead, it got worse. We began to fly in and out of the soup, all the time being forced closer and closer to the waves. I finally had to give up.

"This is really stupid, Duke. I'm going back up. Hang in there."

We broke out at 1,500 feet. That seemed hopeful, anyway, and I climbed on up to 3,000 feet and called Raydon.

"[Cockle] tower, this is Seldom Five One. Do you read?"

"Go ahead, Seldom. We read you loud and clear."

"What's your weather? We're coming in."

"You'll never make it here, Seldom. It's bad. We have zero-zero. Contact Nuthouse to see what's open."[7]

"Roger, Cockle. Switching over."

I pushed the C channel button. "Seldom Five One calling Nuthouse. Do you read?"

"Loud and clear, Seldom. Go ahead."

"We are two planes. We need a heading to the nearest open field."

"There is only one possibility, Seldom—Duxford—and it's closing rapidly. Continue on your heading and give me another call in one minute."

One minute later, I called again. "Hello Nuthouse. One … two … three … four … five. Seldom out."

The controller now had the third leg of a triangulation problem and could give us a heading right to the field. "Roger Seldom. Stand by … turn to one-eight-seven. Call again in three minutes."

I switched back to Raydon. "Cockle, I have Duke with me and we're going to Duxford."

"Roger, Seldom. Good luck."

I switched back to Nuthouse and in three minutes, called again. "Seldom here again Nuthouse. One … two … three … four … five."

"Stand by Seldom. … You're doing okay. Turn to one-eight-five and call Duxford. You should be over the field in two minutes."

"Roger, Nuthouse. Thank you."

I switched then to Channel A. "Hello Duxford, this is Seldom Five One. Do you read?"[8]

"Roger, Seldom. We've been listening. It's bad out, but you can make it. Put your wheels down and come straight in. You should be able to see us in thirty seconds."

"Roger, Duxford."

"We can hear you now, Seldom. You're off to the right slightly."

"Roger."

I let down to the top of the cloud cover, which was now about 500 feet. "When we see the field, Ed, we might have to do some quick maneuvering … stick with me."

"Roger."

I saw an opening ahead, but it wasn't much. We passed over it on the right. The field was there, but I could see only part of the runway. I made a steep left bank and let down, barely making it through the hole. At that point I didn't care what

---

7   "Nuthouse" was the call-sign of the Microwave Early Warning system used for fighter control based at Gulpen on the Continent from November 1944. See Roger A. Freeman, *The Mighty Eighth War Manual*, London, Jane's Publishing Company Ltd, 1985, p. 82.

8   Blick's call-sign during his flying career in England was "Pipeful" and then "Seldom 51." Duxford tower's call-sign at this time was "Rutley."

direction I was going—all I wanted to do was get to the ground. I was underneath the overcast with my right wing in the clouds and my left practically on the trees. I had to do some violent maneuvering to line up with the runway, but then realized I was way too hot and would have to go around.

I jammed the throttle forward. "We've got to go around, Duke."

With a tight turn, I attempted to stay under the overcast and in sight of the field, but as I turned, the scud from the clouds got in the way and I just couldn't take the chance of trying to half-fly contact and instruments so close to the trees. Reluctantly, I pulled up once again through the clouds.

"Dammit, Duke, I lost the field!"

Duke was still there as I continued to circle. "Now where the hell *is* the field?"

"Right behind us I think, Blick," Duke replied.

"Okay."

I continued the turn and spotted the hole, at the same time cutting the throttle. I was still a little hot and too far down the runway. "To hell with it!" I muttered. "I'll land anyway!" and I chopped the throttle all the way back, and put down full flaps. This is it, I thought, I'm committed.

As soon as the wheels touched I was on the brakes, and amid all the screeching and squealing, my plane stopped at the end of the runway—and hard as it was for me to believe, Duke was still there. It wasn't the best landing I'd ever made, for sure, but as they say, "Any landing you can walk away from is a good landing!"

We taxied slowly back to the parking area where the crews were waiting. In Operations, one of the sergeants was smiling. "A little rough, huh Major?"

"Yeah ... just a little."

As we climbed into the jeep, Duke, with his usual smile said, "Gee, that was fun ... let's do it again sometime."

"You hang in there pretty good," I said, "for someone who can't steer past the tail of a P-47!"

The weather was miserable, and according to all the reports we received, it was getting worse everywhere. The weather people claimed the overcast over England was up to 7,000 or 8,000 feet and the reports from the Continent were scary. I wondered if Howard and his group got out. I thought about the remark he had made about the value of their support for the ground troops. There was no way anybody could fly in that kind of soup. The Germans were pushing ahead rapidly with very little opposition. They were due a break in the weather, and it would come eventually ... but when?

I finally got upset enough, with having to hang around Duxford, to call Raydon and have them send my jeep to get us. It was good to get back to familiar surroundings, but the weather was just as unbearable, and there was no sign of it letting up. The reports about the breakthrough kept getting worse, contributing immensely to the already frayed nerves of the pilots.

Thirty

The weather lifted, but it was short-lived, allowing us to fly three missions before it socked in again. On December 24, the Eighth Air Force put up almost 2,000 bombers and the 353rd contributed 80 fighters. The Germans didn't scare easily, however, and continued their push into the Ardennes, making significant gains. The weather had allowed them to regroup and win air superiority over the Ninth Air Force once again, and the Eighth was frustrated—we could not help.

On Christmas day, a repeat show was scheduled with orders to land in France if necessary. The mission was not considered successful, but almost everyone made it back to their bases.

With the predicament in the Ardennes becoming more desperate by the day, we were briefed again on the 26th for the same kind of show. It was zero-zero weather but we all went out again and sat on the runway waiting for the slightest change. It never lifted and the mission was finally scrubbed.

We went out again on the 27th, and after an hour's wait, the weather cleared enough for us to take off, almost completely on instruments. The bombers couldn't make it so we were given permission for a sweep of our own over the Koblenz area. It was uneventful except for the landing. We all made it down, but most of us noticed a few more gray hairs with our next glimpse in the mirror.

Most of our time was spent in the ready room, nervously waiting. We had long since decided it was really our home and we tried to fix it up as comfortably as we could. It was a large Nissen hut, but with all the construction inside it had the look of a normal building partitioned into several rooms. The rounded ceiling was the only remaining tell-tale sign.

The lower part of one end was paneled off with areas for airplane scheduling information: which planes were available, what condition they were in, what pilots were scheduled for the next mission, the position they were flying, etc. There was also a blackboard for chalk talks, used mainly for training sessions and for posting information needing immediate attention.

Above that was our masterpiece. We had designed a permanent board showing all members of the squadron, past and present, with pictures of the aces in the center, and with plenty of room for expansion—the 350th Honor Roll. On both sides, our intelligence officer, Rosentreter, had copied and painted very large pretty girls, leaving off the drapery of course.[1]

Off to the left of that wall was Doc's popular snack bar, and next to that, one of the more creative and ingenious crew chiefs had fashioned a drinking fountain out of a bomb, attaching an old throttle quadrant to it for the handle.

The entrance to the building was to the right, and that doorway led also to the attached hut that housed the group officers and the briefing room. Directly in front of the entrance was the squadron Operations area, partitioned off by a low fence-like structure and gate. It gave our Operations sergeant privacy but availability. He was the fulcrum—the axis around which the squadron revolved. Without him, it would have disintegrated into a shambles of disorganization. As pilots, we knew nothing about the reams of paperwork necessary to run such a large organization. He cut the orders, kept the files tidy, wrote the reports—the equivalent of an executive secretary in a large business.

At the opposite end of the room, the wall was used by intelligence. It displayed any current information about the war, including a large map showing the changing front lines. There were reports of activities, data on new airplanes and weapons—whatever seemed pertinent at the time. There were also aircraft recognition charts and hanging models of the various German and Allied airplanes we were likely to encounter.

In front of that wall was a heavily used ping-pong table. For those who played, there were some wild championship games. I was not the fastest in the world, but I had good reactions and I was right up there with the best. Rosentreter had to be considered the overall champ. I liked to go against him because we played the same kind of game, but Bledsoe was another story. We had faced each other a lot when he was there, but he was terribly frustrating for me. In the first place, he didn't hold the paddle right, and he'd just stand there, right at the edge of the table, with that crazy grin on his face and a steady stream of chatter, and return all my fantastic drives with ease. I'd finally get so upset I'd blow it!

"Attaboy, Blick," he'd say. "Right here ... here's my paddle ... put it right here. ... That's the stuff ... you're doin' great ... right here ... just a little harder ... whatsamatter? You runnin' outta steam?" And all the time grinning like a sick clown. "Right here ... you're slowing down ... give it a big one ... you can do it ... there's

---

1 The artist of the "Raydon Ladies" (there were four ladies in total) is the subject of some debate. Both Bill Tanner and Chauncy Rowan claimed to have had a hand in the painting. Tanner, an accomplished portrait painter, said he did it with the help of intelligence staff—his P-47 carried a very similar piece of artwork. It seems likely that it was therefore a collaborative effort.

a good one for you … just right for you … hit it … harder, Blick … you know you can do it … yakkity yakkity yak. …"

He'd lob it back, high and slow, and it would bounce in exactly the right spot so I couldn't resist the temptation to slam it as hard as I could. But I couldn't keep it up, and Bledsoe would invariably win.

Various kinds of tables and chairs were scattered around the room, including some very comfortable lounge chairs that could be used for reading or sleeping, or just existing. There was a record player over against one wall. The collection of records was sparse, but there was a fair variety, and all became very familiar. Still, after all of this time, whenever I hear Sinatra's *Old Man River*, I see Li'l Joe Furness sitting there in a trance, with his eyes closed and his ear practically in the speaker, listening to that record, over and over again.

There was always a card game in progress—bridge and/or poker. We used any device we could to take our minds off the missions … and the waiting … and the … *depression.*

The wet, dripping blanket of clouds hung there day after day—always the same—the field immersed in a clammy gloom obscuring the runways and eliminating any thought of flight. Even the birds had vertigo. Once in a while the sound of an engine could be heard in the distance, being warmed up by a crew chief, as tense and bored as the pilots, but mostly there were the sounds of frustration and shortened tempers. The mist would lift slightly and we would sense the subtle change. The door would open more often and the conversations would be more hushed in tone—maybe a laugh that wasn't there before—but then the door would close again and they would know there was no longer a need to check.

It was always a relief to fly a mission, if for no other reason than to get rid of that charged-up atmosphere. Doc complained, constantly, about being useless—contributing nothing for the good of the people. Physically, it was true there wasn't much for him to do, but psychologically there was plenty. I was close enough to him to know what he did, but most of the pilots didn't realize the effort he put into it, and how successful he was.

We all had our own individual approaches to the problem of tension build-up. I was never quite sure what was best. With my apparent calmness on the outside, and nervousness kept inside, I sat on one extreme end of the tension scale, but at the other end it was the blow-up-and-release approach. When things got too bad, I would go out and fly around the field a few times in the bad weather, just to release the tension, or just take off to London for a day or two. It seemed to work.

Once again it was posted … MISSION SCRUBBED.

My nerves were catching up to my stomach, and I thought a little flying would help calm my jitters. There was another classmate I hadn't seen since Luke, stationed over in the western part of England with a bomber group. It seemed like a good time to visit. The weather was lousy, but I shrugged that off with the rationalization that my airplane needed to fly as much as I did.

I told Doc, who, of course, called me a damn fool … but then said, "Take me with you."

"I'm a little jumpy, Doc, and I feel the need to be alone—get it out of my system in my own plane."

"I figured as much," he replied, sulking.

I contacted [Staff Sergeant Thomas] O'Connell, my crew chief, who seemed happy to have something to do, and by the time I had my gear all together, the plane was ready to go.

It felt good to be in the air, and especially good to be headed in the opposite direction for a change. My anxieties melted away almost immediately. Temporary as it was, I had escaped!

The ceiling was about 500 feet, and rather than plow up through the clouds, I decided to just relax and enjoy the scenery, even if it did all look the same. The farther west I went, however, the lower I had to fly, the clouds forcing me down until I was somewhere around 200 feet. I began to think Doc was right—that I should seriously wonder what in hell I was doing. There was an old saying that the smartest pilots—the ones who stayed alive—were those who learned how to make a 180-degree turn.

When I was so low I was buzzing the treetops I decided maybe I should be one of the smart ones, and reluctantly started the turn. Halfway through it, everything disappeared! I was completely immersed in the soup! Suddenly I was blindfolded!

As a cadet at Thunderbird, I had been trained in the old tradition of flying "by the seat of your pants!" The theory being, of course, that one should learn to "feel" the attitudes of the plane by the various pressures on your butt. "You can tell the speed by the way the guy wires sing," they said. They even had the needle and ball and the airspeed indicator covered so we couldn't see them. That was fine in the old Stearman, and in the wilds of the Arizona desert where they didn't know what a cloud looked like unless it was dust, but where were the guy wires now? It was a little like shifting gears according to the sound of the engine, or judging your speed in a Model-T by the vibrations.

Later on, when the instruments were uncovered we heard constantly, "Center the needle and ball." The straight-up needle meant that the plane was not banking, and the ball, which worked something like a carpenter's level, meant that the plane was properly aligned and not "slipping"—skidding. If the needle and ball were centered, and the airspeed constant, the plane was flying a straight and level course.

My training was based on those simple and old-fashioned instruments. However, the altimeter had a lag in it—you could actually be going down while it read "up." And the compass was very nervous, always bouncing around and hard to settle down.

Our planes now, though, were equipped with an artificial horizon and a gyro compass, both using a gyroscope, and very accurate and without lag. The artificial horizon allowed the pilot to see the attitude of the plane in relation to the horizon at all times … probably the greatest gadget ever devised for instrument flying. Yet it had a tendency, during very violent maneuvering as in a dogfight, to go all to hell, and maybe get hung up in an odd position. Because of that, and being a product of the old school, I seldom turned it on!

But now, suddenly without visual ground contact, in a turn right on the treetops, and forced to go immediately on instruments, I was completely and utterly disoriented! There was no time! The slightest error and I would be in the trees! My stomach was in my throat! My immediate reaction was to haul back on the stick, which I did. Then I had to try to center the needle. That was easy, but the ball was behaving like it was in a pin-ball machine. In my panic, I overreacted to everything. The plane shuddered before I noticed the airspeed had dropped to near stalling speed—I was probably going straight up! I goosed the throttle and dumped the nose, but because of the lag in the instruments and knowing I had no room above the ground, I was afraid to let the airspeed build. I kept trying to point the plane in the direction of home and the higher ceiling, but the compass was useless. Like on a rollercoaster, I was either near a stall or speeding downward, jerking the stick around like a kid with a toy. I was sick!

The sweat was pouring down, blurring my eyes, and try as I might I just couldn't get the damn thing under control—all I could see in my mind were those trees reaching up to grab me. And the hills—I had no idea whether there were any hills or towns around with steeples and wires. The images kept flashing through my mind as I continued to overreact to every tiny movement of the plane.

It had been hours—so it seemed—and my nerves were shot. My heart was pounding like a drum at twice its normal speed. I was completely and utterly exhausted! I had no more fight in me—I'd had it ... this was it!

I let go of the stick, took my feet off the rudders, and gave up!

"*MY GOD,*" I yelled aloud, "what the hell am I doing!" and I reached again for the stick.

It was a strange and unorthodox approach to the solution, but it worked ... and saved my life.

If a plane is properly trimmed, it is a relatively stable flying machine. In the instant I had given up the controls, momentarily expecting the crash, the plane took over and began to seek its normal flying attitude. It helped, also, that I was calmer, having already accepted the idea I was going to die. I was able to understand more clearly what was happening. I still had a little difficulty with the up and down movement, but I got the plane on a heading toward home and broke out of the mess just about the way I went in ... right on the treetops!

I reached over and turned on the artificial horizon.

Back on the ground, Doc said, "You're back early."

"Yeah," I answered, "weather was bad."

Thirty-one

The weather was even worse in January 1945, but with a dangerously determined effort, the Ninth Air Force won back its air superiority over the front lines. Once again the Allied forces pushed forward, and by the end of the month, they had completely eliminated the Bulge.

Our group flew only sixteen missions, running into the Luftwaffe once and destroying nine aircraft, including two ME262s, the German jets. To add to the problem of the weather, we had bad luck with a series of accidents. Three pilots were killed in take-off accidents and one lost his life crash-landing five miles from the base. Three planes bellied in due to mechanical failure, four were damaged by flak, and two were damaged in take-off accidents.

SNOW! As if the lousy weather wasn't bad enough already.

We hadn't flown for three days. The overworked ground crews had tried to keep the runways cleared, but they couldn't keep up, and finally had to give up the battle, hoping it would stop sometime soon. It did, and they were out for most of the night, hard at it again.

I could see the runway.[1] It looked good, but the banks were threatening, seeming to close in at the far end, leaving only enough room for one plane, not two. At least the visibility was good. I had to admit the landscape was beautiful—everything clean and white, everywhere. Such a change from the usual, dismal gray.

[The weather briefing] had said the ceiling was about 1,000 feet, and that was okay. [The group] could form below and climb up through it together about 4,000 feet on instruments. Maybe it would be better over the Continent.

Lefebre was Jonah, leading the group with the 351st. Haynes was next with the 350th and then Johnson and the 352nd.

The green light, and Lefebre started down the runway [27] with his wingman. I thought he veered a little, but I wasn't sure. It might have just looked that way from

---

1   This is the mission for January 10, 1945. Blick did not fly that day.

where I was. Could it be icy? [The 352nd took off next on runway 35]. When the last flight of the 352nd started, the leader hit the bank with his wing!

"Hold on to it! For God's sake hold on to it," I screamed aloud, but then watched in shock as the pilot over-controlled with the rudder and veered out from the bank and almost into his wingman. Then he swerved back again into the bank. I forgot what I was doing, my eyes fixed on the plane as it lifted slightly, then cartwheeled off to the side, exploding into flames. *Oh my God! He can't get out of that!*

The wingman goosed it and took off as the flames leaped up beside him.

The 350th was taking off [on runway 27]. The smoke was still pouring out of the crashed plane, looking every bit like a bomb burst. I saw the emergency crews with extinguishers trying to gain control of the flames. Nothing burns like gasoline! DISASTER!

"*Good God, another one!*" I said to myself. "*Watch out! What the hell is happening?*" One of the wingmen [Jessup] spun around and slid all the way down the runway dragging a wing. Don Warren skidded, but managed to take off. The rest got off okay.

Good Lord, what a way to start a mission!

Lieutenant Colonel LeFebre, my roommate, finished his tour and moved out. Another squadron CO moved in.[2]

[The 'newcomer'] was another one of my classmates who had been sent to Hamilton Field and then transferred to the 353rd. About five feet ten, [he] was blond and good-looking, with the easy-going manner of a good bedside doctor. I didn't know him all that well, but I found him pleasant and didn't anticipate any problems. I soon found out he wasn't in the room much anyway. About the only time I saw him there was in the morning sleeping, and many times the bed remained untouched. He was either at the officers' club at night or off the base.

It didn't take long for me to discover that, conversationally, he was a bust—I couldn't seem to get into much depth with him. Somehow the talk always drifted around to women. Not that it wasn't an interesting subject, but after three years of talk about flying and women—in that order—I yearned for something a little more mind-stretching. He was quick on the draw and whenever I tried for any depth, he'd come out with a quip that turned everything into humor, albeit some of it very funny I had to admit. He was an excellent person to have around in a party atmosphere, and with him there it always seemed like it was a party atmosphere. He always seemed to have a drink in his hand, and after the first two drinks, his eyes never seemed to focus on anything above the chin. I found myself forever saying, "Look at me when you talk to me!"

Because he was off the base so much of the time, I suspected he was involved with a girl, and owing to some inferences made, that she had a husband off fighting the

---

2   Lieutenant Colonel Fred Lefebre completed his second tour on January 27, 1945.

war on the Continent somewhere. It was not an unusual situation. The involvement, though, whatever it was, never seemed to bother him in his pursuit of other conquests.

There were no rigid rules about parties on the base, and during the long periods of bad weather Rimerman and the base officers were lenient about visitors. Parties were often spontaneous; they just seemed to crop up once in a while. Someone, somewhere, would get the okay, and it would somehow be loosely organized. Once in a while it was a big one—a celebration of something that included the whole base, like a group anniversary or Christmas—but most were smaller and localized, sometimes just the enlisted men, and sometimes only the officers. More usual than not, there would be a few members of the 56th Group around.

Those were the nights that I would seek out Doc and any of the others, like Bill Bailey, who preferred to sit and watch those officers who were not so leery of the camp followers with their questionable physical conditions—of which there seemed to be any number available. Those officers who had found legitimate girlfriends could bring them to the club and enjoy a good time. There was an old beaten-up piano, and several people were good on the keys.[3]

One of those nights, Doc and I sat sipping our drinks, watching the party getting more loaded by the minute. Rimerman and Bailey had been sitting with us for a while. Rimerman was conscientious and always showed, but he wasn't much of a party man, and usually had one or two drinks and then disappeared. Bailey, on the other hand, was too sociable to just sit and talk for any length of time—he liked to meander.

[Blick wrote of Bailey: "While I was still with the squadron, I always thought of him as a kind of clown—quick with the quip. He seemed about as far from being a fighter pilot as you could get. Outwardly, he treated everything so lightly that he came off as being insincere, with no depth, but it was all an act. Later, when I moved to the Wheelhouse and began to know him better, I found out that he was not much different than the rest of us. He was a good pilot, and a good CO. I liked him. He was very sociable, able to talk with anyone, general or otherwise. I don't think he liked fighting a war, but then, who did?"[4]]

"So what's the excuse for this one?" I asked Doc.

"Weather, I suppose. It doesn't take much, and this crummy weather is as good a reason as any. Doesn't look like you're going anywhere tomorrow anyway … so why not?"

"True." I made a gesture toward the bar with my drink. "And the way some of these guys are pouring it down, they've got that all figured out. We haven't been released yet, though … and what happens if they do spring a mission on us?"

---

3 There were well-appointed officers' clubs at Metfield and Raydon with a lounge and bar. The bar was known as "The Auger Inn"—a pun on the demise of unlucky pilots who crashed or "augered in" to the ground.
4 Blickenstaff to Cross, 1998.

Doc shrugged. "They'll fly anyway—they always do. After all this time on the ground, a mission is as good a cure for a hangover as anything."

I thought for a minute. "Does oxygen really work, Doc?"

"I don't know. It should. Everyone always claims they feel better once they start breathing it."

"Do you remember Baer, at Baltimore?" I had to smile at the thought.

"Yeah. ... He wasn't there very long." He paused. "Didn't he go off to Africa or somewhere like that before we got the P-47s?"

"Yeah, he's the one. He was with Balason. I went all through cadets with him, and he was out every night, drinking, when he could get out. He'd come back loaded, just before curfew, and fly just like everyone else the next morning ... damn good pilot, too. I'll swear I could never figure out how he could do it. He was the only guy I've ever known who could walk into any bar at any time and come out with a girl ... free too ... except for the drinks."

"Charm," Doc said. "Can I borrow one of your cigarettes?"

Doc was at it again. He didn't really like cigarettes, always complaining that they tasted like burning paper. Whenever he was giving up smoking he would quit carrying his pipe, thinking of course that if he didn't have it he wouldn't smoke. He always asked if he could "borrow" one. I would usually tease him by reaching into my shirt pocket and pulling out just one cigarette. It was a habit I had developed for my own protection. The cigarette would just sort of appear, and no one would notice, but if the whole pack was taken out, hands would come from everywhere and the whole pack would be gone in no time. Doc would get mad and raise hell when I did that, so this time I brought the whole package out, offered him one, and put it down on the table.

"Maybe so," I continued. "But I never thought he had much sex appeal. But, of course, I wouldn't know that anyway, would I? Maybe he appealed to the mother instinct or something ... or maybe he just knew how to spot horny people."

The decibels had increased, and a few people had gathered around the piano. It wouldn't be long, I thought, before it was "Roll me o—ver ... in the clo—ver. Roll me over, lay me down and do it again."

I pushed through all the hands performing flying maneuvers, to the bar. I ordered two more drinks and wondered, as I had many times, what the bartender, who was a buck sergeant, thought about all the "officers and gentlemen" behaving like just plain old ordinary drunks! And what did he tell his GI buddies back in the barracks?

It took longer than I thought it should, and it seemed that there was an over-abundance of pilots at the bar—more than there ought to be. I looked back, out over the room. With the exception of the girls who were with the studs attempting to make out on the spot, most of the girls were either sitting by themselves or with other girls; it was obvious that the guys had gone to the bar to get refills, but along the way had got involved in conversations about flying. I remembered the studies that had been made, concluding that males would rather chase females than eat. Flying seemed to put sex in second position.

I looked at my watch—it was one o'clock. "I think I'll take off, Doc. You going to hang around?"

"Naw I'm ready. ... How about borrowing another cigarette?"

"Take the rest of the pack. I have more at the house."

Doc grinned. "I'm quitting, remember?"

"Yeah ... that's right. I forgot."

After dropping Doc off at his hut, I drove on to the Wheelhouse. The jeep lights were more of a hindrance than a help. All they did was spread out flat about ten feet ahead, making a solid wall out of the fog. I could almost see better in the dark, without the lights. It didn't matter much, though, either way—the jeep could virtually make it on its own.

I opened the door to find most of the lights on, but there was no one around. I didn't expect to see anyone, anyway; whoever was there should be sleeping. I was tired and ready for it myself.

"What in hell ...!" I said aloud.

My door was bolted on the inside.

I rattled and pounded, but there was no answer. Then it hit me. *Oh shit!* That goddamn [new roommate] is using our room—*my room! What in hell am I supposed to do now?*

I was tempted to break the damn door down, and I'd had just about enough to drink to do it, but I certainly didn't want to wake up Rimerman—I'd already made enough noise. Wake him up and he'd probably kill any more parties for the duration.

I went back downstairs to the living room and sat there getting colder and more furious by the minute. It was warmer upstairs so I went back up and sat down on the top step.

What an asshole. The bastard must have expected me to sit and wait all night while he screwed himself to death—and at that point I hoped he did! That brought on a smile just thinking about it.

I got up and pounded and rattled some more. "C'mon, you bastard—let me in!"

No answer.

I sat down again, and about that time I had a brilliant idea—and enough liquor to release some inhibitions. I remembered the roof over the back stoop, which was just below the bathroom window. I thought I might be able to make it from there to the bedroom window.

The bathroom window was a small one, but I was sure I could climb through it, and the roof wasn't so far down. *I'll give it a try*, I thought. As an ex-gymnast and an alumnus of Muscle Beach in Santa Monica, I felt confident and highly qualified to perform such a feat. If it weren't for the liquor and being so pissed at that louse, I might have tried harder to find another solution.

I went out the window feet first and lowered myself to the roof below. That was easy ... and my confidence level was high. It was only the first step, however. The roof didn't go completely over to the bedroom window—I had to stand on the very edge and lean over to reach the sill. It was a commitment—once there, there was no way back. Leaning over, with my feet on the edge of the roof and my hands on the sill and only the ground below, I was able to raise the window about six inches—certainly not enough to crawl through! It was a complication that hadn't occurred to me. In fact, there was an additional hitch. The sill was slippery! The combination of the heavy fog and mildew greased the surface and my hands kept sliding off.

I looked down. The only light was from the bathroom window and the roof blocked out the light under the window. I couldn't see the ground, and I couldn't go back, so there was nothing to do but forge ahead. Instead of attempting to hang by my hands on the slippery surface, I put my forearms flat on the sill, and from there I could reach in and grab it on the inside. Then, while holding with one hand I raised the window higher. It made me think I'd make a pretty good cat burglar!

My bed was just under the window. *Surely*, I thought, *they wouldn't have the nerve to use my bed!* I could just imagine the terror when all of a sudden out of the darkness above came my foot, and I wondered about such things as just where my foot might land ... I probably should have taken off my shoes.

But they weren't there.

It was black inside—I couldn't see a thing. There was only a thin line of light under the door but it did nothing for the room. I didn't have the nerve to turn the lights on, and I just dropped my clothes and plopped into bed. The last thing I heard was, "No. Go to sleep. ..."

The cold light was just beginning to creep in through the window when I was awakened by thumping and bumping and moans and groans. My watch said six-ten. So what was I supposed to do?

I got up and dressed. All I could see were two lumps in the bed and some blond hair. I said to hell with trying to be quiet—I was still pissed—and I went out the door leaving it unlocked, hoping Tom or someone else would go in later on. Rimerman was an early riser, maybe he would be looking for him. I had to smile. That would be fun.

Upset as I was, I decided not to tell anyone, but couldn't resist the urge to confide in Doc. It helped to get the anger out of my system, and we actually had a good laugh out of it, Doc especially. He bent over double every time he thought about me climbing in the window.

[My new roommate] never mentioned it, and nor did I.

Thirty-two

The weather eased up slightly in February, especially during the latter part of the month, and the Eighth Air Force launched a new, all-out assault on German communications, designed to bring their wheeled communications to a standstill. With forces of over 1,000 bombers, they also continued to pound oil, aircraft and armament objectives.

On the 27th, our squadron found a loaded airfield and we destroyed thirty-eight German airplanes, tying with the previous record of aircraft destroyed by any group in the ETO. Then on the following day we destroyed ten more, making it the leading squadron in the group. The month ended with the group claiming 2 ME262 jets destroyed in the air and 54 aircraft on the ground, along with 113 locomotives, 50 rail cars destroyed, and numerous motor vehicles, oil tanks, gun positions, buildings and barges damaged or destroyed.

On the Eastern Front, the Russians were stopped at the Oder River, about thirty-five miles east of Berlin.

The mission was to sweep the Berlin area ahead of the bombers who were going to Brandenburg, just west of Berlin.[1]

After sitting on the runway for half an hour waiting for the fog to lift—it never did—we finally took off anyway, on instruments. The weather was warmer and had generated the foggy conditions. There was no overcast.

Over the Continent, it was clear with a few scattered clouds, but very hazy. We could see directly below, but in the distance the view was fuzzy and indistinct.

I was Jonah, flying with the 350th. I positioned the squadron at 15,000 feet ahead of the bombers, with the 351st and 352nd ranging out in different directions at 20,000. They were watchful for the worrisome jets.

Very aware that we couldn't engage the German jets in a normal air-to-air encounter, and also knowing that the jet fuel consumption was limited, we had developed the strategy of trying to catch them around airfields or on their return flight when low on fuel. At all times, however, we kept one pilot monitoring the

---

1 Field Order 1647A Target: Brandenburg, February 22, 1945.

bomber radio channel as a safeguard against a surprise attack. Usually, that person was Jonah's element leader, White Three [Ed Duke].

"White Three here, Jonah. The bombers are reporting jets in the vicinity of Brandenburg."

"Roger, White Three. Let's go, Seldom."

I turned back toward Brandenburg and pushed the throttle forward. "Stay alert now," I warned. "Did they say whether they were high or low, White Three?"

"No. I'll see if I can find out."

We had barely completed our turn when I spotted four jets in a diving left turn, strung out in a staggered string formation. "Never mind, White Three. There they are. Ten o'clock low."

"Roger."

I rolled over and headed downward at full throttle in an attempt to build up the speed I knew I'd need.

The jets saw us coming and broke formation.

"I'm going after the first one, Seldom," I announced. "White and Red stay with me. Blue Flight, pick one of the others."

"Okay, Jonah."

The number one jet continued his diving turn right through one of the scattered clouds and I followed, breaking out about 7,000 feet right over the heart of Berlin! The jet outran me easily, even with my increased speed. It was useless to continue.

About the time I decided to abort the chase, I saw another jet coming toward us out of the haze, at about 2,000 feet. I dove again, dropping my wing tanks and jamming the throttle to the wall. This time, by God, I thought, I would have the speed!

The jet pilot hit the deck, right down into the haze. He turned east and I followed, but even though I cut my turn short, I couldn't get close enough to fire. "How in hell do we ever catch these guys?" I asked myself.

The German pilot took me on a thrilling ride, screaming past the tops of buildings and skimming high-tension lines. It was an eerie experience, with the plane fading in and out of the haze, and all the hazards popping out suddenly as if I were riding on one of those scary rides at the Pike.[2] Below, everything raced by my peripheral vision in a blur. After watching the distance between us increase steadily, I reluctantly had to give up.

"It's no use," I told the flight. "Let's go home." I turned back to a heading of two-eighty, and pointed the nose upward.

We were west of the city when I saw still another jet, low in the haze, heading east. "Here we go again," I said to my flight, and, once again, I jammed the throttle forward and rolled over. This time, however, I was determined to be smarter. I aimed

---

2   "The Pike" at Long Beach was one of southern California's largest seaside playgrounds. It closed and was demolished in 1979.

my nose way ahead—leading him—hopefully far enough to come out of the dive close enough to fire. It worked, but I was still farther behind than I thought I'd be. With my built-up speed, I closed in to about 400 yards and opened fire. I rushed it a little, but I could sense my overtaking speed dwindling, and I didn't want to chance losing another one. I saw strikes on the left jet! A thin stream of smoke trailed from it and I was able to close in a little more, to about 300 yards. The German pilot was surprised and started some wild evasive action—I couldn't keep my sights on him. He then dove right down to the treetops and even with one jet damaged, started to pull away. I held my finger down on the trigger … determined. There were more strikes on the same engine, and it scared the German pilot. He pulled up sharply and slowed enough for me to close in a little and hit him again. Smoke poured out of the left jet. I saw the canopy released and watched the pilot bail out, over the right side. The plane rolled off to the left and exploded into the trees. About a second after it hit, I clicked off a picture with my K-25 camera.

I was an ace at last!

[Blick's Encounter Report:

A. Combat
B. 22 Feb., 1945
C. 350th Fighter Squadron
D. 1230
E. Berlin Area
F. Haze up to 2,500 feet; patchy cirrus above in thin layers from 10–15,000 feet
G. Me262
H. One Me262 destroyed in the air
I. I was flying with the 350th Squadron as Jonah on the freelance mission of 2[2] Feb, 1945. While we were patrolling between Brandenburg and Muritz Lake, my white 3 informed me that the bombers had reported jet E/As in the vicinity of Brandenburg. We encountered from northeast of Brandenburg four Me262s and the entire group gave chase. When first seen, these E/A were in a diving turn to the left in a staggered string formation. The E/A broke formation when they reached a southeasterly heading and Seldom Squadron chased one which continued in a left turn. We followed him through a cloud and discovered ourselves over the heart of Berlin, at 7,000 feet. A short time later, still chasing this E/A north of the city we encountered another Me262 at 2,000 feet in the haze coming toward us. I rolled over after him, my flight following, and dropped tanks in an effort to gain more speed. This E/A evidently decided to take advantage of the haze and hit the deck. We chased him for 7 or 8 minutes at full throttle in an easterly direction but were unable to close. Being a bit discouraged and believing that we were near the Russian lines, I decided to break off. After a climbing turn to reassemble the flight we started homeward on a course of 280 [degrees].

We were at about 8,000 feet northwest of Berlin when I noticed another 262 flying east in the haze. I was able to pick up enough speed in the dive to close on this E/A and opened fire at a range of 6 to 700 yards. Strikes were observed in the left jet and a thin stream of smoke began to trail from it. Finding that I was able to close even more, I opened fire again at a range of 4–500 yards. The E/A responded with some rather wild evasive action so that I was unable to keep my sight upon him. The Hun then dove for the deck and started pulling away, but I scored strikes again on the left jet. The E/A pulled up sharply and slowed down enough for me to close and get strikes again. Smoke began to pour out of the left jet. The pilot jettisoned the canopy and bailed out the right side. The plane rolled to the left and split essed into a forest. I rolled over and snapped a picture of the wreckage with my K-25 side camera about two seconds after it went in.

J. I claim one Me262 destroyed in the air.
1,283 rounds fired.

Wayne K. Blickenstaff
Major, Air Corps.]

At the debriefing, we learned that it was a successful mission. Gordon Compton, with the 351st, had a similar experience with one of the other jets, watching the pilot bail out. The group destroyed seventeen locomotives with the 350th getting nine of them.

There was bad news for me, however. Balason was down somewhere, last seen chasing a jet.

I sought out Kolb, who had been leading Blue Flight. Balason had Yellow Flight and was supposed to stick with Blue.

"What happened?" I asked.

"I don't know, Blick. He was there when we took out after the jets. Next time I looked, the whole flight had disappeared."

I talked to John Madson, who was flying Balason's wing, and he said Balason took out after one of the jets, and watched him drop his tanks. The jet flew into a thin stratus cloud and Balason followed. "I flew along the top of the cloud to its end, thinking I'd pick up Balason there," Madson said, "but I never found him and joined up with another flight. He called about fifteen minutes later saying he had joined another flight. That was the last I heard."[3]

Damn!

My throat tightened and my eyes began to fill. I couldn't help it. I started to pace and went for some coffee in an attempt to turn it off. But I couldn't! We had been through so much together! So naïve . ... He was just so damn naïve! Yet so likeable. The crazy sonnavabitch ... why wouldn't he listen?

Damn! I'd have to write his mother. What could I say?

---

3   The editor confirmed with John Madson in August 2015 that he lost Balason in the initial engagement when his own external tanks failed to release properly. Captain John M. Balason chased but then lost the Me262 in clouds near Berlin. While heading home at low altitude (after strafing a train) he received damage from flak and was forced to bail out. Suffering severe burns, he parted company with his flaming aircraft at low level and became a POW. John Balason, *An Autobiography of My Twenty Years in the U.S. Air Force* (unpublished, 1969), courtesy of Balason's daughter Marlene Ehlen.

I thought of all those hours we had spent together—all through cadets and the trip east. And I owed him big time. Without him pulling me through the communication class at Thunderbird, I might have been a bombardier now! I thought about Rimerman catching him sleeping in the Link.

Shit!

I had to stop—I just couldn't let it get to me. It was war, dammit, and I wasn't allowed.

Damn, crazy, naïve idiot! Crazy bastard never did use his head! Too bad he couldn't think as well as he could fly. *How many times did I tell him there's more to fighting this war than flying the damn airplane?* What a waste!

But then … maybe—just maybe—he's okay!

For a change the visibility was good, but we still had to climb up through the clouds. I was leading the group. The bombers were going straight to Kassel this time, no diversionary tactics.[4] On the way home I planned to take the 350th back to Röhrensee airfield to destroy airplanes we had missed on a previous mission. But things had a habit of not working the way we intended.

As usual the flak was heavy at the target, and we had to dawdle around the edges and watch that terrible, lurid, movie-like scene of the bombers plowing into that black hellhole and then, coming out, chaotically, all bruised and beaten up, limping like a flock of geese caught in a volley of buckshot. There was always that twinge of guilt. If they didn't lose more than ten bombers they were lucky. And it was not easy to forget that each plane carried ten men.

Kassel was a favorite target. I was reminded of the earlier days when, over and over again, the bombers were sent to the Ruhr Valley, then the heart of the German industrial strength. It was turned into rubble, looking much like the aftermath of a huge earthquake. I had no way of knowing, but I thought the Germans must have moved what they had left to Kassel.

The cloud cover had broken. There were large clear areas—enough so I wasn't worried about finding the field.

"Jonah here," I said finally, after the bombers were formed up again and on their way out. "I'm going down now, Lawyer and Jockey. You're on your own. Good luck."

In order to find the field, I had to fly contact, so I let down through one of the large holes. The ceiling was lower than I expected, or wanted—about 2,000 feet. It was harder to navigate at lower altitudes.

While looking for landmarks, I saw the white puffs of a locomotive, contrasted sharply against the shadows of the clouds. It was a ready-made target, I thought—one that we could take care of in short order and then continue right on to the airfield.

"Jonah here. I'll be right back. I'm going after that train. White Flight come with me. The rest of you go on."

---

4   Field Order 1675A Target: Kassel, February 28, 1945.

It was a major mistake! The train was armed! I didn't even get a chance to fire my guns! I was ready, all lined up with the engine, when a huge explosion under me heaved my plane upwards and threw it off to the right.

"Oh my God!" I yelled aloud. "What was that?"

The cockpit filled with smoke. I was on fire … I'd had it … there was no time! *This was it!*

My reactions took over. I yanked the stick back to gain enough altitude to bail … I reached down to switch tanks … I released the seat belt and shoulder straps … I opened the canopy … I reached down and switched tanks … I checked the canopy and seat belt. I did all of the emergency procedures at least three times before my mind caught up with my reactions. Then an awareness hit me that the engine was still running and the plane was still flying.

What was I doing? I was halfway out of the plane and it was still running! I couldn't believe it—I'd been ready to jump! Another second and I would have been outside watching the plane fly on …!

"Jonah here," I said into the mike, finally, collecting some of my wits again and settling back down. "I've been hit, but I'm okay. The engine's still running. Hightshoe, take the squadron and go on. I'm going back. Caton, stick with me … we have a long way to go."

"Right, Jonah, I'll be right here."

"Blue Leader here. Okay. Good luck, Blick."

I searched the instrument panel for some indication of what had happened, but everything was in order. The smoke had disappeared. It must have been something else. I closed the canopy and buckled myself back up. The controls were all right. What in the hell happened?

I was up in the scud, just under the clouds, but I didn't want to stay there—I was too good a target. I *had* to find out what condition I was in, though, and I needed the altitude if I had to jump.

I looked over at Caton, right there on my wing. "See if you can get in close enough to find out how much damage there is, Horace."

"Okay."

He flew under my plane and was back in a couple of minutes. "There's a big hole in your left wing right by the wheel. Everything else looks okay. There are some smaller holes around, but they're not bad. The wing looks wet, though."

"Okay, thanks. The plane seems to be flying all right so let's go down to the deck for the trip home."

"Right."

That was it, I thought. What I thought was smoke was probably hydraulic fluid. And that might be a problem, but I'd just have to wait and tackle that later.

The plane continued to check out okay as we made our way over the trees and villages. The gas was fine—tanks hadn't been hit. The coolant and oil were where they should be.

When we hit friendly territory I decided to try for home. "Everything seems fine, Horace. I'm going all the way."

"Okay, Jonah."

Without hydraulic fluid, I wasn't sure what to do about the landing. The wheels should go down if released, just from the force of gravity, but I didn't know that for sure. I could try increasing the G force with a tight turn … that might work. The alternative was to belly it in without even trying to lower the wheels. I'd feel pretty foolish, though, I thought, if I found out later they would have gone down okay.

By the time we were back over the field, I had decided to try the wheels. I made a normal approach and hit the wheel lever. It felt like they went down, but the warning light didn't turn off. Damn! What to do now?

I called the tower. "Jonah here. I'm going to fly by so you can check my wheels—the light's still on."

"Roger, Jonah. Go ahead."

I circled the field and passed back directly over the tower. "You've only got one down, Jonah. The left one is still up and there's a big hole there."

Just one wheel! Wouldn't you know it … now what?

"I know about the hole. I think my hydraulic system is shot."

"Try the manual control, Jonah."

"Okay."

I went around again and tried the crank. The light stayed on and it didn't feel like anything happened. "Look again," I said. "The light's still on."

"Still the same, Jonah. How about trying to pump up the right one? You could belly it in."

"Okay … good idea." I started pumping, but nothing happened … there wasn't enough fluid to do anything.

"It's not working, Tower, I'll just have to take it the way it is."

"How's your gas?"

"Okay … no problem."

"Hold on then. I'm going to call Colonel Rimerman."

I made a few more circles around the field, and noticed the fire truck and ambulance waiting—a little like vultures. Nothing like giving your confidence a big boost, I thought!

"Blick."

"Yes."

"This is Ben … you've got to make a decision."

"You mean there's a choice?"

"We don't know what will happen if you try landing on one wheel. Nobody has ever done it in a P-51. You don't even know if the one wheel is down all the way and locked. You can take your chances with the landing or jump."

I had trouble believing what I'd just heard, "You really serious about bailing out?"

"Yes. It has to be your decision."

The thought of jumping seemed scarier than the landing. Up to then, I hadn't thought much about it ... but all those people were making me a little nervous. And now they're talking about jumping! Forget it!

"I'll land it." I said.

"Okay ... but be careful. Good luck."

Ben was right about one thing, though, I thought. I had no way of knowing whether the right wheel was locked or not. Supposing it collapsed. ...

"I'm going to bounce the wheel on the runway a couple of times to see if it holds," I said.

"Good idea. Go ahead."

I swung around, lined up with the runway and slowed up a little, keeping the power on. About three feet above the runway I shoved the stick forward and rammed the wheel into the asphalt. It was probably a funny sight from the field—like a bird trying to land on one leg—because of the crazy gyrations I had to perform in order to keep the left wing up and away from the runway. I managed to get in one more bounce, but I still wasn't completely satisfied. The wheel felt okay, but maybe I should put a little more strain on it.

"I'm going around once more, Ben. See if it looks okay as I come over."

"Okay."

This time I dropped it hard from about six feet. It still held. The next time I hit the runway I gave it a little left rudder to put some side pressure on the wheel. It still held.

"I'm coming in," I said.

"Roger."

This was it. Once again I lined up with the runway—farther back this time—and cut back the throttle to establish a slow power-on glide right in to the end of the runway. It was so smooth I could barely feel the wheel touch. So far so good. I kept the tail and the wing up as long as possible while the wheel rolled along like it was on glass. I eased the throttle back, and as I slowed, the tail settled down perfectly. To keep the left wing up I had to give it more and more right stick. Then, when I could no longer hold it, the wing settled gently on to the runway, skidding a little, and the plane veered off the strip and stopped ... barely out into the grass.

"Blickenstaff," I said to myself. "That is, without a doubt, the best landing you've ever made!"

The ambulance and fire trucks were screaming out to get the remains and I started to unbuckle my seat belt and get out. I discovered I hadn't even locked the shoulder straps into position. Nervous? Not me!

We looked at the airplane. Aside from the huge hole in the wing, the wingtip was only slightly damaged and the propeller nicked just a little.

Due to the long-range Mustang and with fuel no longer a problem, we were able to penetrate deep into German terrain. Unfortunately, as the missions grew progressively longer, our bodies became progressively more resentful. I had never been a large consumer of liquids, and that helped, but I did drink coffee, and that didn't. Early on, I had developed the habit of going to the john just before a mission, partly because of nervousness and partly because of necessity, but it didn't faze Mother Nature one bit. There was one mission in particular which emphasized, dramatically, the seriousness of the situation.

I had been okay while in unfriendly skies, probably because I was too busy looking over my shoulder to worry about the lesser physical demands, but on the way home over the North Sea, and able to relax a little, the urge to relieve myself became pronounced. It was worrisome, but another half-hour didn't seem too much to ask of my bladder.

Without thinking, I followed my usual procedure of letting down while still over the water—a mistake. At altitude, the air is usually smooth, especially over water, but as I descended, it became noticeably rougher, accentuating my need. I still felt I could wait, however, and clamped down on the muscles a little tighter.

By the time I made landfall, I was sure I'd never make it—the pain was nearly unbearable. Much as I tried, I could no longer force my mind off the problem, and the anticipation made it even worse. The air was much rougher over land and, with every bump, those muscles cramped like a vise. But I was determined to hold on—I was too close for any other alternative. No way was I going to go through an embarrassing debarkation with wet pants.

My usual tight turn toward the end of the runway suffered considerably as I discovered that any G force on my bladder was like a pair of hands squeezing a balloon. The landing was probably a normal one from an outsider's viewpoint, but I was bouncing on rocks, and with each rock it was a near disaster. I ground my teeth all the way to my revetment.

By the time I was out of the plane, I was unzipped and ready to go … but my body forgot how to cooperate. My bladder and my mind were certainly ready and willing, but the muscles were not. The pressure was so extreme and the muscles so cramped, the pain was incredible. I stood there for a good five minutes, suffering, and waiting for those muscles to relax enough to allow the normal function to release. Gradually they did, but not without leaving a mark on my psyche. I vowed never to let it happen again.

The creative geniuses who designed those airplanes thought of everything—except for the sexist gadget called "The Relief Tube." Sexist, because it would be impossible for a female to use. It was a long tube, almost impossible to find, that could be pulled up, like those old cigarette lighters in cars, from somewhere in the depths of the cockpit. It had a funnel-like end you could place in the proper position and pee into, replace, and continue on your merry way, happy as a clam. The only other requirement was to tell the crew chief that it had been used.

I had never used the tube, but after my emotional and painful experience with my cramped muscles, I decided I would quit trying to play the hero and take advantage of it the next time the need became urgent. However, things are never quite as simple as they appear to the designers and engineers.

We were logging six, six and a half, sometimes seven hours on escort missions—a long time strapped into that small, uncomfortable area. The strain of being under a constant threat of becoming a potential statistic didn't help either. But even so, it was a pleasure to be able to fly all those hours and get home without sweating the gas, and I was undeniably happy about that. I still carry the mental scars of being low on fuel—even in a car without the third dimension of altitude to contend with, and that hungry-looking North Sea.

I was alone again, on the way home from another long mission, and beginning to relax a bit, and then came the urge.[5] Although still over land, it seemed safe enough—a good time to try the tube. I still had a long way to go. Why not use it and enjoy a more pleasant ride the rest of the way home.

How naïve …!

First, I made sure the plane was trimmed—I would need two hands. The seat belt, shoulder straps and Mae West had to be first. No problem. The plane remained straight and level … good show. I wasn't too worried about a little erratic flight anyway as there wasn't anyone around.

The jacket was fairly easy, but there were complications with the G-suit, the flight suit and my regular pants. Unzipping in a sitting position, with all the hills and valleys to negotiate, is never an easy operation.

All that took heavy concentration and I needed a third hand, which I didn't have, to keep the plane flying straight and level. I'd suddenly find myself either in a dive, or climbing up into a stall. Each required that I grab the stick to level the plane again. The climb, of course, was the worst—I had to dump the stick forward, which sent me, along with everything else that was loose, including the map case, up to the top of the canopy because there was no longer a safety belt to hold me down. And of course, from that position I could barely control the stick and I couldn't reach the rudders. It was frustrating, and it didn't take long to wonder if it was all worth it. But it *was* a challenge.

The G-suit was a special challenge in itself. It was devised to inflate on those areas around the waist, thighs and calves to keep the blood from rushing away from the upper part of the body and brain to avoid blackouts during excessive G forces

---

5 The relief tube experience scarred Blick enough for him to record it in his war diary for January 5, 1945.

in tight turns or pull-outs from dives. Most pilots would black out with pressures of three or four Gs. With the suit, I once recorded nine Gs in a dogfight, never even feeling the beginning of a blackout—in fact, the wings of a plane were not even designed to withstand that many Gs. The suit would inflate according to the amount of Gs—the more Gs, the more inflation—and, of course, any inflation made the zippers nearly impossible to operate. It was necessary that the plane be kept reasonably level.

It was a struggle, but I finally made it. All that was left, then, was to get into my undershorts and attempt to find the reason for going to all that effort in the first place, which, as I discovered, was all shriveled up with the cold. I couldn't help wishing I had been more heavily endowed.

The whole procedure was complicated even more by the oxygen mask. It, and the bulky tube hanging down from it, made it difficult to lower my head enough to see what I was doing.

I smiled with anticipation when I finally had what I thought was a workable connection between the two relief tubes and let it go, all prepared to sit back in contentment. Once again, however, it was, necessarily, a two-handed operation and I couldn't keep the plane level long enough to enjoy it. Any forward pressure on the stick sent me flying up again, attaching my head to the canopy amid all the debris. It was some picture: Squadron leader Blickenstaff stuck to the canopy, pants open, arms flailing about desperately trying to reach the stick, and peeing upward, all over everything and himself!

But I was determined! If other people could do it …? It went on and on. Each time I'd get everything all lined up and under control, the damn plane would either go into a dive or start climbing, and I'd grab the stick and lose my connection—constantly having to cut off the stream! Not an easy task in itself. And I had no feeling of relief whatsoever!

Tired of the effort, I finally said *to hell with it*, and sat back and let it all go. …

I had to smile, not just with the relief, but at myself and what I would have looked like from an outsider's point of view. Any German watching would surely have told himself, "Why go after that nut when he's going to kill himself anyway!"

Out over the water, I was tempted to leave everything unzipped and unbuckled, but being naturally apprehensive and cautious about my survival in those icy waters, I wasn't about to make the crossing unprepared. I started the long procedure of getting myself back into a reasonable order, but it was easier said than done! It was a little like climbing a mountain—now that I made it up, how do I get down? Zippers were even harder, and all my moving about had dislodged straps so I had to hunt around to find them. And what fit before was too tight, making leg straps and the seat belt nearly impossible.

By the time I was together again, I was almost back to Raydon, with no sense of accomplishment at all, and with the feeling that I would have been better off, psychologically, to have waited, cramped muscles and all. I had to think of the havoc I would have caused had I been leading the squadron home. The other pilots would have thought, for sure, that I had finally cracked, and would have radioed back to the base to have the medics standing by to cart me off to the nearest flak home.

Thirty-three

In March, the 353rd flew twenty-three missions in twenty-one days, making it the busiest month since October. The Luftwaffe was in the air again and we made contact with them on six of our missions, destroying sixty airplanes. Losses, however, were the highest in group history. Twenty planes were lost and eleven damaged. Of those that were lost, one pilot bailed out safely over England when his plane iced up, three were known killed and the rest were MIA … about half surviving as POWs.

The start of the last great offensive action to end the war started in the latter part of the month as General Patton bridged the Rhine River and made his way toward Frankfurt, Germany, in conjunction with the Allied Airborne Army. For want of a better label, someone dubbed it R-Day, and it stuck.

[Blick does not detail here that one of the losses was his wingman for many of his recent missions, First Lieutenant Edward H. Duke, who was lost when his aircraft suffered an oil leak. He was captured but then escaped, returning to Raydon on April 12, 1945. Blick wrote: "Duke was an impressive pilot. I had a few wingmen who could stick with me, right there on the wing, regardless of the situation. Duke was one of the best."[1]]

I met Weep on the way to Rimerman's office. "What's this all about?" I asked.

"You got me," Weep said. "I got this message that he wanted to see me. No reason or anything."

"Yeah, same here."

As always, Rimerman was almost impossible to read, but as we entered I felt sure I saw a slight grin—fleeting though it was.

"I got this communiqué from Wing Headquarters today …" he started "… and it concerns you two."

Oh God, I thought, *what did we do now?* I mulled over the past couple of weeks and couldn't summon up anything that would warrant Wing involvement. I didn't

---

1   Blickenstaff to Cross, 1998.

look, but I could feel Weep tense up, too, obviously doing the same rehashing of past events.

There was a long, uncertain silence, and then Rimerman stood up. *He never stands up.* I thought. What's going on?

Then out of nowhere came a real grin, which turned quickly into a big, genuine smile. "Congratulations," he said. "I'm happy to be the first to acknowledge your promotions to lieutenant colonel!" He shook our hands and said it again, "Congratulations. It's about time."

I was astounded. *Lieutenant colonel!* Two years before, such a possibility had never occurred to me—never entered my mind. I couldn't believe it.[2]

Once out of Rimerman's sight, we took one look at each other and headed straight for the officers' club, deciding then and there that it would be "drinks on us" for anyone who wanted to participate … and as the night went on, hardly anyone didn't. The party grew larger as the word spread—even a few of the 56th Group showed up. The result was a bill for £63 ($252 dollars), which we split.

As far as I was concerned, it was a typical, good-natured party, except for one noteworthy happening, which could probably have been avoided by a good stiff kick in the butt. But Doc didn't have enough guts to do it.

One of the things I had learned as a kid, was that if I didn't talk much except to ask pertinent questions, I came off as being smart. My dad taught me to count to ten before saying anything. It sounded like good advice, but by the time I got to ten, the opportunity to speak was always long gone. And, of course, I had to get older before I realized that's just what my dad had in mind—little kids were to be seen and not heard.

But I grew up with envy and tremendous admiration for all of those "highly intelligent" people who could pull those wonderful words out from somewhere with no effort at all, and talk easily and fluently with confidence and great intellectual sounds. The desire to be able to do it myself was always there.

There were times, however—with the help of a goodly amount of booze—when those inhibitions were released and I felt equally confident. During those periods, it seemed a shame to have to sit back and be the strong, silent type, counting to ten, when I was perfectly able to express myself as well everyone else. So I talked … and the words just flowed, like a Santa Ana breeze. No trouble at all keeping up with the best. But, naturally, I couldn't know whether I was keeping up or not. No one could get a word in edgewise!

With each drink my amazing powers of recall for all those elusive words increased, and along with that came a new-found freedom of expression … and confidence and ego—especially ego! There I was, standing eyeball to eyeball with Dave Schilling, then CO of the 56th Group and one of the leading aces of the ETO, extolling the

---

2   Blick's war diary confirms this was March 10, 1945.

virtues of my P-51 against his P-47. With no way to solve anything at the time, standing at a bar, we even made plans to duel! I knew at the time, of course, that I could have won easily, had it ever come to pass!

Fortunately, it never did, and next morning I was just as happy to let those well-made plans slide away into the world of embarrassing moments—especially after Doc told me about some of my claims I couldn't quite remember.

An escort mission to Berlin, once impossible, was now routine. But, routine or not, it was still a very long and tiring ride. There were no complaints however; it was worth it. The bombers had never felt more secure.

Over the target [on March 18, 1945], the flak was heavy, as usual, and I didn't like to linger there. Too often, the German gunners didn't seem to know, or care, whether they were shooting at bombers or fighters. From the fringes, I could still take pictures of the bombing. Looking down from that height, I had no idea how accurate the bombing was, but that wasn't my job. If the people in intelligence couldn't tell, they could at least make good educated guesses.

I had seen the bombers go through their run countless times but, even so, I had never learned how to steel myself against the sight of that terrible destruction. It was not just the sight of the bombers, who drove resolutely into the flak, living for the moment on pure luck ... but I was never able to rid my mind of those images I couldn't see taking place on the ground—all of those horrified, innocent people ... and the kids. Yes, especially the kids. What must they be going through? What must they think? *Is this to be my life?* My imagination was just too active. I remembered that first night in London, and how scared we were ... and that was only because of a couple of weak, puny bombs!

I broke the group up into flights, spreading them wide to cover as much air space as we could. I was north of Berlin with my flight when Harold Jung called.

"Seldom Yellow Leader here, Jonah. We were just bounced by a Russian fighter."

"Russian! ... Are you sure, Hal?"

"No, not *real* sure, but it didn't look like anything I've seen before, and we didn't take the time to examine it closely. He came charging right into us with all his guns blazing and was gone before we had time to think about what happened. I don't have a flight anymore—we went in four different directions."

"See if you can round them up, and then head for home. It's time to go anyway."

"Roger, Jonah."

"Seldom Yellow Four here, Jonah. My engine is cutting out—I'm losing altitude fast. I must have been hit by that plane. I'm heading east."

That was Page. "Okay, Page," I replied. "You're almost to the Russian lines already. Good luck."

I started another lazy 360, east and north of the bombing area, thinking I might be able to see Page, but he was nowhere in sight. Just then, in a normal check of my instruments, I noticed that my electrical gauges weren't working. At first it didn't register; the engine was purring along as usual—nothing had changed. But almost immediately the significance hit me, and with a huge thump my heart turned completely over—20,000 feet over the eastern edge of Berlin and no generator! *So what do I do now?* In an attempt to cool the feeling of panic that was creeping up from my stomach, I reached over and rapped on the glass, knowing full well it wouldn't do anything—it was just something everyone always did to convince themselves they were doing something positive. Nothing happened of course, and then all of the dire thoughts surfaced. How long would the plane run on battery without a generator? I didn't know. It was still humming along just fine, but we were a long way from home. Maybe I should join Page …?

Then, as I had that thought, the generator kicked back in. My heart calmed. That's just great, I thought, but what now? Will it stay on? What to do? Either I take the chance it stays on, or head east and hope there was a good reason to do it. I had to take action, for sure. I couldn't just dilly-dally around forever, waiting for something to happen.

I continued the circle and when we were once again heading home, there was another call from Page.

"Jonah, this is Page. Do you read?"

"Yes, Page … go ahead."

"I had to belly it in, but I'm on the ground and okay … and I'm pretty sure I'm behind the Russian lines. Goodbye and I'll see you in a couple of months."

Nothing I could do but reply, "Roger, Page. Good luck."[3]

The generator quit again! I had to make a decision. "Jonah here," I said. "I have electrical problems. My generator is not working properly. White Three, you and White Four head on home, and White Two [Gordon], stick with me until I can decide whether to chance the ride home or not."

"Roger, Jonah."

I turned east again, toward the Russian lines. I didn't want to do it. At this late date in the war I had no desire to get stuck in Russia, but that was sure as hell better than being captured by the Germans. Why didn't I know how the damn plane worked? I knew a car would run on the battery a long time and it seemed reasonable that a plane engine would work the same, but I didn't know and I couldn't remember the subject ever coming up.

After another few minutes the generator needle went back up again, and once again my heart became regular. "*Jesus!*" I said aloud. "How can I put up with this?" To hell with it, I thought. I'm going home … I hope. I swung around to the west again. And to my wingman, I said, "I'm going to take the chance and go home, Ray. Stick with me."

"Roger, Jonah."

---

3 Second Lieutenant Garnet D. Page was picked up by Russian troops and eventually made it back to Raydon on April 30, 1945.

The rest of the trip back to base was uneventful … except for the near heart stoppage each time the generator quit. Off and on, off and on! I couldn't get used to it … just as I'd get relaxed, thinking everything was okay, it would cut out, and each time was a new moment of panic until I could calm myself again.

I had to make the same decision about crossing the water, but by then I was able to talk myself into believing that, having gone this far, it would certainly take me the rest of the way. Fortunately it did.

With the generator running some of the time, I never did find out how far the plane would go on battery alone. Not that I really wanted to. …

On March 24, the 353rd's job was to fan out ahead of the Ninth Air Force and give needed air support for them while they were giving close ground support for the troops

Rimerman took A Group out at eight o'clock in the morning with Boone leading B Group. I had the 350th as C Group with five flights and one from the 352nd. We went out at one o'clock. Rimerman did the same, and went out again at two-thirty.

[Major Walker L. Boone from Wyandotte, Oklahoma, joined the squadron on September 25, 1944. He had previously flown a tour of operations with the 78th Fighter Group at Duxford and became squadron operations officer when Bill Price went home on December 6, 1944. Blick wrote of him: "The thing I remember most is that he had a really bad case of combat fatigue. Thinking back on it, I wonder why he hadn't been sent home long before he even came to our group, although, maybe he didn't really show it until then. His mind would wander—he'd start talking on a subject, and soon he'd drift off on to something that had no relation to what he started to say or to the problem at hand. I remember having to stop him many times, when he'd be talking to the squadron about something important and wander off into never never land somewhere. I think he was a good pilot, though, and he certainly had the experience to be put into the position he was in."[4]]

I was flying at 15,000 feet, heading for Zwolle, our assigned area. About two-thirty, Nuthouse called and directed me to patrol the Rhine–Dümmer Lake area—an indication, perhaps, that enemy planes had been spotted. With that thought, the adrenaline started to flow, and I made the turn to the left.

"Muffin here," I said.[5] "Stay alert now. We may have something." I remembered that other day, which then seemed so long ago, when Nuthouse had vectored us into our biggest scoring day.

"Nuthouse to Muffin."

"Roger, Nuthouse. Go ahead."

"Return to assigned area."

"Roger, Nuthouse." The anticipation faded. Now what, I thought. False alarm?

---

4   Blickenstaff to Cross, 1998.
5   Group lead call-sign for A Group was Jonah, B Keylock and C Muffin.

I swung around and headed south again toward the Hersfeld–Kassel area, dropping down to about 7,000 feet. It was clear, but the visibility was hazy and the horizon indistinct. We swept the whole area uneventfully, then turned north again toward Kassel.

Bingo! Just west of Kassel, I saw what looked like about fifteen FW190s, low, around 3,000 feet, heading west toward the front lines. They were carrying bombs. I was so excited I forgot the first rule of survival—keep your head on a swivel—and I didn't see the group of ME109s flying top cover until, fortunately, Louie Lee, my element leader, spotted them.

I dumped the stick forward and went into a right diving turn. I needed a positive identification. "Seldom here—I'm going down after them. Blue Flight, take the top cover. Red, stick with me."

"Roger, Muffin. Blue here."

Both Luftwaffe groups were flying in a line-abreast formation and obviously hadn't seen us yet. I pulled up behind and to the right of the outside aircraft, and found myself staring at the big cross painted on the side of the fuselage. I slipped in behind and opened fire as Red Flight barged right into the center of the formation.

All hell broke loose!

Just as I pulled the trigger the German pilot saw me, jettisoned his bomb, and made a hard right climbing turn. Thanks to the G-suit, I stayed with him, pulling six or seven Gs for about 180 degrees. There were strikes all over the 190's wings and fuselage and it rolled completely over and dove straight into the trees, disintegrating into a puffy ball of smoke.

The rest of my flight had each picked a plane before the Germans broke. [Captain Raymond E. Hartley], my wingman, and Lee chased their planes into the ground. I didn't see Jimmy Hopkins, my White Four.[6] Red Leader was bounced by the 109s from above before he got a chance to shoot—the 109s were vigilant!

I glanced around quickly. It was less than a minute since I had begun firing and what I saw was incredible. There was a great whirling, dogfight, right on the treetops, with black smoke occasionally exploding out of the trees. I couldn't help but think again of those instructors back in the States who told us the days of the old World War I dogfights were over!

Into the muddle of P-51s, 190s and 109s, came Yellow and Green Flights, adding eight more planes to the fray. I saw one of our planes (later identified as John May, Red Four) shoot down a 109 that had bounced Hightshoe, his element leader. At the same time there were four 109s lined up behind him. It all happened so fast no one could get to him. He knew they were there and broke violently to the left, ramming right into one of the 190s and tearing his left wing off. He was just barely

---

6   Second Lieutenant James H. Hopkins was killed in action by enemy fighters.

high enough to bail out. Someone reported later seeing a downed 109 on the ground with a wing embedded in its cockpit.

There were so many airplanes, so close to the ground, going in so many different directions, it was difficult to see anything that made sense. I had to get higher. I yanked the stick back—and unexpectedly climbed right into the path of a 190. Its wings were lit up with flashes, but it barely registered that the plane was firing at me. We missed head-on contact by inches! I leveled off about 5,000 feet.

It was like a disturbed wasps' nest below. Streaks of fire arced toward the ground, exploding in great fireballs, and black smoke poured out of the trees.

There was a lone 109 below, heading off to the left. I rolled and dove toward him but the pilot saw me and broke to the right. While upside down with the trees rushing by overhead, I fired. Because of the dive, my speed was so much faster than the Messerschmitt's. I almost rammed into its tail, but the plane started to break up, forcing me to react quickly to avoid the debris. The 109s canopy came off and the pilot was half out when the plane slammed into the ground in a burst of flame.

I climbed back up with the thought that it must be about time to reform the group. It was incredible—there was no sign of a let-up in the action.

"Muffin break right!" The yell was loud and clear.

Without thinking I jammed full right rudder and yanked the stick! There was a 109 coming down at me from about four o'clock! *Thank you, whoever you are.* I saw no one but the 109.

My hard right turn caught the German by surprise and I wound up in a dive right on the 109's tail. I fired and saw strikes. Smoke came pouring out of the plane and it rolled over and plunged straight into the trees. I was in a perfect position to pull up and snap a picture just as the plane exploded.

Again, I used my speed to climb.

"Blue Leader here—I need some help! I'm on the treetops going around with a couple of 190s!" The call was urgent.

It was Elder! Elder was a major, a friend of Rimerman's who was getting experience with our squadron. I saw him. They were right on the trees—a P-51 and a 190 going around in a circle. The P-51 was firing, but I could see tracers, which meant there were only fifty more rounds in each gun. Two more 190s were on his tail and two others were circling above!

"I see you Blue Leader," I yelled. "This is Muffin. I'll be right there."

"Blue Three here—me too."

As I called, I dove down to latch on to the first plane on Elder's tail. I pulled the trigger and felt my heart miss a beat. Only one gun fired! I was used to the six guns and it seemed like an old 22 rifle.

Damn! What now? Incredibly, though, there were strikes. *What luck!* I couldn't believe it. Smoke poured out of the engine and the plane split-essed into the ground.

Strikes! *Christ!* There were strikes on my wings. The other 190! It was a basic mistake. I was too engrossed in what I was doing to look around. Nothing to do but yank the stick and get the hell out. I glanced back to see a P-51 firing at the plane behind me. It was Hubbell—Blue Three. The other two 190s were nowhere in sight.

Once more I climbed up, thinking again about re-forming the squadron, but saw a 190 circling about 1,000 feet below.

"This is Muffin," I said. "I have a 190 cornered but I need someone with some ammunition left."

"Where are you Muffin?"

"High at 6,000 feet."

"I don't see you. Hang on to him—I'll keep looking."

That's just great! I thought. If I don't do something soon I'll lose him. And everyone's obviously busy with their own thing. Nothing to do but go after him with my one gun. ...

The German pilot hadn't seen me yet. I dove down, going in on his tail from below, hoping to sneak up on him. With only the tracers and one gun, I had to make it good, or I might be in trouble. I waited as long as I could, took careful aim and pulled the trigger. The tracers putt-putted out from the one barrel, looking puny and inadequate, but there were strikes and the plane started to smoke. *What luck!* I actually hit him! The plane slid off to the left and crashed into the ground.

The fifth for the day!

Suddenly it felt quiet. Something had changed. I looked around and could see only Mustangs milling about. Again—*the impression of a peaceful sunny landscape marred only by twenty or twenty-five fires scattered throughout the acres of green below.*

"Muffin here," I said. "Let's go home."

[Blick's Encounter Report:

A. Combat
B. 24 March, 1945
C. 350th Fighter Squadron
D. 1530–1600
E. Northwest of Kassel
F. CAVU [Ceiling and Visibility Unlimited] with slight ground haze.
G. FW190s and Me109s
H. Three FW190s and two Me109s destroyed in the air
I. On the 24th March, 1945, I was leading "C" group composed of the 350th Fighter Squadron and one flight of the 352nd Squadron. We were assigned to patrol the area between Siegen, Stockum, Madfeld and Rosenthal, and had passed Zwolle on the way in when Nuthouse instructed us to patrol between Rheine and Dummer Lake. When N.W. of Dummer, Nuthouse called again and told us to go to our assigned area. So with a heavy heart I turned south and swept uneventfully through our area. We then turned northeast.

We were flying at 6–7,000 feet when we encountered 15 plus 109s at our altitude. These E/A were flying as top cover for 15-plus 190s with belly tanks, at 2–3,000 ft. Both formations were flying line abreast in the west-northwest direction towards the front lines. By means of a right diving turn I pulled up behind and to the side of the right outside A/C in order to positively identify them as E/A. A big white cross on the fuselage satisfied me and I pulled directly astern and opened fire. Just as I pulled the trigger the pilot evidently saw me as he immediately jettisoned his belly tank and reefed his plane to the right. I turned with him for about 180 [degrees] and began to get some strikes. The E/A then rolled over and went straight in. This is confirmed by Lt. Lee.

    Continuing in a climbing turn I picked up an Me109 at about 5,000 feet and opened fire on him. Closing to almost zero range I began to get strikes all over the fuselage and wings. The E/A obligingly leveled out enabling me to get more strikes. It started flaming and pieces came off the wings and tail section. The canopy came off and the pilot attempted to get out, but before he could make it, the E/A rolled over and went into the ground at an angle of 70 [degrees]. Lt. Lee confirms this one. Hurriedly looking around, I was left with a vivid impression of 109s and 190s going down in flames, and the fires of many exploded A/C on the ground. One in particular I watched. A P-51 was shooting at an FW190. They were in a right diving turn, the 190 skidding from side to side. The FW continued to dive and went straight into a clump of trees. I called this P-51 to come up and join me and it turned out to be Lt. Clark. I substantiate Lt. Clark's claim of one FW190 destroyed.

    Thinking that the excitement for the day was over, I started a left orbit at 8–9,000 feet in an attempt to reform the group. I looked back to clear my tail and saw a 109 at four o'clock high bearing down on me. I broke hard right and after a 360 [degree] turn ended up on the E/A's tail in a 50 [-degree] dive. The Me started to smoke after a few strikes and then half rolled into some trees. As I went by, I snapped a picture of the crash with my K-25 camera. This one is also confirmed by Lt. Clark.

    A few minutes later I recognized Major Elder's airplane by the camouflage. As I looked down I saw numerous strikes on a 190 that he was shooting at. This E/A crashed in flames as I started down to help. I could easily cover Major Elder and noticed he was doing very well. He was shooting at another 190 in a left orbit when I saw another 190 close in from his rear. I told him to continue shooting and I would take care of the one behind. Out of the corner of my eye I saw strikes all over his E/A and saw a big crash as it went into the ground. My E/A quit firing at Major Elder as I pulled up on his tail, and leveled out slightly as I started firing. Much to my dismay, only one measly little gun fired. Evidently the first burst hit the E/A as I could see him trailing smoke as I over-shot him. The E/A split S'd but was too low for me to follow him through. I watched him go almost straight into the ground. For a moment it looked as if he would make it but he reversed his split S and unsuccessfully attempted to pull out in the other direction. This destroyed E/A is confirmed by Major Elder and Lt. Clark who was still with me.

    Once again I started a left climbing turn with the hope of reforming. At this time Lt. Clark called in a 190 and I watched him take out after it. The A/C burst into flames and went into the ground. Gradually a few P-51s joined the orbit, but once again the form-up was interrupted when I noticed a 190 approximately 1,000 feet below me in a left orbit. As I only had one gun I continued to circle above him and called someone to come down and finish him off. No one responded so I decided to give it a try. I slid in behind and raked across the cockpit. This E/A also began to smoke and I presume the pilot had been hit as the E/A slid off and crashed into the ground. Lt. Robinson saw this one and confirms it.

    I am duly impressed by the A.P.I. tracer ammunition. Although the first burst probably warns the enemy pilot, it tends to confuse and excite him, so that he takes immediate evasive action and frequently does the wrong thing. This ammunition also enables one to establish the proper line of flight which is half the battle.

Even though my camera exposed only 15 feet of film and my gunnery wasn't as good as it could have been, there is no doubt whatsoever, about the destruction of the A/C. I saw each plane auger into the ground with its pilot and explode. Lt. Clark confirms the destruction of my third (109) and fourth (190) claims.

A few minutes after the fight was over, 5 of us got together and headed out, leaving a few disheartened Huns and many fires in the combat area.

I claim three (3) FW 190s and two (2) Me 109s destroyed in the air.

J. 1,000 rounds fired.

Wayne K. Blickenstaff
Lt. Col., Air Corps
0-728555.]

At the debriefing we tallied up the score. We lost five planes but destroyed twenty-five, making it the 353rd's greatest single day's air victory of the war. Bob Elder also shot down five, which broke another record for the Eighth Air Force. It was the only time two pilots of the same group got five in one engagement.

On the 26th, Weep led the group on an escort mission to Leipzig. Bill Tanner led the 350th and they ran into severe icing conditions, which forced them to abort. The weather was bad everywhere, but Weep luckily missed the ice and plowed up through the clouds to eventually find the bombers. As a mission, however, it was another recognized fiasco—resulting only in the shaking up of the troops. Weep was a nervous wreck by the time he got back.

Tanner, however, ran right into a dreaded thunderhead. He iced up and spun down from about 20,000 feet. He was on the missing list for several hours until we received a report that he was in a hospital in Braintree, about twenty miles south of Raydon.

As soon as I heard, I called Doc and asked if he wanted to go see him.

"You know better than to ask that stupid question Blick," he said. "Are you feeling all right? You know damn well I want to go. I should at least look at him. It's not that I don't trust the English, don't you know … but I should see for myself. After all, I *am* his doctor!"

"Let's go then. If we leave now we can probably be back before dark. Get your stuff and I'll pick you up."

Tanner looked as if he had been enjoying a barroom brawl, but except for a big gash on the side of his head, the wounds were superficial, much to our relief.

"You don't look too good, Bill," I grinned. "What happened?"

"I don't know for sure. We were flying along on instruments, just sailing along like a pelican fishin', when all of a sudden it got dark as hell—darker! I couldn't see anyone. And it was rough—never ever seen it so rough. I was bouncin' around like a tumbleweed in a sandstorm. The plane was out of control and the instruments were useless—they went all to pieces. I couldn't tell what the fuck was happening. The altimeter said I was going up so I kept dumping the stick and gaining speed like crazy—all the time gaining altitude! I was heading straight down, I think, but going up!" He shrugged like he didn't understand.

"And then I saw the ice! It looked like something growing, right there on the wing. I never ran into ice before—did you?" He looked at me, but never gave me a chance to answer. "But I couldn't get down—just kept going up and up and up. Then all of a sudden it changed—the altimeter started dropping and the same thing happened in reverse. I hauled back on the stick but the plane kept going down. I must have been pointing straight up." His hand went skyward. "The next thing I knew I was down to about eighty miles an hour and it stalled! It was maddening! I didn't have the slightest idea where I was or what the hell the attitude of the plane was. The altimeter said I was going down but I could have been right on the trees. I tried everything, but nothing did any good. Then, all of a sudden there was a loud crack—I thought I'd bought it for sure, but then I caught a glimpse of the wing going by. That's when I knew I had to get out!" He had to smile at that. "It wasn't easy because of the wild maneuvers the plane was into—that's probably when I got all banged up. I don't remember anything after that—I must have knocked myself out on something. Next I knew, I wasn't feeling too good, and people were loading me into the back of a car!"

"Wow," I said. "Some story. It sounds like you went right through the middle of a thunderhead. Do you remember what they told us about those things in the weather classes we had? How the winds can go straight up, and then down—as much as 200 miles an hour? That's pretty scary. You were lucky to get out of it as well as you did. The ice didn't help any either. Without it the plane might have been able to take it. Those instructors we had were right when they said to go around them."

"Yeah, I know, but what do you do when you don't even know they're around?" Tanner asked.

"Fly through them I guess!"

Doc had been examining him while we were talking and didn't seem to be very concerned about anything but the gash on his head.

"You think you'll be okay here, Bill, until tomorrow?" he asked. "If you do, I'll go back with Blick tonight and come get you tomorrow. Otherwise I'll stick around."

"Naw, you don't have to do that, Doc, I'll be okay. They seem to be taking good care of me."

"I can't really do much for you while you're here. That's why I want to get you home as soon as I can. They won't be too happy if I start fooling around here. I think you're okay, but I just want to watch that cut. I don't know how deep it is."

On the way out, Doc said quietly, "He's lucky to be alive."

"Yeah, I know."

The next day, Doc took one of the ambulances and picked Tanner up. He looked a lot brighter, and said he felt better. I knew it wouldn't be long before he'd be chomping at the bit again.

Pilots seemed to come in all shapes and sizes, with all sorts of egos and idiosyncrasies, but there was a difference between a good pilot and a good fighter pilot. It was hard to put my finger on it, but I was learning to sense the difference. Without even thinking about it, Bill Tanner was it—the fighter pilot. No mistaking it. He looked and acted the part—no play-acting, just a natural manner. There was something in those lightly slanted and smiling, half-squinting eyes that said, "Don't mess with me, Buddy, I can fly rings around you." And the smart ones didn't dispute it. He didn't try to flaunt it, it was just there—a matter of confidence that seeped out through all of his pores. I had early on felt him out on doing the operations job, but in his Texas accent he let me know he didn't want "nothin' to do with that fuckin' responsibility crap." All he wanted was to get up there and fly, and get rid of "those fucking Germans." And fly he did—every mission if I'd have let him. He wound up with more combat hours than anyone.[7]

Whenever a new batch of pilots came in, Doc and I always played a little game, to see if we could guess which ones would make the best combat pilots. I never told Doc, or anyone for that matter, what I'd use to form my opinion. I'd always look first in the eyes, to see if I could find a hint of that same kind of intensity that Tanner had. I never could, but if I ever saw anything that even resembled it, I knew I had another excellent pilot.

There was no concussion, and after a few days Tanner was up pushing to fly again. He was under strict orders not to fly but, even so, I noticed his name on the schedule and had to take it off twice before he finally had the okay from Doc.

On March 31, I had another promotion, which I was not too happy about. Rimerman gave the squadron to Bob Elder, and transferred me to group, as operations officer. I knew nothing would change all that much, but my responsibility would be to all three squadrons, and after all that time with the 350th, it was not easy. And it would mean that I would take over the group executive position if Bailey was not there.

Then came the rumor that spread over the base like a shock wave.

Glenn Duncan was back!

---

7   Captain William F. Tanner completed two tours of operations, flying 137 missions for a total of 514:50 combat hours.

Thirty-four

In April, 1945, the great air war over Germany was winding down, but until the latter part of the month, the 353rd Group continued its normal activities, flying sixteen missions, all escort but two.

On the 10th, we shot down three Me262s and they were the last aerial victories for the group. On the ground, however, we continued to find targets of opportunity and airdromes filled with aircraft, which we systematically destroyed. The largest score took place on the 16th when the group destroyed 110 airplanes on a field east of Munich. This put us in fourth place in the ETO race for total destroyed, but the next day, we were back in fifth place when the 352nd Group found another field jammed with grounded planes.

Glenn Duncan was *not* back! He was in Paris. The word was out that he had never been captured—that he had eluded the Germans and walked all the way from Hanover to Holland [and hidden] with the Dutch Underground, until he [was able to cross the lines to meet the] advancing Allied Armies relieving them.

On April 10, I flew my last mission. Rimerman had A Group and I took B, on escort to an airfield south of Magdeburg. Our intention was to strafe after the bombers were finished, but there was nothing left for us to strafe—they did a beautiful job of precision bombing.

While watching the bombers, we were informed that there was an ME262 over the target area at 9,000 feet. We saw it and immediately went after it, our flights attempting different approaches knowing full well how hard [it was] catching the jets. I had my sight all lined up and started to fire when Abernathy, coming in at it head-on, blew it away. It was his fifth, making him an ace.

A little later, Clark, who was leading Green Flight, saw another jet, low, probably on its way home, and he and his wingman, McMahan, shared in its destruction.

Gordon Compton, from the 351st, found another ME262 and destroyed it—our last air-to-air victories.

Other than those three encounters, the mission was uneventful.

On April 20, Duncan flew in while the group was landing. He buzzed the tower in an AT-17. Everyone came out to watch, just as they used to when he came home.

He looked a little thinner but seemed in good health. A hero to those of us who knew him, and a legend to those who didn't.

On the 22nd, Ben Rimerman left to take over the 55th Group, and Duncan was once again the 353rd Group's commanding officer. He then left for a rest home visit before going operational, so with Bailey gone, also to a rest home, all of a sudden I was the group commander, group executive officer and group operations officer. Fortunately, nothing very important came up during that period, with the exception of a visit from General Woodbury. That kind of thing is always a little scary in the military—it's never clear why. It could be a social thing, of course, but that always seems highly unlikely, especially when you hardly know the general. More than likely it's an inspection of some kind—a check-up of sorts. He would, for sure, wonder why he wasn't met by someone other than the group operations officer, a lowly lieutenant colonel!

But it went well, and I had help from the group ground officers, who were more accustomed to military procedures. It was lunchtime and we fed him and that helped. When he left he seemed happy enough, and I breathed a sigh of relief, wondering, of course, what kind of grade I received.

The first thing Duncan wanted to do when he returned was, of course, to fly the Mustang. I drove him out to his plane. When the crews heard that he would be back, they had immediately painted up a plane for him, with his dove of peace insignia and twenty-six swastikas.

He had never flown a P-51 so I gave him a complete cockpit check, which didn't take long.[1] I had the feeling he didn't even need it. He had the plane started almost before I could get down off the wing. I drove back to the tower and watched.

He went to the end of the runway, pushed the throttle all the way forward, and sped down the runway. That seemed normal enough, but then the Duncan in him entered and as soon as he was airborne he raised the wheels, held the Mustang down much longer than necessary, then pulled it up—almost straight up—until it slowed a little and he eased it down to normal climbing position. Leave it to him! I had never seen anyone do that before; in fact, I didn't even know a P-51 was capable of it. But that was Duncan—ever the pilot!

There were a few more missions, but they were not very meaningful. The war was ending, and we knew it would be over soon. We began to get rumored reports, mostly truthful, that people were being liberated from the prison camps, and I was really pleased to hear that Balason was one of them.

There wasn't much for me to do except to act like I was doing something useful. I don't remember where we got it, or why, but somehow we had a two-seater P-51 on the field. Doc was after me to give him a ride, and I did. I'm not sure anymore, but I think it was against regulations, but I knew that Doc would never forgive

---

1 Unknown to Blick, or at least not remembered, Duncan had flown the Mustang extensively in February 1944.

me if I didn't take him up. It was a long ride, and we stayed up for over two hours covering a good part of England. It was a thrill for him, and I even let him fly it for a while. After two years of watching all of us go off into the wild blue, at last he was able to get a little feeling of what it was like up there.[2]

On May 7 we heard the news. It was over. May 8 would be designated VE Day. And the celebrations began. The lights came on again in London and I decided I would take another trip just to see what London looked like at night. When I finally did get there, though, only about half of them were on—it had been so long they had forgotten how to work.

On the 17th, Duncan took the two-seater and flew to Paris. He was back later in the day with Colonel Loren McCollom. He was in great shape, with very little evidence of the fire he had encountered as he bailed out. The Germans had taken good care of him.[3] That night we all had a get-together for him and many members of his old group, the 56th, came over. Ben Rimerman also turned up, and I have a picture in my scrapbook of the three of them together in the officers' club: McCollom, Duncan and Rimerman.

On the 28th I took a long, peaceful, sightseeing journey in my airplane, to see what the German countryside really looked like. I flew in the general direction of Frankfurt and then north, low on the Rhine River looking up at the old castles still there. I have photos of some of them caught with my K-25 camera as I went by. I flew over much of the area we had covered so many times, places like Cologne and Kassel, and the Ruhr Valley, and it was a wonderful pleasure to be able to enjoy looking without worrying about being shot at.

I have to admit that I had become somewhat superstitious about my luck running out.

When the war ended, I totaled up my logbook. I had flown 133 missions and logged 456 hours and 55 minutes of combat time, all without a scratch. Not only that, but I had lost seven airplanes with other pilots flying them, forcing me to put out an order stating that no one could fly my plane.

It was not easy to forget all of the close calls I'd had, and all of my friends that had dropped right out of my life. After all of these years, whenever I think of that period of my life, I still ask myself the "Why me?" question.

As pilots, we were paid flight pay as well as our normal salary, and to receive it we were required to fly four hours a month. At the time, I was hesitant, wondering just how long my luck would last, but of course I didn't want to give up the flight pay. We still had a P-47 on the field, so I flew my four hours in it because I felt it was safer! Talk about superstitious. …

On July 18, 1945, the orders came for my return to the States.

---

2   Blick's logbook confirms this 2 hour 45 minute flight took place on April 19, 1945.
3   A South African Medical Corps Doctor, R.J. Rodie, was responsible for the treatment of McCollom's burns. See Cross, *Slybirds*, p. 183.

[Blick's last flights in the P-47 were 1 hour 45 minutes on July 14, and 2 hours 15 minutes on July 18. He left Raydon on July 20, 1945, along with Vic Byers and Weep Junttila, flying to the replacement depot in Stone, Staffordshire, in a special UC-64 arranged by Colonel Duncan. He would never return to England. ...]

2011

I have always considered those four years in the Air Force an interruption in my real life, but at the same time that period of my life was an unbelievable, fascinating experience that I have treasured ever since. It was not something I had planned on doing; in fact, without the war I would never have considered joining any military service. But because I survived, I can look back at my accomplishments with satisfaction and pride, and more than anything else just plain luck.

I was a shy, naïve boy, raised in a small town during the depression, knowing very little about life in the world around me. All of a sudden, I was thrown into a big pool of people from other kinds of worlds and stirred together in a huge stew. We were all the same, yet so very different. We learned from each other about those other lives—something I would probably never have done on my own. Joe Canipelli's medical world, for instance, was far different from my father's, who was a small country veterinarian. And from John Baer, I learned about the affluent world of life in the city, and then there was Bledsoe. Marvin Bledsoe, the smart one who taught me that a person can do anything if he has the conviction and confidence in himself. All good things that would have taken me years to learn in normal circumstances—if I had the kind of opportunity, of course.

With people like Tom Brokaw calling us the greatest generation, we are now thought of as heroes and portrayed standing up straight and proud on pedestals. Yes, I liked wearing a uniform and, yes, I liked flying a plane! Of course I did. I wouldn't be human if I didn't. And of course I feel proud that I'm thought of as being a part of that elite group. But the greatest generation? That's ridiculous. We were just plain normal kids from all over the States just trying to grow up in our own back yards. But then we were attacked, and suddenly all normalcy was gone. We did what we had to do—what anyone would do—we fought back. And in order to do that we had to grow up, fast. And that we did—those of us who had the chance. Many didn't. And it didn't help them at all to be hailed as the greatest generation.

Yes, I treasure those years. And I can do that because I'm still alive. So many of the people I was with are not. For me, and I suspect for all of the men and women in that war, it was a maturing period. We were all very young. Too young, really, to be placed in that position. Contrary to the usual thinking, our children do not become adults when their bodies reach their maximum physical growth. It takes longer for the brain to develop. Yet we were required to be adults, both physically and mentally, before our time. With those of us who survived, the catch-up had to be set aside in the hope that we could someday, when the war was over, go back and find it.

Those of us who could, did, but many were not so fortunate. They were unable to ever again capture the hopes and dreams they once had when their lives were still being formed.

WKB

Epilogue

"The best thing we could do for relatives we love who die is make certain there is some written record of who they are and what they did."—Andy Rooney

Years ago, our dad shared Andy Rooney's quote with us and expressed his desire to one day have his book about his wartime experiences published. After he passed away, we found a copy of the quote in his wallet—perhaps a reminder to us to finish what he could not. It took us longer than we would have hoped, but we are so thankful to Graham Cross for all of his help in pulling all of the pieces together, editing the book, and helping us find a publisher. We love and miss you dad.

Perry Blickenstaff
Gayle Wellborn

APPENDIX I

Blick's War Diary

Blick's "war diary" is reproduced here as he wrote it during World War II. "Doc" Canipelli and Marvin Bledsoe continued to write entries while he was at home on leave during the late summer of 1944. The following list of abbreviations is to aid understanding of various references. Blick used a * to indicate he flew the mission that day.

a/c	aircraft
a/d	airfield
a/s	air-sea rescue
CO	commanding officer
DB	dive-bombing
d/s	detached service (i.e. a posting elsewhere)
e/a	enemy aircraft
ETO	European Theatre of Operations
GAF	German Air Force
MEW	Microwave Early Warning, used for ground control of fighters
NoBall	V-weapon target
NYR	Not Yet Returned
OTU	Operational Training Unit
PW	prisoner of war
Ramrod	escort mission
R/V	rendezvous
SNAFU	Situation Normal All Fucked-Up
Split S	evasive manoeuvre that involves going inverted and reversing the direction of travel by pulling though a partial loop (i.e. a split "S")
Sqdn	squadron
Type 16	high-definition radar control known as "Dwarfbean" and "Nuthouse" from November 1944.
X-C	cross-country flight

12 August, 1943
Great day—the group goes on it's [sic] first operational mission as an operational group. We took a quick look at the enemy coast and came running back. Had some heavy flak over Ostend.

12 August, 1943
Started on a sweep but were called back—we've heard about these things. Called fiascos I believe!!

14 August, 1943*
Made landfall between Ijmoiden [sic] and Noorwijerhout [sic] (egad—what names!) on a sweep. Caught some flak over Hague.

15 August, 1943*
Sweep with landfall north of Knocke [sic]. Flak over Dunkerque.

15 August, 1943
Swept north and west of Ostend to Dunkerque. Rear support to bombers.

16 August, 1943
First bomber escort to the northwest outskirts of Paris. Single 190s and 109s were encountered. Fortier fired a burst at a 190 but makes no claim. He came back with 3 50 cal. Holes in his plane. Seems as if the fort gunners get a little eager—or scared!! We took off from Thorney Island.

17 August, 1943
Penetration with belly tanks for the first time. Col. McCollum [McCollom] led the sqdn. And made r/v at Haamstede. Hurst and Long fired at some 109s but make no claims.

17 August, 1943
Bomber escort with r/v at Malines. A little flak south of Antwerp—no e/a.

18 August, 1943
Sweep with 10/10 cloud coverage and no e/a.

19 August, 1943*
Bomber escort—Halfway between Woensdrecht and Gilze-Rijen. Hurst reported 9 109s about to attack the bombers. Col. McCollum [McCollom] led his flight in and broke it up. Egad! What eyes this guy Hurst has!

23 August, 1943*
Rodeo with no flak over Rotterdam—nothing else.

24 August, 1943*
Bomber escort. Just as we were ready to leave, 20 plus 190s were sighted but we had no combat. On the way back, Fry, flying in Venell's flight, spotted a 190 tailing

Venell. Result—Hurst drew first blood—one destroyed in an excellent head on pass. Group landed at Manston. Fry had us plenty worried but showed up a little later. Had mixed it up with the 190's pal and came home alone in the clouds.

25 August, 1943*
Col. McCollum [McCollom] led the sqdn on a sweep west of Lille and southwest of Hesdin. No enemy aircraft.

27 August, 1943*
Bomber escort—I aborted as an escort to Angelo. No combat.

30 August, 1943
Bomber escort. Took off—circled field and came back; mission cancelled. Another one of those things.

2 September, 1943*
Bomber escort from Thorney Island with Col. Mac leading the sqdn. No e/a.

3 September, 1943*
Bomber escort to about ten miles south of Les Andelys. Landed at West Malling.

5 September, 1943
Tragic day—B flight went to Biggin Hill for some G. C. I. [Ground Control Interception] training. On the [way] down the weather closed in causing Venell to crash into a house and Long to bail out too low. Both were killed. A tough break for B flight and the squadron. Venell was a great guy.

6 September, 1943*
Bomber escort. Dub [Odom] was on my wing and saw a 190 shooting at a 47. I saw it and thought it was a 47 shooting. Am gonna have to get my head out! Perry from the 352nd failed to return.

7 September, 1943
Withdrawal escort with Col. Mac leading the sqdn. Dub [Odom] and Pinky [Lorance] became separated from the sqdn and landed at a bomber base. We were sweating them out for a while.

9 September, 1943
Target escort at Donai airdrome. Good hits reported.

9 September, 1943
Bomber escort—mission aborted.

15 September, 1943
Bomber escort from Thorney Island. Dewey aborted and I thought "Ah, my chance to lead a flight" but looking around I discovered everyone else had gone, too. So I, too, aborted. What a performance!!

16 September, 1943*
Bomber escort from Thorney Island. Walsh and I flew with 351. Saw nothing.

22 September, 1943
Wonder of wonders! E/a seen on a sweep! Fortier's flight was split up by 12 plus bandits. No claims or battle damage.

22 September, 1943*
Swept in between Ostend and Blankenburge [sic] and south to Lille—then Ghent and out.

23 September, 1943
Bomber escort from Ford—nothing happened.

23 September, 1943*
Bomber escort from Ford—nothing happened this time either. I took over Dinse's flight due to oil on his windshield, and most amazingly hit Ford right on the nose.

27 September, 1943
Bomber escort and things really happened. Naturally—I wasn't along. Rimerman and Fry each got one destroyed. Fry confirms the major's. Dewey [Newhart] and Dub [Odom] got one each and shared another. Rosenberg got a probable—has beautiful films. Good deflection shooting. Fortier shot again with no claims. Durant came back on the deck and shot up a convoy. Has the best films I've seen on the art of shooting up a convoy. Pidduck and Furness also fired with no claims. Lowe crash landed out of gas at Ludham—total washout of the plane. Those missions get longer all the time.

2 October, 1943
Bomber escort to Emden. Sqdn was led by Major Duncan. 109s were encountered north of Emden with no claims.

3 October, 1943
Sweep with no e/a—naturally!!!

4 October, 1943
Withdrawal escort from Duren to Sans Van Ghent [sic]. No combat.

8 October, 1943
Dewey's flight went screaming down on the tail of a 210 (probably a 410) with no claim although Pidduck saw strikes. Price tried to attack a 190 that later crashed into a fort.

9 October, 1943
Squadron led by Major Duncan—no e/a.

10 October, 1943
Withdrawal escort. Hurst got another 190—so did Tanner.

14 October, 1943*
Bomber escort to Duren—target was Schweinfurt. E/a popped up just as we were ready to leave so Rimerman told us to take a crack at them and leave. Dewey took Walsh, Fry, and I down into a mess of 190s. I stayed with him and at about 12,000 ft. I looked back expecting to see Fry and lo and behold there were two 190s, right on my ass. Naturally, I didn't stick around very long. Came back on the deck and in the clouds sweating out gas. Made good use of my instrument card. Dewey came back at 30,000 ft and got hit by flak and also by a 190 that "snuck" up behind him. Walsh came back in the clouds—poked his nose out once and got hit. Fry failed to return. Sure hope he got out o.k. Am wondering what happened to him. Peters crashed near Hornchurch and was killed. Dewey claims one destroyed.

18 October, 1943*
Withdrawal escort. Penetration to Turnhout—mission recalled.

20 October, 1943*
Withdrawal escort from Duren. Col. McCollum [McCollom] led the squadron and aborted. Pidduck took over and escorted to Dorosect.

22 October, 1943*
A fiasco to end all fiascos!! We flew instruments all the way up to 35,000 ft. Never got out of the stuff. Rimerman came back alone. Lowe spun out—off his wing. Stone spun out—off Rose's wing. Both are missing. Don't think we'll ever see either again. Rose spun out and came back on the deck. Zolner was hit slightly by flak.

24 October, 1943*
That last one didn't end the fiascos. We got through this time, though—at 34,000 ft. Never found the bombers.

3 November, 1943
Bomber escort—target Wilhelmshaven. No combat although Devane, flying with 352, saw a 47 shoot down a 110.

5 November, 1943
Bomber escort—target Gelsenkirchen. Rimerman claims two 109s damaged. Newman, flying white three, is missing. L'il Joe last saw him going down on the tail of a 190. Hurst's flight was bounced—he got a probable. Price destroyed a 210. Stearns also got a 210. Tanner fired with no claims.

7 November, 1943
Bomber escort—target Duren. Col. Mac led the sqdn. No e/a.

11 November, 1943
Bomber escort—target Munster. No e/a.

13 November, 1943
Bomber escort—target Bremen. Dewey aborted and Dinse took over. Hart dropped behind when his engine didn't catch after his belly tank ran out. He dropped to 8,000 ft before it caught. Dinse and Winder tried to cover him but lost him. By then it was too late to rejoin formation so they tried to fight the whole damn Luftwaffe by themselves. They came back individually—both shot up. Winder landed at Hardwick with a gash in his left shoulder where a 20mm exploded. He'll get the Purple Heart—first one in the group. Dinse got one damaged.

19 November, 1943
Col. Mac led the squadron. No e/a.

25 November, 1943*
Col. Mac is missing!! We've really lost a lot this time. Best C.O. we'll ever see. We had our first dive bombing mission at St. Omer a/d. The Col. was hit by flak as they started their dive. He was flying with the 351st. He got out of the plane o.k.—the 78th saw the chute land. Probably is a PW.

26 November, 1943*
Bomber escort—target Bremen. No e/a.

29 November, 1943*
Bomber escort—target Bremen. Major Duncan led the sqdn. Hurst mixed it up again—no guns fired.

30 November, 1943*
Bomber escort—target Solingen. I led my first flight—and aborted! Was I p'd off!! Belly tank wouldn't draw. No e/a.

1 December, 1943*
Bomber escort—target Leverkusen. I led yellow flight with Rosenberg on my wing. Saw no e/a until time to turn around. We were already overtime. Mixed it up for a while and for the first time fired my guns. Got a damaged 109. Came back on the deck again—sweated more than I ever have. Thought I couldn't possibly get back. Landed at another base. Could have made it home but I didn't believe the gas gauges. Had a hole the size of a watermelon in the bottom of the plane. Flak seems to be pretty good!! Rosie crash landed here out of gas. Cut his nose up pretty bad but he'll be o.k. Devane, flying my no. three, had some battle damage. Ireland got a probable.

4 December, 1943*
Dive bombing—target Gilz Rijen [sic] a/d. Hits were good. Excellent cover by the 56th. No e/a.

5 December, 1943*
Bomber escort—target Paris. No e/a.

11 December, 1943*
Bomber escort—target Emden. Col. Duncan led the sqdn. No action. Hurst landed his flight at Docking.

13 December, 1943*
Bomber escort—target Bremen. Pidduck aborted—Newhart took over the squadron. No e/a seen.

20 December, 1943*
Bomber escort—target Bremen. 2 chutes were seen when a p-47 crashed into a fort. I led yellow flight. No combat.

22 December, 1943*
Withdrawal escort from Osnabruck. I was leading red flight and we mixed it up a little under the bombers but there were no claims. I came back with Pinky [Lorance] and Hart. Devane got hit by the bombers. We saw the p-38s for the first time.

23 December, 1943*
Dive bombing—target Gilze-Rijen a/d. Col. Duncan led the squadron. Hits were good and so was the cover from the 56th.

24 December, 1943*
Flew around the Amiens–Cambria area for an hour at 22,000 ft. Bombers, 47s and everything else in the E.T.O. were in the sky. No e/a, but had some accurate flak thrown up.

30 December, 1943
Bomber escort—target Ludwigshaven. Odom's flight got separated from the rest of the sqdn and ended up in a terrible dogfight with 8 or 10 109s. Odom is missing. Stearns got a damaged. Dub probably got out—we hope.

31 December, 1943
Bomber escort—target Bordeaux. NO combat. Group landed at Exeter and had a rough New Year's Eve—they tell me. I was in London.

4 January, 1944*
Bomber escort—target Munster. Two forts were seen to collide. I led red flight.

5 January, 1944*
Bomber escort—target Elberfeld. Again I led red flight and again nothing happened. Col. Duncan destroyed the only e/a in the sky. Made the 6th for him.

7 January, 1944*
Withdrawal escort. Major Rimerman led the sqdn. Bombers led us astray. We followed them clear around and south of Paris. E/a came in just as we started to leave. Dewey took his flight into them—Walsh fired but makes no claim. Gonnam of 352 got three, making him an ace. Hart, flying my wing, crashed at Eastchurch out of gas. He's o.k.—not hurt. Something always happens to my wingman—can't figure it out. We're still going farther in—with the same am't of gas. Before long, none of us will get back. Each time we conserve a little more!!

11 January, 1944*
Bomber escort—target Brunswick. Another fiasco for us. Bombers were late and strung out. Saw no e/a. I led red flight.

14 January, 1944*
Bomber area escort—target installations along the French coast. Same type mission as on 24 December, and we patrolled just about the same area only this time we were at 17,000 ft. These things have all the earmarks of invasion preparation to me. Beckham took 8 ships down and attacked some poor crew chief madly taxiing a 109 around some field over there. Six of them are sharing a damaged!!

20 January, 1944
The weather closed in rather suddenly and a B-24 came in hotter than hell and cracked up in a ditch at the end of the runway. One guy was killed—a passenger. Ironic—no?!

21 January, 1944
Bomber area escort—same deal—along the "Pas DE Calais" coast. Beckham again took his flight down and pounced on a flight of unsuspecting Huns. He got two of them—making 13. He and Mahurin are having quite a race. Beck seems to stay one behind. Wish I could see things like those boys do. Duncan got another, too. This was a DO 217 on the ground. The 350th saw no action—as usual!!

24 January, 1944*
Bomber area escort with the target Frankfurt. The squadron, led by Col. Duncan, saw a little action again for a change. The bombers were recalled because of weather and we went on what amounted to a sweep deep into Germany—much farther than we were supposed to go. Trip was uneventful until we had withdrawn about half the distance to the coast, when Duncan went screaming down on a flight of 110s flying about 6,000 ft. I was flying his second element and fired at one of the boys, but couldn't hit him—too much deflection. Saw Duncan get his first one and got a good look at the guy as he bailed out. I think they must have been up on a training flight—didn't seem to know what to do when we bounced them. Duncan, Newhart, and Zolner came out on the deck and landed

at Manston—very short on gas. I picked up Price and Chetwood somewhere along the way and we came out at 10,000 ft. What a haul that was! Newhart was fired at a long time by a 190 that was tailing him but the 47s outran him—must have been an old 190!! Zolner hit a tree on the way out—luckey [sic] to get back. Dewey got some O.T.U boy just as he was landing. Claims: Duncan—two 110s, Dewey [Newhart]—110 and 109, Li'l Joe Furness—110, Dinse and Stearns shared a 110, and—I fired my guns!!!!

25 January, 1944*
Dive bombing—target Leeiwarden [sic] a/d. All three squadrons bombed but we didn't see many hits. Jerry is probably having a good laugh over the whole deal. Today made my 40th mission.

29 January, 1944*
Ramrod—freelance at the target which was Frankfurt. I returned about 20 minutes early because of feeling as if I would heave. Nothing was seen anyway except a lot of other 47s.

30 January, 1944
Ramrod—freelance, target Brunswick. Major Rimerman led the sqdn and aborted. Hurst and Fortier aborted also—leaving Dinse as the only flight leader in the crowd. He took his flight down on four 110s but 51s crowded him out—however Walsh and Chetwood are claiming probables. Tanner and Rowan came out early and pounced on two 190s. Tanner got one of them. Beckham also got another.

3 February, 1944*
Bomber escort—target Wilemshaven [sic]. Another weather fiasco—however, not as bad as it has been. Dewey [Newhart] led the sqdn—I had red flight and Hurst was leading blue. The sqdn had a little more action again—something usually happens with Newhart leading. As we were over the target area we saw 12 109s and met them head on. They were about a 1,000 ft. above us and we were at 31,000. The most uneager characters we've seen—acted like they were scared sick. I got a long head on shot at one—did no good—and by the time I got turned around there wasn't an e/a in the sky. All had turned tail and dived for the deck. Dewey got one and damaged another. Ireland also got a couple of damaged. Hurst mushed into Dewey's prop and had his tail chewed off. Nobody saw his chute but he probably got out. Is a terrific loss to the squadron and to B flight. Dewey's plane was in terrible shape—he was lucky to get back. It's amazing the beating these things will take and still fly 300 miles back. Beckham got his usual two destroyed—is now ahead of Mahurin, leading ace in the E.T.O. What a race! What a guy! However, the group didn't fare so well—3 for 3. Kenny and Thornell are missing. Old man Fry is in London!!! What swell news that is. Story will come later.

4 February, 1944*
Bomber escort—target Frankfurt. No action—no e/a, no nuthin'—only a 175 m.p.h. wind. Correction on yesterday's show. Mahurin also got one—so now they are tied with 16 each!!

5 February, 1944*
Bomber escort—target, airfield in France. Trip was around Paris. Today I screwed things up royally. Was leading blue flight and Pappy [Pidduck] aborted—result, my first and only chance (probably) to lead the sqdn. My radio was bad and couldn't hear a damn thing. So, there I was with the squadron and no radio—so I aborted too. What a performance! Had a chance to really do some good and flubbed it. Snafu extreme. Duncan got another—on the deck. Albert of 351 is missing.

6 February, 1944*
Bomber escort—target, airfields in France. Trip was very uneventful—plenty of friends and no e/a. Contrails were beautiful—forming shadows on the undercast below.

8 February, 1944
This is the story on Lt. Dwight A. Fry—missing OCT. 14, 1943, back Jan. 31, 1944.
    Oct. 14th was the famed Schweinfurt raid on which Bomber Command lost 60 heavies. We were penetration support to Duren, Germany.
    As I remember we were flying in red flight (Dewey, Walsh, with Fry no. 4 on my wing) behind Rimerman who was our C.O. at that time. At the time of withdrawal we saw a bunch of e/a below us—so Rimerman told us to take one crack at them and get out. On the way down, two 190s that I didn't see slid in on my tail and started firing. Seeing that, Fry skidded up into the sun and these jokers saw him, broke off me and split up. He singled out the one on the right and shot the hell out of it. The Hun bailed out and Fry—with his usual dislike for the enemy—tried to spill his chute.
    Evidently the other German had his head out and made a tight turn, getting on Fry's tail. With the 190 following, he shoved everything to one corner—pulling out, luckily, right on the tree tops. Looking back, he could still see the Hun blazing away at him. At that time our boy was thinking rather rapidly and figured that if he couldn't out-dive him maybe he could out-zoom him. I have never known Fry to do any acrobatics close to the ground but from what I gather, this was an exception. Pulling up sharply into an immelman [sic] he looked back and Hans was still there. Again he hit the deck, skidding like hell, and with everything forward that rock back there was gaining—so Fry made his first mistake. Thinking he could get more speed, he centred the ball—result [was] one 20mm explosive in his supercharger. The manifold pressure immediately dropped to 48". So with no longer any hope of out-running the 190 he decided he would have to fight—right there on the deck.

Hans was a little afraid to turn right on the tree tops so Fry easily out-turned him—a fact which caused him to make his fatal mistake. We have all learned since it is suicide to reverse a turn in a situation like that, but that's exactly what he did. And, that's when the boy Hans, started getting hits. The last thing Fry remembers about his airplane is when he glanced at his instrument panel and saw the instruments, one by one, disintegrate. Then a 20mm exploded in the cockpit ripping into his side—and tearing his mae west in two. If he were to get out, then was the time—he had had it!! So, zooming up to about 1,000 ft he climbed out—hitting the tail with his ankle [and] breaking 3 bones in his foot. On the way down he was tangled up in the shroud lines and the chute didn't open until about 50 ft above the ground. Then this nice little fellow called Hans strafed him 3 times—but luckily Fry had sense enough to dive behind a rock.

Within an hour and a half Fry was in a bed and had a doctor—and from there on his journey was in comparison to some others, fairly easy. He spent some time touring Belgium and brought some perfume and things for his wife in Paris. From Spain he brought some bananas which are being thoroughly enjoyed by C flight. I would like to write some of his exciting adventures while evading the Hun but they are unwritable at the present time—and are better forgotten anyway.

At any rate, he is back with us—in the best of health—a little changed but not much. It did him a lot of good. Was probably the most terrific "sweating" he will ever do, but now that it is over, seems to him like a bad dream.

From here he goes to a few other fields to give lectures and in about a month home—to Richmond, and Betty.

One by one our flight of that day has returned. First Dewey, then Walsh—a little later I came bouncing in—and now, three months later, Fry. What a guy!

8 February, 1944*

Bomber escort—target Frankfurt. About 5 minutes before r/v my airplane started acting up and Hart and I turned back. About 2 min. later we ran smack into about 20 109s. We almost tangled with them but finally decided there were too many and got the hell out of that particular spot. We went into a steep dive, through compressibility, and pulled out in the clouds. Amazingly enough Hart stayed with me all the way—and is to be congratulated, muchly. We climbed up to about 14,000 ft again and just about the time I thought we were fairly safe, Hart was bounced by two 109s. So, again we came out of a dive in the clouds. We came out at about 5,000 ft hopping from cloud to cloud until they gave out, from there on, on the deck. Nobody fired a shot at us. The rest of the group got into a mix up with 109s around the bombers—resulting in 7 destroyed for the group. Dinse got one that tried to sneak up behind Col. Rimerman—and naturally Beckham got two more making 18 in all. Mahurin was over yesterday and we got to take a look at him. Personally, I'll take Beck to be high scorer.

10 February, 1944*
Bomber escort—target Brunswick. My second trip leading blue flight—naturally nothing happened. We took off in a raging snow flurry. After that, I have no doubt but that we are completely mad!! Luckily, we all returned. Group got three. P-38s got six and lost six. Looks like before long the big shots would get wise and take them off ops. But—guess one for one is o.k. with Fighter Command.

11 February, 1944*
Bomber escort—target Frankfurt again, poor thing. Another milk run—bombers were late. Saw no e/a—almost got some Spits though, or vice versa!

13 February, 1944*
Area support, Pas De Calais—first time on type 16 control. Worked swell too. Controller vectored us into about 10 109s—but nobody got any!! Pappy [Pidduck] had a wonderful bounce but missed it. I started down with blue flight and was cut out by other flights.

14 February, 1944*
Valentine's Day and we go dive bombing. Target was Gillsy [Gilze-Rejin] again—the place has really taken a beating. Makes a good place to practice. I think we [a]re getting a little better—had pretty good hits. Had blue flight again—was my first experience at aiming for the flight.

20 February, 1944*
Bomber escort—target Leipzig. Greatest daylight raid yet—and naturally another damn milk run for us. This time we didn't even [see] any e/a. We must be just about the unluckiest bunch of guys ever to form a group. Made my 50th mission today and I have only a damaged to my credit. Am getting slightly discouraged about the whole thing. Led yellow flight.

21 February, 1944*
Bomber escort. Our bombers hit Gutersloh—or attempted to hit it. Was another milk run for us—nobody saw any e/a. P-47s, P-38s all over the place but no e/a—and me with red flight!!!

22 February, 1944*
Bomber escort—target Schweinfurt again. Duncan has gone stark raving mad! Took his whole squadron down to the deck—deep in Germany—to pounce on an airdrome! Beckham followed with his sqdn. I hope Duncan has learned his lesson but I doubt if he has. There's no excuse for some damn trick like that. Five guys lost, including Beckham—who was hit by flak and bailed out. We're claiming seven—a mighty poor score. Sounds like something the 38s would do. They all came back on the deck—Dunc's windshield was covered solid with black oil. He was lucky to get back. Our squadron saw no e/a, even with Dewey leading. Again I had red flight.

24 February, 1944
Bomber escort—target Schweinfurt. First time operating as two groups. Col. Ben led A group using 108 gal. wing tanks—went to the same place but stayed longer. Duncan led B group and our sqdn. Again, he came back on the deck—all shot to hell. He had Dinse's airplane which is being scrapped. His flight (Stearns, Walsh and Rowan) bounced a flight of 8 190s just west of Steinhuder Lake. Dunc got one and a probable—a JU88 and a ship on the way out. Our boy Stearns did o.k. by himself. Got one—then went round and round on the deck with two more. Got one of those and was chased part way home by the other. Makes 4 for him. Walsh also got one and Rowan shot one down off Walsh's tail. Naturally I was in London at the time!

25 February, 1944
Bomber escort—targets Regensburg and Stuttgart. Group operated again as two groups—but saw no action. The boys with the wing tanks had a good look at the Alps! That's getting in there rather far, I'd say. The 15th A.F. came up from Italy to bomb the same targets. They're really putting this bombing into high gear.

2 March, 1944*
Bomber escort—target Frankfurt. No e/a seen. I had blue flight and flew with 352. Bergeron was low on gas so we landed at Manston. A new t.o. [Technical Order] has come out and they tell me I am to be D flight leader—happy day!![1]

3 March, 1944
Bomber escort—target Berlin!!!! Mission was screwed up in general. Bombers aborted—kinda leery, I guess. Pappy [Pidduck] aborted—also Devane in blue flight—leaving Fortier with the sqdn. Thought sure they would see something, since I wasn't along, but they didn't. P-51s and P-38s went all the way to Berlin on a sweep. Squadron carried 165 gal. belly tanks for the first time—didn't work out too well. Duncan asked for volunteers to join an airdrome strafing squadron. They'll get pilots from the 78th and 361st. Will operate separately and try to get the Hun as he is refuelling. Is a good idea—of course they'll be depending a helluva lot on luck. Although it's what I've wanted for a long time, I didn't volunteer. Against the Jap it would be o.k. but these boys over here are plenty smart—also as yet I have neither paddle prop nor water injection. Until I get them I'm not giving it too much consideration. Beckham was a helluva lot better pilot than I am.

4 March, 1944
Bomber escort—target Berlin. Another fiasco—I'm just as glad I didn't go. Was scheduled in B group but couldn't turn on the radio so never got off the ground. Seems like everybody aborted. B group ended up with about 9 or 10 ships. Neither

---

1   Squadron records confirm D Flight was formed officially on March 7, 1944. See 350th FS records held by the AFHRA, Maxwell, Alabama.

group saw any e/a. Had heavy flak over Cologne. Billy Burkett is missing—cause was probably weather. Another classmate of mine. Weather was bad here with snow etc. but was even worse on the continent. Was up to 25 and 30,000 and down to 2,000. Telephone report tonight was that fighters today destroyed 8 for the loss of 24—which ain't good! 363rd group (P-51s) had 11 n.y.r.s!!!

6 March, 1944
Bomber escort—target Berlin. At last they made it through to the target. Ireland and Fortier [Dawson] were the only pilots to go from the 350th as we were busy trying to get our new (?) planes operational. They have wing racks and water injection. Ireland got all shot up and as he put down his flaps to come in, he slid off on the wing minus the aileron and augered in. He's in a deep coma—Doc doesn't think he'll live. Another of our better pilots gone. Duncan talked him all the way back—he almost bailed—over there.

Bomber claims so far are 93—fighter claims 82 with 69 bombers lost and 11 fighters. A terrific blow to the Luftwaffe. Dunc got two more. 40 bombers were known to be lost to e/a. That part isn't good.

7 March, 1944
Ireland died today of his injuries.

8 March, 1944
Bomber escort—target Berlin. I was scheduled for red flight flying behind Col. Ben, but couldn't go because of my cold—so we put Zolner up there in my plane leading his first flight. He chased a couple guys—got one—and then got hit by flak. It hit him in the main tank and spilled his gas—so he had only enough to get to Holland. Rimerman and Stearns saw him bail out and get picked up by some characters in a black car. Friend or foe—he's o.k. D flight took a helluva beating from his loss. Hart got a long nosed 190—shot it off Price's tail—so D flight got 2 and lost 1. Seems like every one likes to come out on the deck. Rimerman and Stearns were madly shooting at some joker flying down the streets of Hanover. Robertson's flight shot down three 190s in the traffic pattern of some a/d n.w. of Hanover.

Score today is about the same as the 6th—with 35 bombers lost. 56th beat their old record by one—got 29. Mahurin got 3 more making 20, R.S. Johnson got 2 more making 19, also Gerry Johnson got a couple more. The Luftwaffe must be getting well into there [sic] reserves.

Looks like I'll get a new airplane—will make the 5th since I've been in England.

9 March, 1944
Bomber escort—target Berlin. Weather wasn't too good but they went anyway. The Germans just didn't come up. There was just one e/a shot down by fighters and bombers combined. Lost 8 bombers and one fighter. Bombed through 10/10 cloud.

My new plane came in—from the 352nd group. Is a D*15 and looks to be in good condition.

13 March, 1944*
Type 16 control in the Pas DE Calais area—and what a performance that was!! Capt.— led our sqdn—why I don't know. I'm not too sure he should again. Everybody in the squadron had to draw a lot of mercury and we went too far—were all low on gas—and to top it off, some character of a character was breathing on the r/t. No e/a were seen naturally, a little flak, not much. My airplane isn't so hot on gas—and I DON'T like that. Otherwise it's a perfect airplane. I flew blue flight.

D flight is shaping up—hope to have it the hottest flight in the outfit, even without Zolner. Li'l Joe [Furness] will turn out o.k. soon as he leads a few more practice flights. Our set up now is Main on my wing, Pasley on Harts, and Mueller on Joe's.

15 March, 1944*
Bomber escort—target Brunswick. We saw exactly nothing—56th got 25; I give up. CAPT R. S. Johnson got 3 more making 22 for him—two ahead of Mahurin. I had Main on my wing for his first mission—in red flight. What a hot rock he is—smooth as glass.

16 March, 1944*
Bomber escort—target Friedrichshafen. Boy do I have the old r. a. today—and it's from sitting this time!! Four hours on that beaten up dingy—and it was still sore from yesterday. Had a good look at the Alps!—we were that close to Switzerland. Can't understand how we keep avoiding the Luftwaffe—it's amazing. Not one e/a was seen except on the ground. Some of the guys went down on airdromes. Duncan got all shot up again. Incidentally—he is now a full col. From 1st looie to full col. in a year—how about that!! I got hit by a small piece of flak, the boys are getting better and better with that stuff. Flew spare today—took over yellow flight—and finally ended up with Devane in blue flight.

Newman and Dustin are missing from 352—went down on an a/d didn't get back.

17 March, 1944
Dive bomb—target Soesterberg a/d. Group took 24 ships—did low level glide and vertical dive bombing—hits were good.

18 March, 1944
Bomber escort—target Friedrichshafen again. Weather was lousy—saw no e/a; at least they engaged none. Coming out Pappy [Pidduck] took the squadron right over Boulongue [sic]—Garey was hit by flak and landed o.k. at Manston.

20 March, 1944
Bomber escort—target Frankfurt. Am glad I didn't go this time. Was another weather fiasco. Group got up to 20,000 ft—still on instruments—and aborted. In the turn around, Dinse lost Bergeron, Pinky [Lorance], and Main. Got a little rough, I guess. Was sweating out my boy Main for a while—but he made it in good shape. Hope he continues to use his head—and it looks like he will.

22 March, 1944*
Bomber escort—target Berlin, via the northern route. We were slightly late due to a heavy, dense overcast—and bombers were early—so we didn't make r/v until 15 min after we were supposed to leave. Went in a lot farther than we were supposed to. Got into the heaviest flak I've seen, over Hamburg—couldn't get out of it. They're really getting good.

23 March, 1944
Bomber escort—targets in the Brunswick area. No e/a were seen. Rimerman is getting to be as much a milk run kid as I am.
    We finally had our D.F.C. presentation. Also—Devane made Captain.

26 March, 1944
Duncan's buzz boys went out on their first mission to some airdromes south of Paris. Got about 3 or 4 damaged airplanes. One guy is missing [First Lieutenant Kenneth Williams]. Sully [Sullivan] ran into a tree but got back o.k. They blew up a hangar, gun emplacement etc. To me—it doesn't seem to be much of a success.

27 March, 1944
Bomber escort—target, airfields in France, by Orleans, Thot [sic] sure they'd run into something, but they didn't. Didn't even get any flak.
    The buzz boys went out—into the same territory—even they didn't do anything. Didn't lose anybody either, so maybe they had a successful mission.

28 March, 1944*
Bomber escort—target, airfields near La Rochelle, France. Happy day—I led the squadron for the first time. Was a bad day to try experiments—ceiling of 2 or 3 hundred ft, vis less than a mile. Hoey led the group and Vic Byers led the 351st. Everything went o.k. and we finally got together. Was a milk run, naturally. Saw some excellent bombing on one field. Incidentally—yesterday the 56th really took a beating. Got four and lost five! Among the losses were none other than Gerry Johnson AND Mahurin. Mahurin was hit by a rear gunner of a 410—some lucky shavetail, no doubt. Ironic, no? Johnson was hit by light flak and bellied in. One guy tried to land and pick him up but couldn't quite make it. What a blow!

29 March, 1944*
Bomber escort—target Brunswick. I had red flight and aborted—so the group ran into a few!! Squadron didn't do any good but the group got five. Walsh fired, but didn't hit anything.
    The buzz boys went out again and shot up everything in sight. Chetwood got all shot up but Duncan talked him in o.k. They got six—all on the ground. Dunc got 2 or 3 of those and about 8 damaged. Shot up a bunch of trains—villages—people—flak towers—everything. And—amazingly enough—didn't lose anybody. Edwards bailed out in the channel by an air sea rescue launch and was picked up.

1 April, 1944
Bomber escort—target Frankfurt. Weather was bad and every[one] aborted—including the bombers. Li'l Joe [Furness] led his first flight and did o.k.

Buzz boys went farther north and the weather was o.k. They got 3 or 4 destroyed. Rumor has it that Col. Dunc is no longer permitted to fly with them. So, I look for it to be disbanded before long.

I flew a paddle prop today—what a performance!! Makes the old milk bottle feel like an AT-6. What a change. Sure hope we can get them.

Dewey told me today I was to be the next operations officer. Ha—a big dog (?). Looks like it might not be too long either—Pidduck only needs 7 or 8 missions to finish.

5 April, 1944
Fighter sweep—around Hanover. Were originally supposed to strafe airdrome but the weather was so bad they never got down to the ground.

More news—on the q.t. Doc said last night the generals have o.k.'d a 30 day leave home for some of the boys, and Dewey, Willy Price and I have been selected as the first to go! Happy day—that way I'll get to go home and still go with the sqdn if it goes to Burma or somewhere.

Incidentally—the group has been cited!! For the mission of Jan. 7th when Gonnam made ace.

8 April, 1944
Bomber escort—for awhile—the[n] attacks on airfields with each sqdn taking a different one. 352 and 351 didn't do much. 350 shot up quite a bit including a hangar, couple of planes and totally destroyed an engine. Mueller got his trim tabs shot out—came back by himself, holding a lot of back pressure all the way. Was slightly tired!!

9 April, 1944*
Bomber escort—targets around Berlin. I led the squadron again and everything went swell until we hit an overcast. The lead squadron made a turn into me and we got split up—we finally got back together, though. Went all the way to Kiel. Stearns went down on an a/d—got hit and bailed out. Tersian [Terzian] of 351 ran out of gas and bailed out in the channel. Was picked up after about five hours—is o.k. We thot [sic] Li'l Joe [Furness] was down too, but he showed up later—had been flying 5 hours and 50 min!! Had been out circling Tersian. We flew about 375 mi. each way—over water. Longest haul yet.

There's a lot I have to learn about leading a squadron—isn't quite as easy as it looks.

My captaincy came through today—dated 4 or 5 April. Happy day!

10 April, 1944

Bomber escort—target Brussels. Came in at 6:30 this morning with "Briefing at 7:00"! What a performance! Was just a short one—very uneventful. Field order told us to expect another, but they finally released us.

Buzz boys went out—Durant got one on the ground.

Gentile of the 4th group has 23 destroyed in the air and 7 on the ground. R.S. Johnson has 23 also, Gabreski 22. What characters!!

11 April, 1944

Bomber escort—another trip to Denmark. Col. Ben led the squadron—no action. 'Tis getting so the only way to see anything is to go to Berlin.

12 April, 1944*

Bomber escort—bombers aborted and we went on a sweep to Hanover–Bremen–Emden. Had two groups—I had red flight to Col. Rimerman. Had some pretty rough flak at Bremen—that's all.

We're getting the buzz boys' paddle blades. Should be putting mine on soon.

13 April, 1944*

Bomber escort—targets all over Germany. Had two groups—Hoey and Lefebre leading. We missed the bombers!! Those p-blades are colossal. 'Tis amazing what they'll do.

We're all set to move to Raydon tomorrow.

14 April, 1944

We're all moved—looks like it'll be o.k. Living in Nissen huts—one for a flight. In this one we have Doc [Canipelli], Dewey [Newhart], Li'l Joe [Furness], Hart, Mueller, Main, Paslay and Morretto, our new boy.

They tell us we're going to have to give up our p-props. Oh unhappy day!

News that Zolner is a p.w. in Holland!

17 April, 1944

A/d strafing—didn't pan out. Weather got too bad and they aborted.

We're giving up our props to the 56th today!

17 April, 1944

Another Pas De Calais deal. 10/10/overcast—nothing happened.

My airplane came back from the 56th today. Swap wasn't too bad—have a semi-paddle blade.

18 April, 1944

Bomber escort—targets in the Berlin area. The boys made what amounted to a sweep around Hamburg. Bombers were early and were never found. Col. Ben led the sqdn.

I sure haven't been flying much on missions lately. Gotta get on the ball. Am turning into a "gravel scratcher"! Seems like all I do is train new boys.

19 April, 1944*
Bomber escort—targets around and north of the Ruhr. I led the squadron and things went a little better this time—no weather. Fog cleared out right at the last minute. We saw no e/a naturally—millions of bombers—47s, 38s, 51s—everything but e/a.

Devane and Dawson finished up today—we're sweating out what will be done to them.

Looks like Moretto is going to be o.k.—he almost trounced me in a dog fight today.

20 April, 1944
Area support—Pas De Calais. Nothing unusual happened. Looks like all we're doing is stalling for time.

Went down to Winkton to see Howard today. He's in the 404th Fighter Bomber Group. Has been here since the 5th. They have all brand new P-47s with paddle props—and they aren't even operational yet!! Pinky [Lorance] finished today.

21 April, 1944
Bomber escort—targets in the Munich area. Bombers aborted and the fighters were recalled.

22 April, 1944
Bomber escort—target Haam. Rimerman led the squadron and they had a little fun shooting up trains. We got about 6 or 8—351 got about 3 e/a – imagine that – e/a!! Wasn't a deep penetration either. Germans are getting bold again. I was spare and nobody aborted so I came back.

They tell me I am going on d.s. to Scotland for dive bombing—or some such stuff. Up where Duncan and Bailey have been for two weeks—what a performance!

23 April, 1944
Strafing—airdromes and canals. Pappy [Pidduck] led the group with only two flights while Dewey [Newhart] and I had flights on a/s rescue. The squadron shot up a bunch of stuff. Pappy got shot up—he needs one more mission to finish. [3]52nd lost Gonnam and the [3]51st lost Peterson. [3]52nd really lost a good man—this ground work just isn't profitable.

We were out looking for Trudo [Trudeau] who bailed yesterday. Winder finally spotted him and directed the Walrus. He is o.k. after his wet night.

24 April, 1944*
Bomber escort—target Munich. I led the squadron again and what a snafu mission it was. Seems like every time I lead we have an overcast and I'm getting pretty well

p'd off about it. The way it worked out—guess I shouldn't have gone through it all, seein[g] as how ther[e] were holes all around. We finally ended up with seven ships—escorting one combat wing! We finally left them and escorted a lone B-17 all the way to the coast.[2] Duncan got into some more action—was out-turned by a 109 at 20,000 ft. Must have been a real hot rock to turn inside Dunc. Group got one or two destroyed—that's all.

Walsh is going to Scotland instead—and that doesn't make me unhappy.

25 April, 1944
Bomber escort—on type 16 control, n.e. of Paris. They divided the group, Dewey [Newhart] leading our squadron which was B group. Saw nothing.

McKean finished today—Walsh went to Scotland.

26 April, 1944
Bomber escort—target Brunswick. No soap—nothing happened. Dunc led the sqdn.

We were briefed for another mission and were out in the planes—but it was scrubbed.

Yesterday the R.A.F. flying circus came in [No. 1426 Enemy Aircraft Flight]—190, 109 and Ju88. Look to be nice airplanes. Was funny to see them flying around over here.

---

2   Blick and his flight escorted a straggler to the coast after withdrawal. Lieutenant Starr's ship was identified by the bomber pilot and he got a note of thanks. See 350th FS Records, AFHRA, Maxwell, Alabama:

26th May 1944
Dear Lt Starr,

This note is somewhat tardy so please forgive. I happen to be the pilot of the B17 you escorted out of France on April 24th. That happened to be my next to last mission and I finished on the following day. I received my orders to the 12th R.C.D before I could trace your ship number and having just received the same, I am taking this opportunity to thank you for each member of my crew.

Our oxygen system was shot out forcing us to leave formation. I also had a severely wounded waist gunner. I'm telling you, that before you got into recognizable distance, you gave us a hell of a scare, but when we saw you were all P-47s, I can tell you it was the most beautiful sight I have ever seen.

I would like to state that you fellows are sincerely respected and appreciated by every man who flies. Also you have the envy of every bomber pilot, for I know I've wanted to fly your type of ship ever since I received my wings. The cry "P-47s at 12 o'clock, etc" is always music to our ears.

Other words expressing our appreciation for the work you fellows are doing and for the job you did for us on April 24th cannot be really put into words. I want to thank you and I know every other bomber pilot would like to have the same opportunity.

Gratefully yours,
1st Lt Bob Welter.

27 April, 1944
Type 16 control—Pas De Calais, down south; no action.

27 April, 1944
Bomber escort with our squadron dive bombing Florennes a/d. Col. Rimerman led our squadron and the hits were not too good. As they were forming up, Mueller's plane lost power and he pulled a beautiful belly in job in a farmyard about 2 miles from here. He was flying Dunc's new silver job—X the sixth. All this happened when they had climbed only about a 1,000 ft. Before he landed he armed and dropped his bombs and belly tank!! Fast work!

28 April, 1944
Dive bombing—Chateaudon [sic] a/d and ammunition dump. Hits were not very good this time either. P-38s did some beautiful high level bombing.
   Duncan is taking the new D-22 we just got in for X the 7th.

29 April, 1944
Bomber escort—target Berlin. Weather was bad so they met the bombers about the time they were supposed to leave. Newhart aborted and only two flights were together in the squadron. I was spotter and had no business.

30 April, 1944
Bomber escort—ta[r]get Lyon, southern France. The boys saw the Pyranees [sic] today—was quite a trip. Lot of flak, but no e/a.

30 April, 1944
Dive bombing—target Orleans a/d. They really clobbered it in coordination with 38s. Rimerman led our squadron with frags. Had no flak anywhere—what a dream set-up.

1 May, 1944
Bomber escort—target Metz. Not much happened—in fact nothing happened! Looks like Dewey [Newhart] has the squadron and I have operations—and Li'l Joe [Furness] has D flight. Pappy [Pidduck] finished today and will leave us. Price also finished and will go home for 30 days. Walsh and Durant finished yesterday—Walsh will get an extension.
   Begins to look like Mueller got ye olde shaft. Was sent on a/s rescue work and I doubt if we will be able to get him out of it. What a deal—hate to lose him.

5 May, 1944
Pappy [Pidduck] left for wing today. His orders still aren't in so Dewey [Newhart] still doesn't officially have the squadron, but unofficially he does.

7 May, 1944
Bomber escort—targets Osnabrook [sic] and Berlin. No e/a. Hart and Sully [Sullivan] finished up. From the looks of this operations deal, I have quite a job ahead of me.
   Dewey [Newhart] moved up with the wheels today [group field grade officers (major and above) were required to live together in the "Wheelhouse"].

8 May, 1944

Bomber escort—targets Berlin and Brunswick. Withdrawal with the last bunch from Berlin with Col. Duncan leading—and still no e/a! Some of the guys logged five hours.

8 May, 1944

Bomber escort and type 16 control down south in France—no-ball targets.

9 May, 1944*

Bomber escort—targets were airdromes in Northern France. They got us up at 5:30 for a simple milk run that could just as easily been run about noon—can't understand it. Newhart overslept so I was operational again—how about that!

11 May, 1944

Bomber escort—type 16 control with targets all over France. No action. Fortier finished.

11 May, 1944

Gassed up and had another mission an hour after landing. Dinse led the sqdn. Nothing happened—same deal as mission before. Winder finished—will be back.

12 May, 1944

Bomber escort—we were penetration into Frankfurt. Group saw a little action again for a change. Saw more e/a at one time than has ever been seen by this group. Duncan was leading with our squadron and got all shot up again with Bedford's ship. Got back—very luckily—and bellied in here. He leads a charmed life—'tis amazing how he always gets back. He got a 190 and Tanner and Chetwood shared a 109. Looks like the Germans have decided to fight again—in very big bunches. Could be as a last resort—hope so anyway. 56th got 19 today—they're still doing it!!

This job of mine really has my head spinning. Orders came through today, so I'm legally operations officer—hope I can handle it.

13 May, 1944

Bomber escort—target was way to hell and gone in. We were penetration to about 50 miles east of Hamburg. Didn't see anything—and a little gas sweating, that's all. Walsh is back to stay now—is ass't operations.

Mahurin is back!! Will probably talk to us before long—I hope.

19 May, 1944

Bomber escort—target support around Brunswick. Duncan was leading with 352 and they again ran into a great gob of e/a. Dunc did a wonderful job. Led about 4 or 8 ships through 5 waves of Germans firing like mad. Although he didn't get any, they were broken up and never got to the bombers. On the way home he picked up a B-24 that was turning back to let the crew bail out, and talked them home. He's a great guy to talk somebody home.

20 May, 1944*
Bomber escort to airdromes around Paris. I flew again for a change and naturally we saw nothing. Am really going to have to fly now. They raised the tour to 300 hours for those under 180, and it caught me—bad. Probably won't even get home now.

21 May, 1944
Targets—the bombing of trains. Dewey [Newhart] led the group and they really raised hell in general. Flak was terrific. Rowan got hit and had to bail out—was almost finished. The squadron is claiming 5 trains among other things. Mission was very successful in the eyes of the big dogs.

Took an X-C to Atcham today to see Bledsoe. We might get him in this outfit. Hope so—we can use him, now.

22 May, 1944*
Dive bombing—target was two bridges in Liege. We carried a 1,000 pounder under each wing and a 108 gal. belly tank. What a load that was. Was overcast over there and on[l]y a couple of flights hit the target. My flight and Chetwood's went down and couldn't even find the city. While we were hunting we found a radar station and bombed the hell out of it. Chetwood's a damn good man—we'll probably give him A flight. Duncan got all shot up again—right aileron was almost burned off. How long his luck will hold out, I don't know.

Tersian [Terzian] of 351 bailed out. Coffey ran out of gas and bellied in—was almost to the field. Is o.k.—didn't hurt him. One more paddle prop!!!

I should have some good pictures of the bombing. Chetwood's flight's bombs went off just as I was going down firing. Hope they turn out.

23 May, 1944
Bomber escort—Group was late setting course due to insufficient time and weather. They got us up at 6:00 and said briefing immediately!! Made r/v with the wrong bunch of bombers. Dinse led the squadron.

24 May, 1944
Bomber escort—target Berlin. We were withdrawal from east of Hamburg out to sea. Nothing much happened except a lot of flak around Hamburg.

Tanner now has A flight and Chetwood has B. Is a little rough on Tanner but should work out o.k.

25 May, 1944*
Bomber escort—deep into France. We didn't see anything—stooged around the whole time at 10,000 ft; Tanner's flight shot up a train. I had to sweat out Auchincloss and his gas.

27 May, 1944
Bomber escort—target Strasbourg. No e/a seen. Group returned on the deck. Squadron shot up 5 trains. 352 got some planes on an a/d. C[h]etwood did most of the shooting again. He's making a good flight leader. Rimerman led our sqdn.

28 May, 1944
Bomber escort—targets in the Brunswick area. No e/a again. Duncan returned NOT shot up for a change! Mission started as 3 hours and ended up about 5—naturally. Was about the longest one so far. Could have made Berlin easily. Again they hit the deck on the way out—sqdn getting five trains. Chetwood's flight got 4 of them. Moretto bellied in on take-off at Boxted. Another paddle prop!!

29 May, 1944
Bomber escort—target was somewhere in Poland. Group hit the deck again on the way out. Squadron really got hit—flak was something terrific. Bergeron was hit and went in, exploding. McDonald—flying my airplane—was hit and with his right side paralyzed and weak from loss of blood, made it as far as Holland, where he bellied in—couldn't fly it any longer. Said he was too weak to attempt getting out or even burn the plane. Sure hope he's o.k.—was well on his way to becoming one of our hotter combat pilots.

    Dewey [Newhart] finished up today—looks like I'll be C.O. for a while. Hope I can handle it. Guess I'll get the D-25 for my airplane, too.

30 May, 1944*
Bomber escort—a/ds just this side of Berlin. What a deal. We went almost to Berlin—then started to see e/a after everybody was so low they couldn't do anything about it. Poindexter got a couple 190s. Chetwood got some more trains—has 18 now. Edwards was shot down—with the 352nd. Phelan landed out of gas at Woodbridge. I logged 5 hours and 25 min—most, so far.

30 May, 1944*
Dive bombing—a bridge in France. I got some good hits—was one of the few to hit it. Hunter of 351 is missing. Flew 8 hours and 35 minutes today—which isn't bad.

31 May, 1944
Type 16 control. Col. Ben led with our squadron—ran into bad weather, so returned early.

31 May, 1944*
Dive bomb—Gutersloh a/d. Other two squadrons had frags and we had 500 pounders. Again our sqdn did the most good. My flight ALL hit one building—rest of sqdn all hit their assigned area. We're claiming about 5 airplanes, left burning on the ground.

56th bombed 15 min ahead of us and afterwards ran into about 40 plus e/a that we never did see. Zempke [Zemke] got two. Both groups combined, really clobbered the field.

2 June, 1944
Pas De Calais—could very easily be the start of the invasion. Really pounded the area—840 bombers. Walsh led the sqdn.

2 June, 1944
Practically a repeat performance except farther south. Tanner led the squadron—really looked good. Germans broadcasted that the invasion had started. Who knows—maybe it has.

All leaves to the States are temporarily cancelled. Looks like Dewey [Newhart] might have to get an extension. Walsh made captain today—Willy Price's hasn't come through yet.

3 June, 1944*
Type 16 down by Paris. No flak—no e/a—no nuthin'.

4 June, 1944*
Type 16 down by Paris. Nothing doing. Flew my new U for the first time.

4 June, 1944*
Bomber escort—airfields south of Paris, by Orleans. The bombers really clobbered one field.

Hit the 200 hour mark today—now all I have to do is fly another 100!!

5 June, 1944
Pas De Calais—Major Gallup led the sqdn. No action.

The calm before the storm. Looks like tomorrow might be the big day.

6 June, 1944
And I was right!!!!!!!!!! (Doc [Canipelli] insisted on ten exclamation points.) We sat in the briefing room from 10:30 'till 2:00 A.M. Group took off in the dark about 3:00 and was in it's [sic] assigned area at dawn. We were briefed for what is probably the biggest show this earth has ever seen. Everything went off like clockwork—as planned. No e/a at all. Was about 9/10 cloud coverage so the group didn't see much of what went on. Dunc led with our squadron. Tanner, Walsh, Dewey [Newhart], and Li'l Joe [Furness] are getting extensions.

6 June, 1944
Dewey [Newhart] led the sqdn. First two flights had bombs—didn't do much good with them. Had to cruise around under the overcast.

We've had every ship in commission all day. The GIs are doing a good job.

6 June, 1944
Duncan led the sqdn—bombed and clobbered a convoy—shot up some trucks. Furness, Yocum and Brooks slept at Ford. Squadron came back at night.

7 June, 1944*
Dive bomb—briefed to go in at 2,000 ft, Weather was so bad we never got to the assigned area. Flak split us up—I let my bomb go on a railroad track and came home alone. Tanner bombed and strafed a train.

Walsh is missing! Think he made it to the channel, but so far there is no trace of him. Sure hope he's o.k.

7 June, 1944
Dive bomb—Dewey [Newhart] led the sqdn. Were out to get a couple [of] tunnels—and really did. Closed up both ends of both of them.

7 June, 1944*
Rimerman led the sqdn, and I led Blue flight. We clobbered a tunnel. I destroyed two locos and shared in the destruction of two more. Wasn't a bad day's work.

Weather is still bad for the invasion. Group had 9 missions today. Sqdns are going out separately. Duncan was flying with the 351st today and ran into some e/a—he got another.

8 June, 1944
Group went out as a group again today. Dinse led the squadron. Saw and bombed an armored convoy. Starr and Yocum straffed an airdrome. What a character this Yocum is—got a HE111 and 110 and damaged another 110—is the most eager character we've had. Dunc also got one—a Ju52!!

8 June, 1944
Col. Rimerman led the group with our squadron. Weather was bad—was almost a fiasco. Hit a truck convoy—marshalling yards. 351 again ran into some e/a.

8 June, 1944
Duncan led the group—Dewey [Newhart] led the squadron. Flew two hours instruments and let down over there. Duncan was shot up again—flew instruments all the way home—let down and landed with trim tabs!!!—had no elevator control. I think he has more guts than anybody in the E.T.O.—just like a story book character.

Bledsoe finally got here—put him in D flight.

So far since D-Day this group has flown more operational hours and put in more claims than any other group. Have destr[o]yed 35 airplanes and dropped over half the total bombs dropped.

9 June, 1944* [10 June, 1944]
Dive bomb—targets in the Bernay area. My flight and Chetwood's shot up a truck convoy—I got one truck. Was separated from the rest of the squadron and spent about a half hour looking for something to bomb. Finally found a railroad bridge and missed—one bomb hit a bunch of cattle!—tsk! Chetwood's flight went down later on a train and Chetwood was hit. He was going to bail out but we urged him up to the beachhead. I think he's o.k. but the wind might have drifted him back into German hands. The other flights hit some railroad cars—didn't do much good. Coffey mushed into the trees—sure hated to lose him.

10 June, 1944
Rimerman led the squadron—target was a couple of bridges down by Nantes. Weather was so bad they never got there. They did bomb a couple of bridges, though. Was a long mission—some logged 5 hours.

10 June, 1944*
Dewey [Newhart] led the sqdn—I had blue flight. Target was a long tunnel on the river west of Paris. Was a good mission—very successful—really clobbered the tunnel. On the return, the weather was almost closed in and it was dark, but we made it o.k.
  Bledsoe flew my wing on his first mission—wish he'd teach these young hot-rocks how to fly. Best wingman I've had since Hart left.

11 June, 1944
Tanner led the sqdn—did type 16 escort, then hit an airdrome with bombs.
  78th lost 11 yesterday—were jumped by 40 plus e/a while bombing. What a rough performance that was!—Gulp!

11 June, 1944
Rimerman led the sqdn—did a good job on some railroad yards, cars etc. He's still p'd off with the way this sqdn is flying—wish these characters would get on the ball. Guess we can't expect much more though—there's only about 5 originals left. Bledsoe, Rafferty, Graham and Ruscitto are really going to help.
  There's still no word on Walsh or Chetwood—dunno what I'll write Marge [Walsh's wife].

12 June, 1944
This is a mission I hate to write about. What a helluva blow it was. Group went out early to dive bomb and while they were bombing were bounced by 40 plus ME109s. They really clobbered the squadron. I was awakened this morning with the news that Dewey [Newhart] was missing. They hit him and he got as far as the coast where he was hit some more. That's the last that was heard of him—he was calling for help.
  Also, Bedford, Main, Moretto, Phelan, and Peters—are missing!!! What a blow. Ruscitto shot one off Brown's tail or he (Brown) wouldn't be here either.

12 June, 1944*
Duncan got sore and called up wing and got us a sweep to go in there and clean out those guys. Rimerman was about 4 or 5 thousand with 352—351 was about 10,000—and we were at 15. Didn't see anything, then came head on to about 40 109s—same characters. They were about 2,000 ft above us. Tried madly for a long time to catch them—seemed like they were all over the sky. Finally after I was alone I got on the tail of one and followed him through a split s to the deck—such evasive action I have never seen! After fighting for about 5 mins he lost me in a cloud. Never did hit him! He was pretty much a hot rock—must be fresh from the Russian front.

Tanner got 2 and Li'l Joe [Furness] got 2, so we didn't do too bad. Group lost 8 today and got 14—which is not too good.

13 June, 1944*
Another early morning mission—target was a bridge in Tours, France. I got one hit. Rafferty was hit—got back o.k.—ship was pretty bad. One of the 352nd boys—Jones—was hit and gas was running out like mad. He tagged on to me and I took him to the beachhead. Just as he was about ten ft off the ground the ship exploded so I landed to find out that he was o.k. How he got out I'll never know.

Imagine that—I walked on French soil!!! Was first to land and take off again on the beach-head.

Chetwood is back—bellied in a couple [of] miles inside our lines. Has quite a tale. He's o.k.—didn't get hurt.

13 June, 1944
Dive bomb—target—the other bridge at Tours. Everybody missed—did no good whatsoever. Gallup led our squadron. He has officially taken over—will be a good man. I think most of the guys will be satisfied with him.

14 June, 1944
Bomber escort—Dinse led the sqdn and finished up. Nothing spectacular happened.

Incidentally—the other day when Tanner got two that made him our first ace.

14 June, 1944*
We were top cover while the rest of the group dive bombed. Everything worked out swell except that we didn't find anything to shoot at. The other two squadrons hit a marshalling yard and an airdrome with poor results.

15 June, 1944
Gallup took the early one—bomber escort. Again nothing happened. Where are these 40 plus???

Peters is back—down south of London in a RAF hospital. Left leg from knee down is gone. Maybe we can get down to see him tomorrow.

16 June, 1944
Gallup led the group on a short dive bombing mission over the coast. Weather was very bad—ended up a real fiasco.

Saw Peters today—they picked him up in the channel. He lost his foot bailing out—is the most cheerful guy, what a character. Took a lot of guts to do what he did. Was afraid he'd bleed to death so on the way down he took off his belt and made a tournequette [sic]. Lost his dingy so he struggled an hour and a quarter until the boat picked him up. Has no info on what happened to the others. Wants to come back and run the snack bar.

Howard was up today—and had a long chat with him—seems to like it o.k. Has about 20 missions. They're running short missions—all dive bombing. Are planning on moving to France pretty quick.

17 June, 1944
Gallup led the sqdn—escort—area support up by the Zuider Zee. No action.

17 June, 1944*
Type 16—north of Paris; ended up south of Paris. Duncan's no. 4 got a 109. Dunc missed his—lost him in the clouds. Not much else happened.

18 June, 1944
Rimerman led with our squadron—dive bomb with 1,000 pounders. Target was a bridge in Haam. Weather was bad and everybody brought their bombs back.

18 June, 1944
Rimerman led the same mission—same bombs—same bridge—same weather—same flop!

19 June, 1944*
Escort—weather was bad; we all aborted.

19 June, 1944*
Gallup led the squadron—I had red flight. Area escort—Pas De Calais. No action.
Captain Tanner left for the States today. Also—Li'l Joe [Furness] is a captain now.

20 June, 1944
Gallup led—escort, target Berlin. Chetwood's flight got a train—that's about all that happened.

20 June, 1944
Dive bomb—Rimerman led our sqdn; took it back to an a/d they saw packed with planes on the morning mission. They did a good job—was a very successful mission.

21 June, 1944*
Bomber escort—target Berlin; guess we're back to our regular missions again. With my D-25 I could have gone all the way and spent 15 minutes around Berlin—'tis

a good airplane. Nothing exciting happened—Duncan shot up a glider on the ground. Gliders don't count!!

21 June, 1944
Pas De Calais—type 16—nothing happened. Li'l Joe's [Furness] orders came in. He's assigned directly to the States. The boys upstairs must like those 50 hour extensions.

22 June, 1944
Type 16 with 100 pounders. Didn't do much good with the bombs—saw no e/a.

22 June, 1944*
Gallup led the squadron—I had red flight. Bomber escort south and southeast of Paris. My flight chased a bunch of P-51s and got separated from Gallup—so we cruised around for hours by ourselves. Hoey's flight saw a bunch of 109s—got one. That's all that happened. We looked madly for e/a—but no could find.

23 June, 1944
Bomber escort—airfields around Paris. Nobody saw anything—even Duncan.

24 June, 1944
Bomber escort—Rimerman led with our squadron. His flight—Bledsoe, Rafferty, and Paslay—got 7 trains—in the heart of the Ruhr. No e/a seen.

25 June, 1944*
Another birthday—another trip around Paris! Was a good mission—I thought. We escorted the bombers and Duncan leading with the 351st went on a strafing mission. He got almost back and ran into a well camouflaged field with about 25 109s on it. At 15,000 ft I couldn't see an airplane—they were completely hidden from the air. He just happened to stumble onto it. His flight and the rest of their squadron strafed the field but couldn't get in under the trees so didn't do much good.

25 June, 1944
As soon as he returned, Duncan was on the phone—got us a bombing mission back to that field. He led our squadron—show wasn't very good. Bledsoe and Rafferty both got hit. Chetwood—again is on the beach-head. Guess we'll have to give him a leave when he gets back. Poor old Dunc—worked so hard to get the mission going, then it turned out to be such a bad show.
    Li'l Joe [Furness] left for home today.

27 June, 1944*
To spoil a record of months, I aborted for radio. The boys went on a D.B. mission with frags. I had red flight and Gallup had the sqdn. They ran into six 109s trying to get home. Gallup got one—making him an ace. Bledsoe and Benjamin got one just landing; Rafferty hit one already bellied in.

28 June, 1944*
Escort—a/ds around Reims. Didn't see anything—only friendly airplanes.
　Broke Tanner's jinx today—passed him in missions.
　Chetwood called—will be back tonight.
　Starr augured in at the start of runway 27—tried a hot peel off and didn't quite make it. One more flight leader gone. Guess I'll break in Bledsoe.

29 June, 1944
Escort—Rimerman led with 351 and was p'd off at the formation.

30 June, 1944*
Gallup led the squadron—I had red flight—saw a little action again. Gallup led the group and wandered off by himself again after we finished bombing. While we were looking for him, we (I had about a squadron and a hair tagged onto me) ran into ten 109s. Made a head on pass to start things rolling—saw strikes. Made another—just about the closest I've ever come to an airplane—and he was firing like mad. Then I tagged onto another character—hit him—and broke away when he went into a cloud. Would have got him, had I followed!! Yocum stuck right with me the whole time and got a couple damaged, too. Did a good job. Got a truck, also—was proud of my shootin' on that one.

1 July, 1944*
Had another of the same type missions—hit barges with our bombs. Bledsoe led blue flight and did a beautiful job—'course I knew he would.
　Yocum flew 170 hours last month—how about that??
　Took a flight over to Starr's funeral today—had a couple new boys along; they're not too sharp.

4 July, 1944
A short bomber escort mission. Don't think they even saw any flak.

4 July, 1944*
We went on a long haul—almost to the Swiss border—to bomb and strafe rail transportation. We picked on a train first and really stopped it—then attempted to bomb a bridge. I missed, completely, and so did most of the squadron. There were a couple [of] hits on the tracks, though. The other two squadrons hit a marshalling yard and another train. Seemed to me a long way to go, just for that, but we did a little damage. Willy Hargus said he zoomed over the little village nearby and everybody was out watching—was quite a 4th of July show for them.

5 July, 1944*
Another fairly long dive bombing and strafing mission to Orleans. Didn't do much good—everything had been beaten up too much down thataway. I got one

truck—couldn't find anything to drop the bombs on. Finally, my flight dropped on a road bridge—had some fairly good hits.

A couple 109s sneaked up on the tail of one of the new boys in 351 [Claville] and shot him down. Duncan got the boy that did it.

6 July, 1944
Dive bomb—south of Paris. Bailey led the group. They were bounced by about 15 109s and 190s. His no. 4 got one and Gallup got another. Bledsoe and Rafferty got a couple trains. Was a pretty bad show—should have had more destroyed.

6 July, 1944
Strafing—Rimerman led our squadron. Went after road and rail transportation north east of Paris. Got a couple trains—that's about all that happened.

7 July, 1944*
This day will long be remembered by the 353rd—as one of the more tragic. It finally happened—he got shot up a little too much.

Was a long escort mission—target was Leipzig. We escorted from the Zee to a little past Steinhuder Lake. Duncan was flying with 351 and when we left the bombers he went down on an a/d north east of the lake. This time the engine was hit—broke an oil line somewhere. At any rate, he soon had no oil pressure. He remarked how amazing it was "how these things try to keep running with no oil pressure." He kept a running conversation all the way down—how it was blowing cylinders; how it stopped—we even got to hear him belly it in. All the time he was talking we could hear how rough the engine was. Seemed to me that it was almost 5 minutes from the time the engine stopped until he said "I'm on the ground." Last thing he said was "G'bye fellas" and out he went. Was a flashy finish to a flashy career—typically Duncan. He sure hated to go down. One of his remarks was "Sure do wish one of you fellas would come down and pick me up so I could fight again." His no. 2 was looking like mad to find a field to sit down in but couldn't find one.

Poor old Dunc—what an eager character. Don't think there is a guy in the E.T.O. that hates the Hun more. He was almost an institution—doubt if there is a guy in England that hasn't heard of him. He's o.k. though, that's the main thing. Sure hope he gets back. Would give a lot to go to the far east or the pacific with him. He'd go wild over there.

Hoey led a 16 ship squadron out about the time we were coming back—B group. We had one flight in it.

8 July, 1944
Here's a teletype that came in today:

FROM COMFICOM EIGHT 08/0920B
TO COMMANDING OFFICER, 353RD FIGHTER GROUP
BT

CONFIDENTIAL 8/FC/29A I DESIRE TO EXPRESS MY VERY GREAT REGRET AT THE TEMPORARY LOSS OF COLONEL GLENN DUNCAN PD HIS SPLENDID HELP ON EVERY MISSION WILL BE MISSED; HOWEVER HE HAS LEFT A SPLENDID ORGANIZATION IN THE 353RD FIGHTER GROUP THAT I HAVE CONFIDENCE WILL CARRY ON CMA AS THEY KNOW HE WOULD HAVE PD THE GALLANTRY OF COLONEL DUNCAN WAS WELL SHOWN IN HIS FINAL BRAVE MESSAGE QUOTE I WILL BE BACK IN THREE OR FOUR WEEKS UNQUOTE "NEVER QUITTING" COULD WELL BE THE MOTTO FOR THE ENTIRE VIII FIGHTER COMMAND AND INDEED ALL FIGHTERS OF THE ALLIED AIR FORCES EVERYWHERE PD COLONEL DUNCAN'S RECORD TYPIFIES A FIGHTER PILOT'S CREED PD HE WAS OUTSTANDING AS A TWO FISTED FIGHTER LEADER AND A GROUP COMMANDING OFFICER PD
SIGNED KEPNER

8 July, 1944
Area patrol—south of Paris. Briefing was at 0415—tsk, tsk. After all that loss of sleep nothing happened. Gallup led the squadron.

9 July, 1944
Type 16—Hoey led the group with our squadron and amazingly enough they ran into some e/a. Again—nobody in the sqdn did any good. 351 got 5—Auchincloss and Middleton got damaged's. The e/a kept dodging in and out of the clouds and they couldn't get a shot in. Can't understand why we can't do more good. Ferrell got all shot up—came back scared to death—and with good reason.

11 July, 1944
Gallup led the group with the squadron. Were penetration for the bombers bombing Munich. Weather was bad—didn't see any e/a.

11 July, 1944*
Withdrawal support for the same bunch of bombers—nothing seen but friendly fighters and bombers, and clouds.

12 July, 1944*
Escort—target Munich; practically the same as yesterday's show. Had solid overcast—no e/a—nothing happened.
   Looks like Rimerman is definitely C.O. and Bailey is exec. Haven't figured out yet who is 352 C.O.

13 July, 1944
Escort—target Munich. Rimerman led our squadron. They got us up at 0400 this morning but the field was too socked in. They finally scrubbed our penetration and

put us on withdrawal. No e/a—and the weather was bad. Here it is—the middle of summer with weather just as bad as the heart of winter!!

14 July, 1944
Gallup led the group type 16—no e/a seen.

15 July, 1944*
Escort—target Munich again. Hope they did some good today—we sure as hell didn't!!

17 July, 1944
Mission was scheduled about 0900 this morning but by take-off time the field was socked in—completely. So—the mission was scrubbed and another scheduled. This time they got off but were called back just as they were setting course. They tried to pull another but it was scrubbed even before we had a field order. What a performance!!!!

Doc told me last night very much on the q.t. that Gallup's promotion had gone in and mine soon would! How about that! I'm not sweating yet though—too many things can happen. Looks like maybe it might come through while I'm in the States—if I get to the States.

Poindexter is definitely 352 CO.

19 July, 1944
Escort—target Frankfurt. Bailey led the group and Gallup the sqdn. Gallup aborted—came back about 20 min later with a broken elbow [drop tank connector]—took off after they fixed it and caught the rest of the group about the time they reached the point of farthest penetration. What a character! No e/a.

19 July, 1944*
Escort—target Frankfurt. I led B group consisting of 16 ships—and we took off an hour after A group. We picked up the bombers and escorted them all the way to the coast. My navigation turned out o.k.—hit r/v right on the nose. Was real pleased with the way things turned out. We saw all kinds of friendly planes but no e/a.

Have one more mission to go—wish Willy Price would get back so I could finish.

20 July, 1944
Escort—target Leipzig. Rimerman led the sqdn. Didn't see anything—couple characters in 352 got some trains.

20 July, 1944
Same show—B group—16 ships—Poindexter led. They were withdrawal—no e/a.

56th took another beating today. Gabreski went down—strafing an a/d. Seems to me it isn't worth it. Gabby had 23 destroyed and was going home at the end of this week!!!

21 July, 1944
Escort—group went out as three groups. Cles led C with 16 ships, Gallup led A with 24, and Byers led B with 24. Was sort of a messed up deal for a while but went off fairly well after everything was settled. They didn't see anything again. Wonder what has happened to the Luftwaffe.

Two 109s landed intact yesterday at Manston—just gave up. Also they picked up the crew of a scuttled German sub. That—combined with the attempt on Hitler's life—might add up to something; could be the start.

Tech. orders to the P-51 came in today—tsk, tsk.

Where oh where is Willy [Price]???!

24 July, 1944
Type 16—Hoey led the group, down by Paris. Not much happened—did some strafing, couple locos etc.

25 July, 1944
Area support—Gallup led the group; did a little strafing south of Cherbourg.

Jordan and Stump are back. Said Willy [Price], Hart and Winder are sweating out a ride from Atlantic City. Garey and Hargus finished today.

26 July, 1944
Top cover for the 78th as they were dive bombing. Chetwood led the squadron. Not much happened. In fact—nothing happened. 352 shot up a few trains.

27 July, 1944
Escort—target Brussels; no action.

28 July, 1944
Type 16—no action, Gallup led the group.

We are no longer in the 8th Fighter Command, mainly because there no longer is such a thing. We're in the 3rd Bomb Division. No more buzzing, low altitude dog fighting, or acrobatics. Naturally everyone is happy about that!!

We should be fully equipped with the P-51s in a month. At the rate I'm going I'll finish up in 51s. WHERE IS WILLY [PRICE]!!!

29 July, 1944
Escort on type 16—Chetwood led the squadron. Got 5 locos. 352 got 28!!!

30 July, 1944
Sweep-strafing—south of Paris. Gallup led the group—got a bunch of trains, about 17 of them, lots of cars damaged. Aal, flying Bledsoe's airplane, caught a burst of flak in the horizontal fin. Hole was about a foot in diameter. Bledsoe started for the beach-head twice with New's airplane—electrical system went out. He made it home though. 352 got at least 5 planes on the ground—410s and JU88s.

31 July, 1944
Escort—withdrawal from Munich. Chetwood led the sqdn. Nothing happened.

1 August, 1944
Type 16—strafing north of Paris. [Poin]dexter led the group with his last mission. Everybody shot up a lot of stuff. 352 got a couple of 410s on an a/d. Lost two, also. One went straight in [Ames]—other bailed out [Harris], maybe in friendly territory.

2 August, 1944
Dive bombing—everybody shot up everything. Did a lot of good work. Sqdn was separated from Chetwood—blew up a lot of trucks and a couple of ammo trains.
 Rimerman got the only e/a shot down today.

3 August, 1944
Type 16—over Paris; no action.

4 August, 1944
Once again some action. Gallup led the group on an escort mission—target was Hamburg. Group was bounced by about 50 109s from about 27,000ft. A lot of good fights ensued, I guess. Gallup got two, Aal one, Middleton one—and Creekmur augered one in without firing a shot. Gallup got all shot up (following in Duncan's footsteps)—thought he'd have to bail out a couple of times. Yocum was flying his second element and got hit on a head on pass. Looked like he went straight in. What an eager character he was. Group got 17 destroyed—that's our high score so far.
 Price, Hart, and Winder are back—will finish as soon as they get back into the swing of things. They're looking great! Three months since they left.

4 August, 1944
Bombing and strafing—on the first mission they spotted about 35 planes on Plantloon a/d. Went back tonight—350 and 351 bombing flak positions and 352 strafing. Really cleaned house. 353 today destroyed 41 airplanes—how about that!
 Best day we've ever had—a record of some sort.
 Chetwood's captaincy came through today.

5 August, 1944
Bomber escort—targets around Hamburg. Hoey was leading and aborted so Gallup took over. He saw some character shooting at some P-51s so he "went down and shot him." He's on the way to a big score.
Everybody has been congratulating old 353 on the mission yesterday. Makes us all feel pretty good.

6 August, 1944
Escort—targets around Hamburg. Put Gallup up to lead and he didn't show up, so Bledsoe led—did a good job, too. They didn't see anything—didn't even get any flak damage, for a change.

Creekmur spun in today. Was up with Winder and tried a roll at 1,000 ft. Something happened—did another half-roll and went straight in. Was sure a swell egg—hope it doesn't go rough on Winder.

Howard was up today from France—bumming some flower and sugar for their snack bar. Finally got his leaves.

7 August, 1944*
Dive bombing and strafing. My last mission and 'tis a good feeling to be finished. At least for a couple of months. We were looking for buzz bomb trains. Missed with bombs but I got one loco myself and shared one. Bledsoe's flight saw some a/c on the ground—got 4 dest. and one dam. Was a pretty good show. I led the group and Price flew red flight.

7 August, 1944
Price led the sqdn on the same deal. Byers led the group. Got a few trains, trucks, etc.

The Americans are going like mad in Normandy under Patton.

8 August, 1944
Seems like as hard as we try to build up this sqdn—we can't do it. Hart was flying red flight—first mission since back—and was strafing an oil truck. As he got over it, it exploded—knocking him over on his back. He went straight in!!! Sure is tough to lose a guy like that. Was a swell character and an excellent pilot.

Squadron got some trains, trucks, etc. again.

Bailey finished up today—guess we'll go home together.

Howard was up again—stayed last night before going to London on leave.

Americans are 35 miles from Paris!!! At this rate the war will be over before I get back.

—Doc takes over—

9 August, 1944
Two missions today. The first was an escort job. Bombers were to take care of a number of targets such as Stuttgart, Munich, etc. Our bombers aborted because of weather and we failed to r/v.

Second mission—so damn short of planes our sqdn put up only 5 for a dive bombing and strafing job to Lille. Willy [Price] led the flight with Bledsoe as element leader. They got 6 locos and raised mayhem in general.

10 August, 1944
Two missions today. Nothing doing—Blick is sweating out home and Price is getting in the groove as operations officer.

11 August, 1944
A big day for the squadron in a negative sort of a way. Metz augered [sic] in on peel off several hours after Blick left for home. Same deal as Starr. A and B groups

patrolled over Dreux, Chartres, and Orleans. Gallup got one on the ground (his 10th). It is now Lt. Col. Gallup and Maj. Blick. Too bad Blick got away before his orders came but they will be sent to him. It will be a swell break for him to hit the States as a major. Allison nosed up taxiing after landing from the mission.

12 August, 1944
Another day reminiscent of D day—before dawn take-off followed by five separate missions. The idea is to strafe hell out of Jerry trying to get in or out of the pocket between Caen and Falaise. The guys are doing a swell job hitting everything that moves on the ground. Tuttle and Greenwood of 352 had to belly in but both got out o.k.

13 August, 1944
Same deal as yesterday. First pre-dawn mission caught the Jerries on the roads and we destroyed about 150 trucks and vehicles. Curtis of 352 bellied in over there but got out o.k. Devine got hit by flak but made it to the beach-head. McInis and Graham also were hit and it is believed they made it back to our territory. We are getting desperately short of planes.

14 August, 1944
Had the milk run of milk runs today. Didn't have to get up 'till 0900 and then the group escorted some Lancs and Halifaxes (900 of them in all) on airfields in Holland. Little Willy [Price] led and did a good job of it. Saw Oliphant [Oliphint], one of the buzz boys, and he has just returned from France with quite a tale. Had a bad crack up and was discovered by the Germans who treated him badly. He finally escaped.

15 August, 1944
Another escort without incident. Bombers went to varied targets around Leipzig but nothing of incident was encountered. The tempo is beginning to slacken.

16 August, 1944
Repeat performance—some new D-28s came in.

17 August, 1944
A fairly early morning DB mission (disruption of transportation). Rather lean pickings with a few trains and trucks to our credit. Chetwood left for the Z. of I. today—the lucky stiff. Doc is trying to talk Ben [Rimerman] into soloing the cub but Ben is a little abstinate [sic]. Gallup refuses to promote Paslay—the cad!

18 August, 1944
Group had a DB mission today with the primary targets rail traffic between Lille and Rouen. Many trucks were seen around Paris with excellent strafing results. Jerry has a number of Red Cross trucks (suspiciously too many) and he's using them to advantage. Col. Ben led the group and ran into a tree—damn near didn't get back.

Johnson of 351 bailed out near Lille and Swan[e]zy of 352 augered [sic] in over France with no apparent reason.

20 August, 1944
No mission. Telephone message received by S-2 today that Morreto [Moretto] is with the 9th AF and will be here as soon as possible. Auchincloss is now a first lt. Curtis of 352 made it back to our lines in about 48 hours. The group acquired 21 new pilots and we got 8 of them. Their arrival has created a housing shortage. Mueller has arrived along with Junttila of 352. Mueller seems eager to get started.

21 August, 1944
Incredible though it may sound—still no mission. Of course, it is explained by the weather. Until now, those long dreary sieges of winter were almost forgotten. It has been a day of low overcast and a chilly, drizzling rain—a depressing gray shroud that merges the land and the sky with no delineating horizon. All of which presages the weather to come in a month or so. Perhaps an early end to the war will deprive us the opportunity of experiencing another winter in merrie olde England. However—even though we are just now realizing the fruits of our greatest victories in this war—the pendulum has begun to swing to a more sane outlook to the end of this war. The majority realize that it could well last through the winter. Burlingame returned.

23 August, 1944
At last a mission—even though it be DB. Target was rail traffic on line from Lille to Valencennes [sic] and south from Lille. No rail traffic was seen but group got about 30–40 trucks on roads. Fellows are having to use extreme caution in order not to shoot up our own troops.

Moretto had quite a story to tell on his return. After successfully evading several groups of 109s, he was finally hopelessly outnumbered and clobbered. His gas tanks were hit and fire developed so quickly in the cockpit that his hands were badly and painfully burned. Both hands are rather badly scarred but are entirely functional. He was extremely well treated by the French underground and gained ten pounds during his stay. After the Allies began to advance out of Cherbourg, he and a pal walked toward our troops and finally met them after a trek of about 30 miles. He spent most of his time around the Dreux area and believes that another of our bunch is being taken care of in that area.

Gallup became acting group exec, in the absence of Bailey—the job just fits him!! Willy takes over until Blick's return.

25 August, 1944
Withdrawal for 1,400 bombers from the Danish–German area. No action.

26 August, 1944

2 missions today. The first was a DB mission and strafing with rail transport the target. The group worked over south of Brussels area to the tune of 12 locos and a few trucks. Gallup led the mission. The weather was extremely bad and the flak heavy. Knowling's and Smith's planes were shot up. The afternoon's was a ditto of that above but no targets were found—weather remained bad. Hartley of 351 bailed out over the channel.

27 August, 1944

Another 2 mission day. Target was rail transport from Trier south to Metz. The first mission was led by Gallup (Bledsoe led the squadron). The squadron really went to town—getting 6 e/a on a landing strip near Verdun. We also got about 20 locos along with a number of trucks, staff cars and other et-cetera. The second version was to the same area but pickings were rather lean.

28 August, 1944

First mission to the same area as the previous day. The squadron (Gallup, Schilt, Hedler, and others) got 2 HE111s, 2 FW190s in the air and several JU88s on the ground (six in all). We also took heavy toll of locos and other transport. That havoc that this time squadron alone has caused by strafing stretches the imagination. The afternoon show was also DB but this time below Brussels. Willy [Price] and Allison each got one on the ground and Ruscitto one in the air. Benjamin blew hell out of a marshalling yards which contained gas and oil cars. Flame shot up hundreds of feet. The total e/a for the day is 9—our squadron's star is definitely on the ascendancy.

29 August, 1944

Today has been one of the squadron's best days. This is the story—little Willy [Price] was praying for another crack at the landing strip he discovered yesterday and lo and behold an early morning mission to the very area came through. The field had an estimated 20–25 410s on it and our gang was specifically briefed to go out and get them. However, Willy was unable to find the spot (south of Brussels) and ran into another landing strip chock full of 109s. The result was that 4–5 men accounted for 19 destroyed and 7 damaged. Willy got 3, Bledsoe got 4, Benjamin got 6, Hightshoe 3, Aal 2, and Smith 1. Of course with the sweet there is always some bitter—Aal and Smith are NYR and it is fairly certain that both blew up in mid-air and augered [sic] in as a result of direct flak hits. Smith was on another a/d but Aal was with Willy. In addition, the sqdn wrote off 15 locos along with a number of trucks. Bledsoe and Ruscitto got their captaincys [sic] and they caused no little consternation as Winder and Mueller are still first looeys.

—Bledsoe writing—

1 September, 1944
Started off the new month with two missions and good news about the enemy retreating and being disorganized—to say nothing of a rumor that the 300 hour tour will be shortened somewhat.

    Mission no. 1—Winder leading the sqdn with Mueller, up on his first flight since his return from the States—a point which didn't exactly please Col. Ben. Matters weren't helped any, either, when everyone was home except Mueller and Allison who was his wingman. We were sweating him out when the tower reported he was in the area, and coming in on a straight in approach due to battle damage. We finally spotted him several miles from the field with his wheels down and smoking badly. He made it o.k. and said he was hit while passing over an a/d at 1,500 ft. He was flying Z and received a direct hit in the engine causing considerable damage and oil to cover the largest part of the ship. Benjamin was hit causing the left wing to catch fire, but luckily it went out. Hedler was also hit and had a large hole in the tail of his ship—right in front of the right elevator. This strafing is getting rough, indeed. We got several locos and a few trucks.

    Mission no. 2—We got 8 ships up with Ruscitto and Middleton leading the two flights. It was a regular flak run with 500 pounders. We destroyed 15 trucks.

    Pat left to go home.

2 September, 1944
Weather stinko—Doc too, probably!!

3 September, 1944
Strafing mission in north-western Belgium with LeFebre leading the group and Bledsoe the squadron—squadron leader Bledsoe, sounds pretty good. Order came in not to do any more bombing of railroads, as we need them, so our primary targets were trucks and road transportation. The sqdn got 15 or 20 trucks, but bad battle damage on two ships. Bet old Jerry is fooling us with those Red Cross trucks—I saw millions of them !!!!

—Doc again—

5 September, 1944
The P-47s are doing nothing but DB and strafing missions these days while the P-51s are used on escort only. Today's mission was to the Nepple and Rotterdam vicinity. There was the usual haul of trucks etc. Burlingame of 352 got a Do217 in the air. Wouldn't swear to it but I believe this is the first 217 this group ever bagged in the air. Our troops are now in Holland! Perhaps ole Duncan might turn up one of these days. Main is in a hospital in Wales but we haven't been able to get in touch with him as yet. Brown has it second hand that Phelan is in a hospital in France minus a leg [a false rumour—Phelan was KIA 12 June, 1944]. Gabriel and Keywan of the 352nd

also went down the same day. Gabriel has returned with the info that Keywan broke his back on bailing out and is buried in France. This leaves just Newhart and Bedford unaccounted for. One year ago Venell and Long augered [sic] in.

6 September, 1944
Today brought us the missions of missions—fly down the course of the Waal River in Holland and observe for flak positions. Someone must be sore at us!! The 352nd did this without mishap. We and the 351 worked over the Plantlune [sic] area. Auchincloss got a train of 35 tank cars and it's [sic] engine—all of which burned. He picked up a 20mm which blew the hell out of the underside of his right wing. He landed with his right gun bay open and trailing ammo—as cool as a cucumber about the whole thing. The rest of the gang got a few trucks and staff cars.

8 September, 1944
Another DB and strafing mission into Germany—just below Happy Valley [the Ruhr Valley]. There was the usual haul of trucks, staff cars, etc. How the Germans must dread the sight of the old T-bolt blazing away with those 8 fifties. Brimer was hit by flak on the way in and sustained a fractured finger. Barlow of 351 bailed out in Germany.

9 September, 1944
Same mission with orders not to strafe (!!??!!) The gang saw hundreds of juicy trains, etc, but "orders is orders." Benjamin got a 110 as it was going in to land—really clobbered it—this makes our 95th.

Doc and Little Willy [Price] went over to see Main today. He was overjoyed to see someone from the old outfit. He has lost his entire right knee joint and had a compound fracture of his left ankle. He was treated by the Germans (very fairly) and was left behind in Paris when they evacuated the city. A "French specialist" operated on him and the result is that he will be a permanent cripple. Main's story corroborates that of the others who were involved in the fray—hopelessly out-numbered. Main put up a good scrap but finally sustained the injuries described above by 20mm from an e/a. He bailed out and fell into the waiting arms of the Germans. The lad has been through hell and has a long way to go yet. He is to be sent home as soon as possible. Truly, when one considers this story it may be said that Sherman made a gross understatement.

9 September, 1944
Another flak searching mission around the Kassel area. Gang got about 6 locos but little else. Bledsoe took rockets along but they proved to be a fizzle.

10 September, 1944
This group returned to escort at long last. They escorted bombers to various targets in central Germany on withdrawal and target support. Nothing doing.

11 September, 1944
Another escort job to the same area. Although our group and the other P-47 groups saw nothing it was one of the greatest air battles of the war. Approximately 44 bombers were knocked down by e/a and 30 P-51s were lost (mostly due to ground fire). We clobbered 111 in the air and 47 on the ground. The Luftwaffe was aggressive for a change.

12 September, 1944
Back to the same area on the same kind of mission. The Luftwaffe broke precedent by coming up the day after a severe clobbering. Our 51s knocked down approximately 80 and the e/a accounted for another of our bombers.

13 September, 1944
Escort (withdraw[a]l) to Stuttgart which provided many of the new heads an opportunity to see the Alps. No e/a seen and no bombers knocked down. However, the P-51s accounted for 30 more—catching them in scattered groups. Stafford's flight went down on an a/d and got 5 but he and two others of his flight were badly hit. All made it back.

14 September, 1944
Our squadron alone escorted robot B-17 [part of the Aphrodite project] to Denmark on a 5 ½ hour trip—all for nothing as the plane missed. Jake Tersian [Terzian] has returned with quite a tale. He was discovered by the Belgian Gestapho [Gestapo] and put in the local bastil[l]e. He spent his days dreaming of the snack bar back here.

16 September, 1944
The most sensational news of the day is that Zeke Zolner is back in the UK. Ol' Zeke should have a good story for us and we who know him are eagerly awaiting his arrival. Group had an area support mission over Germany just over Koblenz. There is nothing spectacular to report other than the usual haul of locos and trucks. There was surprisingly little damage sustained considering the area in which the group was working.

17 September, 1944
Another D day. Approximately 1,075 Lancs, C-47s, Horsas, and Hamlicars carried air-borne troops over Holland and dropped them. It was quite an impressive sight to watch these many ships come over the field on their way. Our job was to knock out all flak positions and give fighter cover as well. We went in at 3,000 ft and really gave those flak positions hell. 351 lost Greene. It was a tremendous show and evidently went off very well.

18 September, 1944
Another mission in support of the 1st Air-Borne Army. Our job was to knock out flak positions. We were very fortunate in that we lost only one man—Ruscitto. He

was seen to belly in and run for the nearest house. The 56th lost SIXTEEN to flak and the 78th lost 7 to flak.

Approximately 1,000 gliders towed by C-47s went over our base on their way to Holland. What a magnificent and awe-inspiring sight it was.

Zeke Zolner blew in today looking hale and hearty and none the worse for his experiences. It turns out that he was never a PW but made his way to Switzerland with the help of the underground. He evidently had a good time while there as he spent every cent of his pay. Willy [Price] and Rose flew to Paris for an overnight stay.

20 September, 1944
In spite of very poor weather, military necessity dictated a reinforcement of our air-borne troops in Holland by another 1,000 gliders. Again our job was to knock out the flak. However, the visibility was so bad the boys were not able to localize the flak positions. The situation was further complicated by the fact that allied vehicles literally swarmed th[e] dropping area and we didn't dare drop bombs or strafe for fear of hitting our own troops. This latter certainly indicates that our troops have linked up with the airborne army.

Willy [Price] and Rose returned last night from their Paris visit. They report that Paris is as beautiful as it's [sic] women. The French have a warm cordiality toward the Allies—wine women and song are plentiful but the people will trade anything for food and cigarettes. These are much preferred to money in Paris. Rose cracked up his ship (Blick's, incidentally!) trying to land on a grass field near Graves-End!!

21 September, 1944
At last a mission that didn't call for flak busting. The group went out on a MEW control in the Arnheim [sic] area and ran into a gaggle of 190s—our sqdn accounted for 5 while 351 got one. Hally of 351 is MIA.

22 September, 1944
Again the same mission as yesterday but no results. The weather has been decidedly against us since D day.

23 September, 1944
Our big day. Many of our air-borne troops are fighting desperately for their existences and more reinforcements are being sent in to relieve them. A reaction from the Luftwaffe was anticipated and so it developed. Our outfit ran into approximately 100 and our squadron accounted for 15 while the 352nd got 5. The Hun was aggressive and some of the boys (Willy [Price], for one) had a battle royal. Middleton and Auchin[c]loss each got three apiece. Evidently the Luftwaffe has been thrown in to do or die in this most crucial of battles. The sqdn cashed in on the idea concerning combat that ol' Doc has plagged lo these many months. Uncle Benny got his 'chickens' today.

26 September, 1944
Area support for the landing of C-47s in Holland and it was the longest mission accomplished to date. It was done with one belly tank and two wing tanks. Average time logged was 5 1/2 hours. No e/a.

Bledsoe and Doc had a trip to Orconte, France, which naturally included Gay Parree in the itinerary. Paris is indeed a beautiful city and the Parisians are most cordial. Here are a people who really appreciate the Yanks. The Doc had a wonderful opportunity to see the damage and havoc wrought by our air forces.

27 September, 1944
An escort mission for 17s led by Col. Ben to Frankfurt. A five hour milk run. Our squadron got 20 P-51D-10s today.

28 September, 1944
Another escort penetration for B-24s to the Kassel area but there was no reaction. Col. Ben led the squadron for the first time in a long while. The Luftwaffe has been able to recuperate for the past 3–4 months—while the 8th has been doing ground support work. They are beginning to come up in strength again, as in the days of old, and clobber the hell out of the big friends to the tune of 30–40 each mission.

30 September, 1944
Another escort for B-17s all the way around. Mission was to the Seesen area and led by LeFebre—no e/a seen. A beautiful job of precision bombing was done.

2 October, 1944
This day was a milestone in the squadron's history. Led by Benny the Rim—we took 12 P-51s over for the first time. It was an escort job for 17s to the Koblenz area.

In general, the gang is enthusiastic about the 51s. Maybe this is the beginning of many fruitful missions for us.

3 October, 1944
Again an escort mission in 51s and led by Ben! It was a long haul to Nurenburg [sic] but no e/a were encountered. Some of the guys were sweating out gas! Devine landed somewhere near Lille because of coolant trouble. Bledsoe completed his tour today in almost record time of 3 months and 3 weeks!! Somewhat belatedly a word should be said about Middleton, Edwards and Province, since approximately 10 days have passed since they have been missing. It is presumed that they were shot down in combat.

4 October, 1944
No mission—Doc greased ten landings in with the AT-6 today (Bledsoe in the back seat). When Bledsoe and Rafferty leave, Blick will have to check out in the back seat (hint, hint!!).

5 October, 1944
P-51 escort around the route to Berlin—and led by Ben. The guys weren't very impressed with the size of Berlin. No e/a were encountered. It's now a matter of luck as to which group encounters the e/a. The Luftwaffe is now making a mass attack on one combat wing alone. They are mostly in groups of 100 (190s) who use a head on pass in waves of 20—line abreast. When the Luftwaffe attacks [sic] one of our combat wings, the usual result is that one of our combat wings is missing!!

6 October, 1944
Escort to Nurenburg [sic], but again no e/a.

7 October, 1944
Escort to Leipzig all the way around but no results. Yesterday Willy [Price] and Mueller ran into some jet jobs but didn't get them—this was around Hanover [it appears that Mueller actually did score a ME262 victory but did not claim].

7 October to 14 October, 1944, inclusive
These dates are grouped together because there is a paucit[y] of incidents to write about. The group during this time participated in 5 escort missions to various places such as Bremen and Saarbrucken. In general the bombing results have been excellent. Sighting jet con-trails has become a more frequent occurrence—as has been expected. Not since D day has the group experienced such a long period without a victory. To date, no one in our group has shot down an e/a while flying in a P-51. The P-51 still seems a bit tricky for our boys to handle while on the ground—as we have been scourged by heads-up landing and taxiing accidents.

Most of the above missions have been led by Col. Ben with Gallup and LeFebre each leading one apiece. Rafferty got his well deserved captaincy on the 13th. The place doesn't seem quite the same with that character Bledsoe gone.

15 October, 1944
Escort today to Cologne and Gallup leading. Happy Valley still has a respectable amount of flak. No e/a encountered. Nothing else of note except that Bailey arrived from the States today.

17 October, 1944
Escort for big friends all the way around the route. Cologne was the target. Still no e/a. The 78th ran into 20, got 7 and so pulled ahead of us again.

18 October, 1944
Escort to Kassel but again no e/a reaction. The big friends are doing some excellent bombing. Sqdn was led by Winder. Corgan of the 352 bailed out because of a coolant leak. Didn't quite make it to the Sirgfried [Seigfried] Line.

19 October, 1944
Escort to Ludwigshaven area through gobs of weather (cumulus cloud from 5,000 to 30,000 ft plus multi-layered cirrus). No e/a/ encountered. Blick's early return is anticipated.

—Blick talking—

21 October, 1944
Back in the ETO. Arrived today amid rain and dreary, cold weather—what a difference from dear old sunny Calif!!!!

22 October, 1944
Escort around Hamburg—no dice.

24 October, 1944
A transportation strafing mission in the Hamburg area, and P-51s—not so good!
 Mueller's prop came off and he bellied in, in a field in Germany—did a beautiful job. Think he got out. His captaincy came through last night, incidentally. Hedler is missing—how, nobody knows. One guy in 352 found a landing strip loaded with planes—he destroyed 4.

25 October, 1944
Escort around the same area with one sqdn (352) going after the landing strip found yesterday. (They didn't find it, incidentally.) B-24s shot down a 351st boy [French]—he bailed out in the drink but they didn't get him.
 I flew a P-47 today—just to get the feel of the air again. Guess I'm definitely CO.

26 October, 1944
Escort to Hanover—no action. Rafferty finished up. We're getting 10 or 12 new pilots so he'll take charge of the OTU for a couple of weeks. I flew a P-51 today.

27 October, 1944
No mission today but Albertson collided with Edwards of 352 and was killed on a practice escort flight. Edwards came to on the way down and pulled the ripcord—made it o.k.
 Balason!!!!—of all people—called me tonight from the club!! Our replacements are here and he is one of them. What a character he is—went back to the States from the Aleutians and requested further overseas duty. Out walks Bledsoe and in walks Balason—good old 42-H! He's still a second looie, how about that?

30 October, 1944
Escort almost to Leipzig. Our bombers aborted because of weather but the group picked up a bunch of B-24s. Nothing was seen.
 The wheels must be expecting a lot of Germans in the air—maximum effort today and one for tomorrow.

Am almost operational—have 8 hours. 51 is beginning to feel better. Bailey flew today—on Gallup's wing!

2 November, 1944
Another maximum effort with P-47s [the 353rd flew Thunderbolts for the mission]. 8th AF broke their record. Knocked down 132 out of the air—also about 25 on the ground. Abernathy was the only one in 353 to get one. Were a lot of jet jobs up for a change—knocked down a few.

Guess I'll go on the next mission—tour for us is now 180 hours. Figure if everything goes right, it'll take me six months!!

We have to prepare for a lot of maximum effort jobs—looks like the wheels are expecting big Luftwaffe turnouts.

Rimerman is on his way home—LeFebre is acting exec.

4 November, 1944*
I am operational again—took red flight while Willy led the squadron. Was an escort mission to some little target between Hamburg and Berlin. Had over 400 fighters for 300 bombers. No e/a except a couple of jet jobs. From the looks of things, those jets are going to give us trouble. Think they have got a couple of 51s today.

What a cold airplane this 51 is—have NEVER had such a cold ride!! Logged 5 hours and am real tired. That 180 mark looks a long way off. Was my 100th mission today.

5 November, 1944*
Escort to a target a little south of Frankfurt. Penetration, target, and withdrawal support. No e/a. No action of any sort. I led the squadron again.

The P-51 is a nice plane—the only trouble is, the missions are too long. Will have to get my callouses back in shape!!

Ruscitto is here—was gone 6 weeks. Had quite a time—says 'this ground warfare is not for me'.

6 November, 1944
Escort—target, oil refinerys [sic] in the Hamburg area. Didn't see anything. Gave my fanny a rest today and didn't fly. Will probably go the next couple of missions.

8 November, 1944
Escort to oil refinerys [sic] around Leipzig. Bailey led the group for the first time since back, with our squadron. Was a maximum effort with 47s as well [B group flew Thunderbolts]. Cles took his flight down to strafe Plantlune [sic] a/d and was hit—bellied in and got away.

9 November, 1944*
Escort to Saarbrucken—no action. Gallup left for home today—tomorrow I move to the wheel house [housing accommodation for group officers of major rank and above].

10 November, 1944
Escort—Tanner led the squadron. Was a short mission—the sqdn went down to strafe. Hayne's flight got 4 primary trainers on the ground. Jordan took the 47s out also—was a late mission and they made night landings.

Got moved o.k.—looks like it might be pretty nice; am in with LeFebre.

11 November, 1944*
Escort to Koblenze [sic]. I led the group and everything seemed to go off o.k. Weather was good—Mac [Lieutenant Mack, group weather officer] said it would be bad! We saw nothing.

16 November, 1944
Escort to the Aachen area. Weather was extremely bad here at take-off and landing—low visibility. Mission went off o.k. though. We did some sweating—Balason was NYR for a while—got with another group and landed at Manston. Rafferty finally got away yesterday—also Doc left for the flak home. Ard and Asper leave tomorrow.

18 November, 1944*
A little action again for a change. Was a strafing mission to Lechfeld a/d near Munich. Fred's [LeFebre] radio went out and I took over the group. I am still amazed at how well it went off—considering weather etc. Weather was so bad we had to assemble over the channel. My navigation wasn't too good and we almost wound up in Switzerland but—even so—it was near enough correct so that we found the field o.k. and made some perfectly planned passes. Was very successful in that the group got 19 (one in the air) for the loss of none. Our squadron was high this time with 7. Willy's [Price] got one in the air—was a twin engine, escorted by 109s. Immediately upon sighting Willy's P-51s, the 109s broke for the deck. Fine escort!!!

Bombers didn't go out today. 8 groups of fighters destroyed 93 a/c—which isn't bad!

20 November, 1944*
This was positively the most snafu mission I have ever been on!!

Originally we were to strafe oil storage tanks at Nueburg [sic], north of Munich—same show they got us out for 0600 yesterday morning and then scrubbed. Today, from the time we went out to the planes until take-off, they changed the entire mission for us three times—consequently not a soul knew what was going on. Take-off was all messed up—Bailey finally had to abort, finally the bombers aborted—we ran into a solid front up to over 30,000 ft—and finally we came back, well p'd off at the whole show. So—I'm going to London tomorrow!!!

21 November, 1944
Escort—our bombers aborted, but seemed like everyone else's went on ahead and ran into all kinds of e/a. One guy in the 352nd got 6 [Captain William T. Whisner of the 487th Fighter Squadron, 352nd Fighter Group claimed six FW190s destroyed

and one probably destroyed on 21 November 1944. He received credit for five destroyed and two probably destroyed, later revised by the USAF in Study No. 85 to six destroyed].

25 November, 1944
After briefing and scrubbing regularly for the past few days we finally had one. Escort to Mersberg [sic] but no e/a. Got a couple locos on the way home. Elkins bailed out in Germany—Miller got lost, is probably in the channel. 352 lost a couple of guys too. The whole of Fighter Command got about 7 on the ground with something like 29 NYRs. Was a pretty poor show.

26 November, 1944*
Escort to Hanover and we were type 16 control. Was a good mission—at least it was a lot of fun for a change. We had a little more of that old 353rd luck—always not quite in the fight. We were supposed to sweep north of the bombers, so we were unable to reach them when e/a came up from the south—however, the escort took care of them.

As we came away from the target, we happened to look back and see a couple of bombers blow up, so I went rushing back to a bunch of B-24s—unescorted—that were being knocked about by some 190s. I went tearing after the tail end man of a queue of 5 or 6 that blew up a B-24 in my face. I took a long burst at extreme range, trying out my sight, and very luckily missed!! As I closed I discovered it was a P-51 shooting at a 190. So I covered this character while he shot it down—then discovered it was Orzelek, one of our new boys. We got three, counting his—Winder and Boone each scored.

Fighters got about 80 or 90 today—which is very much o.k.

27 November, 1944*
What a day this has been!!! I drew first blood—and what blood!!!!—clobbered 4 Fw190s!

Originally we were going to a little place just south of Berlin to strafe an oil depot, but about three quarters of the way there, Nuthouse vectored us to 200 or 300 enemy fighters, in three bunches. I went to the first bunch—probably 75 190s—and crawled up their ass, shooting down 2 without any trouble whatsoever. The third hit me in a 90 degree deflection shot and we fo[u]ght for a little while and I finally got him. Was trying to catch the main gaggle again when Duke (who did an excellent job all through the show as my wingman) found a 190 on his tail, so we went around with him for a little while—then I was able to knock him down. Was a lot of fun—wouldn't mind a little more!!

Made landfall out and was leaking oil pretty bad so I turned back and landed in France. My oil lines were pretty well shot up and also the throttle linkage. Landed with 5 pounds oil pressure. Came back in a B-26.

Boone got two—Winder, one—Abernathy and a couple others—Moran is missing. Group did o.k. today—got 22 destroyed. This air war is fun—nuts to the strafing.

29 November, 1944*
Bomber escort to Haam [sic]—then a sweep back in with no results. I led B group.

30 November, 1944
Another maximum effort—two group job. This time to Mersberg [sic]. Willy [Price] led B group. Every[body] was expecting an all out effort on the part of the Hun as well, but he didn't show up. He picks the damnedest time to come up—the other day must have been a mistake. Bombers bombed visually for a change.

2 December, 1944
Escort to just a little south of the Ruhr. No e/a were seen. 357th got 7 and the 56th dug up 10 somewhere.

Doc and I went over to see Hop [Wallace Hopkins—former 350th CO then with the 361st Fighter Group]—he just got back from leave. Came back with Byers—Vic was at Atlantic City 26 days!!

Keatley was over yesterday—is flying with the 78th.

Rumor has it that we might move to France—but naturally, 'tis just a rumor!

4 December, 1944*
Escort to Koblenz area to bomb railway yards. I led A group—Weep [Junttila] took B. Nothing much happened—our bombers were practically lost most of the time. Have a P-51 K now—has an Aero prop; am anxious to try it.

5 December, 1944*
Escort to Berlin—my longest haul yet. Bailey led A group and LeFebre led B. Group got mixed up with a bunch of 190s north-east of Berlin—naturally, at the time, I was south-west of the city. Drove up to the fight but it was all over when I got there. On the way out Tanner ran into about 30 190s on the deck by Dummer Lake—destroyed one and got a probable, but in the meantime, Deeds and Cowen were shot down from under him.

Group got 10—357 got 20 again. All toll [sic] the fighters got 83—which isn't bad. My fanny is really sore tonight!!!

6 December, 1944
Escort to Leipzig—Willy [Price] led the group and finished. Was glad to see him get through—was sweating him out. He's a happy boy tonight. Boone will be operations. They didn't see anything—not much action except that the visibility was practically nil on take-off AND landing. Everybody made it o.k. though.

10 December, 1944
Escort to Koblenz again—no action. Boone led the squadron.

11 December, 1944*
Escort to Geisen [sic]. I led A group—Weep [Junttila] had B. No action—1,532 bombers!!!

12 December, 1944*
Practically the same show as yesterday only this time we went to Frankfurt. Bombers did a good job bombing visually—targets were rail yards and transportation. Fred [LeFebre] led A and I had B.

15 December, 1944*
Escort to Hanover. Weep [Junttila] was leading and aborted so I took over. Weather was bad—bombers were late and the mission was generally snafu. I doubt if we even got to Hanover.
    Fred [LeFebre] is a Lt. Col. as of yesterday—also, Balason's first came through.
    Grainger's engine almost cut out and he landed at a field about 3 miles from the front lines.

16 December, 1944
Escort to Stuttgart. Weather was bad—especially on the return. Although it was right on the deck everybody made it o.k. except Kolb and Prescott who landed 234 miles north of here—almost in Scotland. What a performance!!

17 December, 1944
No mission so I went over to see Carter. Ran into Bob Baughman—has been about five years since I last saw him.
    Grainger, Kolb and Prescott are back.

18 December, 1944*
Escort to Frankfurt—with extremely bad weather. Bombers ran into a solid bank of cloud from 30,000 ft to the deck, and we lost them.
    On the way out, Duke and I landed at St. Trond to see Howard and find out about getting some champagne. Stayed with LT. Col. G and managed to pick up 4 bottles—out of the kindness of his heart. What a set up they have—are living in an old German rest camp. Nice buildings—steam heat, and pretty Belgian maids to wait on the tables.
    Duke developed an oil leak in his airplane and taxied into a 47 with mine—chewing the tail off the 47 but not hurting the "Betty E."

19 December, 1944
Took off from St. Trond practically on instruments—couldn't get home so we rode the homing station to Duxford on C channel. Weather was plenty rough.

21 December, 1944
Finally got disgusted with hanging around Duxford, so I sent for my jeep and we rode back in it. Weather has been zero-zero all this time.
    Rimerman is back—took about a month and a half—flew both ways.

23 December, 1944
Escort to the Frankfurt area with Boone leading A group and Com[p]ton leading B. Was socked in at take-off but cleared up later enabling them to get off about half an hour late. They didn't see anything.

56th did it again—got about 35 in the air. Schilling got 5, making about 34 for him!!!

The Germans have had time to rebuild and reorganize and seem to be making an all out effort to stop our shows.

24 December, 1944
Escort to airfields around the same area and north. Bombers were intercepted while still over friendly territory—first time they have attempted anything like that. Looks like they're throwing up everything—we're going to have to beat them out of the skies once again. Combat from now on—it seems—is inevitable, if the weather is good. Today was the biggest show yet—almost 2,000 bombers went over from the 8th, itself. Three Five Three put up 80 fighters.

Col. Bill [Bailey] led A group and saw nothing—however, Winder, flying with B group, ran into a few. Winder got 2. Abernathy, leading his first flight, also got 2 and Lee, our Chinese boy, got one—his third or fourth mission. Hightshoe is NYR—might be on the continent.

Haynes was bounced while flying escort to 2 PRU spits—going to Leipzig. He had 4 ships and says they were lucky to get back. Jessup, flying his element, got one.

357th got 31!!!

25 December, 1944
Escort—just over the lines.

The situation [the German attack in the Ardennes] is desperate. The Hun has made great gains around the La Roche area. The 9th AF has lost air superiority and we are unmercifly [sic] weathered in. Again—the weather is playing a big part in the war for the Germans. The situation must be bad when we receive orders such as today—we were to escort the bombers and then land in France if the weather closed in, and operate from there if we couldn't get back. As it turned out, they did get back, with one destroyed, that's all.

Hightshoe is back—had landed at St. Dizier, where the 361st is now based. His news about the situation is very bad—we have to do something, pronto.

26 December, 1944
The day after Xmas—and the situation is even worse. The Hun has broken through in another place, and we still can't get over there to help. This field has been about the only one in England that has been open—and it was socked in solid this morning. We were briefed for the same show as yesterday and I was scheduled to lead. Got out to the runway but couldn't see 100 ft until too late to take off. It's imperative that we get over there to help those boys—the Germans are running all over our

army and 9th AF. Tomorrow we'll probably take off on instruments. These must be the reserves we've been waiting for them to throw at us. They're all young, eager Germans that know no better!!!

27 December, 1944*
We were awakened early again—briefed, hoping to get off in support of the bombers, but we were socked in completely. So we waited and waited—pulled out on the runway and waited and waited, finally taking off almost on instruments about 1145. Had permission to go on a sweep into Koblenz. Was a short mission and try as we could, we couldn't scare up the promised e/a. So finally we came back to a field—actually worse than at take-off. Was just about the roughest time I've ever had landing—but everybody made it o.k.

The crisis, I believe, is passed. It seems to me that the situation is a little stagnant at present. The next couple of days will tell. The weather is supposed to lift and if it does everything will go a little better. Again we carried our stuff [things needed for living away from Raydon], preparing to land in France. I had A group, Weep [Junttila] led B.

28 December, 1944*
Escort—just over the lines—no action. Continent was all fogged in just as we have been. I doubt if the GAF flew at all.

Ground situation has eased slightly. I have a hunch we have again achieved air superiority over the lines—I hope!!!!

29 December, 1944*
Escort to Frankfurt—Col. Bill [Bailey] led A group and I had B. Not much happened—Winder cracked up on take-off—wasn't hurt. Flew my airplane once again—finally got it back from Duxford.

30 December, 1944
Escort to Kassel—Boone led the group. Didn't see a thing—where is the Hun??

They told me tonight that I would not fly unless I lead the group—all of which will prolong my stay here. AT LEAST two months—gulp!!

31 December, 1944
Escort to the Koblenz area—nobody saw a thing except three guys in the 352nd, who managed to destroy one of about 30 they discovered down low.

Big party tonight so I guess I'll fly tomorrow. Will probably be the only one feeling good enough to fly.

1 January, 1945
After the big party last night we briefed for the first long show in quite a while. B[a]iley decided to go so I was scrubbed. It was escort all the way round Hamburg from in via the North Sea down and around Frankfurt. But the base was socked in at take-off and for a couple of hours afterward—so Maguire led a reduced effort sweep into the Koblenz area. Group got one.

2 January, 1945*
Escort to Koblenz—via the long route around Dummer lake and the Ruhr. Should have been a good show and we expected to see something but evidently the weather was a little bad for them. Either that or they are trying to recover from the beating they took yesterday.

Yesterday they got a little offensive—strafed our airdromes, trains, troops, etc. Dogfights were even going on over Brussels. Am wondering if Howard is o.k. at St. Trond and if their airplanes were hit!!

Allison had a coolant leak and bellied in somewhere in the Antwerp area. Certainly hope he's in friendly territory. Winder and Ferrell finished.

3 January, 1945
Another blow to the group, especially to 352—one of the unpredictables. Poindexter developed a coolant leak shortly after take-off and bellied in about 3 or 4 miles from the field. He was hot—hit a couple of stumps and a ditch and the airplane caught fire. He never got out. He was one of our best combat pilots.

Mission was escort to Achshaffenburg [sic] near Frankfurt. No Jerries—10/10 the whole way.

5 January, 1945*
What a—mission this was. Reminded me of the one so long ago when the B-24s led us astray. This time it was B-17s—they were supposed to bomb Haneau [sic] but I figure they were miles off course. Led us a merry chase and bombed through clouds.

Allison got back o.k. yesterday—cool, calm, and collected.

Had my first experience with the relief tube—and it is one I will never forget!!

6 January, 1945
Sweep in the Manheim [sic] area. Bailey led the group and they couldn't pick up anything. Thought sure they would run into something. Rimerman led our blue section.

7 January, 1945
Escort—just over the front lines. Again no action. Evidently the Hun is again recuperating to gain strength before once more attempting the impossible!! Had a squadron GI party which seemed to go off fairly well—at least everybody got looped on beer. Allison led the squadron.

10 January, 1945
Sweep in the Ludwigshaven area. Nothing exciting happened—that is, on the mission. Take-off was about the most nerve wracking I've seen. The last two days have been GREAT—for those who like the snow. Runways were covered yesterday and the snow was pushed off forming a bank along the side of the runway. Forkin, of 352, hit the bank—almost cartwheeled—and crashed, exploding as he hit. Plane burned like mad but—amazingly enough—he got out, only bruised. Jessup,

Warren, and a 351 character did the same thing but they were able to control the airplane and not crack up. LeFebre led the group—has two more to go. Haynes led the squadron.

13 January, 1945*
Escort to the same areas—Frankfurt. Had a pretty good weather problem on take-off—500 ft ceiling with a 4,000 ft top. G Lee—our Chinese boy—evidently spun out and augered in. Hated to see that boy go. Was one of our better pilots anyway, and the Chinese part made everybody want to see him get through.

Am half through now [his second tour]. Wish the next half would go as fast—but will probably take twice as long.

14 January, 1945
Another big day for the 8th AF but not so big for us. Was an escort mission to the outskirts of Berlin. Naturally we were not in on the big fight. 357th got an all time high of 53 ½ destroyed—gulp! We got 9 with the 350 getting none. The 8th had about 150 destroyed from the fighter flash reports. Haven't heard what the bombers did. They did good bombing visually for a change. Was a good show—will leave quite a few empty tables at the Luftwaffe chow house. My 4 destroyed [27 November, 1944] came through as confirmed today.

15 January, 1945
Escort to—or practically to—Munich. Bailey led the group and Rimerman our sqdn. Nothing was seen—no action of any kind.

Claims were over 240 yesterday—bombers included. 357th got 56—the score of scores.

16 January, 1945
Escort to Madgeburg [sic]—Rimerman led the group with our squadron. Weather socked in a couple of hours after take-off and the group landed in France—Columier [sic]—east of Paris. Was pretty bad all over England—we were listening to some of the boys from other groups that tried to get home. Heard at least 4 say they were bailing out. Tanner aborted and had a rough time getting in. Was a long show—1,200 miles round trip!! Took up Tanner's ship on a test hop and tried out our new [homing] beam on D channel. Really works great—should do wonders to decrease talk on A channel on the way home.

17 January, 1945*
Escort to the Osnabruck area. We managed to get 17 ships off today in the group. Meanwhile, scattered remnants of yesterday's mission have returned—still leaving, however, a good half of the group somewhere in France.

Rumor has it that Maguire was shot down by a straggling Fort that he was escorting—may have made it to friendly territory.

What a fiasco that was yesterday—a good day for the Hun.

18 January, 1945
Escort to the Frankfurt area—Boone led the group. We were able to get about 36 ships in the air. Half landed on the continent but all but three got back. Rimerman, LeFebre, and the rest still aren't back. We're released tomorrow so they should be able to make it then.

20 January, 1945
Same show as the last. Weep [Junttila] led and Seppala led our squadron. Another weather fiasco with nothing happening. The rest of the group got back yesterday.

23 January, 1945
Escort to the western part of the Ruhr. Naturally nothing happened. One of the 351 boys [Nicklebur] bellied in in friendly territory—engine just stopped.

    LeFebre finished his second tour—leaving Vic [Byers] as 351 CO. Maguire is back—bellied in right inside the front lines.

29 January, 1945
Escort to Kassel with no action. Col. Ben [Rimerman] led with our sqdn—take off was bad again with all the snow and ice on the runways. Several didn't make it. Larsen got off, barely—engine still wouldn't run right, so he dropped tanks, bent it around, and made an emergency landing on another runway. Robinson's engine wouldn't take power so he pulled up the wheels and bellied in on the runway. Evans of 352 came in to land, forgot to put his wheels down—and bellied in!!!

    Russians have been going like mad. Entire GAF has moved to that front so we will again be strafing rail traffic I'm sure. They are only 100 miles from Berlin and still going strong. Sure hope they can keep it up—maybe we'll be out of here before we expected.

1 February, 1945
Tanner, Duke, and Agnew [squadron records indicate Lanoue also] flew escort to Gen. Partridge today. The target was just inside the Ruhr. The General went over to observe the bomb hits, bomber formation, etc.

3 February, 1945*
I flew again for a change—what's gonna happen! Was an escort mission to Berlin. Rimerman led A group and I had B. Was a swell mission—weather and everything—but the Hun just didn't come up. We were able to see the Oder River well, and many fires around the Russian lines.

    Rimerman's flight and a couple other's went down to strafe—got a couple of locos—that's about all. Sepalla [Seppala] was hit and bellied in east of Hamburg—got out o.k. Was the only good group operations officer we've had.

    If we can't get the Hun up on a show like that, guess we'll never see him again. Incidentally, the Russians are only 40 miles from Berlin!!

6 February, 1945
Escort to the Leipzig area—Col. Ben leading. No e/a were seen by any groups. Bombers were off course—probably never hit the target. Weather was bad and we thought for a while they were going to have to divert to the continent, but they made it home o.k.

Russians have finally stopped at the Oder River. Germans say the Reds have several bridgeheads on the Western side—which makes them about 35 miles from Berlin.

Vic [Byers] has moved in and is settled [likely refers to the "Wheelhouse" for group field grade officers and above].

7 February, 1945
Have been painting the squadron operations room—looks pretty nice—light blue and burnt sienna.

8 February, 1945
Escort to Merseberg. Col. Ben [Rimerman] led the group and Tanner the squadron. Bombers were all messed up—no e/a seen.

9 February, 1945
Escort to Madgeburg [sic]. Col. Bill [Bailey] led the group and Boone the squadron. Boone broke an elbow [wing tank connector] on take-off—landed, took off again but never found the group. Our outfit never saw a thing but several of the groups found small formations of e/a. 20th group raised hell with an a/d—got 38 destroyed on the ground.

Gen. Partridge was here on his inspection while the group was gone. Inspected the troops as well as the base. Seemed well pleased.

14 February, 1945*
Escort to Chemnitz. Got to fire my guns a little anyway. Compton had B group and stayed with the bombers while I took A down to the deck. Weather was very bad on the way in but was o.k. from the target out—and very good for strafing. Group got 23 locos and a lot of small stuff.

Was no e/a up—479th ran into 5 and the 356th 7 and that's all. Was a little interesting for a change anyway—is getting more and more like around D-Day only this is much, much farther in.

15 February, 1945
Escort to Rhuland [sic]—oil. Was our longest mission to date. Was scheduled almost seven hours and a lot logged well over that. Should have seen some Jerries but they didn't come up. Liebold nosed up at some RAF field in Belgium [B-75]. Orzelek bellied it in somewhere over there [A-83]—we had guys scattered all over the place. They think Orzelek was the guy that was breathing over the radio—everybody was really sore; went on the whole time. Benny [Rimerman] threatens to send him to a/s rescue.

17 February, 1945
What a fiasco this was. Was originally an escort mission—again to Rhuland [sic]—but the weather was so bad they changed it twice after they were airborne. Finally ended up as an area support in the Frankfurt area. Boone led the group—a few did some strafing, got several locos. Weather at take-off was an overcast with a 200 ft ceiling with tops at about 800 ft. As they were crossing the channel, they ran into more and flew instruments from 4,000 to 20!!

351st lost a new boy [McKenney]—augered in just off the field; evidently was because of weather.

19 February, 1945
Escort into the Ruhr. Naturally they saw nothing—Compton led the show. Other groups were strafing farther in and really raised hell in general. The 55th—among other things—got 81 locos!!! 171 locos in two days!!

20 February, 1945
Escort to Nurnburg. Weep [Junttila] led the group and Boone the squadron. Weather was bad and nothing was seen.

Other groups were again strafing—more locos!

21 February, 1945
Escort to Nurnburg again—only this time we were to do the strafing. Bailey led with our squadron—didn't do much. Balason, leading yellow flight, caught a loco. Group did a little good though—destroyed 9 locos and some other stuff. Weather was bad for strafing—poor vis.

Rumor has it that I am flying again tomorrow—of all things!!

22 February, 1945*
A good show for a change. We were to sweep the Berlin area and north of there ahead of the bombers to try to pick up groups of e/a forming up. Weather was bad for take-off and we delayed a half hour but still made an instrument take-off. We were late over Berlin but still made it before the bombers. Northwest of Berlin we chased 4 ME262s, during which Compton got one. Part of our squadron was chasing one which made a couple of diving circles—one taking us over the heart of Berlin at 7,000 ft. I finally broke off this character with my flight when I spotted another. This guy we chased right on the deck for what seemed like hours at full throttle—but couldn't catch him. He led us over flak positions, airdromes, etc.—almost augered into high tension lines a couple of times—what a wild ride!

Finally said 'what the hell' and broke off—climbed up to about 8,000 ft and spotted another. This time we had altitude on him and I managed to get close enough to shoot. Hit him about three times in the left jet—and he pulled it up and bailed. Caught a picture of the plane as it went in with my side camera. This makes me—at long last—an ace!!

Those were the only e/a encountered. Squadron got 9 locos—group got 17 all toll [sic]. Balason is NYR—sure hope he's o.k.; was last seen chasing a jet.

23 February, 1945
Escort around the Manheim [sic] area and out north of the Ruhr—or vice versa!!

Was a long haul with no e/a spotted. Byers led the group with Tanner B group. 352 got 5 planes on the ground—twin engine stuff. The usual locos were strafed—the German transportation system is pretty well shot now. Before long it will be in the same condition as France before D-Day.

24 February, 1945
Escort to Hamburg—Boone leading. Nothing was seen—couldn't even find a loco to strafe.

We have a new major in the group—classmate of Rimerman's. I have a hunch 350 will be taken over by him—at least one of the squadrons. That's probably why there [sic] are flying me again tomorrow. Maybe I can finish now. And does that make me unhappy—Hell no!!

I think also that my L.C. [lieutenant colonelcy] has gone in—we'll see in a couple of weeks.

25 February, 1945*
Escort to Munich. Not much happened—our squadron didn't pay too much attention to the bombers. We flew the course at about 9–10,000 ft—looking for trains, low flying aircraft, etc., but saw nary a thing. Got some swell K-25 pictures of airfields, bombing, and one of the Alps. Got one loco—that's all we could dig up.

26 February, 1945
Escort to Berlin—Allison led the squadron. Nothing was seen—not even a jet. Bombers bombed on instruments—Germans have decided not to fly at all, I guess. Another major came into the group—that should cinch my being able to fly a little more.

27 February, 1945
What a field day this has been for the squadron!!! Never has anything happened like this before.

The mission, led by Weep [Junttila], was escort to Leipzig. On the return trip Boone, with our squadron, spotted a well camoflaged [sic] strip with about 50 plus airplanes of assorted kinds. He tested for flak and found none so the squadron proceeded to set up a gunnery pattern. They destroyed 38 planes, Boone getting 7— Kolb, 5—which ties the record set by the squadron of the 357th group. This makes us—finally—the top squadron in the group—with 15 or 20 to spare!! 352 blew up a marshalling yard—in fact, a good time was had by all; except 351.

28 February, 1945*
Escort to Kassel. Had a little more fun today—and did some SWEATIN'. We (our squadron) were going back to the same a/d as yesterday and clean out the rest of the planes. We left the bombers at the target and went down to the deck, through an overcast. While on the road to the a/d I spotted a train so I figured I could go down and get it—then continue on. While over the train I was clobbered by a burst of flak in the left gun bay and wheel well. Thot [sic] for a while I was on fire when I saw all the stuff coming out—but on closer inspection discovered it was hydraulic fluid. Gas tanks were not hit, so I was able to make it back o.k. Only one wheel came down and I couldn't get left one down or the right one back up—so bounced it on the runway on two passes, then decided to bring it in on one wheel. Made it o.k. with only slight damage to the plane. Engine is o.k. and the prop only nicked.

The rest of the squadron did mighty good again—got ten destroyed on another a/d—never found the right one. Was flak this time—had several battle damages but everybody made it back o.k.

48 in two days for old 350—which is dam [sic] good, and everybody knows it.

1 March, 1945
Escort—west of Munich. Davis led the squadron and stayed with the bombers while Col. Ben [Rimerman] with 351 and 352 hit the deck at the target. They shot up a little stuff. Johnson of 352 caught a liaison plane landing—made short work of it. Group got 25 locos.

2 March, 1945
Looks like the Luftwaffe decided to come up again. Was a Berlin show—target Rhuland [sic], and we were on the lead box for a change. Bailey led the group and Boone the squadron. So far the group has 15 destroyed. Kolb was returning early and hasn't been heard of since. Sure hope he's in Belgium. Agnew, Lanoue, Lee and Page each got one. Makes the 8th for Lanoue in three shows. Boone pulled up behind one character and only one gun fired!!—didn't hit him. Bailey got two and so did Byers. Waggoner and Cundy of 352 each got three apiece. Group got most in the air of all groups. 357 and 339 went to the deck and strafed—against orders.

3 March, 1945*
Escort to Brunswick—Weep [Junttila] led the group. We went on a sweep around Dummer lake—didn't see a thing. If we had seen anything we really could have clobbered them; 350 was really flying. Group saw jets—but didn't shoot any down. Grainger finished.

4 March, 1945
Escort to Luneburg. Boone led the group but aborted. Bombers were very much disorganized—weather was bad and they didn't bomb their target.

5 March, 1945
Escort—just over the lines—down south in the Frankfurt area. Davis led the squadron—nothing happened.

8 March, 1945
Escort in the same area—Kolb led the squadron. There has been a ban on strafing because of a plane shortage for the 8th. Results of that will be many missions like this—without any exciting happenings.

10 March, 1945
Sweep in the Kassel area—Boone led the squadron. Nothing happened—10/10 overcast. Benny [Rimerman] led the group. Jessup finished.

11 March, 1945
Escort to Hamburg—Boone led the squadron and Bailey the group. Cundy of 352 had coolant trouble—couldn't see—tried to bail out, but never made it—hit the tail. Went in the drink 40 miles off the coast of Lowestoff [sic].

Tanner taxied into our two-seater—hope I don't have to fine him. Will put him into operations after Boone finishes his next three missions.

I was originally scheduled to fly today but when my L.C. [lieutenant colonelcy] came through last night I decided to pitch a wild one, and that we did—Weep [Junttila] and I, everybody, for that matter. Our bill was 63 pounds—which we split!!!! Lt. Col.—never expected to see that. The next one is a big jump—one that I'll never make in the States.

12 March, 1945*
Sweep—working on MEW control in the Frankfurt area; 10/10 overcast—uneventful. Elder flew my element—does damn good.

14 March, 1945
Sweep in the Steinhuder Lake area. Allison led the squadron and finished. Maguire took 351 on a little private sweep and ran into about 15 109s. The squadron got 11—Mac getting two and Markham three. Was a good show—no NYRs. Am glad to see 351 get a few—they're pretty far behind. Bombers bombed Hanover.

15 March, 1945
Escort to Berlin—Col. Bill [Bailey] leading. Davis led the squadron and finished. Nothing was seen—not even any flak. Must have run out of flak at Berlin! Weather was bad on return—but everybody made it in o.k. including Carter and 7 others from the 56th.

16 March, 1945
Our first night flying in P-51s. Eight pilots from each squadron went off o.k.—hope it works as well every time.

17 March, 1945
Escort to Leipzig—Col. Ben [Rimerman] leading our squadron. Weather was bad and they didn't see a thing. Duke had engine trouble and bailed out near Cologne—which side we don't know. Fix from Nuthouse [callsign for MEW (Microwave Early Warning) fighter control] said EAST!! Sure hope it was in friendly territory—hate to lose him.

18 March, 1945*
Escort to Berlin—and again I did some sweatin'. While north of Berlin my generator quit and I turned and headed for the Russian lines. Plane seemed to run o.k. with all the electrical switches off, so after a while I decided to try for home—and made it, all the way here.

Jung's flight was bounced by a Russian fighter and a short time later Page bellied in inside the Russian lines—might have been hit by this fighter. Page called after landing, saying he was o.k. and would see us in a couple of months.

351 had a boy [Campbell] bail out around Steinhuder Lake—engine trouble—and no e/a were seen!!!

19 March, 1945
Escort to Rhuland [sic]—we saw nothing. 351 had a boy bail out in Germany [no recorded loss, Blick possibly means Hahn of 352 who became a POW] and another [Frye] spin out in the Channel—352 had one [actually Matula of 351] belly land in Belgium; is o.k.

Other groups saw quite a few jets and other e/a. 78th was high with 32 destroyed. Total was not more than 50 or 60.

21 March, 1945
Strafing—Achmer a/d—Boone leading. We were to break off escort and strafe—just as the bombers finished dropping. Everything worked out swell except that the 4th group busted into our pattern and broke it up. But—even so—we came out way up on top for the day. Group total was 28, 352 getting none. Our squadron got 19—11 or 12 of them jets. Boone and Gus[t]ke shared 8—and Lanoue got three more, bringing his total to 11!! We had no pilot losses—one airplane—and several battle damages including my airplane, in which Gus[t]ke hit a tree. 351 lost 2 [actually three, Gilmer, Eddy and Brock] and 352, one [Michel].

22 March, 1945
Escort to an a/d north of Dummer Lake. Tanner led the sqdn and swept the Dummer Lake area. Saw nothing. Weather was CAVU and the bombing excellent.
The 4th—on area support at Rhuland [sic] for the 15th AF—caught 15 190s, got 11.

23 March, 1945
Sub minimum sweep of the Kassel–Frankfurt area. 8 ships per squadron. Larsen led ours and didn't see a thing.

All indications lead to another D day for Monty's [British General Montgomery] troops in Holland tomorrow.

Haynes got back today—full of wild tales of the States—looks healthy and eager to go!

24 March, 1945*

♪ What a day—what a day!!!!!! ♪ Another D day is right—I believe they call it R day. They crossed the Rhine last night and have been dropping supplies, reinforcements all day. Last Thursday Patton's troops crossed in a massive operation with utmost secrecy, headed for Frankfurt. Today the 15th AF bombed Berlin!! If the weather will only hold out—what confusion those Germans will be in. The armies are really off to the races.

Our part was patrol south east of the Ruhr. Col. Ben [Rimerman] took A group out early this morning. Our squadron came back early and I took it out as B group about 1300. We were near Kassel and ran into about 15 190s with belly tanks and about the same no. of 109s covering them. Result was a fierce battle in which we knocked down 25 (maybe more with NYR claims). I had a helluva battle and ended up with 3 190s and 2 109s destroyed—augered in!! Major Elder also got 5—both g[r]oup records. Was quite a sight, seeing all those e/s [sic] going down in flames and the fires from the crashes. The Hun is defeated and he certainly knows it. Rimerman took the rest of the group out again and didn't see a thing—so again the 350 comes through. We have destroyed over 100 e/a in less than a month. 'Tis some record—the boys are getting hot, and plenty eager. These e/a were heading for the lines—and I'm sure not one of them got there!!!

But—with the good, there is also the bad. Onkey is evidently MIA—two others are definitely on the continent o.k. and 4 others, including Larsen, are NYR [Hopkins, May, Larsen, Grizzle and Onkey did not return]. Nobody saw a thing of any of them. Sure hope Larsen gets back—is a good man.

I got hit again—in the wing—along with several others, so into the hangar goes Betty E. again—just got it out today. We'll only have about 12 airplanes tomorrow.

25 March, 1945

Released—Hubble is back with claims of two 109s destroyed which makes a total of 27. That many in the air for one squadron is a group record.

26 March, 1945

Escort to Leipzig—Weep [Junttila] led the group and Tanner the squadron. Weather was very bad with 350 running into the worst. Almost everybody came back in our squadron due to severe icing conditions, but the other two squadrons hit it a little easier and finally found the bombers—even so, Weep was plenty shaky from the ordeal.

Had a real scare from Tanner. He iced up and spun down from 20,000 ft. Thought he went straight in until a report came through from a hosp. in Brintree [Braintree]. Doc and I went over to see him and found him pretty well beaten up but o.k. Has a gash on the side of his head. Plane broke up in the spin and he bailed at the last minute—is a lucky boy.

27 March, 1945
O'Neil is back from the continent with one destroyed.
I am acting exec. in Bailey's absence.
Patton's tanks reported to have reached Nurnburg!! The old boy's really going again. What a name he has made for himself.
Tanner is back—in our hospital. Looks a lot better than yesterday.
I have a new airplane—D-20.

30 March, 1945
Escort to Hamburg—Compton led the group and Kolb the squadron. A few jets were sighted, that's all.

31 March, 1945
Escort to Madgeburg [sic]—Boone led the group and finished his second tour. There's a lot of guys sweatin' out what happens to him now. A lot of jets were seen. Tordoff of 352 got one—and Long, flying with them, ran into some 109s and knocked down three of them. Looks like Long and Elder are having a little race between them.
Elder has officially taken over 350 with Tanner as operations and Kolb as ass't.
I am group operations—and exec. in Bailey's absence. After 28 months with 350 it's a little hard to leave.
Good news—Duke is with the 9th AF headquarters. Am happy to hear that he's o.k.

1 April, 1945
Released—in today's Sunday Graphic was a picture of a group of liberated prisoners, liberated when our army over-ran the camp at Wetzlar—and among them was Balason, which, naturally we were happy to see.
Two of Long's 109s of yesterday were SPITFIRES—gulp!!!

2 April, 1945
Escort—targets were airfields in Denmark. Bombers aborted, due to weather. Byers led—Bailey led the 352nd and Benny [Rimerman] led blue section of 350 with Elder leading the sqdn!!!

3 April, 1945
Escort to Kiel with Bailey leading. Bombers bombed through partial cloud—we saw nothing.
Is beginning to look as if the war for the 8th is rapidly coming to an end. We—at present—are doing little or no good—have no targets to bomb. Teletype came

through today that stated no bombing within 25 miles of Berlin. Looks like they could easily send one division home—I'll take it!!!

Looks like I'm in the same position as the 8th AF. Am not needed anymore and yet they still won't let me fly and finish—even though they know how much I want to go home.

What a performance!!

4 April, 1945
Escort—again to Kiel. Rimerman leading—no nothing.

5 April, 1945*
At last I flew again—escort to Nurnburg. Weather was bad—went across the channel in a violent rainstorm, forming up at landfall in, then climbed to 27,000 ft on instruments!!! Finally found the bombers but were split up so escorted by flights. Didn't see anything and came back on the deck.

6 April, 1945
Escort to Leipzig—Bailey leading. Solid overcast—mission was very snafued.

Yesterday Compton strafed an airstrip with his wingman and got 4 planes.

7 April, 1945
Escort to Hamburg. Weep [Junttila] led—Rimerman took B group with 351. The Luftwaffe came up again for a change. Looks like maybe we'll see them for a while again. Might be a last stand of some sort. (Seems to me I said that before!) 351 ran into them today getting 7 with McGraw getting three.

Total for today was about 65 with everyone getting in on it—suggesting that the Hun has been told to get up there regardless, with no thought toward formation.

We have Dummer Lake now—how queer it will be to fly around there and have it occupied by Allied troops. Times have certainly changed—used to be a mighty long mission to go to Dummer and back!!

8 April, 1945*
Sweep—I led A group and patrolled the Stendal area. Bailey led B group and was stooging around Nurnburg. Between the two groups we covered most of Germany—nary an e/a in the sky. We were over Berlin at about 10,000 ft for a while. Coming out I took a good look at Hanover—and it is completely demolished.

9 April, 1945
Escort—to Munich. Byers led—Bailey, Weep [Junttila], [John B.] Rose, and Elder also flew. All the wheels are flying nowadays. Guess Rimerman and I'll go tomorrow. 351 caught a couple of jets on the ground.

Duke is back—and what a story he has. Was captured by the Germans and escaped after 12 days. Had it pretty rough all the time—no food. Is quite mad at the Germans—and rightly so. Looks o.k. but is a trifle thin and nervous.

10 April, 1945*
Escort to an airfield south of Madgeburg [sic]. Col. Ben [Rimerman] took A group and I had B. We were going to strafe after the bombers bombed but saw nothing on the field, so didn't. Watched them do some beautiful precision bombing. Caught an ME 262 and was almost ready to shoot when Abernathy clobbered him head on. Makes 'Ab' an ace. Clark got one in the air and so did Compton. Clark and Caton finished today.

Gr[e]at news just came in. Duncan is alive and well!!!! Can't say more—but will later.

11 April, 1945
Escort—to fields in the Munich area. Sounds a little like the D day era with all the fields being bombed the way they are. Junttila led the group and finished up—will be drunk out for him tonight. Rimerman took B group—saw nothing.

Yesterday was the day of days as far as ground claims go—the field order said no strafing!!!! Somebody should be fried. 326 planes on the ground with the 339th getting 105!!

15 April, 1945
Looks like the war is just about over—our troops are as near Berlin as the Russians. 'Ike' [Eisenhower] said that organized resistance would be declared over very shortly.

We haven't had a mission since the 11th—however the other two wings pulled a sneak strafing show the other day and cleaned up. 56th got 95 on the ground.

President Roosevelt's untimely death is a great blow to the world. It's a shame he couldn't have lived to see the end of this thing.

Page is o.k. in Russia—so our news says.

16 April, 1945
Area support—way over on the other side of Munich. Col. Ben [Rimerman] led and just about everybody else went. Each sqdn picked out a/ds to strafe. 351 got about 55—350, 40, and 352 got 15 making a total of 110. A few NYRs might have more. It's a big score—wish it did more good. Isn't worth the price though. Prescott and Howie bellied in in enemy territory, Greenfield made a one-wheeled landing on the continent, and McMullen is on the continent.
The 8th piled up a real score today—something like 630 destroyed. 78th got 120; 339th got 118, 55th got 60 some—was practically all our wing. We passed 352 and 257 [357?] to put us in 4th place.

17 April, 1945
Escort—to Dresden. Johnson led with 352 and went on a sweep to the same area as yesterday. Managed to pick up 18 planes. Lamb and Lancaster were hit and are MIA. The gunners on the fields were re[a]dy today. It's just not worth it—to lose good men on planes that are not being used anyway. Besides—our armies will capture the fields shortly anyway.

352nd group passed us again with 66. 55th got 9 in the air (????) and 38 on the ground, as trade for 4 MIAs as well as Col. Righetti—and that is a real loss to them. 78th got 15 and 357 a couple—so we're in 5th place.

18 April, 1945
Escort to the same area—is the only place we can go now. Compton led the group—saw a couple of jets, gave chase but didn't catch.
　　Rumors are flying thick and fast. The last 'straight dope' has us going straight home. Sure hope so.

19 April, 1945
Escort—same area. The 8th is hitting tactical targets now. No luck—saw jets but couldn't catch. Elder led the group.
　　The big news of the day is that Duncan is in Paris. Called Johnson today, telling him to paint his [Duncan's] name on an airplane—he was going to fly. Would certainly be great to have him back. He naturally has his eye on the Pacific. Sure would be swell for him to take this group over.
　　He has been all this time working in the Dutch underground. Had the chance to come back several times but preferred to help finish the Germans that way [Blick is reporting second hand here rather than providing a factually accurate account of Duncan's activities in the Netherlands while evading]. One in a million that boy. Was never a PW—walked all the way from Hanover to Holland without being caught.
　　He should be rolling in here in three or four days—we're all mighty anxious to see him.

20 April, 1945
Escort—just west of Berlin. Johnson led—no action.
　　Duncan flew in today!!!! Buzzed the field in the AT-17 while the group was landing. Everybody came out to watch just as they used to whenever he came in. What a character—same old Dunc—quite a bit thinner but in good health. A real hero in the eyes of most of us around here—and a legend to those who never knew him. Dunc will take this group and Rimerman will go to the 55th.

22 April, 1945
Rimerman left today for the 55th group. Duncan is once again our CO. Looks like I'll have my hands full for a while. He is going to the rest home before he goes operational so that will leave me with operations, exec, and CO—gulp!

24 April, 1945
Escort to the RAF—target Berchesgaden [sic] (?). Elder led. Was a snafued mission from the start. Field order came in ten minutes after briefing time. That was about 0425. Field was fogged in—350th didn't have their planes ready, so they finally got off on instruments an hour late!! Saw nothing.

30 April, 1945
Page is back from Russia with a lot of wild tales about the Russians.

Harris of 352 is back—had been a PW for 9 months. Escaped while on a march south of Nurnburg. Was 7 months at Sagan. Roomed with Bedford, Corgan, and Cles. Gonnam was there and possibly many others. Harris has a rough story to tell—wish I could relate it here—is about 50 pounds lighter.

Also, two more boys are back—new boys that I didn't know. There should be more soon.

Clark, Caton, Hightshoe, and Abernathy are gone—home.

Elder is now a Lt. Col.—was a mistake giving it to him before Byers.

7 May, 1945
IT'S OVER!!!!!! At long last. Tomorrow is legally VE day. The celebrating has started and will continue for a couple of days, and that's o.k. by me—this is one day I really intend to celebrate. I imagine the British will really go mad—6 years they have been sweating this out. Seems like a long time to me and that has only been two years.

Half the battle has been won—I only hope the next half doesn't take as long. We'll wait and see.

14 May, 1945
Beckham walked in last night, really looks great—so happy to see everybody and be back he cried.

15 May, 1945
Saw Stearns today—looks a little thin but otherwise o.k. Wants to go home—can't say that I blame him!

17 May, 1945
Dunc went over to Paris yesterday in a two seater 51 and walked in tonight with McCollom. Is good to see him. He's another that is plenty happy to be back. Hardly shows where he was burned. Is beginning to look like the old gang around here.

And that just about winds up this little diary of operations in the ETO for old Three Five Three. If it's all the same to the powers that be, I'll let someone else continue this—in the Pacific.

APPENDIX 2

"Captain Blickenstaff Gives Good Dope on Bombing"

In the summer of 1944, the Eighth Fighter Command canvassed its pilots for good practice for ground-attack missions. The result was internally published as Down to Earth—Fighter Attack on Ground Targets *(August 30, 1944). Blick contributed to this "manual" for fellow fighter pilots and his "Good Dope" is reproduced as printed here.*

"In my opinion any consideration of air to ground firing would not be complete without touching dive bombing. Being a member of the group that pioneered in dive bombing in this theatre, I am particularly interested in it. After experimenting both in practice and operational dive bombing missions, we soon found certain principles that were essential to success. For instance, vertical dive bombing requires individual aiming and releasing from an altitude of not more than 10,000 feet. Without these essentials, accuracy is sacrificed. Coordinated flying is of course necessary and without that old ball in the center one cannot reasonably expect to do accurate dive bombing. It is to be emphasized that the plane must be properly trimmed. In this connection, it is well to remember that aileron as well as rudder trim must constantly be used. This means a well planned run without having to hurry through it. For the average pilot tenseness due to flak encountered is the main cause for haste and sloppy flying. Thus provisions should be made to neutralize flak as soon as possible. For this purpose we carry a flight with frags [fragmentation] or 250 pound general purpose bombs to take care of the flak positions. Another effective means of neutralizing the ground fire is to detail a flight to observe for and strafe any fire encountered.

"After 'D' day the types of targets and frequent bad weather prohibited the use of vertical dive bombing. As a consequence glide bombing and skip bombing were used. It was soon found by operational experience that the glide had to be at least 30 degrees, otherwise, even the 1,000 pounders would fail to stick. This likewise required coordinated flying during the dive. Proper briefing to include thorough study of contour and flak maps pays dividends. Contour maps are especially necessary for planning attacks on bridges. Glide bombing allows us to release within 2,000 feet of the target with the result that greater accuracy is accomplished. In this connection, it is well to warn against releasing too close to the target when instantaneous fuses are used. Sad experience taught us that 500 feet was needed for 250 pounders, 800 feet for 500 pounders and 1,500 feet for 1,000 pounders. These are minimum altitudes.

"The majority of mistakes made in ground strafing are due to the pilots disregarding his training in ground gunnery both in flying school and OTU. Too frequently the novice puts the pip [gun sight] directly on the target and attempts to judge his error by watching his strikes. The result is that in the beginning of the pass he shoots below the target and his attempts at correction spraying bullets above and around the target. This habit can be corrected by leaving the pip above the target at the beginning of the pass and as the range decreases allowing the pip to drop on to the target.

"In strafing convoys it is best for a flight to make a line abreast attack, perpendicular to the road. Each pilot should pick a target and concentrate on it alone, during the pass. Wild spraying causes very little damage. After the pass, the wing man should keep his leader in sight so that they can form up and establish a good gunnery pattern with several runs on the target. Train busting is a great sport. Two precautions are worth mentioning here. First of all a train needs very little if any lead and can be considered as a stationary target. Secondly it is well to look over every train carefully and neutralize any small arm defenses if present; then the locomotive is easy meat.

"Out of the experience gained in airdrome strafing by many pilots, a number of fundamental rules developed. First of all one should have a good mental picture of the flak defenses of an airdrome before attacking. It is a good practice to pick a reference point several miles from the airdrome and get down on the deck and fly to it. This is the only practical method of navigating on the deck to an airdrome and still achieve an element of surprise. Once over the drome pull up to about 50 feet so that a target can be selected and destroyed. Then back to the deck until out of the range of the flak guns. If those tracers begin to get uncomfortably close a little weaving is the only logical evasive action. Even if no responses from the ground defenses is experienced during the first pass, one should attempt subsequent passes prayerfully. During any pass flights should be line abreast, and if possible have a flight at 5,000 or 7,000 feet to disperse and neutralize flak."

APPENDIX 3

Blick's Aircraft

Unknown P-47 Thunderbolt at Goxhill. Blick wrote in his diary when Lieutenant Zolner was lost on March 8, 1944, in his aircraft: "Look's like I'll get a new airplane. Will make the 5th since I've been in England." The sequence of aircraft indicates, therefore, that there is an unidentified first LH-U. The group did receive some early D models at Goxhill, replacing them when they went operational. An undated US newspaper report held by the Blickenstaff family describes how Blick painted two girls on his aircraft and "when they were finished … he could find no appropriate name until it dawned upon him that 'Hell's Belles' would be indicative." Numerous photos of the various females that Blick painted on aircraft exist but none located feature a name. It seems likely that "Hell's Belles" was either the first or an early P-47.

P-47D-2-RE 42-7988 LH-U. This aircraft had a rough career with the squadron, suffering its first mishap when the ferry pilot delivering it to Goxhill dinged the propellers on the runway when landing on July 20, 1943. It next shows up in an abort by Blick on August 27 and an early return on September 15, 1943. It suffered battle damage on September 27 and photographic evidence shows damage on November 3, 1943 (Blick was not flying it on either occasion). It is currently only possible to confirm the codes. No photos located show either artwork or name for this aircraft. According to the Individual Aircraft Record Card, the Ninth Air Force took the aircraft and sent it for salvage on November 11, 1943, subsequent to damage sustained on November 3.

P-47D-6-RE 42-74647 LH-U. This is the first aircraft for which photos are available showing nude female artwork painted by Blick on the port and starboard side of the aircraft. No name is confirmed in any photograph. This aircraft stayed with the 350th Fighter Squadron until moving to the 56th Fighter Group at nearby Halesworth, sometime after receiving battle damage on February 24, 1944. The 56th recoded it as LM-V, but retained Blick's eye-catching artwork. By April 14, 1944, a photographer snapped it, along with many other P-47s, a P-38, a B-17 and even some Mosquitoes at BAD 1 Burtonwood. The aircraft had a rough career while with the squadron. On November 12, 1943, Second Lieutenant Robert S. Hart nosed up the aircraft, damaging the propeller. Then on December 1, 1944, Blick recorded he had "a hole the size of a watermelon on the bottom of the plane. Flak seems to be pretty good!!"

P-47D-5-RE 42-8557 LH-U. Blick's fourth aircraft did not last very long. It failed to return when it was hit by flak while flown by First Lieutenant John Zolner on the March 8, 1944, mission. A photo is available of an LH-U with different female artwork (but no serial number). Given the cooler vent configuration on the LH-U in the photograph is not that of a D-15, and given the different female artwork, it seems likely that the photo is of the fourth LH-U.

P-47D-15-RE 42-76320 LH-U. Blick's fifth aircraft arrived on March 9, 1944. Blick wrote in his diary: "My new plane came in from the 352nd group. Is a D*15 and looks to be in good condition." He took it for a test flight on March 11 and recorded "TEST—NEW 'U' (5th plane)" in his log. On March 13 he noted in his diary: "My airplane isn't so hot on gas—and I DON'T like that. Otherwise, it's a perfect airplane." The aircraft was lost when Second Lieutenant Joseph C. McDonald was hit by flak and had to belly in on May 29, 1944. Blick recorded: "MacDonald—flying my airplane—was hit. ... Guess I'll get the D-25 for my airplane too." There is no available photograph of this aircraft with the 350th FS.

P-47D-25-RE 42-26402 LH-U. This aircraft arrived early in June (Blick's log records a test hop in a D-25 on June 1) but was lost along with Major Dewey E. Newhart on the disastrous June 12, 1944, mission.

P-47D-25-RE 42-26416 LH-U *Soubrette* (the Individual Aircraft Record Card records it as a D-30). Blick named the seventh LH-U *Soubrette* but Phil Rossi painted the artwork on the cowl. Blick explained: "The first couple, of course, were the P-47s that I had drawn the nudes for and which soon became too much trouble to keep putting back on. After that, I tried to think of something different. I wasn't married and didn't have a steady girlfriend at the time, so I saw the French 'Soubrette' and liked the sound, so that's what I used. It really had no particular meaning for me—other than the dictionary meaning which was 'A saucy, coquettish, flirtatious, frivolous young woman.'"[1] Following the harrowing series of losses in his personal aircraft, Blick banned other pilots from flying *Soubrette*, but finished his first tour on August 7, 1944, and would not return to the squadron until October that year.

---

1   Blickenstaff letter to Cross, January 24, 1991.

In the meantime, Captain John B. Rose wrote off *Soubrette* on September 19, 1944, when he crashed the aircraft into a canteen building at RAF Rochester.

P-51D-10-NA 44-14726 LH-U *The BETTY E.* On Blick's return to the group they had already converted to the Mustang and he recorded "P-51 MY NEW U" in his logbook when noting an hour-long flight on October 27, 1944. Blick named the aircraft *The BETTY E* and explained the name came about "when I met the girl on my leave back to the States. I hardly knew her but it was something more tangible to put on the plane."[2] He was flying this aircraft when he scored his four victories on November 27, 1944, and received battle damage to the aircraft's oil line, forcing him to land at Denain/Prouvy, France. Blick hitched a ride home in a B-26 but the aircraft remained in France until December 8 when it transferred back to station engineering at Raydon. The aircraft subsequently moved to the 352nd Fighter Squadron.

P-51K-1-NT 44-11353 LH-U *BETTY E.* On December 4, 1944, Blick recorded: "Have a P-51K now—has an Aero prop, am anxious to try it" in his diary. He got the chance on December 7, recording "P-51K MY NEW U" in his logbook. There are two early photos of the aircraft available showing three rows of checkers probably taken at some point in December 1944. Blick left the aircraft at Duxford after landing there on December 19 and did not fly it again until December 29, when he recorded in his diary: "Flew my airplane again—finally got it back from Duxford." The aircraft was damaged by flak that caused Blick's "one-wheeled" landing at Raydon on February 28, 1945. Blick recorded in his diary: "The Betty E—Fixed up" on March 13, 1945. It received damage again on March 21 when he recorded "several battle damages including my airplane, in which Gus[t]ke hit a tree." Blick was flying this aircraft when he scored his five victories on March 24, 1945, but it received battle damage in that encounter (his log also suggests he was flying it for his ME262 victory on February 22, 1945, but does not confirm). His diary entry for the 24th confirmed "I got hit again—in the wing—along with several others, so into the hangar goes Betty E. again—just got it out today." After repair, the aircraft became LH-Z *JayHawk Jalopy*, belonging to First Lieutenant Albert B. Brimer.

P-51D-20-NA 44-72374 LH-U *BETTY E.* Blick recorded "P-51D-20 MY NEW U" in his log on March 27, 1945. Several photographs confirm the identity and port markings of this aircraft. The aircraft was still with the squadron and listed in their engineering records as of July 1945. The Colchester diary also details the name *Delores* on the starboard side of the aircraft. Blick confirmed: "Delores was my crew chief's wife. Her name was on the right side of the plane. I think his name was Sgt.

---

2   Blickenstaff letter to Cross, January 24, 1991.

O'Connell." (Staff Sergeant Thomas O'Connell, 32278924, originally of B Flight).[3] The *Delores* starboard name may well have applied to earlier Mustangs but there is no available evidence either way. This aircraft left the squadron in the summer of 1945 and later joined the Swiss Air Force via Speke Air Depot.

---

3   Blickenstaff email to Cross, November 26, 2000.

APPENDIX 4

Blick's Aerial Claims

December 1, 1943	ME109 damaged (air)	Solingen
June 30, 1944	ME109 probable (air)	W Châlons
June 30, 1944	ME109 damaged (air)	W Châlons
November 27, 1944	4 × FW190 destroyed (air)	Steinhuder Lake/ Brunswick
February 22, 1945	ME262 destroyed (air)	Berlin
March 24, 1945	3 × FW190 destroyed (air)	NW Kassel
March 24, 1945	2 × ME109 destroyed (air)	NW Kassel

APPENDIX 5

Blick's Promotions

Blick entered service on January 28, 1942, as an aviation cadet and entered active service after graduating in Class 42-H on August 27, 1942.

Second lieutenant, August 27, 1942.

First Lieutenant, April 21, 1943.

D Flight commander, March 7, 1944.

Captain, April 4, 1944.

350th Fighter Squadron operations officer, May 8, 1944.

Major, August 9, 1944.

350th Fighter Squadron commander, November 9, 1944 (from September 21, 1944, but on leave in the US and did not return to the squadron until October 21, 1944).

Lieutenant colonel, March 7, 1945.

353rd Fighter Group operations officer, April 2, 1945.

APPENDIX 6

Blick's Awards

European African Middle Eastern (EAME) Campaign Medal with six Bronze Stars.

Distinguished Unit Badge, March 22, 1945, for operations September 17 to 23, 1944.

Air Medal (September 20, 1943) with Seven Oak Leaf Clusters: 1st, November 5, 1943; 2nd, December 20, 1943; 3rd, December 31, 1943; 4th, unknown; 5th, unknown; 6th, unknown; 7th, May 23, 1945.

Distinguished Flying Cross (January 28, 1944) with Three Oak Leaf Clusters: 1st, April 27, 1944; 2nd, unknown; 3rd, June 21, 1945, for action February 22, 1945.

Silver Star for action November 27, 1944 (awarded May 8, 1945).

French Croix de Guerre (awarded March 18, 1946).

APPENDIX 7

Blick's Missions

Key
WM = Wingman   SL = Squadron lead   R = Red Flight
UK = Unknown   GL = Group lead   B = Blue Flight
EL = Element lead   W = White Flight   Y = Yellow Flight

APPENDIX 7: BLICK'S MISSIONS • 327

No.	Date	Field Order	Type	Role	Position	Target/Mission	Duration	Remarks
1	09-Aug-43	W28/95	Sweep	WM	R#2	Netherlands	01:48	
2	14-Aug-43	34/102	Escort	EL	R#3	Netherlands	01:36	
3	15-Aug-43	36/104	Sweep	WM	W#4	Belgium/France	01:42	
4	18-Aug-43	108/40	Escort	EL	B#3	Gilze-Rijen	01:56	
5	23-Aug-43	43/111	Sweep	EL	B#3	Rotterdam	01:42	
6	24-Aug-43	44/112	Escort	EL	B#3	Villacoublay	01:48	
7	25-Aug-43	46/114	Sweep	EL	B#3	Dunkirk/Le Touquet	01:48	
8	27-Aug-43	116	Escort	EL	B#3	Saint-Omer	01:30	
9	31-Aug-43	119	Escort	EL	B#3	Paris	01:24	Estimated.
10	02-Sep-43	50/120	Escort	EL	B#3	Brussels	01:54	
11	03-Sep-43	51/121	Escort	EL	B#3	Meulan	01:54	
12	06-Sep-43	55/125	Escort	EL	W#3	Stuttgart	02:30	
13	16-Sep-43	63/133	Escort	EL	B#3	Nantes/	01:48	
14	22-Sep-43	139	Sweep	WM	R#2	Lille Ghent	01:36	
15	23-Sep-43	142	Escort	UK	UK	Nantes	02:12	
16	26-Sep-43	145	Escort	UK	UK	Nantes	02:12	
17	14-Oct-43	156	Escort	EL	R#3	Schweinfurt	03:10	
18	18-Oct-43	162	Escort	EL	R#3	Düren	01:50	
19	20-Oct-43	163	Escort	EL	R#3	Düren	02:30	
20	22-Oct-43	165	Escort	EL	R#3	Cambrai	01:50	
21	24-Oct-43	166	Escort	EL	R#3	Saint Andre	02:20	
22	25-Nov-43	190	Dive-bombing	EL	W#3	Saint-Omer/Ft Rouge	01:50	
23	26-Nov-43	191	Escort	EL	W#3	Bremen	03:00	

No.	Date	Field Order	Type	Role	Position	Target/Mission	Duration	Remarks
24	29-Nov-42	192	Escort	EL	B#3	Bremen	02:50	
25	01-Dec-43	194	Escort	FL	Y#1	Solingen	03:40	First flight lead.
26	04-Dec-43	195	Dive-bombing	EL	B#3	Gilze-Rijen	02:15	
27	05-Dec-43	196	Escort	EL	B#3	Paris	03:00	
28	11-Dec-43	198	Escort	EL	B#3	Emden	03:20	
29	13-Dec-43	199	Escort	EL	B#3	Bremen	03:00	
30	20-Dec-43	204	Escort	FL	Y#1	Bremen	03:05	
31	22-Dec-43	207	Escort	FL	R#1	Osnabrück	03:10	
32	23-Dec-43	W37	Dive-bombing	EL	Y#3	Gilze-Rijen	02:00	
33	24-Dec-43	209	Escort	EL	Y#3	Pas-de-Calais	03:20	
34	04-Jan-44	212	Escort	FL	R#1	Munster	03:00	
35	05-Jan-44	213	Escort	FL	R#1	Neuse/Elberfeld	02:50	
36	07-Jan-44	215	Escort	EL	W#3	Ludwigshafen	03:45	
37	11-Jan-44	216	Escort	EL	B#3	Halberstadt/Brunswick	03:10	
38	14-Jan-44	217	Escort	EL	B#3	French coast	03:10	
39	24-Jan-44	222	Escort	EL	W#3	Frankfurt	03:40	
40	25-Jan-44	W40	Dive-bombing	EL	R#3	Leeuwarden	02:20	
41	29-Jan-44	226	Escort	FL	R#1	Frankfurt	03:10	
42	03-Feb-44	233	Escort	FL	R#1	Wilhemshaven	03:00	
43	04-Feb-44	234	Escort	EL	B#2/3	Frankfurt	02:30	
44	06-Feb-44	236	Escort	EL	B#3	Nancy	03:00	
45	08-Feb-44	237	Escort	EL	B#3	Frankfurt	02:30	
46	10-Feb-44	239	Escort	FL	B#1	Brunswick	02:45	

APPENDIX 7: BLICK'S MISSIONS • 329

47	11-Feb-44	240	Escort	EL	B#3	Frankfurt	02:45	
48	13-Feb-44	242	Escort	FL	B#1	Pas-de-Calais	03:00	
49	14-Feb-44	W46	Dive-bombing	FL	B#1	Gilze-Rijen	01:45	
50	20-Feb-44	245	Escort	FL	Y#1	Leipzig	02:50	
51	21-Feb-44	246	Escort	FL	R#1	Gütersloh	02:45	
52	22-Feb-44	247	Escort	FL	R#1	Gotha	03:10	
53	02-Mar-44	257	Escort	FL	B#1	Frankfurt	03:15	
54	13-Mar-44	267	Escort	FL	B#1	Pas-de-Calais	03:30	
55	15-Mar-44	269	Escort	FL	B#1	Brunswick	03:30	
56	16-Mar-44	270	Escort	FL	Y#1	Friedrichshafen	04:00	
57	22-Mar-44	277	Escort	FL	R#1	Berlin	04:00	
58	28-Mar-44	283	Escort	SL	W#1	Chartres	03:45	First squadron lead.
59	29-Mar-44	284	Escort	FL	R#1	Brunswick	02:00	
60	09-Apr-44	292	Escort	SL	W#1	Gdynia	04:30	
61	12-Apr-44	296	Escort	FL	R#1	Schweinfurt	03:45	
62	13-Apr-44	298	Escort	FL	R#1	Augsburg	03:20	
63	19-Apr-44	305	Escort	SL	W#1	Kassel	03:00	
64	24-Apr-44	312	Escort	SL	W#1	Oberpfaffenhofen	04:45	
65	09-May-44	333	Escort	SL	W#1	Laon/Jouvincourt	03:05	
66	20-May-44	343a	Escort	SL	W#1	Villacoublay/Orly	03:25	
67	22-May-44	347	Dive-bombing	SL	W#1	Liège	03:35	
68	25-May-44	350	Escort	SL	W#1	Nancy	04:35	
69	30-May-44	354	Escort	SL	W#1	Magdeburg	05:25	
70	30-May-44	W62	Dive-bombing	SL	W#1	Verberie/Compiègne	03:10	

330 • ACE IN A DAY

No.	Date	Field Order	Type	Role	Position	Target/Mission	Duration	Remarks
71	31-May-44	W63	Dive-bombing	SL	W#1	Gütersloh	03:40	
72	03-Jun-44	363	Type 16	SL	W#1	Rouen	03:25	
73	04-Jun-44	365	Type 16	SL	W#1	Saint-Quentin	03:15	
74	04-Jun-44	368	Type 16	SL	W#1	St Avord	03:45	
75	07-Jun-44	373	Dive-bombing	SL	W#1	NW Paris	02:25	
76	07-Jun-44	375	Dive-bombing	FL	B#1	Pas-de-Calais	03:25	
77	10-Jun-44	380	Dive-bombing	SL	W#1	L'Aigle	03:30	
78	10-Jun-44	381	Dive-bombing	FL	B#1	Beauvais	02:55	
79	12-Jun-44	383	Sweep	SL	W#1	Paris	03:40	
80	13-Jun-44	385	Dive-bombing	SL	W#1	Tours	04:10	
81	14-Jun-44	389	Dive-bombing	SL	W#1	Compiègne	03:35	
82	17-Jun-44	394	Sweep	SL	W#1	Dreux	03:25	Individual record has 4:25.
83	19-Jun-44	399	Sweep	SL	W#1	Dreux	02:20	
84	19-Jun-44	400	Sweep	FL	R#1	Pas-de-Calais	03:00	
85	21-Jun-44	407	Escort	SL	W#1	Berlin	04:45	
86	22-Jun-44	412	Escort	FL	R#1	Paris	04:00	
87	25-Jun-44	417	Escort	SL	W#1	Paris	04:15	
88	27-Jun-44	420	Dive-bombing	FL	R#1	Épernay	00:00	Abort—mission but no time credit.
89	28-Jun-44	421	Escort	SL	W#1	Laon/Jouvincourt	03:40	
90	30-Jun-44	424	Dive-bombing	FL	R#1	Longueville	04:10	
91	01-Jul-44	425	Dive-bombing	SL	W#1	Noyon	03:30	
92	04-Jul-44	429	Dive-bombing	SL	W#1	Dijon	04:30	
93	05-Jul-44	430	Dive-bombing	SL	W#1	Orleans	04:35	

APPENDIX 7: BLICK'S MISSIONS

#	Date	Mission	Type			Location	Time	Notes
94	07-Jul-44	436	Escort	SL	W#1	Leipzig	04:25	
95	11-Jul-44	441	Escort	SL	W#1	Munich	02:45	
96	12-Jul-44	442B	Escort	SL	W#1	Munich	03:50	
97	16-Jul-44	450	Escort	SL	W#1	Munich	04:45	
98	19-Jul-44	456	Escort	GL/SL	W#1	Saarbrücken	03:30	First group lead.
99	07-Aug-44	490	Dive-bombing	GL/SL	W#1	Saint-Omer/Cambrai	03:40	First tour complete.
	First Tour Total Hours						**300:00**	
100	04-Nov-44	1286A	Escort	FL	R#1	Merseburg	05:00	Second tour—P-51 from here.
101	05-Nov-44	1288A	Escort	SL	W#1	Ludwigshafen	04:15	
102	09-Nov-44	1299A	Escort	SL	W#1	Saarbrücken	04:00	
103	11-Nov-44	1306A	Escort	GL/SL	W#1	Lahnstein	03:55	
104	18-Nov-44	1317A	Sweep	GL/SL	W#1	Lechfeld	05:15	
105	20-Nov-44	1320A	Escort	SL	W#1	Ansbach	02:45	
106	26-Nov-44	496A	Escort	SL	W#1	Misburg	04:30	
107	27-Nov-44	1343A	Sweep	SL	W#1	Annaburg	03:00	
108	29-Nov-44	1348A	Escort	GL/SL	W#1	Hamm	04:30	
109	04-Dec-44	1370A	Escort	GL/SL	W#1	Giessen	04:45	
110	05-Dec-44	1374A	Escort	SL	W#1	Berlin	05:50	
111	11-Dec-44	1408A	Escort	GL/SL	W#1	Giessen	04:05	
112	12-Dec-44	1412A	Escort	GL/SL	W#1	Darmstadt	05:05	
113	15-Dec-44	1422A	Escort	GL/SL	W#1	Hanover	04:00	Estimated.
114	18-Dec-44	1430A	Escort	SL	W#1	Mainz	03:45	
115	27-Dec-44	1456A	Sweep	GL/SL	W#1	Koblenz	03:00	
116	28-Dec-44	1458A	Escort	SL	W#1	Bonn area	03:40	

No.	Date	Field Order	Type	Role	Position	Target/Mission	Duration	Remarks
117	29-Dec-44	1463A	Escort	GL/SL	W#1	Frankfurt	04:45	
118	02-Jan-45	1479A	Escort	GL/SL	W#1	Koblenz	04:10	
119	05-Jan-45	1491A	Escort	GL/SL	W#1	Hanau	04:25	Estimated.
120	13-Jan-45	1513A	Escort	GL/SL	W#1	Mainz	04:15	
121	17-Jan-45	1525A	Escort	GL/SL	W#1	Paderborn	04:30	
122	03-Feb-45	1586A	Escort	GL/SL	W#1	Berlin	05:45	
123	14-Feb-45	1622A	Escort	GL/SL	W#1	Chemnitz	05:30	
124	22-Feb-45	1650A	Sweep	GL/SL	W#1	Magdeburg	05:15	
125	25-Feb-45	1662A	Escort	GL/SL	W#1	Neuburg	05:45	
126	28-Feb-45	1675A	Escort	GL/SL	W#1	Kassel	05:05	
127	03-Mar-45	1690A	Escort	SL	W#1	Hanover/Brunswick	04:50	
128	12-Mar-45	1742A	Sweep	GL/SL	W#1	Frankfurt	05:30	
129	18-Mar-45	1779A	Escort	GL/SL	W#1	Berlin	05:30	
130	24-Mar-45	1828A	Sweep	GL/SL	W#1	Kassel	04:20	
131	05-Apr-45	1903A	Escort	GL/SL	W#1	Grafenwöhr	05:30	
132	08-Apr-45	1918A	Escort	GL/SL	W#1	Stendal	05:30	
133	10-Apr-45	1936A	Escort	GL/SL	W#1	Zerbst	05:00	
Second Tour Total Hours							156:55	
Total Combat Hours							456:55	

APPENDIX 8

350th Fighter Squadron Losses

1	01-Mar-43	2nd. Lt. Meyer Rothblatt	KIFA	Seen to dive into Chesapeake Bay.
2	24-Mar-43	2nd. Lt. Roy J. Reigard	KIFA	Mid-air collision with F/O Bowen.
3	05-Sep-43	Capt. Irvin E. Venell	KIFA	Crashed in poor weather.
4	05-Sep-43	1st. Lt. Harold W. Long	KIFA	Crashed in poor weather.
5	14-Oct-43	2nd. Lt. Robert C. Peters	KIA	Crashed returning from mission.
6	22-Oct-43	2nd. Lt. Walter B. Stone	KIA	Disorientated in poor weather over France.
7	22-Oct-43	1st. Lt. Alan W. Lowe	KIA	Disorientated in poor weather over France.
8	05-Nov-43	1st. Lt. Robert L. Newman	KIA	Possibly hit by enemy fighters.
9	30-Dec-43	1st. Lt. William W. Odom	KIA	Hit by enemy fighters.
10	03-Feb-44	Capt. Wilford F. Hurst	KIA	Mid-air collision with Capt. Newhart.
11	06-Mar-44	1st. Lt. Robert N. Ireland	KIA	Hit by enemy fighters and crashed in UK.
12	29-May-44	1st. Lt. Arthur C. Bergeron	KIA	Hit by flak.
13	07-Jun-44	Capt. Francis T. Walsh	KIA	Possibly hit by flak. Ditched in Channel.
14	10-Jun-44	2nd. Lt. Martin D. Coffey	KIA	Hit ground while strafing.
15	12-Jun-44	Major Dewey E. Newhart	KIA	Hit by enemy fighters.
16	12-Jun-44	2nd. Lt. John J. Phelan	KIA	Hit by enemy fighters.
17	28-Jun-44	1st. Lt. John F. Starr	KIFA	Crashed while landing at Raydon.
18	04-Aug-44	2nd. Lt. Denny L. Yocum	KIA	Hit by enemy fighters.
19	04-Aug-44	2nd. Lt. Harry Y. Aldridge	KIA	Hit by flak.
20	06-Aug-44	1st. Lt. Thomas C. Creekmur	KIFA	Crashed during a slow roll at low level.
21	08-Aug-44	1st. Lt. Robert S. Hart	KIA	Hit by explosion while strafing.
22	11-Aug-44	2nd. Lt. Robert A. Metz	KIFA	Crashed while landing at Raydon.
23	13-Aug-44	2nd. Lt. George W. McInis	KIA	Hit by flak.
24	13-Aug-44	2nd. Lt. Max K. Graham	KIA	Hit by flak.

25	29-Aug-44	Capt. William D. Smith	KIA	Hit by flak or ground explosion.
26	29-Aug-44	2nd. Lt. Olger I. Aal	KIA	Hit by flak.
27	23-Sep-44	2nd. Lt. Gerald F. Province	KIA	Possibly hit by enemy fighters.
28	23-Sep-44	Capt. Ellis S. Middleton	KIA	Possibly hit by enemy fighters.
29	23-Sep-44	2nd. Lt. John G. Edwards	KIA	Possibly hit by enemy fighters.
30	24-Oct-44	1st. Lt. Robert W. Hedler	KIA	Hit by flak.
31	27-Oct-44	1st. Lt. Marvin E. Albertson	KIFA	Mid-air collision with Lt Edwards.
32	27-Nov-44	1st. Lt. George C. Moran	KIA	Hit by enemy fighters.
33	05-Dec-44	1st. Lt. Alvin L. Deeds	KIA	Hit by enemy fighters.
34	05-Dec-44	2nd. Lt. Noah N. Cowen	KIA	Hit by enemy fighters.
35	13-Jan-45	2nd. Lt. George S. Lee	KIFA	Lost control in overcast.
36	24-Mar-45	2nd. Lt. James H. Hopkins	KIA	Hit by enemy fighters.
37	24-Mar-45	2nd. Lt. Wiley Grizzle	KIA	Hit by enemy fighters.
38	15-Apr-45	2nd. Lt. William O. Fitch	KIFA	Fire in flight.
39	16-Apr-45	2nd. Lt. Donald E. Howie	KIA	Hit by flak or ground explosion.
40	16-Apr-45	1st. Lt. Walter S. Prescott	KIA	Hit by flak.

Index

3rd Bomb Division 282
4th Fighter Group 81, 83, 171, 265, 310
18th Fighter Squadron 72
20th Fighter Group 305
31st Fighter Group 66
50th Control Squadron 147
55th Fighter Group 182, 306, 314, 315
56th Fighter Group 81–2, 83, 84, 87, 89, 127, 138, 171, 194–5, 213, 230, 243, 261, 262, 263, 265, 269, 272, 281, 291, 300, 309, 314
65th Fighter Wing 84
66th Fighter Wing 84
78th Fighter Group 80–2, 83, 112, 151, 233, 253, 260, 274, 282, 291, 293, 298, 310, 314, 315
80th Fighter Group 58
81st Fighter Group 55
90th Fighter Squadron 58
91st Fighter Squadron 55, 56
92nd Fighter Squadron 56
93rd Fighter Squadron 56
326th Fighter Squadron 59
328th Fighter Group 55, 56, 59, 61
329th Fighter Squadron 59
339th Fighter Group 171, 308, 314
343rd Fighter Group 72
350th Fighter Squadron ix, xi, 63, 65, 72, 74, 78, 85, 109, 112, 115, 117, 120, 123, 125, 139, 142, 147, 150, 153, 161, 176, 207, 211, 212, 217, 219, 220, 236, 240, 255, 260, 264, 267, 283, 298, 303, 307, 308, 311, 312, 314, 315
351st Bombardment Group 58
351st Fighter Squadron 65, 83, 85, 105, 108, 111, 112, 121, 123, 139, 140, 143, 153, 162, 163, 192, 194, 211, 217, 220, 251, 253, 263, 264, 266, 273, 277, 279, 283, 286, 287, 289, 291, 304, 307, 308, 309, 310, 312, 313, 314
352nd Fighter Group 241, 261, 296, 314, 315
352nd Fighter Squadron 65, 83, 85, 87, 105, 106, 108, 110–2, 123, 139, 142, 153, 156, 163, 171, 182, 176, 182, 183, 211, 212, 217, 250, 252, 255, 262, 264, 266, 269, 275, 280–3, 285, 286, 288, 289, 291, 294, 297, 301, 302, 304, 307, 308, 310, 312, 314
353rd Fighter Group x–xi, 56, 63, 66, 73, 109, 111, 127, 136, 167, 171, 233, 241, 261, 283, 295, 297
355th Fighter Group 171
357th Fighter Group 171, 300, 303, 305, 307, 308, 314, 315
361st Fighter Group 76, 260, 298, 300
404th Fighter Group 198, 266
479th Fighter Group 305
482nd Bombardment Group 93
487th Fighter Squadron 296
508th Bombardment Squadron 58

Aal, Olger I. 167, 282, 283, 287
Abernathy, Robert W. 241, 295, 298, 300, 314, 316
Adair, Phillip 47
Adams, Robert H. 55
Agnew, William M. 177, 304, 308
Air Sea Rescue 116, 132, 263, 266, 268, 305
Albert, Edgar J. 257
Albertson, Marvin E. 294
Alder, (Luke Field) 45
Aleutians, The 177, 178, 294
Allen, James G. 55
Allison, Ralph T. 194, 285, 287–8, 302, 309
Alps, The 290, 307
Ames, Kenneth 283
Angelo, Walter L. 90, 91, 250
Aphrodite operation 290
Ard, John M. 296
Ardennes 206, 300
Argiropulos, Theodore 30, 32, 38
A.P.I (Armor Piercing Incendiary Ammunition) 237
Arnold, Henry H. 114, 121
Asper, Harold E. 296
Atcham, Shropshire 270
Atlantic City, New Jersey 171, 282, 298
Auchincloss, Bayard C. 138–9, 270, 280, 289, 291
Auger Inn 213
"Axis Sally" 81

Baer, John H. (pseudonym) 24, 27–8, 30, 36, 38, 44, 50–1, 55, 57, 59, 62, 64, 63, 65, 70–1, 73, 143, 178, 214, 245
Bailey, William B. 81, 105, 142, 145, 157, 159, 160, 163, 166, 168, 213, 242, 266, 279–81, 284, 286, 293, 295, 296, 298, 300, 301, 302, 303, 305, 306, 308, 309, 312, 313
Balason, John M. 24–8, 30, 34, 36, 38, 44, 47, 55, 59, 62, 63, 64, 65, 66, 71, 72–3, 143, 177–8, 179–82, 194, 197, 202–21, 220, 242, 294, 296, 299, 307, 312
Baltimore, Maryland 60, 62, 63, 65, 70, 72, 76, 77, 128, 133, 134, 143, 178, 214
Bangor, Maine 168
Barlow, Albert W. 289
Battle of the Bulge 194
Beattie, Robert F. 55
Beckham, Walter C. 109, 111, 120, 121, 255, 256, 258, 259, 260, 316
Bedford, Richard L. 153, 274, 289, 316
Behr Jr., John H. 55, 59, 62, 63, 64
Belgium 249, 268, 270
  Brussels 89, 265, 282, 287, 302
  Saint Trond 198, 200, 299
Bell, Bob 8, 51
Bell P-39 Airacobra 56, 57, 59, 60, 65, 70, 74, 109

336 • ACE IN A DAY

Benjamin, Swift T. 161, 277, 287–9
Bennett, Robert M. 51, 55
Bergeron, Arthur Clarence 133, 260, 262, 271
Betner, Raymond J. 24, 38, 51, 55
Biggin Hill, Kent 104, 250
Bill's Buzz Boys 122, 127, 132, 260, 263, 264, 265, 285
Bjorkman, Henry B. "Hank" (Group Intelligence Officer) 121
Black, Eugene J. (Joseph Bridges in text) 29–30
Bledsoe, Marvin V. 6–8, 136, 140, 146–7, 150, 156, 164–5, 167–8, 176, 177, 207–8, 245, 248, 270, 274, 277, 278, 279, 282–4, 287, 288, 292, 294
    Arrives at Raydon 145, 273
    In England 133–5
    P-47 Aerial collision 58–9
    Training 9, 10, 12–13, 16, 18, 21, 23, 25, 30, 37–8, 42, 44, 50–1
Blevins, Hilary 16, 18
Blickenstaff, Wayne K.
    Ace in a day 234–8, 311
    and Betty Evans 169
    and Duncan 114–5, 119, 125, 242
    and "Doc" Canipelli's role 191
    and loss of Robert S. Hart 168
    Award of Silver Star 189
    Baltimore 63–76
    Career summary ix
    Character 154–5
    Commands "D" Flight 125, 260
    D-Day 141–2, 272–3
    Encounter reports 115–6, 118, 120, 160–1, 187, 219–20
    Enlistment 4
    First Mustang flight 176
    Goxhill 80–2
    Group operations officer 240
    Hamilton Field 53–60
    Instructor controversy 164–6
    Instructors Plan 135, 136, 146–7, 154
    June 12, 1944 disaster 152–4, 160, 274
    Lands and takes off from Beachhead 156–60, 275
    Last mission 241, 314
    Me262 victory February 22, 1945 218–20, 306
    Metfield 82, 124, 144, 213
    Millville gunnery 72, 75
    Mitchel Field 61–2
    Morse Code, problems with 22, 33, 36, 39
    Move into the "Wheelhouse" 192–3, 295–6
    Names aircraft "Betty-E" 177
    Near crash with Moretto 128–31
    on Squadron need for replacements 128, 133
    One-wheeled landing 223–4, 308
    Promotions 168, 229–30
    Relief tube problems 225–8
    Squadron Operations Officer 132, 268
    Thoughts on bombing 231
    Thoughts on fighter pilots 128
    Thoughts on Medals 189–90
    Thoughts on second tour 173, 175
    Training 8–13, 14–54
    Wheelhouse escapade 215–6
    Youth 1–3
Blickenstaff, Ralph (brother) 169
Boeing B-17 Flying Fortress 93, 105, 118, 135, 195, 197, 244, 267, 292
Boggs, Cadet 38
Boldman, Cadet 39

Bolken, Cadet Magnus G. 39, 42
Boone, Walker L. 233, 297, 298, 300, 301, 304, 305, 306, 307, 309, 310, 312
Borders, Andrew J. 56
Boxted, Essex 271
Bradley, Jack T. 55
Braintree, Essex 238, 312
Brentwood, Essex 108
Bressler, Clyde 16–23, 29–30
Bridges, Cadet Gerald Joseph 8, 29–30
Broadhead, Joseph E. 56
Broady, Donald M. 58–9
Brock, Thomas C. 310
Brokaw, Tom 245
Brooklyn, New York 144
Brooks, Joseph B. 273
Brown, Harold C. 153, 274, 288
Buchannan, Brian 8, 29, 38
Budesa, Paul G. 56, 59, 62, 63, 65
Burkett, William R. 47, 56, 261
Burlingame, Gordon S. 56, 286
Byers, Vic L. 51, 56, 244, 263, 282, 284, 298, 304, 305, 307, 308, 313, 315

Cagle, Henderson 24, 30
Cagney, Jimmy 40
Caldwell, Kenneth 56
California 2, 5, 36, 37, 39, 42, 55, 57, 77, 79, 100, 134, 144, 169, 171, 192, 215, 218, 230
    Chino 1, 3, 36, 51, 169
    Hamilton Field, San Rafael 52–3, 54, 56, 58, 61, 100
    Los Angeles 5, 24, 39, 55, 100
    March Field, Riverside 55
    Minter Field, Bakersfield 36, 42–3, 44, 56
    Pomona 1–2, 4, 55, 169
    Victorville Army Flying School 51–2
Callsigns 85, 90, 148, 233
Camp Kilmer, New Jersey 72, 78
Campbell, Jerry M. 310
Canipelli, Joseph (Flight Surgeon, 350th Fighter Squadron), ix, xi, 66, 69–70, 76, 91–2, 93–104, 108, 117, 121, 122–4, 127, 130–2, 136–7, 141, 143–4, 146–7, 149, 161, 164–5, 180, 181, 182, 190–1, 193, 207–9, 213–6, 230–1, 239–40, 242, 245, 248, 261, 264, 265, 272, 281, 285, 288, 289, 292, 296, 312
Cannon, James 56
Carrington, Dick 10, 11, 22, 38, 47, 53, 58, 135
Caton, Horace E. 177, 222, 314, 316
Cessna AT-17 241, 315
Chambers, Verlin E. 56
Chennault, Claire 65
Chesapeake Bay 65, 74
Chetwood, Kenneth 118, 147–8, 149, 160, 166, 256, 263, 269–71, 274, 275, 276, 278, 282, 283, 285
Childress, Jesse M. 63
Christian, Shannon 81, 120, 138–9
Christy, Donald B. 56
Clark, Jack 237–8, 241, 314, 316
Class 42-H August 1942 52, 66, 68, 294
Claville, Daniel L. 279
Cles, Leslie P. 56, 111, 282, 295, 316
Coffey, Martin D. 147, 149, 270, 274
Colchester, Essex 127, 145
Compton, Gordon B. 220, 241, 300, 305, 306, 312, 313, 314, 315

INDEX • 337

Consolidated B-24 Liberator 175, 255, 269, 292, 294, 297, 302
Corgan, Robert D. 293, 316
Corrigan, Donald J. 88
Corrigan, "Wrong Way" (aviator) 4
Cowen, Noah N. 177, 183, 298
Creekmur, Thomas C. 167, 283, 284
Cundy, Arthur C. 308, 309
Curtis, Victor N. 285–6
Curtiss Wright AT-9 Fledgling 52
Curtiss Wright P-40 Warhawk 65, 70, 72, 75, 109, 178

Davis, Lonnie M. 308, 309
Dawson, Melvin P. 123, 124, 128, 266
D-Day June 6, 1944 141–2, 146, 152
Debden, Essex 83
Deeds, Alvin L. 298
Denmark 265, 290, 312
Devane, John L. 116, 128, 252, 253, 254, 260, 262, 263, 266
Devine, Gerald P. 285, 292
Dinse, Charles W. "Chuck" 69, 77–8, 114, 119, 140, 251, 253, 256, 258, 260, 262, 269, 270, 273, 275
Dinse, Pat 77–8
Dive-bombing 109, 111–2, 122, 139, 262, 268, 270, 271
Doolittle, Jimmy H. 189
Dornier Do 217, 255
Dorsey, Tommy 81, 98–9
Douglas C-47 Skytrain 290, 292
Douglas C-54 Skymaster 168
Douglas DC-3 63
Drop tanks 89, 122, 171, 253, 260, 270
Dubois, Lawrence G. 56
Duncan, Glenn E. 81, 105–6, 108–9, 114, 114–5, 117–9, 121, 122, 123–5, 133, 141–3, 145, 150–1, 153, 155, 161, 162–3, 167, 240–2, 244, 251, 253–64, 266, 267, 268, 269, 271, 273, 275–7, 279–80, 283, 288, 314–6
Dundalk, Maryland 63, 143
Duke, Edward H. 177, 183, 185–8, 194–5, 198, 200–5, 218, 229, 297, 298, 304, 310, 312, 313
Durant, Charles O. 116, 251, 265, 268
Dustin, Harry H. 262
Duxford, Cambridgeshire 83, 204, 205, 299, 301
Dyer, Joseph E. 177

Eaker, Ira C. 83
Eastchurch, Kent 117, 255
Eddy, Bruce A. 310
Edwards, Edmund B. 294
Edwards, Francis L. 139, 263, 271
Edwards, John G. 292
Eighth Air Force 105, 175, 206, 217, 295, 303, 313
Eighth Bomber Command 83, 105, 132
Eighth Fighter Command 89, 111, 114, 115, 171, 259, 282, 297
Eisenhower, Dwight D. 314
Elder, Robert A. 235, 237, 240, 307, 309, 311, 312, 313, 315
Elkins, Frank E. 177, 297
Enemy Aircraft Flight No. 1426 267
English Channel 83, 116, 118, 127, 138, 203, 263, 310
Evans, James R. 169, 304

Ferrell, Arthur E. 180, 280, 302
Fifteenth Air Force 260, 310, 311

Flak 84, 86, 91, 116, 135, 140, 147, 156, 162, 231, 253, 262, 263, 270, 273
Flak Homes (Rest Homes) 164, 228
Focke Wulf 190 87, 90, 106, 107, 111, 116, 119, 122, 139, 154, 186, 234, 235–8, 249, 250, 251, 252, 256, 260, 261, 267, 269, 271, 279, 287, 293, 297, 310, 311
Ford, West Sussex 251, 273
Forkin, Thomas J. 302
Fortier, Robert E. 71, 85, 128, 249, 251, 260, 261
France 109, 140, 156, 161, 162, 188, 249, 254, 262, 263, 268, 271, 274, 275, 278, 282, 285, 286, 287
  Ft. Rouge Airfield, St. Omer, 112, 253
  Lille 250, 284, 285, 286, 292
  Normandy 145, 152, 284
  Orleans 263, 268, 272, 278, 285
  Paris 140, 150, 167, 249, 254, 255, 257, 258, 263, 267, 270, 272, 274, 277, 276, 279, 280, 282, 284, 289, 291, 292, 303, 315, 316
  Pas de Calais 83, 112, 118, 132, 255, 259, 262, 265, 266, 268, 272, 276, 277
Franklin 45, 46, 48–50, 52
French, Bernard J. 176, 294
Fry, Betty 77, 258
Fry, Dwight 76, 77, 87, 88, 88, 91, 93–107, 108, 120–1, 249–52, 256–8
Frye, James E. 310
Furness, Joseph F. "Li'l Joe" 74–5, 85, 119, 125, 132, 140, 153, 154, 156, 208, 251, 252, 256, 262, 264, 265, 268, 272, 273, 275–7

Gabreski, Francis S. 265, 281
Gabriel, John R. 288–9
Galbreath, Howard L. (childhood friend), 3, 51, 169, 198, 200–3, 266, 276, 282, 299, 302
Gallup, Kenneth W. 155, 156, 161, 166–7, 272, 275–8, 279–83, 285–7, 293, 295
Garey, Abel H. 157, 164, 166, 262, 282
Geiger Field, Washington 58
Gentile, Dominic S. 265
Germany 83, 115, 140, 178, 217, 219, 252, 253, 254, 259, 260, 262, 271, 287, 293, 295, 296, 302, 305, 307, 308, 310, 312, 313, 314, 315
  Berlin 122–3, 126, 137, 138, 178, 179, 184, 217, 218, 231, 232, 260, 261, 263, 264, 265, 268, 270, 271, 276, 293, 295, 297, 298, 304, 306, 309, 310, 311, 313, 315, 314
  Bremen 253, 254, 265, 293
  Brunswick 184, 255, 256, 259, 262, 263, 267, 269, 271, 308
  Cologne 115, 261, 293, 310
  Dümmer Lake 233, 236, 298, 302, 310, 313
  Düren 105–6, 251, 252, 257
  Emden 93, 251, 254, 265
  Frankfurt 118, 166, 179, 194, 198, 229, 243, 255, 257, 258, 260, 262, 264, 269, 281, 292, 295, 299, 300, 301, 303, 304, 306, 309, 310, 311
  Giessen 194, 196, 299
  Haam 266, 276, 298
  Hamburg 269, 270, 283, 294, 295, 304, 307, 312, 313
  Hanover 261, 264, 265, 294, 297, 299, 313, 315
  Kassel 221, 234, 236, 289, 292, 293, 301, 304, 308, 309, 310, 311
  Kiel 264, 312, 313
  Koblenz 175, 179, 194, 206, 290, 296, 298, 301, 302
  Leipzig 123, 162, 259, 279, 281, 285, 293, 294, 295, 298, 300, 305, 307, 310, 311, 313

Ludwigshafen 117, 254, 294, 302
Magdeburg 138, 139, 241, 303, 305, 312, 314
Merseburg 297, 298, 305
Munich 164, 266, 280, 281, 283, 284, 296, 303, 307, 308, 314
Nuremberg 292, 293, 306, 313, 316
Osnabruck 254, 268, 303
Ruhr Valley 221, 243, 266, 289, 298, 302, 304, 305, 306, 307, 310, 311
Schweinfurt 83, 105, 252, 257, 259, 260
Steinhuder Lake 162, 184, 279, 309, 310
Stuttgart 260, 284, 290, 299
Wilhelmshaven 119, 252, 256
Geurtz, Robert P. 108
G-Forces 22, 225
Gilmer, Harry U. 310
Glendale, Arizona 55
Gonnam, Jesse W. 255, 264, 266, 316
Gordon, Ray C. 232
Gottlieb, Robert C. 64
Goxhill, Lincolnshire ix, 80, 81
Graham, Max K. 285
Graham, Milton H. 136, 147, 156, 274
Grainger, Lester M. 299, 308
Granbo, 60
Gravesend, Kent 291
Green, Earl W. 142
Greene, Robert N. 290
Greenfield, Bernard 314
Greenland 168
Greenwood, Raymond P. 285
Grier, (Luke Field) 45
Grimes, Robert H. 56
Grimsby, Lincolnshire 80
Grizzle, Wiley 311
G-Suit 226, 234
Gustke, Richard N. 310

Hahn, Richard E. 310
Halesworth, Suffolk 82, 83, 84
Hally, Lloyd G. 291
Hammett, W. A. (primary flight instructor, William Handel in text) 24, 25–8,33, 36
Hargus, William W. 164, 278, 282
Harris, Delbert E. 283, 316
Hart, Robert S. 117, 125–6, 139, 140, 164, 167, 168, 253, 254, 258, 261, 262, 265, 268, 274, 282, 283, 284
Hartley, Alex S. 287
Hartley, Raymond E. 234
Hatch, William E. 60
Haynes, Harry E. 181, 211, 300, 311
Hazing 14, 38, 52
Hazington, Mr. (Blick's art teacher) 11
Hedler, Robert W. 176, 287, 288
Heinkel He111 162, 273, 287
Hempstead, Long Island 61
Herfurth, Herman 87
Hess, Myra (concert pianist) 103
Higgins, William A. 56
Hightshoe, Melville W. 222, 234, 287, 300, 316
Hill, W. M. 39–41, 42–3
Hoey, Charles J. 263, 265, 277, 279–83
Hopkins, James H. 234, 311
Hopkins, Wallace 67, 68, 72, 76, 298
Hornchurch, Essex 252
Howie, Donald E. 314

Hubbell, William R. 236, 311
Hughes, Howard 198
Hunter, Harry 140, 271
Hurst, Wilford F. 90, 110, 119–20, 249, 250, 252, 253, 254, 256

Iceland 168
Immelmann (aerial maneuver) 27, 121
Ipswich, Suffolk 82
Ireland, Robert N. 116, 123–5, 253, 256, 261

Jacobus, Henry R. 56
Jessup, John E. 212, 300, 302, 309
Johnson, Dwight W. 286
Johnson, Gerald W. 261, 263
Johnson, Robert S. 261, 262, 265
Johnson, Wilton W. 308, 314, 315
Jones, Thomas W. 157–60, 275
Jordan, William J. 282, 296
Jung, Richard F. 177, 231, 310
Junkers Ju52 143
Junkers Ju88 260, 267, 282, 287
Junttila, Wilbert H. 183, 184, 194, 196, 229, 230, 238, 244, 286, 298, 299, 301, 304, 306–9, 311, 313, 314

K-14 Gunsight 188
K-25 Camera 196, 219, 220, 243, 307
Kanner, (Commander, Thunderbird Field) 15–6
Kenney, David C. 120, 256
Kentucky 99–100
Kepner, William E. 108, 114, 122, 127, 132, 163, 280
Keywan, Richard V. 288–9
Kilmer, Alfred Joyce 78
Kolb, Herbert G. 299, 307–9, 312

La Guardia Airport, New York 58
Lamb, James W. 314
Lancaster, Billy J. 314
Langley, Virginia 65, 178
Lanoue, Roland J. 304, 308, 310
Larsen, Carl A. 304, 310, 311
Lee, George S. H. 300, 303
Lee, Louis W. 234, 237, 308
Leeper, Don (friend) 169
Lefebre, Frederick H. 113, 192–3, 199, 211, 212, 265, 288, 292, 293, 295, 296, 298, 299, 303, 304
Lemmon, Cadet 39
Leonard, Jack 99
Lindbergh, Charles (aviator) 4
Link Trainer 47, 67, 72
Liverpool, United Kingdom 133
Lockheed P-38 Lightning 82, 114, 254, 259–60, 266, 268
London, United Kingdom 93, 95, 96–7, 102, 103, 104, 243, 254, 260, 296
Long, Harold W. 104, 249, 289, 250
Long, William M. 312
Lorance, Tom "Pinky" 109–10, 117–8, 128, 250, 254, 262, 266
Lowe, Allen E. 56, 59, 62, 63, 65, 109, 111, 251, 252
Lowestoft, Suffolk 108, 309
Luftwaffe 105, 114, 121, 124, 122, 139, 145, 153, 175, 229, 234, 253, 261, 262, 282, 290, 291, 292, 293, 295, 303, 308, 313
Luke, Frank 44
Luke Field, Phoenix, Arizona 42, 43, 45, 46–7, 50, 53, 56, 66, 134–5, 208

Madson, John A. 220
Maguire, William J. 56, 301, 303, 304, 309
Mahurin, Walker M. 256, 257, 258, 261, 262, 263
Main, Earl C. 125, 153, 262, 265, 269, 274, 288–9
Manston, Kent 118, 182, 250, 256, 260, 262, 282
Markham, Gene E. 309
Martin, Cadet 39
Martin B-26 Marauder 111, 189, 297
Matula, John 310
May, John F. 234, 311
McCollom, Loren G. 87, 88, 89, 90, 91, 109–11, 112–3, 114, 115, 243, 249, 250, 252, 253, 316
McCool, Cadet 39, 42
McDonald, Joseph C. 133, 271
McInis, George W. 285
McKean, Roland R. 56, 59, 61, 63, 267
McKenney, Paul M. 306
McMahan, Bruce D. 241
McMullen, Joseph D. 314
Messerschmitt Me109 91, 106, 107, 111, 117, 119, 120–1, 122, 124, 143, 154, 161, 167, 234, 235–8, 252, 253, 254, 256, 257, 258, 259, 267, 269, 274, 277, 278, 279, 282, 283, 287, 296, 309, 311
Messerschmitt Me110 116, 118, 119, 252, 255, 256, 273, 289
Messerschmitt Me210 251, 252
Messerschmitt Me262 175, 179, 211, 217, 218–20, 241, 293, 306, 314
Messerschmitt Me410 263, 282, 283, 287
Metfield, Suffolk ix, 82, 144
Metz, Robert A. 284
Michel, Alvin 310
Microwave Earl Warning (MEW) Control 84, 204, 291, 309, 310
Middleton, Ellis S. 167, 280, 283, 288, 291, 292
Miller, A. Glenn 81, 98
Miller, William L. 177
Millville, New Jersey 72, 75
Missouri 68, 69
Mitchel, John Purroy 61
Mitchel Field, New York 52, 58–9, 61, 62, 63, 65, 134
Montgomery, Bernard L. 311
Moran, George C. 298
Moretto, Geoffred F. 125, 128–31, 138–9, 153, 265, 266, 271, 274, 286
Morris, Joseph A. 64, 81, 83, 85, 87, 88
Mott, Charles R. 56
Mueller, Carl W. 125, 133, 175, 262, 264, 265, 268, 286–8, 293, 294

Netherlands 84, 90, 106, 139, 204, 233, 236, 249, 251, 256, 276, 291, 302
 Gilze Rijen 89, 116, 249, 253, 254, 259
 Hague, The 84, 86, 253
 Plantloon 283, 295
 Rotterdam 84, 249, 288
New, Almon W. 282
New Brunswick, New Jersey 78
New Orleans, Louisiana 66
Newhart, Dewey E. 66, 68, 69–70, 72, 73, 75–6, 81, 93, 105–7, 114, 119, 117–21, 128, 132, 134, 140–3, 146, 147, 150–1, 152–3, 154, 190, 192, 250–5, 256, 257, 259, 264, 265, 266, 267, 268–71, 272, 273, 274, 289
Newman, Robert A. 262
Newman, Robert L. 108, 252

Nicklebur, John M. 304
Ninth Air Force 152, 169, 188, 198, 206, 211, 233, 286, 300, 301
No-Ball Targets 269
Norfolk, United Kingdom 82, 93, 251 253, 254
Norfolk, Virginia 65
North Africa 72, 73, 82
North American AT-6 Texan 47, 57, 147, 264, 292
North American P-51 Mustang 120, 166, 175–6, 223, 231, 234, 235, 236, 237, 242–3, 260, 266, 277, 282, 283, 290, 293, 296, 309, 316
 Cold 179, 295
 First Group Mustang mission 292
 Performance 179
 Range 171
North Sea 188
Northern Ireland 80, 189

O'Connell, Thomas (Crew Chief) 209
Odell, Cadet (Thunderbird Field) 16–22
Odom, William W. "Dub" 87, 89, 95, 117, 250, 251, 254
Oliphint, John H. 285
O'Neil, Francis 312
Onkey, John 311
Orzelek, Frank J. 177, 297, 305
Ostersen, (Williams Field) 8–9

Page, Garnet D. 231–2, 308, 310, 314, 316
Palladium Theater, Los Angeles 98
Partridge, Earle E. 305
Paslay, Harold P. 125, 164, 262, 265, 285
Pathfinders H2S "Stinkey"/H2X "Mickey" 93
Patton, George S. 229, 284, 311, 312
Pearl Harbor attack 3, 44, 75, 198, 202
Perry, Earl W. 250
Peters, Edwin H. 153, 160, 274–6
Peters, Robert C. 108, 252
Peterson, Cletus W. 266
Phelan, John J. 153, 271, 274, 288
Philadelphia, Pennsylvania 62, 63
Phister, (Base Adjutant, Williams Field) 9–10
Phoenix, Arizona 8, 37, 49, 50
Pidduck, Stanley R. 67, 68, 75, 81, 83, 85, 94, 109–10, 111, 114, 132, 251, 252, 254, 257, 259, 260, 262, 264, 266, 268
Pittsburgh, Pennsylvania 156
Poindexter, James N. 137, 153, 166, 171, 271, 281, 283, 302
Poland, 271, 315
Post, Wiley (aviator) 4
Prescott, Walter A. 177, 299, 314
Price, William F. 118, 132, 155–6, 164–8, 176, 178, 233, 251, 252, 256, 261, 264, 268, 272, 281–4, 285, 287, 289, 291, 293, 296, 298
Province, Gerald F. 292
Pyrenees Mountains 268

Qualline, E. A. (advanced instructor) 47, 49
Queen Mary (liner) 78–9, 97, 174
Quesada, Elwood R. 63

Rafferty, Vernon G. 136, 147, 156, 158, 176, 179, 274, 275, 277, 279, 292–4, 296
Ranckin, 45
Raydon, Suffolk ix, 127, 132, 146, 160, 168, 189, 198, 203, 205, 228, 229, 244, 265, 301
Red Cross 80, 98–101

Reigard, Roy J. 59, 62, 65, 75
Republic P-47 Thunderbolt 58, 61, 65, 81–2, 83, 111, 114, 116, 118, 153, 160, 166, 171, 175–6, 179, 188, 202, 203, 205, 207, 214, 231, 250, 252, 254, 256, 259, 266, 267, 288, 289, 290, 294, 295, 296, 297
   Compressibility 74, 87
   Paddle blade propellors 122, 260, 264, 265, 266, 271
   Problems 73–4, 82
   Ruggedness 119
   Safe aircraft 177, 243
Rhine River 229, 243
Richmond, Virginia 59, 77, 258
Righetti, Elwyn G. 315
Rimerman, Ben 72–3, 76, 89, 94, 105–12, 114, 115, 117, 122, 125, 126, 133, 136–7, 137–8, 142–3, 145, 153, 163, 175, 178, 190, 192, 213, 216, 223, 224, 229, 233, 235, 240–3, 251, 252, 255, 256–8, 260–1, 263, 265, 266, 268, 271, 273–6, 279, 280, 281, 283, 285, 288, 291–3, 295, 299, 302, 303, 304, 305, 307, 308, 309, 310, 311, 312, 313–5
Robertson, Raynor E. 261
Robinson, George W. 177, 237, 304
Rodie R. J. Doctor. 243
Rooney, Andy 247
Roosevelt, Franklin Delano President 3, 314
Rose, John B. 252, 291, 313
Rosenberg, Joseph 116, 251, 253
Rosentreter, Edward M. (350th Intelligence Officer) 72, 182, 207
Rothblatt, Meyer 74
Rowan, Chauncy 207, 256, 260, 270
Ruscitto, James O. 136, 147, 153, 176, 274, 287–8, 290, 295

Salt Lake City, Utah 10, 21
Schilling, David C. 230, 300
Schilt, John L. 180, 287
Schwartz, Cadet (Minter Field) 38–9
Schwarz, Eric (psychologist) 171
Scotland 80, 266, 267, 299
Sebloux, Rod Cadet 47
Seppala, Leslie W. 304
Sheets, Millard (artist) 14
Sinatra, Frank 98–9, 208
Smith, William D. 287
Squadron ready room 206–8
Stafford, Charles L. 290
Starkey, Operation 83
Starr, John F. 138–9, 154, 161, 267, 273, 278, 284
Stars and Stripes (newspaper) 98
Stearman PT-17 Primary Trainer 25, 209
Stearns, Richard A. 117, 119, 126, 252, 256, 260, 261, 264, 316
Stone, Staffordshire 244
Stone, Walter B. 111, 252
Strafing 121, 136, 175, 176, 265, 266
Stump, Hassel D. 282
Sullivan, John A. 263, 268
Supermarine Spitfire 74, 81, 107, 158, 259, 312

Swanezy, John J. 286
Switzerland 262, 291, 296

Tanner, William F. 122, 153–6, 181, 182, 207, 238–240, 251, 252, 256, 269, 270, 272, 274–6, 278, 296, 298, 303, 304, 305, 307, 309, 311, 312
Tennessee 99
Terzian, Jack 264, 270, 290
Thornell, Lloyd A. 120, 256
Thorney Island, West Sussex 249, 250, 251
Thunderbird Field, Phoenix, Arizona 13–4, 28, 30, 38, 39, 42, 46, 49, 148, 201
Tordoff, Harrison B. 312
Tour of duty length 127, 270, 295
Travis, R. B. 62
Trudeau, Paul J. 266
Turner, Roscoe (aviator) 4
Tuttle, James M. 285
Tuttle, Robert S. 161
Type 16 Control 259, 262, 267, 269, 271, 272, 274, 276, 277, 280, 282, 283, 297

Van Cau, H. T. (Jacksen) 34–6
VE Day 243, 316
Venell, Irvin E. 104, 249, 250, 289
Vultee "Vibrator" BT-13/15 39, 42

Wade, 56
Waggoner, Horace Q. 308
Wallace, Charlie (father's friend) 169
Walsh, Francis T. 77, 87, 91, 105–6, 108, 117, 125, 132, 140–2, 143–4, 251–2, 255, 257, 260, 263, 267, 268, 272, 273–4
Walsh, Marge 77, 143–4, 274
Warren, Donald W. 303
Weather conditions (poor) 111, 137–9, 183, 192, 194–5, 199, 203–5, 208–11, 261, 264, 274, 276, 280, 286, 299
Welter, Bob 267
West Malling, Kent 250
West Point Military Academy, New York 52
Wheelhouse, The, Great Wenham, Suffolk 132, 190–2, 215, 268, 305
Whisner, William T. 296
Whitehead, Ennis (Luke Field) 44
Williams, Kenneth 263
Williams Field, Arizona 8, 11, 38
Winder, John H. 109, 140, 164, 167, 253, 269, 282–4, 287–8, 293, 297, 298, 300, 301, 302
Winkton, Dorset 198, 266
Woodbridge, Suffolk 271
Woodbury, Murray C. 242

Yellot, Henry W. 56
Yocum, Denny L. 161, 167–8, 273, 278, 283

Zemke, Hubert 84, 85, 86, 272
Zolner, John "Zeke" 116, 118, 119, 126, 128, 252, 255, 256, 261, 262, 265, 290–1